Provincial Museum of Alberta

Natural History

Occasional Paper No. 14

1991

BIBLIOGRAPHY OF THE FAMILY CATOSTOMIDAE (CYPRINIFORMES)

John Clay Bruner

Department of Zoology
University of Alberta
Edmonton, Alberta
Canada, T6G 2E9

Prepared and Published by:

Natural History Section
Provincial Museum of Alberta
12845-102 Avenue
Edmonton, Alberta
T5N 0M6

NATURAL HISTORY OCCASIONAL PAPER SERIES

Occasional Paper titles are Published by the Provincial Museum of Alberta on subjects pertaining to the natural history of Alberta. Potential contributors are requested to submit manuscript proposals to the Assistant Director, Curatorial, Provincial Museum of Alberta, 12845-102 Avenue, Edmonton, Alberta T5N 0M6.

CATALOGUING IN PUBLICATION DATA

Bruner, John Clay, 1950-
Bibliography of the Family Catostomidae (Cypriniformes)

(Provincial Museum of Alberta natural history occasional paper, ISSN 0838-5971 ; no. 14)

ISBN 0-7732-0539-X

1. Catostomidae - Bibliography. 2. Fishes - Bibliography. 3 Fishes, Fossil - Bibliography. I. Provincial Museum of Alberta. Natural History Section. II. Series: Natural history occasional paper; no. 14. III. Title.

Z7996.F5B78 1991 [QL638.C27]   016.597'52

CONTENTS

PREFACE

This bibliography lists 2000 references for unpublished and published reports, articles, Master of Science theses, Doctoral dissertations, maps, and books relating to the Family Catostomidae (Order Cypriniformes). Both living and fossil forms are included. A list of all the sources of information is given in order that future workers on suckers may continue from where this bibliography stops. Indices are provided for Master of Science theses, Doctoral dissertations, common names and scientific names. Entries for Master of Science theses, Doctoral dissertations and scientific names list references alphabetically by author(s) and year. The listings of the scientific names include subspecies names and use the names that the author(s) used in the publication.

An attempt has been made to compile everything ever published on the Family Catostomidae (Order Cypriniformes). I do not pretend that I have succeeded in listing every reference ever published on the Catostomidae, but I tried. It is hoped this bibliography will save the user's valuable research time. The systematic index to the papers uses the spelling of the scientific names as they appeared in the original paper. However, I have not seen every one of the 2000 papers indexed in this bibliography and often was forced to rely on the abstract services. I have noticed these sometimes update spellings for scientific names without noting the change from the original author's usage. Besides the variation in spelling, one also must be aware of the various synonyms for each species. Five hundred and thirty five taxonomic categories were used to index the 2000 papers down to subspecies.

Some people may argue my spellings of the author's names Charles Alexandre Le Sueur and Bernard Germain Étienne La Cepède. I prefer to use the name as it appeared on the publication. For "Citoyen La Cepède" my authority is *The National Union Catalog Pre-1956 Imprints*, Vol. 310, Mansell Information/Publishing Limited, London, U.K., 698pp., NL 0011071. American Fisheries Society has been inconsistent in their spellings of these authors' names in their various editions of their list of fish names. Charles Alexandre Le Sueur's last name is spelled as LeSueur in the second edition (Bailey et al. 1966) and as Lesueur in the third (Bailey et al. 1970) and fourth (Robins et al. 1980) editions. Bernard Germain Éienne La Cepéde's last name is spelled as Lacépède in the second and third editions and as Lacepède in the fourth edition.

Also, I always tried to use the full name of an author when it was known to me. This helps prevent combining papers by different authors who have the same last name and initials (for example, Carl Hubbs and Clark Hubbs).

Common names are listed when they are known to me. The first common name listed is usually the one established by the American Fisheries Society's list. Subsequent names are additional common names which have been used for suckers. Sometimes it is helpful to know what the common names of a hundred years ago were in order to establish what species the author is discussing. Although the worker should be warned, it is a dangerous precedent to use common fish names in establishing what species the author was discussing.

This bibliography was compiled using the holdings of the library of the University of Alberta and the following references:

1. AGRICOLA. 1970-1990 (December). National Agricultural Library, Technical Services Division, United States Department of Agriculture. Beltsville, Maryland.

2. Atz, James W. 1971. Dean Bibliography of Fishes 1968. American Museum of Natural History. New York, New York. 512pp.

3. Atz, James W. 1973. Dean Bibliography of Fishes 1969. American Museum of Natural History. New York, New York. 853pp.

4. The Biological Abstracts. 1970 to 1987. Vol. 51, 1970 to Vol.83(7), April 1, 1987.

5. The Bibliography of Fossil Vertebrates. 1939 to 1983. The Geological Society of American and continued by the Society of Vertebrate Paleontology. 1939-1983.

6. Blackwelder, Richard E. 1972. Guide to the Taxonomic Literature of Vertebrates Iowa State University Press, Ames, Iowa. pp. 1-259.

7. Carlander, Kenneth D. 1969. Handbook of Freshwater Fishery Biology Volume One. Iowa State University Press, Ames, Iowa. 752pp.

8. Carter, Neal M. 1968. Index and List of Titles, Fisheries Research Board of Canada and associated Publications, 1900-1964. Fisheries Research Board of Canada, Ottawa. Bulletin 164:1-649.

9. Carter, Neal M. 1973. Index and List of Titles, Fisheries Research Board of Canada and associated Publications, 1965-1972. Fisheries Research Board of Canada, Ottawa. Miscellaneous Special Publication No. 18:1-588.

10. Cvancara, Victor. 1977-1987. Current References in Fish Research. Volumes 2, 4-11. Eau Claire, Wisconsin.

11. Dean, Bashford. 1916. A Bibliography of Fishes. Enlarged and edited by Charles Rochester Eastman. American Museum of Natural History. University Press, Cambridge, Mass. Volume I. 718pp.

12. Dean, Bashford. 1917. A Bibliography of Fishes. Enlarged and edited by Charles Rochester Eastman. American Museum of Natural History.University Press, Cambridge, Mass. Volume II. 697pp.

13. Dean, Bashford. 1923. A Bibliography of Fishes. Extended and edited by Eugene Willis Gudger, with the Cooperation of Arthur Wilbur Henn. American Museum of Natural History. University Press, Cambridge, Mass.Volume III. 707pp.

14. Hay, Oliver Perry. 1902. Bibliography and Catalogue of the Fossil Vertebrata of North America. Bull. U.S. Geol. Surv. No. 179. 868pp.

15. Hay, Oliver Perry. 1929. Second Bibliography and Catalogue of the Fossil Vertebrata of North America. 2 volumes. Publ. Carnegie Inst. Washington. No. 390. 2003pp.

16. Reed, Clyde F. 1955. Index to Copeia 1913-1954. Part I-Author Index. The Science Press, Lancaster, Pennsylvania. pp. 1-106.

17. Reed, Clyde F. 1956. Index to Copeia 1913-1954. Part II-Subject Index. The Science Press. Lancaster, Pennsylvania. pp. 1-332.

18. Reed, Clyde F. 1965. Index to Copeia 1955-1964 Supplement. Paul M. Harrod Co. Towson, Maryland. pp. 1-329.

19. Zoological Record. 1864-1990. Zoological Record. Volumes 1 to 126.

In order to be sure of getting every possible reference for a particular species of sucker, it is suggested that the worker search the 148 references under the category "Catostomidae" which I have not been able to scan personally. Included in this bibliography are 21 Master of Science theses and 39 Doctor of Philosophy Dissertations and a few provincial and state reports which are not normally covered by the abstract services. I would appreciate learning of any errors or corrections to this bibliography.

ACKNOWLEDGEMENTS

I wish to thank my wife, Sarah Derr Bruner, for help in editing this bibliography. I also wish to thank Randy Reichardt, Reference Librarian, University Library, University of Alberta, for help in obtaining some obscure references and Bob Gregorish, Computer Programmer/Anaylst, University of Alberta, for technical help in writing the computer program. Bob Fedun, University Computing Systems, University of Alberta, helped in answering my questions about Microsoft Word 4.0. Ms. Clara Richardson, scientific artist, Field Museum of Natural History, drew the illustration of the Longnose Sucker (*Catostomus catostomus*) from a specimen collected in Lake Michigan, Chicago, Illinois, which is deposited at the fish collections of the Field Museum of Natural History. This bibliography was prepared as part of Dr. Mark V. H. Wilson's Paleontology 620 seminar course at the University of Alberta.

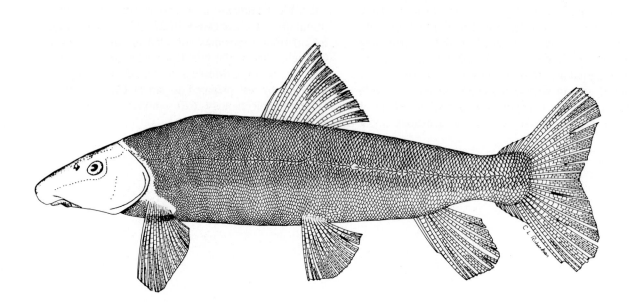

Longnose Sucker (*Catostomus catastomus*) from Lake Michigan.

AUTHOR INDEX

Aadland, L. P., and J.J. Peterka. 1981. The effect of artificial reefs on fish distribution, relative abundance and fishing success in Jamestown Reservoir, North Dakota. North Dakota State Game and Fish Department. 1981:1-16.

Abbott, Charles Conrad. 1861. Descriptions of Four New Species of North American Cyprinidæ. Proceedings of the Academy of Natural Sciences of Philadelphia, 1860. Philadelphia:473-474.

Adams, C. C., and T. L. Hankinson. 1928. The ecology and economics of Oneida Lake fish. Roosevelt Wildl. Ann. Vol. 1(3&4):241-358.

Adams, L. A. 1928. Modifications and associated structures of the first three vertebrae in the Buffalo fish *Ictiobus urus*. Transactions of the Illinois Academy of Science Acad. Sci. Vol. 20:116-120.

Adams, L. A. 1931. Determination of age in fishes. Transactions of the Illinois Academy of Science. Vol. 23(3):219-226.

Adelman, I. R. 1980. Uptake of ^{14}C-glycine by scales as an index of fish growth: effect of fish acclimation temperature. Transactions of the American Fisheries Society. Vol. 109(2):187-194.

Afanasiev, V. I. 1985. Fish with argulosis. Veterinariya, Moscow. 1985(9):43-44.

Agassiz, John Louis Rodolphe. 1850. Lake Superior. Its physical character, vegetation, and animals, compared with those of other and similar regions. Gould, Kendall, and Lincoln. Boston. 428pp.

Agassiz, John Louis Rodolphe. 1854. Notice of a Collection of Fishes from the Southern Bend of the Tennessee River in the State of Alabama. Amer. J. Sci. and Arts, Ser. 2, Vol. 17:297-308;353-369.

Agassiz, John Louis Rodolphe. 1855. Synopsis of the ichthyological fauna of the Pacific slope of North America, chiefly from the collections made by the expedition under the command of Capt. C. Wilkes, with recent additions and comparisons with eastern types. Amer. Journ. Sci. Vol. 2. Ser. 19:71-99;192-231.

Ahlgren, M. O. 1990. Diet slection and the contribution of detritus to the diet of the juvenile white sucker (*Catostomus commersoni*). Canadian Journal of Fisheries and Aquatic Sciences Vol. 47(1):41-48.

Ahlgren, M. O. 1990. Nutritional significance of facultative detritivary to the juvenile white sucker (*Catostomus commersoni*). Canadian Journal of Fisheries and Aquatic Sciences. Vol. 47(1):49-54.

Aliff, J.U., and D. Smith, H. Lucas. 1977. Some metaxoan parasites from fishes of middle Georgia. Transactions Am. Microsc. Soc. Vol. 96(1):145-148.

Allen, E. R. 1946. Fishes of Silver Springs, Florida. Silver Springs, Florida. 36pp.

Allis, Edward Phelps. 1909. The Cranial Anatomy of the Mail-cheeked fishes. Zoologica, Stuttgart. Vol. 22. Heft 57:1-219pp.

Allis, Edward Phelps. 1919. On certain features of the otic region of the chondrocranium of *Lepidosteus* and comparison with other fishes and higher vertebrates. Proc. Zool. Soc. Lond., 1919:245-266.

Al-Rawi, T. R. 1964. Reading of scales of river carpsuckers, *Carpiodes carpio*. M.S. thesis Iowa St. Univ. Lib. 75pp.

Amedjo, S. D., and John C. Holmes. 1990. Color, size, and maturation of *Pomphorhynchus bulbocolli* (Acanthocephala) in white sucker, *Catostomus commersoni*. Journal of Parasitology. Vol. 75(5):798-800.

Amin, O. M. 1981. On the crustacean ectoparasites of fishes from southeast Wisconsin. Trans. Am. Microsc. Soc. Vol. 100(2):142-150.

Amin, Omar A. 1985. Acanthocephala from lake fishes in Wisconsin (USA): *Neoechinorhynchus robertbaueri*, new species from *Erimyzon sucetta*, with a key to species of the genus *Neoechinorhynchus* from North American freshwater fishes. Journal of Parasitology. Vol. 71(3):312-318.

Amin, Omar M. 1968. Deformed individuals of two species of suckers, *Catostomus insignis* and *C. clarkii*, from the Gila River system, Arizona. Copeia 1968(4):862-863.

Amin, Omar M. 1969. Helminth fauna of suckers (Catostomidae) of the Gila River System, Arizona 1. *Nematobothrium texomensis* McIntosh and Self, 1955 (Trematoda) and *Glaridacris confusus* Hunter, 1929 (Cestoda) from buffalofish. American Midland Naturalist. Vol. 82:188-196.

Amin, Omar M. 1974. Intestinal helminths of the white sucker, *Catostomus commersoni* (La Cepède), in SE Wisconsin. Proceedings helminth. Soc. Wash. Vol. 41(1):81-88.

Amin, Omar M. 1975. *Acanthocephalus parksidei* sp.n. (Acanthocephala: Echinorhynchidae) from Wisconsin fishes. Journal of Parasitology. Vol. 61(2):301-306.

Amin, Omar M. 1977a. Helminth parasites of some southwestern Lake Michigan fishes. Proceedings helminth. Soc. Wash. Vol. 44(2):210-217.

Amin, Omar M. 1977b. Distribution of fish parasites from two southeast Wisconsin streams. Transactions Wis. Acad. Sci. Arts Lett. Vol. 65:225-230.

Amin, Omar M. 1982. Adult trematodes (Digenea) from lake fishes of southeastern Wisconsin, with a key to species of the genus *Crepidostomum* Braun, 1900 in North America. Proceedings Helminthol. Soc. Wash. Vol. 49(2):196-206.

Amin, Omar M. 1984. Camallanid and other nematode parasites of lake fishes in southeastern Wisconsin. Proc. Helminthol. Soc. Wash. Vol. 51(1):78-84.

Amin, Omar M. 1985. *Acanthocephala* from lake fishes in Wisconsin: *Neoechinorhynchus robertbaueri* n. sp. from *Erimyzon sucetta* (La Cepède) with a key to species of the genus *Neoechinorhynchus* Hamann, 1892, from North American freshwater fishes. Journal of Parasitology. Vol. 71(3): 312-318.

Amin, Omar M. 1986a. Caryophyllaeidae (Cestoda) from the lake fishes in Wisconsin [USA] with a description of *Isoglaridacris multivitellaria*, new species from *Erimyzon sucetta* (Catostomidae). Proc. Helminthol. Soc. Wash. Vol. 53(1):48-58.

Amin, Omar, M. 1986b. Acanthocephala from lake fishes in Wisconsin: Host and seasonal distribution of species of the genus *Neoechinorhynchus*. Journal of Parasitology. Vol. 72(1):111-118.

Amin, O. M. 1987. Acanthocephala from lake fishes in Wisconsin: ecology and host relationships of *Pomphorhynchus bulbocolli* (Pomphorhynchidae). Journal of Parasitology. Vol. 73(2):278-289.

Amin, O. M., and J. C. Vignieri. 1986. Acanthocephala from lake fishes in Wisconsin: the giant nuclei pattern in *Neoechinorhynchus robertbaueri* and *Neoechinorhynchus prolixoides* (Neoechinorhynchidae). Proceedings helminth. Soc. Wash. Vol. 53(2):184-193.

Amin, Omar M., and Ernest H. Williams, Jr. 1983. *Acanthocephalus alabamensis* sp.n. (Acanthocephala: Echinorhynchidae) from Alabama fishes. Journal of Parasitology. Vol. 69(4): 764-768.

Anderson, E. D., and L. L. Smith, Jr. 1971. A synoptic study of food habits of 30 fish species from western Lake Superior. Univ. Minn. Agric. Exp. Stn. Tech. Bull. 279. 199pp.

Anderson, I. G., and G. A. D. Haslewood. 1970. Comparative studies of bile salts. 5 ^{alpha}-chimaerol, a new bile alcohol from the White sucker *Catostomus commersoni* (La Cepède). Biochem J., Tokyo. Vol. 116:581-587.

Anderson, W. D. 1964. Fishes of some South Carolina coastal plain streams. Quart. J. Fla. Acad. Sci. Vol. 27:31-54.

Andreasen, J. K. 1976. Systematics and status of the family Catostomidae in southern Oregon. Dissertation Abstr. int. (B) Vol. 36(7):3259.

Andreasen, J. K., and J. R. Barnes. 1975. Reproductive life history of *Catostomus ardens* and *C. discobolus* in the Weber River, Utah. Copeia 1975(4):643-648.

Andrews, C. W. 1946. Effect of heat on the light behaviour of fish. Trans. Roy. Soc. Can. (3) Vol. 40(5):27-31.

Andrews, L. M., and C. W. Threinen. 1968. Surface water resources of Shawano County. Wisconsin Department of Natural Resources Lake and Stream Classification Project. 147pp.

Andryushchenko, A. I., and V. I. Glebova. 1979. Overwintering of the buffalo in fish ponds. Rybnoe Khoz., Kiev. No. 28:11-14.

Andryushchenko, A. I., and T. G. Litvinova. 1978. [The growth of two year old black buffalo being reared on various feeds.] Rybnoe Khoz., Kiev. No. 27:25-29.

Andryushchenko, A. I., and T. G. Litvinova, N. F. Grishchenko, E. P. Garbareva. 1986. [Survival of young of the wide mouth buffalo and their dependence on water hydrogen indices]. Rybn. Khoz. Resp. Mezhved. Temat Nauchn Sb. No. 40:24-27.

Andryushchenko, A. I., and A. M. Tretyak. 1989. Some questions on the technology of rearing the wide mouth buffalo in cooler reservoirs of the Burshyn HEP..Rybn. Khoz. Resp. Mezhved. Temat Nauchn Sb. No. 43:9-12.

Andryushchenko, A. I., and N. V. Yurkevich. 1983. Breeding of the bigmouthed buffalo and some features of its biology during the early stages of development. Rybnoe Khoz., Kiev. No. 36:13-17.

Angelescu, N. 1982. Buffalo fish in the Romanian waters. Vinatorul Pesc. Sportov. Vol. 34(2):12.

Angelescu, N., and G. Cazacu, C. Cazacu. 1980. Notes on the biology and systematization of the buffalofish (*Ictiobus*, Catostomidae) introduced in Romania's waters. Buletinul Cerc. pisc. (N.S.) Vol. 2(1-2):73-83.

Anonymous. 1915. Rearing buffalofish in ponds. Fisheries Service Bulletin, 1915. United States Fisheries Service Bulletin. Vol. 7:4-5.

Anonymous. 1921. A noteworthy production of buffalofish. Fisheries Service Bulletin, 1921. United States Fisheries Service Bulletin. Vol. 78:4.

Anonymous. 1957. Alabama Dept. of Conserv., 1957. Report for fiscal year, October 1, 1955 - September 30, 1956. 205pp.

Anonymous. 1958a. Alabama Dept. of Conserv., 1958. Report for fiscal year, October 1, 1956 - September 30, 1957. 200pp.

Anonymous. 1958b. Methods for canning suckers. Canada Dept. Fish., Trade News. Vol. 10(10):16.

Anonymous. 1961. Iowa Conservation Commission, Biology Section. Calculated total lengths at each annulus for various species of fish taken from De Soto Bend, September 25-29, 1961. 13pp. mimeo.

Anonymous. 1964. Montana Fish and Game Department, 1964. Age and growth studies. D.-J. Completion Rep., F-23-R-7 (Jobs I,II):6pp. mimeo.

Anonymous. 1965a. Chapter 15. Gallery of Fresh-water Fishes. pp. 247-294. **IN:** Melville Bell Grosvenor. (ed.) Wondrous World of Fishes. National Geographic Society, Washington, D. C. 367pp.

Anonymous. 1965b. U.S. Bureau of Commercial Fisheries, Mobridge, S.D. Missouri River reservoir commercial fishing, investigations. A documentation of 1963-1964 activities and findings. 74 pp. mimeo.

Anonymous. 1972. IPN virus from white sucker. FAO Aquacult. Bull. Vol. 5(1):14-15.

Anonymous. 1973. Quantifying evolutionary phenomena: widely adaptable American fishes. Research News Univ. Divn. Res. Dev. Admin. Vol. 24(4):?pp.

Anonymous. 1978. Environmental Assessment Report Hickory/Spring Creek Flood Control. Report to the Illinois Department of Transportation Division of Water Resources. De Leuw, Cather and Company. Chicago, Illinois. 128pp.

Anonymous. 1981. Environmental Assessment Hickory/Spring Creek Flood Control Project.Report to the Illinois Department of Transportation Division of Water Resources. De Leuw Cather, Cather & Company. 168pp.

Arai, Hisao P., and R. H. Kussat. 1967. Observations on the distribution of parasites of certain catostomid fishes of the Bow River, Alberta. Canadian Journal of Zoology. Vol. 45:1287-1290.

Arai, Hisao P., and Dwight R. Mudry. 1983. Protozoan and metazoan parasites of fishes from the headwaters of the Parsnip and McGregor Rivers, British Columbia [Canada]: A study of possible parasite transfaunations. Canadian Journal of Fisheries and Aquatic Sciences. Vol. 40:(10):1676-1684.

Arldt, Th. 1907. Die Entwicklung der Kontinente und ihrer Lebewelt: ein Beitrag zur vergleichenden Erdgeschichte. 730pp.

Arldt, Th. 1912. Die Fauna der alten Tierregionen des Festlandes. Neues Jahrb. Min., Geol. Pal., Beil.-Bd. Vol. 34:633-782.

Arldt, Th. 1923. Zur Ausbreitungsgeschicte der Fische, besonders der Fische der Kontinentalen Gewässer. Arch. Hydrobiol. Vol. 14:478-522, 673-719.

Arruda, J. A., and M. S. Cringar, D. Gilliland, S. G. Haslouer, J. E. Fry, R. Broxterman, K. L. Brunson. 1987. Correspondence between urban areas and the concentration of chlordane in fish from the Kansas River. Bull. Environ. Contam. Toxicol. Vol. 39(4):563-570.

Atton, F. M., and R. P. Johnson. 1955. First records of eight species of fishes in Saskatchewan. Canadian Field Naturalist. Vol. 69:82-84.

Averyanov, O. V., and V. N. Dubrovin, R. A. Aslanova. 1980. [Oxygen consumption of the big-mouthed buffalo in its early stages of development.] Rybnoe Khoz., Mosk. 1980(11):29-31.

Ayres, William O. 1855. Description of new species of Californian fishes. Proc. Calif. Acad. Nat. Sci. 1854-57. Vol. 1:23-77.

Badenko, L. V., and T. F. Shuvatova, V. I. Zhivonkina. 1983. Physiological conditions of the large-mouth buffalo (*Ictiobus cyprinellus* Val.) at formation of brood stocks in ponds of the Don River Estuary and the Miussk Firth. pp. 30-41. **IN:** J. B. Bukhanevich, E. V. Soldatova, L. V. Badenko, and N. K. Strubalina. (editors). Use of inland water bodies of the Azov and Caspian Sea basins for fishing and aquaculture. Collected papers. Min. of Fisheries, USSR. All Univ. Res. Instit. of Mar. Fish. & Ocean. (UNIRO). Moscow. 166 pp.

Bachanan, C. C., and M. W. Coleman. 1987. The cui-ui. Natl. Audubon. Soc. Annu. Rep. (NY) 1987:425-436.

Backus, Richard H. 1957. The Fishes of Labrador. Bulletin of the American Museum of Natural History. Vol. 113(4):273-338.

Bagenal, T. B. 1978. Chapter 4. Aspects of Fish Fecundity. pp. 75-101. **IN:** Shelby D. Gerking. (ed.) Ecology of Freshwater Fish Production. John Wiley and Sons. New York, N. Y. 520pp.

Bailey, B. E., and A. W. Lantz, P. J. Schmidt. 1951. Utilization of freshwater fish, trimmings, and offal. Progress Reports of Fisheries Research Board Pacific Coast Stations. No. 88:66-67.

Bailey, M. M. 1969. Age, growth, and maturity of the longnose sucker. *Catostomus catostomus*, of western Lake Superior. Journal of the Fisheries Research Board of Canada Vol. 26(5):1289-1299.

Bailey, Reeve M. 1943a. Progress report-Fisheries Research in Spirit and Okoboji Lakes. Quart. Rep. Iowa Coop. Wildl. Fish. Res. Units, 1943 (July-Sept.):11-13.

Bailey, Reeve M. 1943b. Fisheries research in Clear Lake, Iowa. Quart. Rep. Iowa Coop. Wildl. Fish. Res. Units, 1943 (July-Sept.):14-17.

Bailey, Reeve M. 1959. A new catostomid fish, *Moxostoma (Thoburnia) atripinne*, from the Green River drainage, Kentucky and Tennessee. Occ. Pap. Mus. Zool. Univ. Mich. No. 599:1-19.

Bailey, Reeve M., and Marvin O. Allum. 1962. Fishes of South Dakota. Univ. Mich. Mus. Zool. Misc. Publ. No. 119. 131pp.

Bailey, R. M., and W. N. Eschmeyer. 1988. Case 2598. *Ictiobus* Rafinseque, 1820 (Osteichthyes, Cypriniformes): proposed conservation. Bull. Zool. Nomencl. Vol. 45(1):36-37.

Bailey, Reeve M., and John E. Fitch, Earl S. Herald, Ernest A. Lachner, C. C. Lindsey, C. Richard Robins, W. B. Scott. 1970. A List of Common and Scientific Names of Fishes from the United States and Canada. (Third Edition). American Fisheries Society Special Publication No. 6. Washington, D.C. 150pp.

Bailey, Reeve M., and Ernest A. Lachner, C. C. Lindsey, C. Richard Robins, Phil M. Roedel, W. B. Scott, Loren P. Woods. 1966. A List of Common and Scientific Names of Fishes from the United States and Canada. Second Edition. American Fisheries Society Special Publication No. 2. 102 pp.

Bailey, Reeve M., and Gerald R. Smith. 1981. Origin and Geography of the Fish Fauna of the Laurentian Great Lakes Basin. Canadian Journal of Fisheries and Aquatic Sciences. Vol. 38(No. 12):1539-1561.

Bailey, Reeve M., and Howard E. Winn, C. Lavett Smith. 1954. Fishes from the Escambia River, Alabama and Florida, with Ecologic and Taxonomic Notes. Proc. Acad. Nat. Sci. Phila. Vol. 106:109-164.

Baird, Spencer Fullerton, and Charles Girard. 1854. Descriptions of new species of fishes collected by Mr. John H. Clark on the U. S. and Mexican Boundary Survey, under Lt.-Col. Jas. D. Graham. Proc. Acad. Nat. Sci. Philad., 1853 (1854):387-390.

Baird, Spencer Fullerton, and Charles Girard. 1855. Descriptions of new species of fishes collected in Texas, New Mexico and Sonora, by Mr. John H. Clark, on the U. S. and Mexican Boundary Survey, and in Texas by Capt. Stewart Van Vliet, U.S.A. Proc. Acad. Nat. Sci. Philad., 1854(1855):24-29.

Bajkov, A. 1927. Reports of the Jasper Park Lakes Investigations, 1925-26. I. The Fishes. Contr. Canad. Biol. Toronto. Vol. 3(16):377-404.

Bajkov, A. 1928. A preliminary report on the fishes of the Hudson Bay drainage system. Canadian Field Naturalist. 42:96-99

Baker, J. P. 1981. Aluminum toxicity to fish as related to acid precipitation and Adirondack surface water quality. Dissertation Abstr. int. (B). Vol. 41(12):4384.

Baker, M. R. 1986. Revision of *Hedruris* Nitzsch (Nematoda: Habronemtoidea) from aquatic vertebrates of North America. Canadian Journal of Zoology. Vol. 64(7):1567-1572.

Baker, S. C., and M. L. Armstrong. 1987. Recent collections of fishes from the Spring River drainage in northeast Arkansas. Arkansas Acad. Sci. Proc. Vol. 41:p. 96.

Balan, A. I., and V. A. Prikhod'ko, I. M. Sherman, O. M. Tarasova, V. V. Isaevich, O. E. Semenyuk. 1977. [On the question of acclimating the large-mouth buffalo *Ictiobus cyprinellus* (Val.) in the inland water bodies of the Ukraine.] Rybnoe Khoz., Kiev. No. 22:46-50.

Ball, R. C. 1949. Experimental use of fertilizer in the production of fish-food organisms and fish. Mich. Agric. Exp. Sta. Tech. Bull. 210:1-28.

Ballard, W. W. 1982. Morphologenetic movements and fate map of the cypriniform teleost, *Catostomus commersoni* (La Cepède). Journal Exp. Zool. Vol. 219(3):301-321.

Baltz, Donald M., and Peter B. Moyle. 1984. Segregation by species and size classes of rainbow trout, *Salmo gairdneri*, and Sacramento sucker, *Catostomus occidentalis*, in three California (USA) streams. Environmental Biol. Fishes. Vol. 10(1-2):101-110.

Baltz, D. M., and B. Vondracek, L. R. Brown, P. B. Moyle. 1987. Influence of temperature on microhabitat choice by fishes in a California stream. Transactions of the American Fisheries Society. Vol. 116(1):12-20.

Bangham, Ralph V., and James R. Adams. 1954. A survey of the parasites of freshwater fishes from the mainland of British Columbia. Journal of the Biological Board of Canada. Vol. 11(6):673-708.

Barber, D. L., and J. E. Mills Westermann. 1975a. Morphological and histochemical studies on a PAS-positive granular leukocyte in blood and connective tissues of *Catostomus commersonii* (La Cepède) (Teleostei: Pisces). American Journal of Anatomy. Vol. 142(2):205-220.

Barber, D. L., and J. E. Mills Westermann. 1975b. 'Rodlet cells' in *Catostomus commersonii* (Teleostei:Pisces): secretory cells or parasite? Experientia. Vol. 31(8):924-925.

Barber, D. L., and J. E. Mills Westermann. 1983. Comparison of nuclear DNA content of rodlet cells and erythrocytes in some freshwater teleosts. Journal of Fish Biology. Vol. 22(4):477-484.

Barber, D. L., and J. E. Mills Westermann. 1985. Reappraisal of nuclear DNA content of rodlet cell types compared to several cell types from some freshwater teleosts, using two methods of microdensitometry. J. Fish Biol. Vol. 27(6):817-826.

Barber, D. L., and J. E. Mills Westermann. 1986. The rodlet cells of *Semotilus atromaculatus* and *Catostomus commersoni* (Teleostei): Studies on its identity using histochemistry and DNase I-gold, RNase A-gold, and S1 nuclease-gold labeling techniques. Canadian Journal of Zoology. Vol. 64(4):805-813.

Barclay, L. A., Jr. 1974. Home ranges and movements of small stream fishes in Alabama. Dissertation Abstr. int. (B):Vol. 35(3):1456.

Barnhart, M. C., and E. C. Powell. 1979. *Lissorchis kritskyi* sp. n. (Digenea: Lissorchiidae) from the river carpsucker, *Carpiodes carpio* (Rafinesque). Proceedings helminth. Soc. Wash. Vol. 46(1):47-51.

Barnhart, R. 1955. Survey of Lake Loveland Reservoir, Larimer County, Colorado. Colo. Fish. Res. Unit Quart. Rep. 2(1&2):31-40.

Barnickol, P. G., and W. C. Starrett. 1951. Commercial and sport fishes of the Mississippi River between Caruthersville, Missouri, and Dubuque, Iowa. Illinois Nat. Hist. Surv., Bull. Vol. 25(5):267-350.

Barton, B. A. 1980. Spawning migrations, age and growth, and summer feeding of white and longnose suckers in an irrigation reservoir. Canadian Fld. Nat. Vol. 94(3):300-304.

Barton, B. A., and B. F. Bidgood. 1980. Competitive feeding habits of rainbow trout, white sucker, and longnose sucker in Paine Lake, Alberta. Fisheries Research Report, Calgary, Alberta. No. 16:1-27pp.

Barwick, D. H., and P. L. Hudson. (undated). Food and feeding of fish in Hartwell Reservoir tailwater, George-South Carolina. Proc. Annu. Conf. Southeast Assoc. Fish Widl. Agencies Vol. 39:185-193.

Bass, J. C., and C. D. Riggs. 1959. Age and growth of the river carpsucker, *Carpiodes carpio* (Rafinesque), of Lake Texoma. Proc. Okla. Acad. Sci. Vol. 39:50-69.

Bassett, H. N. 1957. Further life history studies of two species of suckers in Shadow Mountain Reservoir, Grand County, Colorado. MS thesis Colo. St. Univ. 112pp.

Basu, Satyendra Prasanna. 1959. Active respiration of fish in relation to ambient concentrations of oxygen and carbon dioxide. Journal of the Fisheries Research Board of Canada. Vol. 16(2):175-212.

Batraeva, M. N. and E. K. Saurskaya. 1982. Effect of climatic conditions in various aquatic zones on the uterine stages of the buffalo. pp. 16-18 **IN:** Gvozdev, E. V. (editor). The animal world of Kazakhstan and the problems of its conservation. Nauka, Alma Ata. 211pp.

Bauer, Bruce H., and Branley A. Branson, Strant T. Colwell. 1978. Fishes of Paddy's Run Creek and the Dry Fork of the Whitewater River, Southwestern Ohio. Ohio J. Sci. Vol. 78(3):144-148.

Baugh, T. 1979. Nature vacuum cleaners. Freshwater mar. Aquar. Vol. 2(3):14-15.

Baughman, J. L. 1946. An interesting association of fishes. Copeia 1946(4):263.

Baumann, Paul C. 1984. Cancer in wild freshwater fish populations with emphasis on the Great Lakes. J. Great Lakes Res. Vol. 10(3):251-253.

Baxter, George T., and James R. Simon. 1970. Wyoming Fishes. Wyoming Game Fish Dep. Bull. No. 4. Cheyenne, Wyoming. 168pp.

Beamish, R. J. 1972a. Lethal pH for the white sucker *Catostomus commersoni* (La Cepède). Transactions of the American Fisheries Society. Vol. 101(2):355-358.

Beamish, R. J. 1972b. Factors affecting the age and size of the white sucker *Catostomus commersoni* at maturity. Dissertation Abstr. Int. Vol. 32B(9):5529.

Beamish, R. J. 1973. Determination of age and growth of populations of the white sucker (*Catostomus commersoni*) exhibiting a wide range in size at maturity. Journal of the Fisheries Research Board of Canada. Vol. 30(5): 607-616.

Beamish, R. J. 1974. Growth and survival of white suckers (*Catostomus commersoni*) in an acidified lake. Journal of the Fisheries Research Board of Canada. Vol. 31(1):49-54.

Beamish, R. J., and E. J. Crossman. 1977. Validity of the subspecies designation for the dwarf white sucker (*Catostomus commersoni utawana*) Journal of the Fisheries Research Board of Canada. Vol. 34(3):371-378.

Beamish, R. J., and H. H. Harvey. 1969. Age determination in the white sucker. Journal of the Fisheries Research Board of Canada. Vol. 26(3):633-638.

Beamish, R. J., and H. H. Harvey. 1972. Acidification of the La Cloche Mountain lakes, Ontario, and resulting fish mortalities. Journal of the Fisheries Research Board of Canada. Vol. 29(8):1131-1143.

Beamish, R. J., and W. L. Lockhart, J. C. Van Loon, Harold H. Harvey. 1975. Long term acidification of a lake and resulting effects on fishes. Ambio Vol. 4:98-102.

Beamish, R. J., and G. A. McFarlane. 1983. The forgotten requirement for age validation in fisheries biology. Transactions of the American Fisheries Society. Vol. 112(6):735-743.

Beamish, R. J., and H. Tsuyuki. 1972. A biochemical and cytological study of the longnose sucker (*Catostomus catostomus*) and large and dwarf forms of the white sucker (*Catostomus commersoni*). Journal of the Fisheries Research Board of Canada. Vol. 28(11):1745-1748.

Bean, L. S. 1936. Fish yield on the National Forests. Region Nine. Proc. N. Amer. Wildl. Conf. 1:301-304.

Bean, Tarleton Hoffman. 1879. Descriptions of two species of fishes collected by Prof. A. Dugès in central Mexico. Proc. U. S. Nat. Mus. Vol. 2:302-306.

Beatty, S. A. 1937. The measurement of the spoilage of fresh fish. Progress reports of Fisheries Research Board Atlantic Coast Stations. No. 20:3-5.

Beck, R. V. 1952. Introduction of suckers into the Upper San Joaquin River drainage, California. Calif. Fish. Game Vol. 38:407-408.

Becker, George C. 1959. Distribution of central Wisconsin fishes. Trans. Wisc. Acad. Sci., Arts, Lett. Vol. 48:65-102.

Becker, George C. 1964a. The fishes of Lakes Poygan and Winnebago. Trans. Wisc. Acad. Sci., Arts, Lett. Vol. 53:29-52.

Becker, George C. 1964b. The fishes of Pewaukee Lake. Trans. Wis. Acad. Sci. Arts Lett. Vol. 53:19-27.

Becker, George C. 1966. Fishes of southwestern Wisconsin. Trans. Wis. Acad. Sci., Arts, Lett. Vol. 55:87-117.

Becker, George C. 1976. Inland fishes of the Lake Michigan drainage basin. Argonne Natl. Lab. ANL/ES-40. Vol. 17. 237pp.

Becker, George C. 1983. Fishes of Wisconsin. University of Wisconsin Press, Madison, Wisconsin. 1052pp.

Beecher, H. A. 1979a. Anomalous occurrence of lip projection on *Carpiodes cyprinus*. Florida Scient. Vol. 42(1):62-63.

Beecher, H. A. 1979b. Comparative functional morphology and ecological isolating mechanisms in sympatric fishes of the genus *Carpiodes* in northwestern Florida. Dissertation Abstr. int. (B) Vol. 40(6):2557-2558.

Beecher, H. A. 1980. Habitat segregation of Florida carpsuckers (Osteichthyes: Catostomidae: *Carpiodes*). Florida Scient. Vol. 43(2):92-97.

Beers, G. D. 1955. Effects of a threadfin shad introduction upon black crappie and buffalo fish populations in Roosevelt Lake. M.S. Thesis Univ. Ariz. Lib. 57pp.

Behmer, D. J. 1965a. Length-weight relationship and spawning of river carpsuckers, *Carpiodes carpio*, in Des Moines, Iowa. M.S. Thesis Iowa St. Univ. Lib. 54pp.

Behmer, D. J. 1965b. Spawning periodicity of the river carpsucker, *Carpiodes carpio*. Proc. Iowa Acad. Sci. Vol. 72:253-262.

Behmer, D. J. 1966. Length-weight relationships as a measure of "condition" of river carpsuckers, *Carpiodes carpio*, in the Des Moines River. Ph.D. Disser. Iowa St. Univ. Lib. 154pp.

Behmer, D. J. 1969. A method of estimating fecunditiy; with data on river carpsucker, *Carpiodes carpio*. Transactions of the American Fisheries Society. Vol. 98(3):523-524.

Behmer, D. J. 1969. Schooling of river carpsuckers and a population estimate. Transactions of the American Fisheries Society. Vol. 98(2):520-523.

Behnke, Robert J. 1981. Chapter 4. Systematic and Zoogeographical Interpretation of Great Basin Trouts. pp. 95-124. **IN:** Robert J. Naiman and David L. Soltz (eds.). Fishes in North American Deserts. John Wiley and Sons. New York, N.Y. 552pp.

Behnke, Robert J., and Ralph M. Wetzel. 1960. A preliminary list of the fishes found in the fresh waters of Connecticut. Copeia 1960(2):141-143.

Bell, D. A., and Mary Beverly-Burton. 1980. Prevalence and intensity of *Capillaria catostomi* (Nematoda: Trichuroidea) in white sucker (*Catostomus commersoni*) in southern Lake Huron, Canada. Environmental Biol. Fishes Vol. 5(3):267-271.

Bendell-Young, Leah I., and Harold H. Harvey. 1986. Uptake and tissue distribution of manganese in the white sucker (*Catostomus commersoni*) under conditions of low pH. Hydrobiologia. Vol. 133(2):117-126.

Bendell-Young, Leah I., and Harold H. Harvey. 1986. Metal concentration and calcification of bone of white sucker (*Catostomus commersoni*) in relation to lake pH. Water, Air, and Soil Pollution. Vol. 30(3-4):657-664.

Bendell-Young, Leah I., and Harold H. Harvey. 1989. Concentrations and distribution of Fe, Zn and Cu in tissues of the white sucker (*Catostomus commersoni*) in relation to levels of metals and low pH. Hydrobiologia. Vol. 176-177:349-354.

Bendell-Young, Leah I., and Harold H. Harvey, Jeffrey F. Young. 1986. Accumulation of cadium by white suckers (*Catostomus commersoni*) in relation to fish growth and lake acidification. Can. J. Fish Aquat. Sci. Vol. 43(4):806-811.

Bennett, D. K. 1979. Three late Cenozoic fish faunas from Nebraska. **IN:** Kansas Academy of Science, 111th annual meeting (anonymous), Kans. Acad. Sci., Trans. Vol. 82(2):146-177.

Bennett, D. H., and O. E. Maughan, D. B. Jester, Jr. 1985. Generalized model for predicting spawning success of fish in reservoirs with fluctuating water levels. North American Journal of Fisheries Management. American Fisheries Society. Vol. 5(1):12-20.

Bennett, G. W., and W. F. Childers. 1957. The smallmouth bass, Micropterus dolomieui, in warm-water ponds. J. Wildlife Mgmt. Vol. 21(4):414-424.

Bennett, G. W., and W. F. Childers. 1966. The lake chubsucker as a forage species. Progr. Fish-Cult. Vol. 28(2):89-92.

Bensley, B. A. 1915. The fishes of Georgian Bay. Contributions to Canadian Biology. 1911-1914 Volume (Fasc. II). Fresh water fish and lake biology:1-51.

Berg, Leo Simonovich. 1912. Faune de la Russie Poissons. III(1):1-336.

Berg, Leo Simonovich. 1932. Les poissons des eaux douces de l'U.R.S.S., 3rd ed. Leningrad. I, 1-543.

Berg, Leo Simonovich. 1936. Note on *Coregonus* (*Prosopium*) *cylindraceus* (Pallas). Copeia 1936(1):57-58.

Berg, Leo Simonovich. 1940. Classification of fishes, both recent and fossil. Trav. Inst. Zool. Acad. Sci. URSS Vol. 5:85-517.

Berg, Leo Simonovich. 1949. Fresh-water fishes of Soviet Union. Tabl. Anal. Faune U.R.S.S. II. Vol. 29:467-925.

Berg, Leo Simonovich. 1964. Freshwater fishes of the U.S.S.R. and adjacent countries. Volume 2, Washington, D.C. 1-496. [translation of 1949].

Berigina, I. A. 1976. The structure of the digestive tract in the genus *Ictiobus* (Cypriniformes, Catostomidae). 2. The digestive tract of *Ictiobus bubalis* (Raf.) Annalen naturh. Mus. Wien Vol. 16(5):859-866.

Berkman, Hilary E., and Charles F. Rabeni, Terence P. Boyle. 1986. Biomonitors of stream quality in agricultural areas: Fish vs. invertebrates. Environ. Manage. Vol. 10(3):413-420.

Berner, Lester M. 1948. The intestinal convolutions: new generic characters for the separation of *Carpiodes* and *Ictiobus*. Copeia, Ann Arbor. 1948(2):140.

Berner, Lester M. 1951. Limnology of the lower Missouri River. Ecol. Vol. 32(1):1-12.

Bernhardt, R. W. 1957. Growth of fish in the waters of the Huntington Wildlife Forest. M.S. Thesis Syracuse Univ. 93pp.

Bernstein, J. W., and S. M. Swanson. 1989. Hematological parameters and parasite load in wild fish with elevated radionuclide levels. Adv. Environ. Sci. Technol. Vol. 22:47-64.

Berry, C. R., Jr. 1984. Hematology of four rare Colorado River Fishes. Copeia 1984(3):790-793.

Berst, A. H. 1961. Selectivity and efficiency of experimental gill nets in South Bay and Georgian Bay of Lake Huron. Transactions of the American Fisheries Society. Vol. 90(4):413-418.

Berst, A. H., and A. M. McCombie. 1963. The spatial distribution of fish in gill nets. Journal of the Fisheries Research Board of Canada. Vol. 20(3):735-742.

Beverly-Burton, Mary. 1984. Monogenea and Turbellaria. pp. 5-209. **IN:** L. Margolis and Z. Kabata (ed.) Guide to the parasites of fishes of Canada. Part I. Can. Spec. Publ. Fish. Aquat. Sci. Vol. 74:209pp.

Bigelow, N. K. 1923. The food of young Suckers (*Catostomus commersonii*) on Lake Nipigon. Publications of the Ontario Fisheries Research Laboratory No. 21. Univ. Toronto Studies Biol. Ser. Vol. 24:81-115.

Birkenholz, D., and A. W. Fritz. 1956. Fishes of Little Wall Lake, Iowa. Ia. St. Univ. Coop. Fish. Unit. 21pp. typewritten.

Birt, T. P., and R. E. Dillinger, Jr., J. M. Green, W. S. Davidson. 1990. Transferrin variation in the longnose sucker, *Catostomus catostomus*, from the Yukon and Mackenzie Rivers. Biochem. Syst. Ecol. Vol. 18(1):75-79.

Bissett, E. D. R. 1927. Freshwater Fish of Manitoba. Can. Field-Nat. Vol. 41:127-128.

Black, Edgar C. 1953. Upper lethal temperatures of some British Columbia freshwater fishes. Journal of the Fisheries Research Board of Canada. Vol. 10(4):196-210.

Black, Edgar C. 1955. Blood levels of hemoglobin and lactic acid in some freshwater fishes following exercise. Journal of the Fisheries Research Board of Canada. Vol. 12(6):917-929.

Black, G. A., and J. M. Fraser. 1984. Dynamics of prevalence of *Ligula intestinalis* (L.) in *Catostomus commersoni* (La Cepède). J. Fish Biol. Vol. 25(2):139-146.

Black, J. J. 1984. Environmental implications of neoplasia in Great Lakes fish. Mar. Environ. Res. Vol. 14(1-4):529-534.

Black, J. J., and M. Holmes, P. P. Dymerski, W. F. Zapisek. 1979. Fish tumor pathology and aromatic hydrocarbon pollution in a Great Lakes estuary. Environmental Sci. Res. Vol. 16:559-565.

Blackwelder, Richard E. 1972. Guide to the Taxonomic Literature of Vertebrates. Iowa State University Press, Ames, Iowa. 259pp.

Blatchley, W. S. 1938. The Fishes of Indiana. The Nature Publishing Co. Indianapolis, Indiana. 121pp.

Bleeker, P. 1864. Notices sur quelques genres et espèces de Cyprinoides de Chine. Nederl. Tydschr. Dierk. Vol. 2: 18-29.

Bligh, E. G. 1970. Mercury contamination in fish. 20th Annu. Inst. Public. Health Insp., Winnipeg, Manitoba. Oct. 19-23, 1970. Interpretive Articles of the Fisheries Research Board of Canada. No. 200. p. 10-19.

Bligh, E. G. 1971. Environmental factors affecting the utilization of Great Lakes fish as human food. Limnos Vol. 4:13-19. Interpretative Articles of the Fisheries Research Board of Canada. No. 201. pp. 13-19.

Blinova, R. D., and A. N. Burlakova, E. M. Zaitseva. 1980. Feeding relations between the carp and black buffalo reared together in water bodies of Middle Volga. Sbornik nauch. Trud. gos. nauchno-issled. Inst. ozern. rechn. rybn. Khozyaist. No. 158:70-75.

Blouin, E. F., and A. D. Johnson, D. G. Dunlap, D. K. Spiegel. 1984. Prevalence of black spot (*Neascus pyriformis*: Trematoda: Diplostomatidae) of fishes in Brule Creek, South Dakota. Proceedings helminth. Soc. Wash. Vol. 51(2):357-359.

Bond, Carl E. 1953. Occurrence of the mountain-sucker, *Pantosteus jordani*, in the Williamette River System, Oregon. Copeia 1953(2):116.

Borges, M. H. 1950. Fish distribution studies, Niangua Arm of the Lake of the Ozarks, Missouri. Journal of Wildlife Management. Vol. 14(1):16-33.

Borgmann, Uwe, and Karen M. Ralph. 1985. Feeding, growth and particle-size-conversion efficiency in white sucker larvae and young common shiners. Environ. Biol. Fishes. Vol. 14(4):269-279.

Borgmann, Uwe, and Karen M. Ralph. 1986. Effects of cadmium, 2,4-dichlorophenol and pentachlorophenol on feeding, growth, and particle-size-conversion efficiency of white sucker [*Catostomus commersoni*] larvae and young common shiners [*Notropis cornutus*]. Arch. Environ. Contam. Toxicol. Vol. 15(5):473-480.

Borgstrom, Georg. 1978. Chapter 19. The Contribution of Freshwater Fish to Human Food. pp. 469-491. **IN:** Shelby D. Gerking. (ed.). Ecology of Freshwater Fish Production. John Wiley & Sons. New York, New York. 520pp.

Boschung, Herbert T., Jr., and James D. Williams, Daniel W. Gotshall, David K. Caldwell, Melba C. Caldwell, Carol Nehring, Jordan Verner. 1983. The Audubon Society Field Guide to North American Fishes, Whales, and Dolphins. Alfred A. Knopf Publ., New York, N. Y. 848pp.

Bosley, C. E. 1960. Pre-impoundment study of the Flaming Gorge Reservoir. Wyo. Game Fish Comm. Fish Tech. Rep. Vol. 9:81pp.

Bosley, T. R., and J. V. Conner. 1984. Geographic and temporal variation in numbers of myomeres in fish larvae from the lower Mississippi River. Transactions of the American Fisheries Society. Vol. 113(2):238-242.

Boucher, R., and R. Schetagne, E. Magnin. 1985. Mercury levels in fish of the La Grande 2 and Opinaca reservoirs (Québec, Canada) before and after impoundment. Rev. Fr. Sci. Eau. Vol. 4(2-3):193-206.

Bouck, G. R., and R. C. Ball. 1967. Distribution of low mobility proteins in the blood of fishes. Journal of the Fisheries Research Board of Canada. Vol. 24(3):695-697.

Boulenger, G. A. 1904. Teleosti (Systematic part). The Cambridge Natural History. Vol. 7:539-727; text-figs. 325-440.

Bower, S. M., and P. T. K. Woo. 1977a. Morphology and host specificity of *Cryptobia catastomi* n.sp. (Protozoa:Kinetoplastida) from white sucker (*Catostomus commersoni*) in southern Ontario. Canadian Journal of Zoology. Vol. 55(7):1082-1093.

Bower, S. M., and P. T. K. Woo. 1977b. Division and morphogenesis of *Cryptobia catastomi* (Protozoa: Kinetoplastida) in the blood of white sucker (*Catostomus commersoni*). Canadian Journal of Zoology. Vol. 55(7):1093-1099.

Bower, S. M., and P. T. K. Woo. 1979. The prevalence of *Trypanosoma catostomi* in white sucker (*Catostomus commersoni*) from southern Ontario. Journal Wildl. Dis. Vol. 15(3):429-431.

Bowman, M. L. 1954. Some aspects of the life history of the black redhorse (*Moxostoma duquesnei* Le Sueur), with reference to its association with the smallmouth bass (*Micropterus dolomieu* La Cepède) in two south central Missouri streams, the Niangua and the Big Piney. M.S. Thesis Univ. Mo. 39pp.

Bowman, M. L. 1959. Life history of the black redhorse, *Moxostoma duquesnei* (Le Sueur), in Missouri. Ph.D. Thesis. University of Missouri, Columbia. 144pp.

Bowman, M. L. 1970. Life history of the Black redhorse, *Moxostoma duquesnei* (Le Sueur), in Missouri. Transactions of the American Fisheries Society. Vol. 99:546-559.

Boyadjiev, A. 1983. First results from buffalo propagation in our country. pp. 145-154. **IN:** A. M. Boyadzhiev, Kh, M. Tomasyan, P. G. Petrov. (editors). 30th Anniversary Freshwater Fish. Res Inst., Plovdiv, Sofia. 234pp.

Bozek, M. A., and L. J. Paulson, G. R. Wilde. 1990. Effects of ambient Lake Mohave temperatures on development, oxygen consumption, and hatching success of the razorback sucker. Environ. Biol. Fishes. Vol. 27(4):255-263.

Bradley, R. W., and J. R. Morris. 1986. Heavy metals in fish from a series of metal-contaminated lakes near Sudbury, Ontario [Canada]. Water Air Soil Pollut. Vol. 27(3/4):341-354.

Brady, L., and A. Hulsey. 1959. Propagation of buffalofishes, 1959. Proc. S.E. Assoc. Game Fish Comm. Vol. 13:80-90.

Branson, Branley A. 1961. Observation on the distribution of nuptial tubercles in some catostomid fish. Trans. Kansas Acad. Sci. Vol. 64:360-372.

Branson, Branley A. 1962. Comparative cephalic and appendicular osteology of the fish Family Catostomidae. Part I, *Cycleptus elongatus* (Le Sueur). Southwest. Nat. Vol. 7:81-153.

Branson, Branley A., and Donald L. Batch. 1974. Fishes of the Red River Drainage, Eastern Kentucky. The University Press of Kentucky. Lexington, Kentucky. 67pp.

Branson, Branley A., and Donald L. Batch, S. Rice. 1981. Collections of fishes from the Little Sandy River and Tygarts Creek Drainages, Kentucky. Transactions Ky. Acad. Sci. Vol. 42(3-4):98-100.

Branson, Branley A., and Clarence J. McCoy, Jr., Morgan E. Sisk. 1960. Notes on the freshwater fishes of Sonora with an addition to the known fauna. Copeia 1960(3):217-220.

Branson, Branley A., and George A. Moore. 1962. The lateralis components of the acoustico-lateralis system in the sunfish family Centrarchidae. Copeia 1962(1):1-108.

Breder, C. M., Jr. 1920. Some notes on *Leuciscus vandoisulus* (Cuv. and Val.) Copeia 1920(No. 82):35-38.

Breder, C. M., Jr., and D. E. Rosen. 1966. Modes of reproduction in fishes. Am. Mus. Nat. Hist. N. Y. 941pp.

Brett, J. R. 1944. Some lethal temperature relations of Algonquin Park fishes. Univ. Toronto Stud. Biol. Ser. No. 52. 49pp.

Brett, J. R. 1956. Some priniciples in the thermal requirements of fishes. Quarterly Review of Biology. Vol. 31(2):75-87.

Brett, J. R., and A. L. Pritchard. 1946. Lakes of the Skeena River drainage. I. Lakelse Lake. Progress Reports of Fisheries Research Board Pacific Coast Stations.Issue No. 66:12-15.

Brett, J. R., and A. L. Pritchard. 1946. Lakes of the Skeena River drainage. II. Morice Lake. Progress Reports of Fisheries Research Board Pacific Coast Stations. Issue No. 67:23-26.

Brezner, J. 1956. Some aspects in the life history of the northern river carpsucker, *Carpiodes carpio* (Rafinesque), in the Niangua Arm of the Lake of the Ozarks. M.S. Thesis Univ. Mo. 79pp. typewritten.

Brezner, J. 1958. Food habits of the northern river carpsucker in Missouri. Progr. Fish-Cult. Vol. 20(4):170-174.

Brienholt, J. C., and R. A. Heckmann. 1980. Parasites from two species of suckers (Catostomidae) from southern Utah. Great Basin Nat. Vol. 40(2):149-156.

Briggs, T., and C. Bussjaeger. 1972. Allocholic acid, the major component in bile from the river carpsucker, *Carpiodes carpio* (Rafinesque) (Catostomidae). Comparative Biochem. Physiol. (B) Vol. 42(3):493-496.

Brimley, C. S., and W. B. Mabee. 1925. Reptiles, amphibians and fishes collected in eastern North Carolina in the autumn of 1923. Copeia 1925(No. 139):14-16.

Brittan, Martin R., and John D. Hopkirk, Jerrold D. Conners, Michael Martin. 1970. Explosive spread of the Oriental goby *Acanthogobius flavimanus* in the San Francisco Bay-Delta Region of California. Proceedings of the California Academy of Sciences. Fourth Series. Vol. 38(No. 11):207-214.

Britton, J. C., and C. E. Murphy. 1977. New records and ecological notes for *Corbicula manilensis* in Texas. Nautilus, Philad. Vol. 91(1):20-23.

Bronte, C. R., and D. W. Johnson. 1984. Evaluation of the commercial entanglement-gear fishery in Lake Barkley and Kentucky Lake, Kentucky. N.A.J. Fisheries Management. Vol. 3(2):78-83.

Brothers, E. B. 1984. Otolith Studies. pp. 50-57. **IN:** Moser, H. G. et al., (ed.) Ontogeny and Systematics of Fishes. American Society of Ichthyologists and Herpetologists Special Publication Number 1. Allen Press, Inc., Lawrence, Kansas. 760pp.

Brousseau, R. A. 1976. The pectoral anatomy of selected Ostariophysi. Cypriniformes and Siluriformes. Journal Morph. Vol. 150(1):79-116.

Brown, C. J. D. 1971. Fishes of Montana. Agric. Exp. Stn. Mont. State Univ. Big Sky Books, Bozeman. 207pp.

Brown, C. J. D., and R. C. Ball. 1943. A fish population study of Third Sister Lake. Transactions of the American Fisheries Society. Vol. 72:177-185.

Brown, C. J. D., and R. J. Graham. 1954. Observations on the longnose sucker in Yellowstone Lake. Transactions of the American Fisheries Society. Vol. 83:38-46.

Brown, E. H., Jr. 1960. Little Miami River headwater-stream investigations. Ohio Dept. Nat. Resources Div. Wildl. 1-143.

Brynildson, C., and J. Truog. 1958. The structure of the forage fish populations in Milner Branch, Grant County, October 7-10, 1958. Wisc. Conserv. Dep. Invest. Memo. No. 247. 8pp.

Buchanon, T. M. 1973. <u>Key</u> <u>to</u> <u>the</u> <u>Fishes</u> <u>of</u> <u>Arkansas</u>. Arkansas Game and Fish Commission. 1-68pp.

Bucholz, M. 1957. Age and growth of river carpsucker in Des Moines River, Iowa. Proc. Iowa Acad. Sci. Vol. 64:589-600.

Buck, D. H., and Frank B. Cross. 1952. Early limnological and fish population conditions of Canton Reservoir, Oklahoma, and fishery management recommendations. Okla. A. M. Coll. Res. Found. 110pp.

Bulkley, R. V., and S.-Y. T. Leung, J. J. Richard. 1981. Organochlorine insecticide concentrations in fish of the Des Moines River, Iowa, 1977-78. Pesticides Monit. J. Vol. 15(2):86-89.

Bulkley, R. V., and R. Pimental. 1983. Temperature preference and avoidance by adult razorback suckers. Transactions of the American Fisheries Society. Vol. 112(5):601-607.

Bur, M. T. 1976. Age, growth and food habits of Catostomidae in Pool 8 of the upper Mississippi River. Univ. Wisc., LaCrosse. MS Thesis. 107pp.

Burns, J. W. 1966. Western sucker. Inland Fisheries Management, A. Calhoun (ed.). Calif. Dept. Fish Game:516-517.

Burr, Brooks M. 1979. Observations on spawning and breeding coloration of *Moxostoma lachneri* in Chattahoochee River, Georgia. Georgia Journal of Science. Vol. . Sci. Vol. 37(3-4):205-207.

Burr, Brooks M., and D. A. Carney. 1984. The blacktail redhorse, *Moxostoma poecilurum* (Catostomidae) in Kentucky with other additions to the state ichthyofauna. Transactions Ky. Acad. Sci. Vol. 45(1-2):408-414.

Burr, Brooks M., and R. C. Heidinger. 1983. Reproductive behavior of the bigmouth buffalo *Ictiobus cyprinellus* in Crab Orchard Lake, Illinois. American Midl. Nat. Vol. 110(1):220-221.

Burr, Brooks M., and M. A. Morris. 1977. Spawning behavior of the shorthead redhorse, *Moxostoma macrolepidotum*, in Big Rock Creek, Illinois. Transactions of the American Fisheries Society. Vol. 106(1):80-82.

Bussjaeger, C. E. 1973. A comparative study of bile salts in sucker fishes (Family Catostomidae). Dissertation Abstr. int. Vol. 34B(4):1364.

Bussjaeger, C. E., and T. Briggs. 1978. Phylogenetic implications of bile salts in some catostomid fishes. Copeia. 1978(3):533-535.

Buth, Donald G. 1977a. Biochemical identification of *Moxostoma rhothoecum* and *M. hamiltoni*. Biochemical Syst. Ecol. Vol. 5(1):57-60.

Buth, Donald G. 1977b. Alcohol dehydrogenase variability in *Hypentelium nigricans*. Biochemical Syst. Ecol. Vol. 5(1):61-63.

Buth, Donald G. 1978. Biochemical systematics of the Moxostomatini (Cypriniformes, Catostomidae). Dissertation Abstr. int. (B) Vol. 39(5):2170-2171.

Buth, Donald G. 1979a. Duplicate gene expression in tetraploid fishes of the tribe Moxostomatini (Cypriniformes: Catostomidae). Comparative Biochem. Physiol. (B) Vol. 63(1):7-12.

Buth, Donald G. 1979b. Genetic relationships among the torrent suckers, genus Thoburnia. Biochemical Syst.. Ecol. Vol. 7(4):311-316.

Buth, Donald G. 1979c. Creatine kinase variability in *Moxostoma macrolepidotum* (Cypriniformes: Catostomidae). Copeia 1979(1):152-154.

Buth, Donald G. 1980. Evolutionary genetics and systematic relationships in the catostomid genus *Hypentelium*. Copeia 1980(2):280-290.

Buth, Donald G. 1982. Glucosephosphate-isomerase expression in a tetraploid fish, *Moxostoma lachneri* (Cypriniformes, Catostomidae): evidence for 'retetraploidization'? Genetica. Vol. 57:171-175.

Buth, Donald G. 1983. Duplicate Isozyme Loci in Fishes: Origins, Distribution, Phyletic Consequences, and Locus Nomenclature. pp. 381-400. **IN:** Isozymes: Current Topics in biological and Medical Research. Genetics and Evolution. Volume 10: Alan R. Liss, Inc. New York, N.Y.

Buth, Donald G. 1984. The application of electrophoretic data in systematic studies. Annual Review of Ecology and Systematics. Vol. 15:501-522.

Buth, Donald G., and C. B. Crabtree. 1982. Genetic variability and population structure of *Catostomus santaanae* in the Santa Clara Drainage. Copeia 1982(2):439-444.

Buth, Donald G., and R. W. Murphy, L. Ulmer. 1987. Population differentiation and introgressive hybridization of the flannelmouth sucker and of hatchery and native stocks of the razorback sucker. Transactions of the American Fisheries Society. Vol. 116(1):103-110.

Butler, J. L. 1960. Development of the Weberian apparatus of a catostomid fish. Proc. Iowa Acad. Sci. Vol. 67:532-543.

Buynak, G. L., and H. W. Mohr, Jr. 1978a. Larval development of the white sucker (*Catostomus commersoni*) from the Susquehanna River. Proceedings Pa. Acad. Sci. Vol. 52(2):143-145.

Buynak, G. L., and H. W. Mohr, Jr. 1978b. Larval development of the northern hog sucker (*Hypentelium nigricans*), from the Susquehanna River. Transactions of the American Fisheries Society. Vol. 107(4):595-599.

Buynak, G. L., and H. W. Mohr, Jr. 1979. Larval development of the shorthead redhorse (*Moxostoma macrolepidotum*) from the Susquehanna River. Transactions of the American Fisheries Society. Vol. 108(2):161-165.

Buynak, G. L., and H. W. Mohr, Jr. 1980. Key to the identification of sucker larvae in the Susquehanna River near Berwick, Pennsylvania. Proceedings Pa. Acad Sci. Vol. 54(2):161-164.

Cagnolaro, L., and C. Violani. 1988. Introductions to the anastatic report of 'Vertebratorum Synopsis...' by E. Cornalia (1849). Atti Soc. Ital. Sci. Nat. Mus. Civ. Stor. Nat. Milano Vol. 129(4):433-434.

Cahn, A. R. 1927. An ecological study of the southern Wisconsin fishes. The brook silverside (*Labidesthes sicculus*) and the cisco (*Leucichthys artedi*) in their relations to the region. Ill. Biol. Monogr. Vol. 11(1):1-151.

Call, M. W. 1960. A study of the Pole Mountain beaver and their relation to the brook trout fishery. Wyo. Game Fish Comm., Univ. Wyo. Coop. Res. Proj. 2. M.S. thesis:93-219.

Call, R. E. 1887. Memoranda on a collection of fishes from the Ozark Region of Missouri. Proc. Davenport Acad. Nat. Sci. Vol. 5:73-80.

Cameron, J. N. 1974. Evidence for the lack of by-pass shunting in teleost gills. Journal of the Fisheries Research Board of Canada. Vol. 31(2):211-213.

Cameron, J. N. 1975. Morphometric and flow indicator studies of the teleost heart. Canadian Journal of Zoology. Vol. 53(6):691-698.

Campbell, K. P. 1974. Competition between brown trout (*Salmo trutta*) and white suckers (*Catostomus commersoni*). Dissertation Abstr. int. (B) Vol. 34(8):4126-4127.

Campbell, R. S. 1935. A study of the common sucker, *Catostomus commersoni* (La Cepède), of Waskesiu Lake. M.A. Thesis. Univ. Sask. 48pp.

Canfield, H. L. 1922. Care and feeding of buffalofish in ponds. U. S. Bur. Fish., Econ. Circ. 56:3pp.

Canton, S. P., and L. D. Cline, R. A. Short, J. V. Ward. 1984. The macroinvertebrates and fish of a Colorado stream during a period of fluctuating discharge. Freshwater Biol. Vol. 14(3):311-316.

Caraiman, G., and Z. Pogan. 1981. The buffalo fish in the course of acclimatization at the Cefa - Bihor fishery. Nymphaea. Vol. 8-9:483-501.

Carbine, W. F. 1943. The artificial propagation and growth of the common white sucker, *Catostomus c. commersonii* and its value as a bait and forage fish. Copeia, Ann Arbor 1943(1):48-49.

Carbine, W. F., and V. C. Applegate. 1948. The fish population of Deep Lake, Michigan. Transactions of the American Fisheries Society. Vol. 75:200-237.

Carl, G. Clifford. 1936. Food of the Coarse-scaled Sucker (*Catostomus macrocheilus* Girard). J. biol. Board Canada. Vol. 3(1):20-25.

Carl, G. Clifford, and Wilbert Amie Clemens, Casimir Charles Lindsey. 1977. The Fresh-water Fishes of British Columbia.British Columbia Provincial Museum. Handbook No. 5. Province of British Columbia. 7th printing. 3rd edition revised. 192pp.

Carlander, Kenneth D. 1942. An investigation of Lake of the Woods, Minnesota, with particular reference to the commercial fisheries. Minn. Bur. Fish. Res. Invest. Rep. Vol. 42:1-534. typewritten.

Carlander, Kenneth D. 1943. Growth rate of the spottailed minnow, *Notropis hudsonius* (Clinton), in Minnesota waters. Minn. Bur. Fish. Res. Invest. Rep. Vol. 50:3 pp. typewritten.

Carlander, Kenneth D. 1944a. Notes on the coefficient of condition, K, of Minnesota fishes. Minn. Bur. Fish. Res. Invest. Rep. 41 (revised):40pp. typewritten.

Carlander, Kenneth D. 1944b. Notes on the minor species of fish taken in the commercial fisheries at Lake of the Woods, 1939 to 1943. Minn. Bur. Fish. Res. Invest. Rep. Vol. 42(Suppl. 2):27 pp. typewritten.

Carlander, Kenneth D. 1948. Some changes in the fish population of Lake of the Woods, Minnesota, 1910 to 1945. Copeia 1948(4):271-274.

Carlander, Kenneth D. 1949. Project No. 39. Yellow pike-perch management. Progr. Rep. Iowa Coop. Wildl. Fish. Res. Units, 1949 (Jan.-Mar.):44-57.

Carlander, Kenneth D. 1952. Project 37. Farm ponds. Quart. Rep. Iowa Coop. Wildl. Fish. Res. Units. Vol. 17(4):23-25.

Carlander, Kenneth D. 1955. Standing crops of named fishes in North American lakes and reservoirs. Journal of the Fisheries Research Board of Canada. Vol. 12(4):543-570.

Carlander, Kenneth D. 1969. Handbook of freshwater fishery biology. Vol. 1. Iowa State Univ. Press. Ames, Iowa. 752pp.

Carlander, Kenneth D. 1978. History of the Fish Population of Lake Laverne, Iowa State University Campus. Iowa State Journal of Research. Vol. 52(4):425-433.

Carlander, Kenneth D., and L. E. Hiner. 1943a. Preliminary report on fisheries investigations, Leech Lake, Cass County. Minn. Bur. Fish. Res. 18pp. typewritten.

Carlander, Kenneth D., and L. E. Hiner. 1943b. Fisheries investigation and management report for Lake Vermilion, St. Louis County. Minn. Bur. Fish. Res. Invest. Rep. Vol. 54:1-175.

Carlander, Kenneth D., and R. B. Moorman. 1949. Project 37. Management of small ponds for fish production. Quart. Rep. Iowa Coop. Wildl. Fish. Res. Units, 1949 (July-Sept.):54-83.

Carlander, Kenneth D., and J. W. Parsons. 1949. Project No. 39. Yellow pike-perch management. Progr. Rep. Iowa Coop. Wildl. Fish. Res. Units, 1949 (April-June):49-52.

Carlander, Kenneth D., and Lloyd L. Smith, Jr. 1945. Some factors to consider in the choice between standard, fork or total lengths in fishery investigations. Copeia 1945(1):7-12.

Carnes, W. C., Jr. 1958. Contributions to the biology of the eastern creek chubsucker, *Erimyzon oblongus oblongus* (Mitchill). N. C. State Coll., Raleigh. M.S. Thesis. 69pp.

Carson, R. 1943. Fishes of the Middle West. U.S. Fish Wildl. Serv. Conserv. Bull. 34:44pp.

Carter, John G., and Vincent A. Lamarra, Ronald J. Ryel. 1986. Drift of larval fishes in the upper Colorado River. J. Freshwater Biol. Vol. 3(4):567-578.

Carter, John G., and R. A. Valdez, Ronald J. Ryel, Vincent A. Lamarra. 1985. Fisheries habitat dynamics in the upper Colorado River. J. Freshwater Ecol. Vol. 3(2):249-264.

Casteel, Richard W. 1976. Fish remains in archaeology and paleo-environmental studies. Academic Press, London, New York and San Francisco. 1-180pp.

Casteel, Richard W., and D. P. Adam. 1977. Pleistocene fishes from Alameda County, California. J. Res. U. S. Geol. Surv. Vol. 5(2):209-215.

Casteel, Richard W., and Michael J. Rymer. 1981. Pliocene and Pleistocene fishes from the Clear Lake area: Geol. Surv. Prof. Pap., 1141, pp. 231-235. IN: Robert J. McLaughlin, et al., ed., Research in The Geyers-Clear Lake geothermal area, northern California.

Casteel, Richard W., and J. H. Williams, C. K. Throckmorton, et al. 1979. Fish remains from Core 8, Clear Lake, Lake County, California. U.S. Geol. Surv., Open-file Rep., No. 79-1148, 101pp.

Cavender, T. M. 1968. Freshwater fish remains from the Clarno Formation, Ochoco Mountains of North-central Oregon.--The Ore Bin (Oregon Department of Geology and Mineral Industries, Portland). Vol. 30(7):125-141.

Cavender, Ted M. 1986. Chapter 19. Review of the Fossil History of North American Freshwater Fishes. pp. 699-724. IN: Hocutt, Charles H., and E. O. Wiley (eds.). The Zoogeography of North American Freshwater Fishes. John Wiley and Sons. New York, N.Y. 1985(1986). 866pp.

Chadwick, James W., and Steven P. Canton. 1983. Coal mine drainage effects on a lotic ecosystem in Northwest Colorado, USA. Hydrobiologia. Vol. 107(1):25-34.

Chaicharn, A., and W. L. Bullock. 1967. The histopathology of acanthocephalan infections in suckers with observations on the intestinal histology of two species of Catostomid fishes. Acta zool., Stockh. Vol. 48:19-42.

Chalanchuk, S. M. 1985. Recruitment, growth and condition of a population of the white sucker, Catostomus commersoni, in Lake 223 (Canada), an experimentally acidified lake. Can. Tech. Rep. Fish Aquat. Sci. No. 1396:1-18.

Chan, G.-L. 1981. A study of some parasites of the white sucker, Catostomus commersoni (La Cepède), and the fathead minnow, Pimephales promelas Rafinesque, in a reservoir and its contiguous streams. Dissertation Abstr. int. (B) Vol. 42(5):1753.

Chan, D. K. O., and R. Gunther, H. A. Bern. 1978. The isolated trout rectum bioassay for urotensin II: assessment for specificity and precision. General comp. Endocr. Vol. 34(3):347-359.

Chang, C.-Y., and G. I. Ji. 1978. A new species of Pseudomurraytrema from gills of Myxocyprinus asiaticus. Acta hydrobiol. sin. Vol. 6(3):349-352.

Chapman, D. W. 1978. Chapter 1. Production in Fish Populations. pp. 5-25. IN: Shelby D. Gerking (ed.) Ecology of Freshwater Fish Production. John Wiley & Sons. New York, N. Y. 520pp.

Chatto, D. A. 1979. Effect of salinity on hatching success of the cui-ui. Progressive Fish-Culturist. Vol. 41(2):82-85.

Chau, Y. K., and P. T. S. Wong, G. A. Bengert, J. L. Dunn, B. Glen. 1985. Occurrence of alkyllead compounds in the Detroit and St. Clair Rivers. Journal Great Lakes Research. Vol. 11(3):313-319.

Cherry, D. S., and K. L. Dickson, J. Cairns, Jr., J. R. Stauffer. 1977. Preferred, avoided, and lethal temperatures of fish during rising temperature conditions. Journal of the Fisheries Research Board of Canada. Vol. 34(2): 239-246.

Chew, Robert D., and Martin A. Hamilton. 1985. Toxicity curve estimation: Fitting a compartment model to median survival times. Trans. Am. Fish Soc. Vol. 114(3):403-412.

Chien, Shin Ming. 1969. Monogenean parasites of *Hypentelium nigricans* with description of a new species. J. Parasitology. Vol. 55:737-739.

Chien, Shin Ming, and Wilmer A. Rogers. 1970. Four New Species of Monogenetic Trematodes, Genus *Pellucidhaptor* from Fishes of Southeastern U.S. Journal of Parasitology. Vol. 56(3):480-485.

Chlebeck, A., and G. L. Phillips. 1969. Hematological study of two buffalofishes *Ictiobus cyprinellus* and *I. bulbalus* (Catostomidae). Journal of the Fisheries Research Board of Canada Vol. 26:2881-2886.

Chovelon, A., and L. George, C. Gulayets, Y. Hoyano, E. McGuinness, J. Moore, S. Ramamoorthy, S. Ramammoorthy, P. Singer, K. Smiley, A. Wheatley. 1984. Pesticide and PCB levels in fish from Alberta (Canada) Chemosphere. Vol. 13(1):19-32.

Chranilov, Ivar N. S. 1926. Der Schwimmblasenapparat bei Catostomus und einige allgemeine Erwägungen über den Weber'schen Apparat dei Ostariophysi. Anat. Anz. Jena. Vol. 61(3-4):49-69.

Christensen, B. M., and R. L. Calentine. 1983. *Penarchigetes macrorchis* sp. n. (Cestoidea: Caryophyllaeidae) from the lake chubsucker, *Erimyzon succeta* (La Cepède), in western Kentucky. Proceedings helminth. Soc. Wash. Vol. 50(1):112-116.

Christensen, B. M., and P. K. Wellner, L. N. Gleason. 1982. Two new species of *Lissorchis* Magath (Digenea: Lissorchiidae) from the spotted sucker, *Minytrema melanops* (Rafinesque), with a key to species. Proceedings helminth. Soc. Wash. Vol. 49(1):22-27.

Christensen, G. M. 1972. Effects of metal cations and other chemicals upon the in vitro activity of two enzymes in the blood plasma of the white sucker, *Catostomus commersoni* (La Cepède). Chemico-biological Interactions. Vol. 4(5):351-361.

Christenson, L. M. 1957. Some characteristics of the fish populations in backwater areas of the Upper Mississippi River. M.S. Thesis Univ. Minn. 125pp.

Christenson, L. M. 1974. Notes on the blue sucker, *Cycleptus elongatus* (Le Sueur), in the lower Chippewa and Red Cedar rivers, Wisconsin. Wis. Dep. Nat. Resour. Res. Rep. 75. 7 pp.

Christenson, L. M., and L. L. Smith. 1965. Characteristics of fish populations in upper Mississippi backwater areas. U.S. Fish Wildl. Serv. Circ. 212: 53 pp.

Chung, Y.-T. 1980. A study of the relationship between body length and several scale measurements of the northern hogsucker. Quarterly J. Taiwan Mus. Vol. 33(3-4):283-288.

Chung, Y.-T. 1981. A study on the histopathology in the Wolffian ducts of *Hypentelium nigricans* (Osteichthyes: Catostomidae) caused by *Phylladistomum superbum* (Trematoda:Gorgoderidae). Quarterly J. Taiwan Mus. Vol. 34(3-4):237-240.

Cicerello, Ronald R., and Robert S. Butler. 1985. Fishes of Buck Creek, Cumberland River Drainage, Kentucky [USA]. Brimleyana. 0(11):133-160.

Ciepielewski, W. 1985. Experimentally increased fish stock in the pond type Lake Warniak. Changes of ichthyofauna between 1970 and 1983. Ekol. Polska-Polish J. Ecol. Vol. 33(1):37-60.

Cincotta, Dan A., and Robert L. Miles, Michael E. Hoeft, Gerald E. Lewis. 1986. Discovery of *Noturus eleutherus, Noturus stigmosus*, and *Percina peltata* in West Virginia, with discussions of other additions and records of fishes. Brimleyana No. 12:101-122.

Cincotta, Dan A., and J. R. Stauffer, Jr. 1984. Temperature preference and avoidance studies of six North American freshwater fish species. Hydrobiologia Vol. 109(2):173-178.

Cincotta, Dan A., and J. R. Stauffer, Jr., C. H. Hocutt. 1982. Fish responses to temperature to assess effects of thermal discharge on biological integrity. Water Resour. Bull. Vol. 18(3):437-450.

Cincotta, Dan A., and J. R. Stauffer, Jr., C. H. Hocutt. 1984. The effects of rapid temperature decreases by five freshwater fish species. Archiv Hydrobiol. Vol. 99(4):529-536.

Clark, C. F. 1960. Lake St. Mary's and its management. Ohio Dept. Nat. Resources Div. Wildl. Publ. W-324:107pp.

Clarke, R. F., and J. W. Clarke. 1984. New county records for Kansas fishes and amphibians. Transactions Kans. Acad. Sci. Vol. 87(1-2):71-72.

Clarkson, R. W., and W. L. Minckley. 1988. Morphology and foods of Arizona catostomid fishes: *Catostomus insignis, Pantosteus clarki*, and there putative hybrids. Copeia 1988(2):422-433.

Clay, W. M. 1975. The Fishes of Kentucky. Kentucky Department of Fish and Wildlife Resources. Frankfort, Kentucky. 1-416pp.

Cleary, R. E. 1956. The distribution of the fishes of Iowa. (pp. 276-324). **IN:** J. R. Harlan and E. B. Speaker (eds.) Iowa Fish and Fishing. Iowa State Cons. Comm., Des Moines. 377pp.

Clemens, Howard P., and W. Waynon Johnson. 1964. Specificity of the gonadal hydration factor in the pituitary of some freshwater fishes. Copeia 1964(2):389-398.

Clemens, W. A. 1939. The fishes of Okanagan Lake and nearby waters. Bull. Fish. Res. Bd. Can. Vol. 56:27-38.

Clemens, W. A., and J. R. Dymond, N. K. Bigelow. 1923. Food studies of Lake Nipigon fishes. Univ. Toronto Studies. Publ. Ontario Fish. Res. Lab. 25:103-165.

Clemens, W. A., and J. R. Dymond, N. K. Bigelow, F. B. Adamstone, W. J. K. Harkness. 1923. The food of Lake Nipigon fishes. Publ. Ontario Fish. Res. Lab. Vol. 16:171-188.

Clemens, W. A., and D. S. Rawson, J. L. McHugh. 1939. A biological survey of Okanagan Lake, British Columbia. Bull. Fish. Res. Bd. Canada. 56. 70pp.

Clifford, H. F. 1972. Downstream movements of white sucker, *Catostomus commersoni*, fry in a brown-water stream of Alberta. Journal of the Fisheries Research Board of Canada. Vol. 29(7):1091-1093.

Clifford, T. J., and S. Facciana. 1972. *Philometra nodulosa* in Wyoming white suckers. Progressive Fish-Culturist. Vol. 34(4):235-236.

Coble, Daniel W. 1966. Alkaline phosphatase in fish scales. Journal of the Fisheries Research Board of Canada. Vol. 23(1):149-152.

Coble, Daniel W. 1967. The white sucker population of South Bay, Lake Huron, and effects of the sea lamprey on it. Journal of the Fisheries Research Board of Canada Vol. 24(10):2117-2136.

Coble, Daniel W., and Gordon B. Farabee, Richard O. Anderson. 1985. Comparative learning ability of selected fishes. Canadian Journal of Fisheries and Aquatic Sciences. Vol. 42(4):791-796.

Cochran, P. A. 1985. Size - selective attack by parasitic lampreys: consideration of alternate null hypothesis. Oecologia. Vol. 67(1):137-141.

Cockerell, T. D. A. 1906. The fossil fauna and flora of the Florissant (Colorado) shales. Univ. Colorado Stud. Vol. 3:157-176.

Cockerell, T. D. A. 1908. The fishes of the Rocky Mountain region. Univ. Colorado Stud. Vol. 5:159-178.

Cockerell, T. D. A. 1910. The scales of the clupeid fishes. Proc. Biol. Soc. Wash. Vol. 23:61-63.

Cockerell, T. D. A. 1911. The scales of fresh-water fishes. Biol. Bull. Vol. 20:367-376.

Cockerell, T. D. A. 1913. Observations on fish scales. Bull. U. S. Bur. Fish. Vol. 32:1912(1913):117-174.

Cockerell, T. D. A. 1914. Some fossil fish scales. Zool. Anz. Vol. 45:189-192.

Cockerell, T. D. A., and Edith M. Allison. 1909. The scales of some American Cyprinidae. Proc. Biol. Soc. Wash. Vol. 22:157-163.

Coker, R. E. 1930. Studies of common fishes of the Mississippi River at Keokuk. U. S. Dep. Commer. Bur. Fish. Doc. 1072:141-225.

Cole, H., and D. Barry, D. E. H. Frear, A. Bradford. 1967. DDT levels in fish, streams, stream sediments, and soil before and after DDT aerial spray application for fall cankerworm in northern Pennsylvania Bull. environm. Contam. Toxicol. Vol. 2:127-146.

Combs, D. L., and J. P. Harley, J. C. Williams. 1977. Helminth parasites of the spotted sucker and golden redhorse from the Kentucky River. Transactions Ky. Acad. Sci. Vol. 38(3-4):128-131.

Combs, D. L., and J. C. Williams, J. P. Harley. 1976. New host records for *Anonchohaptor muelleri* (Trematoda: Monogenea) from catostomid fishes of the Kentucky River. Proceedings helminth. Soc. Wash. Vol. 43(1):84.

Comeau, Napoléon A. 1915. Report on the fisheries expedition to Hudson Bay in the auxiliary schooner Burleigh, 1914. Ann. Rept. Canada Dept. Naval Serv. 1913-1914, p. 69-85 of appendix. Studies Supplement Biological Board of Canada.

Comiskey, C. E., and D. A. Etnier. 1972. Fishes of the Big South Fork of the Cumberland River. Journal Tenn. Acad. Sci. Vol. 47(4):140-146.

Cone, D. K. 1983. *Myxobolus subcircularis* Fantham, Porter, and Richardson, 1939 from the white sucker (*Catostomus commersoni*) in New Brunswick, Canada. Journal of Parasitology. Vol. 69(2):427-428.

Cone, D. K., and A. O. Dechtiar. 1984. *Gyrodactylus fryi*, new species (Monogenea) from *Esox masquinongy* in Ontario (Canada). Canadian Journal of Zoology. Vol. 62(6):1089-1090.

Cone, D. K., and M. Wiles. 1985. Trophozoite morphology and development site of two species of *Myxobolus* (Myxozoa) parasitizing *Catostomus commersoni* and *Notemigonus crysoleucas* in Atlantic Canada. Canadian Journal of Zoology. Vol. 63(12):2919-2923.

Contreras-Balderas, S., and R. Rivera-T. 1972. Una localided nueva para *Cycleptus elongatus* (Le Sueur) en el Rio Bravo Mexico y Estados Unidos (Pisces: Catostomidae). Revista Soc. Mexicana Hist. nat. Vol. 33:47-49.

Cook, F. A. 1959. Freshwater fishes in Mississippi. Miss. Fish Game Comm., Jackson. 239pp.

Coomer, C. E., Jr., and D. R. Holder, C. D. Swanson. 1977. A comparison of the diets of redbreast sunfish and spotted sucker in a coastal plain stream. Proceedings a. Conf. SEast. Ass. Fish Widl. Agencies. Vol. 31:497-596.

Cooper, Edwin Lavern 1983. Fishes of Pennsylvania and the northeastern United States. Pennsylvania State University Press, University Park. 243pp.

Cooper, Edwin Lavern, and C. C. Wagner, G. E. Krantz. 1971. Bluegills dominate production in a mixed population of fishes. Ecology. Vol. 52(2):280-290.

Cooper, G. P. 1936a. Some results of forage fish investigations in Michigan. Transactions of the American Fisheries Society. Vol. 65(1935):132-142.

Cooper, G. P. 1936b. Importance of forage fish. Proc. N. Am. Wildl. Conf. Vol. 1:305-310.

Cooper, G. P., and R. N. Schafer. 1954. Studies on the population of legal-size fish in Whitmore Lake, Washtenaw and Livingstone counties, Michigan. Trans. N. Amer. Wildl. Conf. Vol. 19:239-258.

Cooper, G. P., and G. N. Washburn. 1949. Relation of dissolved oxygen to winter mortality of fish in lakes. Transactions of the American Fisheries Society. Vol. 76(1946):23-33.

Cooper, J. J. 1983. Distributional ecology of native and introduced fishes of the Pit River system, northeastern California, with notes on the modoc sucker. California Fish Game Vol. 69(1):39-53.

Coots, M. 1965. Occurrences of the Lost River Sucker, *Deltistes luxatus* (Cope), and Shortnose Sucker, *Chasmistes brevirostris* Cope, in Northern California. Calif. Fish Game. Vol. 51:68-73.

Cope, Edward Drinker. 1868. On the distribution of freshwater fishes in the Allegheny region of southwestern Virginia. Journ. Acad. Nat. Sci. Philad., 1868. Vol. 6:207-247.

Cope, Edward Drinker. 1870. A partial synopsis of the Fishes of the Fresh Waters of North Carolina. American Philosophical Society Proceedings. Vol. 11:448-495.

24

Cope, Edward Drinker. 1871. Report on recent reptiles and fishes, obtained by naturalists of the Hayden expedition for the survey of Wyoming and contiguous territories in 1870. 2. [4] Ann. Rept. U. S. Geol. Surv. Wyoming and Territ. 1870 (1871):432-442.

Cope, Edward Drinker. 1872a. Observations on the systematic relations of the fishes. Proc. Amer. Assoc. Adv. Science, 20th meeting, Indianopolis, 1871:317-343.

Cope, Edward Drinker. 1872b. On the Tertiary coal and fossils of Osino, Nevada. Proc. Amer. Philos. Soc. Vol. 12:478-481.

Cope, Edward Drinker. 1872c. The Fish-beds of Osino, Nevada. Amer. Naturalist. Vol. 6:775-776.

Cope, Edward Drinker. 1873. On the extinct vertebrata of the Eocene of Wyoming, observed by the expedition of 1872, with notes on the geology. 6. Ann. Rept. U.S. Geol. Surv. Territ. embracing portions of Montana, Idaho, Wyoming, and Utah; being a report of progress of the explorations for the year 1872. Pt. 2, 545-649.

Cope, Edward Drinker. 1874a. Report on the vertebrate palæontology of Colorado.Annual Report Geol. and Geog. Surv. Territories for 1873, F. V. Hayden, U.S. Geologist, Washington, D. C.:427-533.

Cope, Edward Drinker. 1874b. Supplementary notices of fishes from the fresh-water Tertiaries of the Rocky Mountains. Bull. U.S. Geol. and Geog. Surv. of the Terrs. Vol. 1(No. 2):49-51.

Cope, Edward Drinker. 1874c. Ichthyology of Utah. Proceedings of the American Philosophical Society. Vol. 14:122-139.

Cope, Edward Drinker. 1875. On the fishes of the Tertiary shales of the South Park. Bull. U. S. Geol. and Geog. Surv. Territories 2nd series, No. 1:3-5.

Cope, Edward Drinker. 1879. Fishes of Klamath Lake, Oregon. Am. Nat. Vol. 13:784-785.

Cope, Edward Drinker. 1881. A new genus of Catostomidæ [Lipomyzon]. Amer. Naturalist. Vol. 15:59.

Cope, Edward Drinker. 1883. On the Fishes of the Recent and Pliocene Lakes of the Western part of the Great Basin, and of the Idaho Pliocene Lake. P. Ac. Nat. Sci. Philad.:134-166.

Cope, Edward Drinker. 1885. The Vertebrata of the Tertiary formations of the West. Books I and II. Report U.S. Geolog. Survey of the Territories, F. V. Hayden, U. S. Geologist in charge, 1884, Washington. Vol. 3:1-1009.

Cope, Edward Drinker. 1889a. The vertebrate fauna of the Equus beds. Amer. Naturalist. Vol. 23:160-165.

Cope, Edward Drinker. 1889b. The Silver Lake of Oregon and its region. Amer. Naturalist. Vol. 23:970-982.

Cope, Edward Drinker. 1894. Fossil Fishes from British Columbia. P. Ac. Philad. 1893 (1894):401-402.

Cope, Edward Drinker, and H. C. Yarrow. 1875. Report upon the Collections of Fishes [freshwater] made in portions of Nevada, Utah, California, Colorado, New Mexico, and

Arizona during the years 1871-1874. **IN:** Wheeler's Rep. Geogr. Explor. W. of 100th mer., v. Zoology. Washington, 4 to., chapter 6:639-700, pls. 26-32.

Cope, O. B. 1969. Effects of DDT spraying for spruce budworm on fish in the Yellowstone River system. pp. 325-343. **IN:** Cox, G. W. (ed.) <u>Readings</u> <u>in</u> <u>conservation</u> <u>ecology.</u> Appleton-Century-Crofts, New York.

Corbett, B. W., and P. M. Powles. 1983. Spawning and early-life ecological phases of the white sucker in Jack Lake, Ontario. Transactions of the American Fisheries Society. Vol. 112(2B):308-313.

Corbett, B. W., and P. M. Powles. 1986. Spawning and larva drift of sympatric walleyes (*Stizostedion vitreum vitreum*) and white suckers (*Catostomus commersoni*) in an Ontario stream [Canada]. Transactions of the American Fisheries Society. Vol. 115(1):41-46.

Cornelius, R. R. 1966. A morphological study of three Iowa carpsuckers. Proc. Iowa Acad. Sci. Vol. 73:177-179.

Cowley, D. E., and J. E. Sublette. 1989. Food habits of *Moxostoma congestum* and *Cycleptus elongatus* (Catostomidae, Cypriniformes) in Black River, Eddy County, New Mexico. Southwest Nat. Vol. 32(3): 411-413.

Crabtree, C. B., and D. G. Buth. 1981. Gene duplication and diploidization in tetraploid catostomid fishes *Catostomus fumeiventris* and *C. santaanae*. Copeia 1981(3):705-708.

Crabtree, C. B., and Donald G. Buth. 1987. Biochemical systematics of the catostomid genus *Catostomus*: assessment of *C. clarki, C. plebeius* and *C. discobolus* including the zuni sucker, *C. d. yarrowi*. Copeia 1987(4):843-854.

Crawford, D. R. 1923. The significance of food supply in the larval development of fishes. Ecology New York. Vol. 4:147-153.

Cross, Frank B. 1967. <u>Handbook</u> <u>of</u> <u>Fishes</u> <u>of</u> <u>Kansas.</u> Misc. Publs. Mus. Nat. Hist. Univ. Kans. No. 45:1-357.

Cross, Frank B., and Joseph T. Collins. 1975. <u>Fishes</u> <u>in</u> <u>Kansas.</u> University of Kansas. Museum of Natural History. Public Education Series no. 3. 189pp.

Cross, Frank B., and Richard L. Mayden, J. D. Stewart. 1986. Chapter 11. Fishes in the Western Mississippi Basin (Missouri, Arkansas and Red Rivers). pp. 363-412. **IN:** Hocutt, Charles H., and E. O. Wiley. (eds.) <u>The</u> <u>Zoogeography</u> <u>of</u> <u>North</u> <u>American</u> <u>Freshwater</u> <u>Fishes.</u> John Wiley and Sons. New York, New York. 866pp.

Cross, Frank B., and Artie L. Metcalf. 1963. Records of three lampreys (*Ichthyomyzon*) from the Missouri River system. Copeia 1963(1):187.

Cross, Frank B., and G. A. Moore. 1952. The fishes of the Poteau River, Oklahoma and Arkansas. Amer. Midl. Nat. Vol. 47:396-412.

Cross, Jeffrey N. 1985. Distribution of fish in the Virgin River, a tributary of the lower Colorado River (USA). Environ. Biol. Fishes Vol. 12(1):13-22.

Crossman, E. J. 1962. The Redfin Pickerel, *Esox a. americanus*, in North Carolina. Copeia 1962(1):114-123.

Crossman, E. J. 1976. Quetico fishes. Royal Ontario Museum. The Quetico Foundation. Toronto, Canada. 86pp.

Crossman, E. J., and R. G. Ferguson. 1963. The first record from Canada of *Minytrema melanops*, the spotted sucker. Copeia 1963(1):186-187.

Crossman, E. J., and S. J. Nepszy. 1979. First Canadian record of the black buffalo (Osteichthyes: Catostomidae). Canadian Fld. Nat. Vol. 93(3):304-305.

Culbertson, G. 1904. A note on the breeding habits of the Common or White Sucker. P. Indiana Ac. 1903:65-66.

Cumbra, Stephen L., and Don E. McAllister, Richard E. Morlan. 1981. Late Pleistocene fish fossils of *Coregonus, Stenodus, Thymallus, Catostomus, Lota* and *Cottus* from the Old Crow Basin, northern Yukon, Canada. Canadian J. Earth Sci. Vol. 18(11):1740-1754.

Curry, Kevin D. 1980. Use of a Wabash River tributary for sucker (Catostomidae) reproduction. Dissertation Abstr. int. (B) Vol. 41(1):54.

Curry, Kevin D., and Anne Spacie. 1979. Distribution of Stream Fishes in Tippecanoe County, Indiana. Proceedings of the Indiana Academy of Science. Vol. 88:182-188.

Curry, Kevin D., and Anne Spacie. 1980. Temperature-controlled recirculating system for hatching catostomid larvae. Progressive Fish-Culturist. Vol. 42(3):151-152.

Curry, Kevin D., and Anne Spacie. 1984. Differential use of stream habitat by spawning catostomids. American Midland Naturalist. Vol. 111(2):267-279.

Curtis, M. A., and M. E. Rau. 1980. The geographical distribution of diplostomiasis (Trematoda: Strigeidae) in fishes from northern Québec, Canada in relation to the calcium ion concentrations of lakes. Canadian Journal of Zoology. Vol. 58(7):1390-1394.

Cuvier, Georges, and Achille Valenciennes. 1844. Histoire naturelle des poissons. Paris. Vol. 17:1-497.

Cvancara, V. A., and S. F. Stieber, B. A. Cvancara. 1977. Summer temperature tolerance of selected species of Mississippi river acclimated young of the year fishes. Comparative Biochem. Physiol. (A) Vol. 56(1):81-85.

Dahl, F. H., and R. B. McDonald. 1980. Effects of control of the sea lamprey (*Petromyzon marinus*) on migratory and resident fish populations. Canad. J. Fish. Aquat. Sci. Vol. 37(11):1886-1894.

Dalquest, Walter W. 1962. The Good Creek formation, Pleistocene of Texas, and its fauna. Journ. Paleontol. Vol. 36(3):568-582.

Dauble, Dennis D. 1980. Life history of the bridgelip sucker in the central Columbia River. Transactions of the American Fisheries Society. Vol. 109(1):92-98.

Dauble, Dennis D. 1986. Life history and ecology of the large-scale sucker (*Catostomus macrocheilus*) in the Columbia River [Washington, U.S.A.]. American Midland Naturalist. Vol. 116(2):356-367.

Dauble, Dennis D., and R. L. Buschbom. 1981. Estimates of hybridization between two species of catostomids in the Columbia River. Copeia. 1981(4):801-810.

Davis, J. T. 1955. Contributions to the ecology of fishes of Perche Creek, Missouri. Part I. Movement of fishes. Part II. Age and growth of the northern river carpsucker, *Carpiodes carpio carpio* (Rafinesque). M.A. Thesis Univ. Mo. 75pp.

Davis, J. T. 1960. Fish populations and aquatic conditions in polluted waters in Louisiana. La. Wildl. Fish Comm. Bull. Vol. 1(1960):121pp.

Davis, Kenneth B., and Nick C. Parker. 1986. Plasma corticosteroid stress response of fourteen species of warmwater fish to transportation. Transactions of the American Fisheries Society. Vol. 115(3): 495-499.

Dawe, C. J., and M. F. Stanton, F. J. Schwartz. 1964. Hepatic neoplasms in native bottom-feeding fish of Deep Creek Lake, Maryland. Cancer Res. Vol. 24(7):1194-1201.

Dawson, George Mercer. 1896. Report on the area of the Kamloops map-sheet, British Columbia. 1895.Geological Survey of Canada, Annual Report, New Series. Volume 7, p. 76D.

Dawson, L. E., and K. L. Uebersax, M. A. Uebersax. 1978. Stability of freshwater sucker (*Catostomus* spp.) flesh during frozen storage. Journal of the Fisheries Research Board of Canada. Vol. 35(2):253-257.

Day, D. 1979. Endangered animals in Utah and adjacent areas. Great Basin Nat. Mem. Vol. 3:35-40.

Deacon, James Everett. 1960. Fish populations of the Neosho and Marais des Cygnes Rivers, Kansas, Following Drought. University of Kansas, Ph.D. Thesis, Zoology. 113pp.

Deacon, James Everett. 1961. Fish populations, following a drought, in the Neosho and Marais des Cygnes Rivers in Kansas. Univ. Kansas Mus. Natur. Hist. Publ. Vol. 13(9):359-427.

Deacon, J. E., and P. B. Schumann, E. L. Stuenkel. 1987. Thermal tolerances and preferences of fishes of the Virgin River system (Utah, Arizona, Nevada). Great Basin Nat. Vol. 47(4):538-546.

Dechtiar, A. O. 1968. *Neoechinorhynchus carpiodi* n. sp. (Acanthocephala: Neoechinorhynchidae) from quillback of Lake Erie. Canadian Journal of Zoology. Vol. 46:201-204.

Dechtiar, A. O. 1969. Two new species of monogenetic trematodes (Trematoda: Monogenea) from nasal cavities of catostomid fishes. Journal of the Fisheries Research Board of Canada Vol. 26(4):865-869.

Dechtiar, A. O. 1972a. Parasites of fish from Lake of the Woods, Ontario. Journal of the Fisheries Research Board of Canada. Vol. 29(3):275-283.

Dechtiar, A. O. 1972b. New parasite records for Lake Erie fish. Technical Rep. Gt. Lakes Fish. Comm. No. 17:1-20.

Dechtiar, A. O., and W. A. Dillon. 1974. Redescription of *Anonchohaptor anomalum* Mueller 1938 and a description of *Icelanonchohaptor fyvili* n.sp. (Monogenoidea: Dactylogridae). Journal of the Fisheries Research Board of Canada. Vol. 31(12):1863-1866.

Decker, L. M. 1989. Coexistence of two species of sucker, *Catostomus*, in Sagehen Creek, California, and notes on their status in the Western Lahontan Basin. Great Basin Nat. Vol. 49(4):540-551.

DeKay, James Ellsworth. 1842. Zoology of New York; or The New York Fauna. Comprising detailed descriptions of all the animals hitherto observed within the state, with brief notices of those occasionally found near its borders. **IN:** Natural history of New York [State] Geological Survey. Albany, 1842. Vol. I:pts. 3 and 4. 102 pls. 4°.

Dempster, R. P., and P. Morales, F. X. Glennon. 1988. Use of sodium chlorite to combat anchorworm infestations of fish. Prog. Fish-Cult. Vol. 50(1):51-55.

Dence, Wilford A. 1940. The occurrence of "free living" *Ligula* in Catlin Lake, central Adirondacks. Copeia 1940 (2):140.

Dence, Wilford A. 1948. Life history, ecology and habits of the dwarf sucker, *Catostomus commersonii utawana* Mather, at the Huntington Wildlife Station. Roosevelt Wildl. Bull. Vol. 8(4):82-150.

Denison, Samuel G., and Carl R. Carlson, John L. Dorkin, Jr., Cecil Lue-Hing. 1978. Fish Survey of Northeastern Illinois Streams. Paper presented at the108th Annual Meeting of the American Fisheries Society Kingston, Rhode Island. The Metropolitan Sanitary District of Greater Chicago. 40pp.

Denoncourt, R. F. 1975. Key to the families and genera of Pennsylvania freshwater fishes and the species of freshwater fishes of the Susquehanna river drainage above Conowingo Dam. Proceedings Pa. Acad. Sci. Vol. 49(1):82-88.

Desser, S. S., and R. Lester. 1975. An ultrastructural study of the enigmatic 'rodlet cells' in the white sucker, *Catostomus commersoni* (La Cepède) (Pisces: Catostomidae). Canadian Journal of Zoology. Vol. 53(11):1483-1494.

Deutsch, M., and V. E. Engelbert. 1970. Erythropoiesis through clone cell formation in peripheral blood of the White sucker, *Catostomus commersoni*, studied after labeling with ^{3}H-thymidine for various exposure intervals. Canadian Journal of Zoology. Vol. 48:1241-1250.

Deutsch, W. G. 1978. *Lernaea cyprinacea* on two catostomid fishes. Proceedings Pa. Acad. Sci. Vol. 52(1):57-59.

Devault, D. S. 1985. Contaminants in fish from Great Lakes harbors and tributary mouths. Arch. Environ. Contam. Toxicol. Vol. 14(5):587-594.

Devine, A., and E. Stevens. 1985. Great horned owl feeding on sucker. Conn. Warbler Vol. 5(4):48-49.

Diercks, K. J., and T. G. Goldsberry. 1970. Target strength of a single fish. J. acoust. Soc. Am. Vol. 48:415-416.

Dietz, E. M. C., and K. C. Jurgens. 1963. An evaluation of selective shad control at Medina Lake, Texas. Tex. Parks Wildl. Dept. IF Rep., 5:1-32.

Dill, W. A. 1944. The fishery of the lower Colorado River. Calif. Fish Game. Vol. 30(3):109-211.

Dobie, J. 1952. A method of calculating fish production in rearing ponds. Progr. Fish Cult. Vol. 14(1):22-26.

Dobie, J. 1962. Role of the tiger salamander in natural ponds used in Minnesota for rearing suckers. Progr. Fish Cult. Vol. 24(2):85-87.

Dobie, J. 1966. Food and feeding habits of the walleye, *Stizostedion vitreum vitreum*, and associated game and forage fishes in Lake Vermilion, Minnesota, with special reference to the tullibee, *Coregonus (Leucichthys) artedi*. Minn. Fish. Invest. Vol. 4:39-71.

Dobie, J. 1969. Growth of walleye and sucker fingerlings in Minnesota rearing ponds. Verh. int. Ver. Limnol. Vol. 17:641-649.

Dobie, J. R., and O. L. Meehean, G. N. Washburn. 1948. Propagation of minnows and other bait species. Circ. U. S. Fish Wildlife Serv. No. 12:1-113.

Dobie, J. R., and O. L. Meehean, S. F. Snieszko, F. N. Washburn. 1956. Raising bait fishes. U.S. Fish Wildl. Serv. Circ. 35:124pp.

Dobie, J., and J. B. Moyle. 1956. Methods used for investigating productivity of fish-rearing ponds in Minnesota. Minn. Fish. Res. Unit Spec. Publ. 5:54pp.

Donahue, J., and R. Stuckenrath, J. M. Adovasio, et al. 1978. Meadowcroft Rocksheter. pp. 140-180. **IN:** A. L. Bryan (ed.) Early Man in America; from a circum-Pacific perspective. Occas. Pap. Dep. Anthropol., Univ. Alberta, No. 1.

Dorkin, John L., Jr. 1980. The Fishes of Hickory Creek. University of Illinois at Chicago Circle. Chicago, Illinois. M.S. Thesis. 121pp.

Dorosev, S. I., and V. K. Vinogradov. 1976. Rezultati aklimatizacije severnoamerickih riba u SSSR-u. Ichthyologia. Vol. 8(1):35-43.

Douglas, Neil H. 1974. Freshwater Fishes of Louisiana. Claitor's Publishing Division. Baton Rouge, Louisiana. 443pp.

Douglas, P. A. 1952. Notes on the spawning of the Humpback Sucker, *Xyrauchen texanus* (Abbott). Calif. Fish Game. Vol. 38:149-155.

Douglas, P. A. 1957. Humpback sucker, *Xyrauchen texanus*. (Abbott). Data for Handbook of Biological Data. 5p.

Drew, Wayland, and Don Baldwin, Alan Emery, Wayne McLaren, Robert Collins. 1974. The Illustrated Natural History of Canada. The Nature of Fish. Natural Science of Canada Limited, Toronto, Ontario. 160pp.

Driscoll, C. T., Jr., and J. P. Baker, J. J. Bisogni, Jr., C. L. Schofield. 1980. Effect of aluminum speciation on fish in dilute acidified waters. Nature, Lond. Vol. 284(5752):161-164.

Dryer, W. R. 1966. Bathymetric distribution of fish in the Apostle Islands region, Lake Superior. Transactions of the American Fisheries Society. Vol. 95(3):248-259.

Dugal, L. C. 1962. Proximate composition of some freshwater fish. Circulars of the Biological Station, London, Ontario. No. 5:1-6.

Duméril, A. M. Constant. 1856. Ichthyologie analytique ou classification des poissons, suivant la méthode naturelle, a l'aide de tableaux synoptiques. Mém. Acad. Sci. France. Vol. 27:1-511.

Dunbar, M. J., and H. H. Hildebrand. 1952. Contribution to the study of the fishes of Ungava Bay. Journal of the Biological Board of Canada. Vol. 9(2):83-128.

Dunham, A. E., and Gerald R. Smith, J. N. Taylor. 1979. Evidence for ecological character displacement in western American catostomid fishes. Evolution, Lawrence, Kansas. Vol. 33(3):877-896.

Dunst, R. C., and T. Wirth. 1972. Appendix O, the Chippewa Flowage fish population. pp. 0-43. **IN:** Chippewa flowage investigations. Part IIIA. Appendixes. Inland Lakes Demon. Stn. Proj., Upper Great Lakes Reg. Comm.

Duru, C., and A. D. Johnson, E. Blouin. 1981. *Neascus pyriformis* Chandler, 1951 (Trematoda: Diplostomatidae), redescription and incidence in fishes from Brinle Creek, South Dakota. Proceedings helminth Soc. Wash. Vol. 48(2):177-183.

Dwyer, W. P., and C. E. Smith. 1989. Metacercariae of *Diplostomum spathaceum* in the eyes of fishes from Yellowstone Lake, Wyoming. J. Wildlife Dis. Vol. 25(1):126-129.

Dyakonov, Yu. N. 1980. [The feeding and feeding relations of carp and buffalo fish fry reared together.] Sbornik gos. nauchno-issled. Inst. ozern rech. ryb. No. 29:21-27.

Dymond, J. R. 1936. Some fresh-water fishes of British Columbia. Report of the British Columbia Commissioner of Fisheries for 1935. Studies from the Board's [FRB] Establishments. No. 144:60-72.

Dymond, J. R. 1937. New records of Ontario fishes. Copeia 1937(1):59.

Dymond, J. R. 1947. A List of the freshwater fishes of Canada east of the Rocky Mountains, with keys. Royal Ont. Mus. Zool. Toronto Misc. Pub. No. 1. 1947:1-36.

Dymond, J. R. 1964. A history of Ichthyology in Canada. Copeia 1964(1):2-33.

Dymond, J. R., and J. L. Hart. 1927. The fishes of Lake Abitibi (Ontario) and adjacent waters. Univ. Toronto Studies Biol. Ser. 29:1-19.

Dymond, J. R., and J. L. Hart, A. L. Pritchard. 1929. The fishes of the Canadian waters of Lake Ontario. Univ. Toronto Stud., Ont. Fish. Res. Lab. Publ. Vol. 37:1-35.

Dymond, J. R., and W. B. Scott. 1941. Fishes of Patricia portion of the Kenora District, Ontario. Copeia 1941(4):243-245.

Eastman, Charles Rochester. 1917. Fossil fishes in the collection of the United States National Museum. Proc. U.S. Nat. Mus. Vol. 52:235-304.

Eastman, Joseph T. 1977. The pharyngeal bones and teeth of catostomid fishes. American Midl. Nat. Vol. 97(1):68-88.

Eastman, Joseph T. 1980. The caudal skeletons of catostomid fishes. American Midl. Nat. Vol. 103(1):133-148.

Eaton, J., and J. Arthur, Hermanutz, R. Kiefer, L. Mueller, R. Anderson, R. Erickson, B. Nordling, J. Rogers, H. Pritchard. 1985. Correlations of laboratory and field data. Biological effects of continuous and intermittent dosing of outdoor experimental streams with chlorpyrifos. ASTM (Am. Soc. Test Mater.) Spec. Tech. Publ. No. 891:85-118.

Eaton, J. G., and J. M. McKim, G. W. Holcombe. 1978. Metal toxicity to embryos and larvae of seven freshwater fish species. - 1. Cadium. Bulletin envir. Contam. Toxicol. Vol. 19(1):95-103.

Eaton, T. H., Jr. 1935. Evolution of the upper jaw mechanism in teleost fishes. J. Morphol. Vol. 58(1):157-172.

Eddy, Samuel. 1957. How to know the freshwater fishes. Wm. C. Brown Co., Dubuque, Iowa. 253pp.

Eddy, Samuel. 1969. The Freshwater Fishes. 2nd ed. Wm. C. Brown Company Publishers. Dubuque, Iowa. 286pp.

Eddy, Samuel, and Kenneth D. Carlander. 1939. Growth of Minnesota fishes. Minn. Conserv. Vol. 69:8-10.

Eddy, Samuel, and Kenneth D. Carlander. 1940. The effect of environmental factors upon the growth rates of Minnesota fishes. Proc. Minn. Acad. Sci. Vol. 8:14-19.

Eddy, Samuel, and Kenneth D. Carlander. 1942. Growth rate studies of Minnesota fish. Minn. Dept. Conser. Fish. Res. Invest. Rep. 28:64pp. mimeo.

Eddy, Samuel, and T. Surber. 1947. Northern fishes. Univ. Minn. Press. Minneapolis. 414pp.

Eddy, Samuel, and Roy C. Tasker, James C. Underhill. 1972. Fishes of the Red River, Rainy River, and Lake of the Woods, Minnesota, with Comments on the Distribution of Species in the Nelson River Drainage. Bell Museum of Natural History. University of Minnesota Occassional Papers Number 11:1-24.

Eddy, Samuel, and James C. Underhill. 1974. Northern fishes. Univ. Minn. Press, Minneapolis. 414pp.

Eder, S., and C. A. Carlson. 1977. Food habits of carp and white suckers in the South Platte and St. Vrain Rivers and Goosequill Pond, Welsh County, Colorado. Transactions of the American Fisheries Society. Vol. 106(4):339-346.

Edwards, Elizabeth A. 1983. Habitat suitability index models: bigmouth buffalo. Wash. D. C.: Western Energy & Land Use Team, Div. of Biol. Service, Res. & Devel., F. & Wildlife Service, U.S. Dept. of the Interior. 23 pp.

Edwards, L. F. 1926. The protractile apparatus of the mouth of the Catostomid fishes. Anat. Rec. Philadelphia. Vol. 33:257-270.

Eigenmann, Carl H. 1895. Results of explorations in western Canada and the northwestern United States. Bull. U. S. Fish Comm. Vol. 14. 1894(1895):101-132.

Eigenmann, Carl H., and Rosa Smith. 1893. New Fishes from Western Canada. Am. Nat. Vol. 27:151-154.

Eigenmann, Rosa Smith. 1891. Description of a New Species of Catostomus (C. rex) from Oregon. American Naturalist. Vol. 25 (July 295):667-668.

Elkin, R. E., Jr. 1954. The fish population of two cut-off pools in Salt Creek, Osage County, Oklahoma. Proc. Okla. Acad. Sci. Vol. 35:25-29.

Ellis, Max M. 1934. Arsenic storage in game fish. Copeia 1934(2):97.

Ellis, Max M., and B. B. Jaffa. 1918. Notes on Cragin's darter, *Catonotus cragini* (Gilbert). Copeia 1918(No. 59):73-75.

Ellis, Max M., and G. C. Roe. 1917. Destruction of log perch eggs by suckers. Copeia 1917 (No. 47): 69-71.

Elrod, J. H., and T. J. Hassler. 1971. Vital statistics of seven fish species in Lake Sharpe, South Dakota 1964-1969. Special Publs. Am. Fish. Soc. No. 8. 1971:27-40.

Elser, H. J. 1961. Record Maryland fish. Md. Conserv. Vol. 38(2):15-17.

Elsey, C. A. 1946. An ecological study of the competitor fish in Pyramid Lake, Jasper, with special reference to the northern sucker. M.A. Thesis. Univ. Sask. 61pp.

Embody, G. C. 1915. The farm fishpond. Cornell Reading Courses, Country Life Ser., 3:213-252.

Emel'Yanova, N. G., and A. P. Makeeva. 1983. The ultrastructure of egg membranes of the bigmouth buffalo, *Ictiobus cyprinella* (Catostomidae) under normal conditions and with sticky envelopes removed.. Vopr Ikhtiol. Vol. 23(1):81-86.

Emery, Alan R. 1973. Preliminary comparisons of day and night habits of freshwater fish in Ontario Lakes. Journal of the Fisheries Research Board of Canada. Vol. 30(6):761-774.

Emery, Lee. 1976. Fish Species Lists of the U.S. Waters of the Great Lakes. Appendix II. pp. 201-206. **IN:** John Boreman (ed.). Great Lakes Fish Egg and Larvae Identification: Proceedings of a Workshop. U.S. Fish and Wildlife Service National Power Plant Team Ann Arbor, Michigan. FWS/OBS-76/23 220pp.

Engel, J. M. 1978. Management of endangered coolwater fishes. Special Publs. Am. Fish. Soc. No. 11:159-160.

Engstrom-Heg, R., and R. T. Colesante, G. A. Stillings. 1988. Prey selection by three esocid species and a hybrid esocid. Am. Fish Soc. Spec. Publ. No. 15:189-194.

Ergens, R. and R. A. Kudentsova, Iu. A. Strelkov. 1980. Record of *Gyrodactylus spathulatus* Mueller, 1936 (Monogenea: Gyrodactylidae) from *Catostomus catostomus* in east Siberia. Folia-Parasit. Praha Vol. 27(1):p. 52.

Erman, D. C. 1972. A fisherman survey of the Madison-Firehole rivers in Yellowstone National Park, 1969. Transactions of the American Fisheries Society. Vol. 101(2):352-355.

Erman, D. C. 1973. Upstream changes in fish populations following impoundment of Sagehen Creek, California. Transactions of the American Fisheries Society. Vol. 102(3):626-629.

Erman, D. C. 1986. Long term structure of fish populations in Sagehen Creek, California. Transactions Am. Fish. Soc. Vol. 115(5):682-692.

Erokhina, L. V., and V. K. Vinogradov, V. V. Vychegzhanina. 1976. Ovary development on buffalo. Trudy uses. nauchno-issled. Inst. prud. ryb. Khoz. Vol. 25:59-66.

Erokhina, L. V., and N. V. Voropaev, A. K. Bogeruk, V. F. Krivtsov. 1976. Nutrition of buffalos during their rearing in ponds. Trudy vses. nauchno-issled. Inst. prud. ryb. Khoz. Vol. 25:73-81.

Eschmeyer, R. W. 1942. The catch, abundance, and migration of game fishes in Norris Reservoir, Tennessee, 1940. J. Tenn. Acad. Sci. Vol. 17(1):90-114.

Eschmeyer, R. W., and R. H. Stroud, A. M. Jones. 1944. Studies of the fish population on the shoal area of a TVA main-stream reservoir. J. Tenn. Acad. Sci. Vol. 19(1):70-122.

Eschmeyer, William N. 1990. Catalog of the Genera of Recent Fishes. California Academy of Sciences. San Francisco, California. 697 pp.

Eshelman, Ralph E. 1975. Geology and paleontology of the Pleistocene (late Blancan) White Rock fauna from North-central Kansas. Papers on Paleontology, No. 13. (Claude W. Hibbard memorial Volume 4). 60pp.

Estep, Marilyn L. F., and Steven Vigg. 1985. Stable carbon and nitrogen isotope tracers of trophic dynamics in natural populations and fisheries of the Lahontan Lake system, Nevada [USA]. Can. J. Fish Aquat. Sci. Vol. 42(11):1712-1719.

Evans, James W., and Richard L. Noble. 1979. The Longitudinal Distribution of Fishes in an East Texas Stream. The American Midland Naturalist. Vol. 101(2):333-343.

Evans, R. S., and R. A. Heckmann, J. Palmieri. 1976. Diplostomatosis in Utah. Proceedings Utah Acad. Sci. Arts Letters Vol. 53(1):20-25.

Evans, W. A. 1950. Notes on the occurrence of the bigmouth buffalo in Southern California. Calif. Fish Game Vol. 36:435-436.

Everhart, W. H. 1958. Fishes of Maine. 2nd ed. Maine Dept. Inland Fish. Game. Augusta, Maine. 94pp.

Everhart, W. H., and W. R. Seaman. 1971. Fishes of Colorado. Colo. Game, Fish Parks Div. 75pp.

494 Evermann, Barton Warren. 1893a. A reconnaissance of the streams and lakes of western Montana and northwestern Wyoming. Bull. U. S. Fish Comm. Vol. 11:1891 (1893):3-60.

Evermann, Barton Warren. 1893b. Description of a new Sucker, *Pantosteus jordani*, from the upper Missouri basin. Bull. U.S. Fish Comm. Vol. 12:1892 (1893):51-56.

Evermann, Barton Warren. 1896. A report upon Salmon Investigations in the headwaters of the Columbia River, in the State of Idaho, in 1895; together with notes upon the Fishes observed in that State in 1894 and 1895. Bull. U.S. Fish Comm. f. 1896:149-202.

Evermann, Barton Warren. 1899. Report on investigations by the U.S. Fish Commission in Mississippi, Louisiana, and Texas, in 1897. Rep. U.S. Fish. Comm. f. 1898:287-310.

Evermann, Barton Warren. 1916. Notes on the fishes of the Lumbee River. Copeia 1916 (No. 36):77-80.

Evermann, Barton Warren, and U. O. Cox. 1894. Report upon the Fishes of the Missouri River basin. Rep. U.S. Fish Comm. f. 1894:325-429.

Evermann, Barton Warren, and E. L. Goldsborough. 1907.The fishes of Alaska. Bull. U.S. Bur. Fish. Vol. 26:219-360.

Evermann, Barton Warren, and W. C. Kendall. 1895. A list of the species of fishes known from the vicinity of Neosho, Missouri. Bull. U.S. Fish Comm. Vol. 14:469-472.

Evermann, Barton Warren, and Seth Eugene Meek. 1898. A report upon Salmon Investigations in the Columbia River Basin and elsewhere on the Pacific Coast in 1896. Bull. U.S. Fish Comm. Vol. 17:201-208.

Ewers, L. A., and M. W. Boesel. 1935. The food of some Buckeye Lake fishes. Transactions of the American Fisheries Society. Vol. 65:57-70.

Faber, D. J. 1967. Limnetic larval fish in northern Wisconsin lakes. Journal of the Fisheries Research Board of Canada. Vol. 24(5):927-937.

Fago, Don. 1982. Distribution and relative abundance of fishes in Wisconsin   1. Greater Rock River Basin. Technical Bull. Dep. nat. Resour. Wisc. No. 136:1-120.

Fago, Don. 1984a. Distribution and relative abundance of fishes in Wisconsin (USA): 3. Red Cedar River Basin. Wis. Dep. Nat. Resour. Tech. Bull. No. 143:1-26.

Fago, Don. 1984b. Relative Abundance of Fishes in Wisconsin IV. Root, Milwaukee, Des Plaines, and Fox River Basins. Wisconsin Department of Natural Resources. Technical Bulletin No. 147:1-128pp.

Fang, P. W. 1934. Notes on *Myxocyprinus asiaticus* (Bleeker) in Chinese fresh-waters. Sinensia Vol. 4:329-337.

Farmer, G. J., and F. W. H. Beamish, P. F. Lett. 1977. Influence of water temperature on the growth rate of the landlocked sea lamprey (*Petromyzon marinus*) and the associated rate of horst mortality. Journal of the Fisheries Research Board of Canada. Vol. 34(9):1373-1378.

Fassbender, R. L., and J. J. Weber, L. M. Nelson. 1970. Surface water resources of Green Lake County. Wis. Dep. Nat. Resour. Lake and Strm. Classif. Proj. 72pp.

Fedoruk, A. N. 1971. Freshwater fishes of Manitoba: checklist and keys. Department of Mines, Manitoba. 1-130.

Fernholz, W. B. 1966. Mississippi River commercial fishing statistics, 1965. Wis. Conserv. Dep. Div. Fish. Mgmt. Stat. Rep. 31pp.

Fernholz, W. B. 1971. Mississippi River commercial fishing statistics, 1970. Wisc. Dep. Nat. Resour. Bur. Fish Mgmt. Stat. Rep. 24pp.

Fernholz, W. B. 1972. Mississippi River commercial fishing statistics, 1971. Wis. Dep. Nat. Resour. Bur. Fish Mgmt. Stat. Rep. 24pp.

Fernholz, W. B., and V. E. Crawley. 1976. Mississippi River commercial fishing statistics, 1975. Wis. Dep. Nat. Resour. Bur. Fish Wildlife Mgmt. Stat. Rep. 25pp.

Fernholz, W. B., and V. E. Crawley. 1977. Mississippi River commercial fishing statistics, 1977. Wis. Dep. Nat. Resour. Bur. Fish Wildl. Mgmt. Stat. Rep. 22pp.

Ferris, Stephen D. 1983. Tetraploidy and the evolution of catostomid fishes. Chapter 2. pp. 55-93. **IN:** Turner, Bruce J. (ed.) Evolutionary Genetics of Fishes. Plenum Press. New York, New York. 636pp.

Ferris, Stephen D., and D. G. Buth, Gregory S. Whitt. 1982. Substantial genetic differentiation among populations of *Catostomus plebius*. Copeia 1982(2):444-449.

Ferris, Stephen D., and S. L. Portnoy, Gregory S. Whitt. 1979. The roles of speciation and divergence time in the loss of duplicate gene expression. Theoretical Popul. Biol. Vol. 15(1):114-139.

Ferris, Stephen D., and Gregory S. Whitt. 1978. Phylogeny of tetraploid catostomid fishes based on the loss of duplicate gene expression. Systematic Zool. Vol. 27(2):189-206.

Ferris, Stephen D., and Gregory S. Whitt. 1980. Genetic variability in species with extensive gene duplication: the tetraploid catostomid fish. American Nat. Vol. 115(5):650-666.

Fickeisen, D. H., and J. C. Montgomery. 1978. Tolerances of fishes to dissolved gas supersaturation in deep tank bioassays. Transactions of the American Fisheries Society. Vol. 107(2):376-381.

Figueroa, J. and S. D. Morley, J. Heierhorst, C. Krentler, K. Lederis, D. Richter. 1989. Two isotocin genes are present in the white sucker *Catostomus commersoni* both lacking introns in their coding regions. EMBO (Eur. Mol. Biol. Organ) J. 8(10):2873-2877.

Fingerman, Sue Whitsell, and Royal D. Suttkus. 1961. Comparison of *Hybognathus hay* Jordan and *Hybognathus nuchalis* Agassiz. Copeia 1961(4):462-467.

Finke, A. H. 1967. A five-year summary of commercial fishing for carp, buffalo, sheepshead, catfish and bullhead on the Wisconsin portion of the Mississippi River. Proc. 23d Annu. Meet. Upper Miss. R. Conserv. Comm. 33pp.

Finnell, Joe C. 1955. Growth of Fishes in Cutoff Lakes and Streams of the Little River System, McCurtain County, Oklahoma. Proceedings of the Oklahoma Academy of Science. Vol. 36:61-66.

Finnley, D. [Editor]. 1978a. Plan maps recovery of cui-ui population. Endangered spec. tech. Bull. Vol. 3(2):3.

Finnley, D. [Editor]. 1978b. Rulemaking actions- April 1978. Protection sought for bonytail chub, razorback sucker. Endangered Spec. tech. Bull. Vol. 3(5):6.

Fischthal, J. H., and D. O. Carson, R. S. Vaught. 1982. Comparative size allometry of the digenetic trematode *Lissorchis attenuatus* (Monorchiidae) at four intensities of infection in the white sucker. Journal of Parasitology. Vol. 68(2):314-318.

Fish, M. P. 1929. Contributions to the early life histories of Lake Erie fishes. Buffalo Soc. Nat. Sci., Bull. 14(3):136-187.

Fish, M. P. 1932. Contributions to the early life histories of 62 species of fishes from Lake Erie and its tributary waters. Bull. U.S. Bur. Fish. Vol. 47(10):293-398.

Fisher, A. W. F., and K. Wong, V. Gill, K. Lederis. 1984. Immunocytochemical localization of urotensin I neurons in the caudal neurosecretory system of the white sucker (*Catostomus commersoni*). Cell Tissue Res. Vol. 235(1):19-23.

Fisher, H. J. 1962. Some fishes of the lower Missouri River. Amer. Midl. Nat. Vol. 68(2):424-429.

Fisher, S. G., and D. E. Busch, N. B. Grimm. 1981. Diel feeding chronologies in two Sonoran Desert stream fishes, *Agosia chrysogaster* (Cyprinidae) and *Pantosteus clarki* (Catostomidae). Southwestern Nat. Vol. 26(1):31-36.

Flemer, D. A., and W. S. Woolcott. 1966. Food habits and distribution of the fishes of Tuckahoe Creek, Virginia, with special emphasis on the bluegill, *Lepomis m. macrochirus* Rafinesque. Chesapeake Sci. Vol. 7(2):75-89.

Flick, W. A., and D. A. Webster. 1961. Brandon Park. Fish management report, 1961. Cornell Univ. Dept. Conserv. 47pp. mimeo.

Foerster, R. E. 1937. Increasing the survival rate of young sockeye salmon by removing predatory fishes. Progress Reports of Fisheries Research Board Pacific Coast Stations. No. 32:21-22.

Fogle, N. E. 1961a. Report of fisheries investigations during the third year of impoundment of Oahe Reservoir, South Dakota, 1960. S.D. Dept. Game Fish Parks D-J Proj., F-1-R-10 (Jobs 9-12):57 pp. mimeo.

Fogle, N. E. 1961b. Report of fisheries investigations during the second year of impoundment of Oahe Reservoir, South Dakota, 1959. S.D. Dept. Game Fish Parks D-J Proj., F-1-R-9 (Jobs 12-14):43pp.

Fogle, N. E. 1963a. Report of fisheries investigations during the fourth year of impoundment of Oahe Reservoir, South Dakota, 1961. S.D. Dingell-Johnson Proj., F-1-R-11 (Jobs 10-12):43pp.

Fogle, N. E. 1963b. Report of fisheries investigations during the fourth year of impoundment of Oahe Reservoir, South Dakota, 1962. S.D. Dingell-Johnson Proj., F-1-R-12 (Jobs 10-12):43pp. (The title is "fourth year," but the report apparently refers to the fifth year of impoundment).

Follett, W. I. 1967. Fish remains from coprolites and midden deposits at Lovelock Cave, Churchill County, Nevada. Rep. Calif. archaeol. Surv. Vol. 70:93-116.

Forbes, Stephen Alfred. 1884. A catalogue of the native fishes of Illinois. Report of the Illinois State Fish Commissioner for 1884:60-89.

Forbes, Stephen Alfred. 1890. Studies of the food of freshwater fishes. Bull. Illinois State Lab. Nat. Hist. Vol. 2:433-473.

Forbes, Stephen Alfred., and Robert Earl Richardson. 1908. The fishes of Illinois. Illinois State Laboratory of Natural History. 357pp.

Forbes, Stephen Alfred., and Robert Earl Richardson. 1920. The fishes of Illinois. Illinois Natural History Survey Division. 2nd edition. Springfield, Illinois. 357pp.

Forney, J. L. 1957a. Bait fish production in New York ponds. N.Y. Fish Game J. Vol. 4(2):150-194.

Forney, J. L. 1957b. Raising bait fish and crayfish in New York ponds. Cornell Ext. Bull. Vol. 986:3-30.

Forster, J. R. 1773. An account of some curious fishes sent from Hudson Bay. Phil. Trans. Roy. Soc. London. Vol. 63(1):149-160.

Foskett, D. R. 1947. Lakes of the Skeena River drainage. V. Bear Lake. Progress Reports of FRB Pacific Coast Stations. No. 70:10-12.

Fourine, J. W., and J. J. Black, A. D. Vethaak. 1988. Exocrine pancreatic adenomas in the greater redhorse, *Moxostoma valenciennesi* Jordan, and in the European flounder, *Platichthys flesus* (L.). J. Fish Dis. Vol. 11(5):445-448.

Fowden, M. 1980. 'Sucker squeezin' at Sunshine. Wyoming Wildl. Vol. 44(3):14-17.

Fowler, Henry Weed. 1904. Notes on Fishes from Arkansas, Indian Territory, and Texas. P. Ac. Philad. Vol. 55:242-249.

Fowler, Henry Weed. 1914a. Notes on catostomid fishes. Philadelphia Proc. Acad. Nat. Sci. 1913(1914) Vol. 65:45-60.

Fowler, Henry Weed. 1914b. Fishes in polluted waters. Copeia 1914(No. 5):4.

Fowler, Henry Weed. 1914.c The long-nosed dace in the Hackensack, New York. Copeia 1914 (No. 11):3.

Fowler, Henry Weed. 1916a. Notes on New Jersey fishes, several new to the state. Copeia 1916 (No. 27):10-12.

Fowler, Henry Weed. 1916b. Records of northern New Jersey fishes. Copeia 1916 (No. 31):41-42.

Fowler, Henry Weed. 1917. Some notes on the breeding habits of local catfishes. Copeia 1917 (No. 45):32-36.

Fowler, Henry Weed. 1918. The fishes of Perry County, Pennsylvania. Copeia 1918 (No. 63):89-91.

Fowler, Henry Weed 1919. A list of the fishes of Pennsylvania. Proc. Biol. Soc. Washington. Vol. 32:49-74.

Fowler, Henry Weed. 1921. The fishes of Bucks County, Pennsylvania. Copeia 1921 (No. 98):62-68.

Fowler, Henry Weed. 1922. Records of Fishes from the Southern and Eastern United States. Proc. Acad. Nat. Sci. Phila. Vol. 74:1-27.

Fowler, Henry Weed. 1925. Records of fishes in Pennsylvania 1924. Copeia 1925 (No. 140):23-24.

Fowler, Henry Weed. 1945. A Study of the Fishes of the Southern Piedmont and coastal Plain. The Academy of Natural Sciences of Philadelphia Monographs. No. 7:1-408.

Fowler, Henry Weed. 1948a. Fishes of the Nueltin Lake Expedition, Keewatin, 1947. Part 1 - Taxonomy. Proc. Acad. Nat. Sci. Phila. Vol. 57:141-152.

Fowler, Henry Weed. 1948b. A list of the fishes recorded from Pennsylvania. Rev. ed. Bull. Pa. Bd. Fish. Comm. Vol. 7:3-26.

Fowler, Henry Weed. 1958. Some new taxonomic names of fishlike vertebrates. Notul. Naturae, Philad. No. 310:1-16.

Franke, E. D., and S. MacKiewicz. 1982. Isolation of *Acanthamoeba* and *Naegleria* from the intestine contents of freshwater fishes and their potential pathogenicity. Journal of Parasitology. Vol. 68(1):164-166.

Franzin, W. G. 1984. Aquatic contamination in the vicinity of the base metal smelter at Flin Flon, Manitoba, Canada - a case history.Advances envir. Sci. Technol. Vol. 15:524-550.

Franzin, W. G., and G. A. McFarlane. 1981. Fallout, distribution and some effects of Zn, Cd, Du, Pb, and As in aquatic ecosystems near a base metal smelter on Canada's Precambrian Shield. Canadian Tech. Rep. Fish. Aquat. Sci. No. 990:46-68.

Franzin, W. G., and B. R. Parker, S. M. Harbicht. 1986. First record of the golden redhorse, *Moxostoma eythrurum*, new record, from the Red River in Manitoba [Canada]. Can. Field-Nat. Vol. 100(2):270-271.

Franzin, W. G., and G. A. McFarlane. 1987. Comparison of Floy anchor tags and fingerling tags for tagging white suckers. N. Am. J. Fish Manage. Vol. 7(2):307-309.

Fraser, D. F., and T. N. Mottolese. 1984. Discrimination and avoidance reactions towards predatory and nonpredatory fish by blacknose dace, *Rhinichthys atratulus* (Pisces: Cyprinidae). Zeitschrift Tierpsychol. Vol. 66(2):89-100.

Fraser, D. I., and A. Mannan, W. J. Dyer. 1962. Proximate composition of Canadian Atlantic fish. III. Sectional differences in the flesh of a species of Chondrostrei, one of Chimaerae, and of some miscellaneous teleosts. Journal of the Fisheries Research Board of Canada. Vol. 18(6):893-905.

Fraser, G. A., and Harold H. Harvey. 1982. Elemental composition of bone form white sucker (*Catostomus commersoni*) in relation to lake acidification. Canadian Journal of Fisheries and Aquatic Sciences. Vol. 39(9):1289-1296.

Fraser, Grant A., and Harold H. Harvey. 1984. Effects of environmental pH on the ionic composition of the white sucker (*Catostomus commersoni*) and pumpkinseed (*Lepomis gibbosus*). Canadian Journal of Zoology. Vol. 62(2):249-259.

Fredeen, F. J. H., and J. G. Saha, L. M. Royer. 1971. Residues of DDT, DDE, and DDD in fish in the Saskatchewan River after using DDT as a blackfly larvicide for twenty years. Journal of the Fisheries Research Board of Canada. Vol. 28(1):105-109.

Frederick, L. L. 1975. Comparative uptake of a polychlorinated biphenyl and dieldrin by the white sucker (*Catostomus commersoni*). Journal of the Fisheries Research Board of Canada. Vol. 32(10):1705-1709.

Fredrickson, L. H., and M. J. Ulmer. 1965. Caryophyllaeid cestodes from two species of redhorse (*Moxostoma*). Proc. Iowa Acad. Sci. Vol. 72:444-461.

Freeman, H. W. 1952. New distribution records for fishes of the Savannah River Basin, South Carolina. Copeia 1952(4):269.

Frey, D. G., and H. Pedracine. 1938. Growth of the buffalo in Wisconsin lakes and streams. Trans. Wis. Acad. Sci., Arts, Lett. Vol. 31:513-525.

Frick, H. C. 1965. Economic aspects of the Great Lakes fisheries of Ontario. Bulletins of the Fisheries Research Board of Canada. Number 149: 160pp.

Fried, B., and J. G. Kitchen. 1966. Morphological variation of *Triganodistomum attenuatum* Mueller and Van Cleave 1932 (Trematoda) from the white sucker, *Catostomus commersoni* (La Cepède). Proc. Pa. Acad. Sci. Vol. 39(2):68-72.

Fried, B., and J. G. Kitchen, R. S. Koplin. 1969. An intestinal helminth study of *Catostomus commersoni* from the Bushkill Creek, Northampton County, Pennsylvania, with observations on seasonal distribution of Triganodistomum sp. (Trematoda) and Fessisentis sp. (Acanthocephala). Proc. Pa. Acad. Sci. Vol. 38(2):1965:95-98.

Fried, B., and R. S. Koplin. 1967. Morphological variation of *Fessisentis vancleavei* Haley and Bullock 1953 (Acanthocephala) from the white sucker, *Catostomus commersoni* (La Cepède). Proc. Pa. Acad. Sci. Vol. 40(2):1967:53-58.

Friedrich, George W. 1933. A catalog of the fishes of central Minnesota. Copeia 1933(1):27-30.

Fry, F. E. J. 1960. Requirements for the aquatic habitat. Pulp Paper Mag. Can. 1960 (Feb.):8p.

Fry, J. P. 1962. Harvest of fish from tailwaters of three large impoundments in Missouri. Proc. 16th Conf. Southeastern Assoc. Game and Fish Comm.: 405-411.

Frych, I. V., and A. M. Tretyak, V. V. Romanyuk. 1989. The wide-mouth buffalo in temperate waters. Rybn. Khoz. 1989 (8):65-66.

Fuiman, Lee A. 1979. Descriptions and comparisons of catostomid fish larvae: northern Atlantic drainage species. Transactions of the American Fisheries Society. Vol. 108(6):560-603.

Fuiman, Lee A. 1983. Growth gradients in fish larvae. Journal of Fish Biology. Vol. 23(1):117-123.

Fuiman, Lee A. 1984. Ostariophysi: Development and Relationships. pp. 126-137. **IN:** Moser, H. G., et al.(ed.). Ontogeny and Systematics of Fishes. American Society of Ichthyologists and Herpetologists. Special Publication Number 1. Allen Press, Inc., Lawrence, Kansas. 760pp.

Fuiman, Lee A. 1985. Contributions of developmental characters to a phylogeny of catostomid fishes, with comments on heterochrony. Copeia 1985(4): 833-846.

Fuiman, L. A., and L. Corazza. 1979. Morphometrics and allometry: implications for larval fish taxonomy. pp. 1-17. **IN:** R. Wallus, and C. W. Voigtlander. (editors). Proceedings of a workshop on freshwater larval fishes. Tennessee Valley Authority, Division of Forestry Fisheries & Wildlife Development, Norris. Tennessee. 241 pp.

Fuiman, Lee A., and J. R. Trojnar. 1980. Factors affecting egg diameter of white suckers (*Catostomus commersoni*) Copeia 1980(4):699-704.

Fuiman, Lee A., and D. C. Witman. 1979. Descriptions and comparisons of catostomid fish larvae: *Catostomus catostomus* and *Moxostoma erythrurum*. Transactions of the American Fisheries Society. Vol. 108(6):604-619.

Fujihara, M. P. and F. P. Hungate. 1971. Chondrococcus columnaris disease of fishes: influence of Columbia river fish ladders. Journal of the Fisheries Research Board of Canada. Vol. 28(4):533-536.

Fujihara, M. P. and F. P. Hungate. 1972. Seasonal distribution of *Chondrococcus columnaris* infection in river fishes as determined by specific agglutinins. Journal of the Fisheries Research Board of Canada. Vol. 29(2):173-178.

Funk, J. L. 1957. Movements of stream fishes in Missouri. Transactions of the American Fisheries Society. Vol. 85:39-57.

Funk, J. L., and R. S. Campbell. 1953. The population of larger fishes in Black River, Missouri. pp. 69-82. **IN:** J. L. Funk, et al. The Black River Studies. Univ. Missouri Studies. Vol. 26(2):1-136.

Gabel, J. A. 1974. An experimental trap net fishery, Lake Oahe, South Dakota, 1965. Technical Pap. Bur. Sport. Fish. Wildl. No. 82:1-9.

Gadd, Ben. 1986. Handbook of the Canadian Rockies. Corax Press. Jasper, Alberta, Canada. 876pp.

Galasun, P. T., and A. I. Andryushchenko, V. V. Grusevich. 1984. Biological priniciples of introducing new species for aquaculture (*Ictalurus punctatus* and *Ictiobus cyprinellus*) into Ukrainian (USSR) waters. Aquaculture. Vol. 42(3-4):333-342.

Gale, N. L. and B. G. Wixson. 1986. Fish from Missouri's Lead Belt: to eat or not to eat. Environmental Geochem. Health Vol. 8(1):3-10.

Gammon, J. R. 1973. The effect of thermal input on the populations of fish and macroinvertebrates in the Wabash River. Purdue Univ. Water Res. Cent., Tech. Rep. No. 32. 106pp.

Gammon, J. R. 1977. The status of Indiana Streams and Fish from 1800 to 1900. Proceedings of the Indiana Academy of Science for 1976. Vol. 86:209-216.

Garman, H., 1890. A preliminary report on the animals of the Mississippi bottoms near Quincy, Illinois in August, 1888. Part I. Illinois State Lab. Nat. Hist., Bull. Vol. 3:123-184.

Garman, Samuel. 1881. New and little-known reptiles and fishes in the museum collections. Bull. Mus. Comp. Zool. Harv. Coll. Vol. 8(3):85-93.

Garth, W. A., and J. S. Dendy. 1952. Fertilization of eggs from a Catostomid fish, *Moxostoma poecilurum*, killed by rotenone. Copeia 1952(1):43.

Gasaway, C. R. 1970. Changes in the fish population in Lake Francis Case in South Dakota in the first 16 years of impoundment. U.S. Bur. Fish. Wildl. Techn. Pap. 56. 30pp.

Geen, G. H. 1958. Reproduction of three species of suckers (Catostomidae) in British Columbia. M.Sc. Thesis, University of British Columbia, Canada.

Geen, G. H., and T. G. Northcote. 1968. Latex injection as a method of marking large catostomids for long term study. Transactions of the American Fisheries Society. Vol. 97:281-282.

Geen, G. H., and T. G. Northcote, G. F. Hartman, C. C. Lindsey. 1966. Life histories of two species of catostomid fishes in Sixteenmile Lake, British Columbia, with particular reference to inlet stream spawning. Journal of the Fisheries Research Board of Canada. Vol. 23(11):1761-1788.

Gehlbach, F. R., and R. R. Miller. 1961. Fishes from archaeological sites in northern New Mexico. Southwestern Nat. Vol. 6:2-8.

Georgescu, R., and P. Dascalescu, G. Caraiman. 1984. Contributions regarding the evolution of an episode of eritrodermatita to *Ictiobus cyprinellus*, *I. bubalus*, and *I. niger* (Catostomidae). Bul. Cercet Piscic Ser. Nova 37(1-2):84-90.

Gerking, Shelby D. 1945. The distribution of the fishes of Indiana. Indiana Dep. Conserv. Indiana Univ. Dep. Zool., Invest. Indiana Lakes and Strms. Vol. 3(1):1-137.

Gerking, Shelby D. 1947 The use of minor postglacial drainage by fishes in Indiana. Copeia 1947(2):89-91.

Gerking, Shelby D. 1953. Evidence for the concept of home range and territory in stream fishes. Ecology Vol. 34(2):347-365.

Gerking, Shelby D. 1955. Key to the fishes of Indiana. Invest. Ind. Lakes. Vol. 4:49-86.

Gerlack, Jim. 1973. Early development of the quillback carpsucker, *Carpiodes cyprinus*. M.S. Thesis. Millersville State College, Millersville, Penna.

Gilbert, Carter R. 1961. *Notropis semperasper*, a new cyprinid fish from the upper James River System, Virginia. Copeia 1961(4):450-456.

Gilbert, Carter R., and Benjamin R. Wall, Jr. 1985. Status of the catostomid fish *Erimyzon oblongus* from eastern Gulf slope drainages in Florida and Alabama [USA]. Fla. Sci. Vol. 48(4):202-207.

Gilbert, Charles Henry 1885. Notes on the Fishes of Kansas. Bull. Washburn Coll. Vol. 1:10-16 & 97-99.

Gilbert, Charles Henry 1891. Report of Explorations made in Alabama during 1889, with notes on the Fishes of the Tennessee, Alabama, and Escambia Rivers. Bull. U.S. Fish Comm. Vol. 9(1889):143-159.

Gilbert, Charles Henry. 1893. Report on the fishes of the Death Valley expedition, collected in southern California and Nevada in 1891, with descriptions of new species. North Amer. Fauna, 1893, no. 7, pt. 2:228-234.

Gilbert, Charles Henry 1898. The fishes of the Klamath Basin. Bull. U.S. Fish Comm. Vol. 17:1-13.

Gilbert, Charles Henry, and Barton Evermann. 1894. A report upon investigations in the Columbia river basin, with descriptions of four new species of fishes. Report of the Commissioner of fish and fisheries on investigations in the Columbia river basin in regard to the Salmon fisheries. Report Comm. Fish & Fisher., Washington:19-54.

Gilbert, Charles Henry, and N. B. Scofield. 1898. Notes on a collection of Fishes from the Colorado Basin in Arizona. P.U.S. Mus. Vol. 20:487-499.

Gill, Theodore Nicholas. 1861. On the classification of the Eventognathi or Cyprini, a suborder of Teleocephali. Proc. Acad. Nat. Sci. Phila. 1861:6-9.

Gill, Theodore Nicholas. 1872. Arrangement of the families of fishes, or classes Pisces, Marsipobranchii, and Leptocardii. Smithsonian Miscel. Coll. No. 247:1-49.

Gill, Theodore Nicholas. 1875. On the geographical distribution of fishes. Ann. Mag. Nat. Hist. Vol. 15(4):251-255.

Gill, Theodore Nicholas. 1885. Teleostei. Stand. Nat. Hist. Vol. 3:98-298.

Gill, Theodore Nicholas. 1893. Families and subfamilies of fishes. Mem. Nat. Acad. Sci., Vol. 6:125-138.

Gill, Theodore Nicholas. 1905. The family of cyprinnids and the carp as its type. Smithson. Misc. Coll. Vol. 48:195-217.

Gill, V. E., and G. D. Burford, K. Lederis, E. A. Zimmerman. 1977. An immunocytochemical investigation for arginine vasotocin and neurophysin in the pituitary gland and the caudal neurosecretory system of *Catostomus commersoni*. General comp. Endocr. Vol. 32(4):505-511.

Girard, C. F. 1857. Researches upon the cyprinoid fishes inhabiting the fresh waters of the United States west of the Mississippi valley, from specimens in the museum of the Smithsonian Institution. Proc. Acad. Natur. Sci. Philadelphia (1856), Vol. 8:165-213.

Giurca, R., and N. Angelescu. 1978. Les poissons-chat. Vinatorul Pesc. Sportiv 1978(10):4.

Glass, N. R. 1969. Discussion of calculation of power function with special refernce to respiratory metabolism in fish. Journal of the Fisheries Research Board of Canada. Vol. 26:(10):2643-2650.

Gleason, Larry N. 1984. Population composition and dispersal pattern of *Pomphorhynchus bulbocolli* in *Hypentelium nigricans* from the West Fork of Drake's Creek, Kentucky (USA). American Midland Naturalist. Vol. 112(2):273-279.

Gleason, Larry N., and B. M. Christensen, Yui Tan Chung. 1983. Archinephric duct lesions caused by *Phyllodistomum superbum* and *P. lysteri* (Digenea:Gorgoderidae) in catostomid fishes. Journal Wildl. Dis. Vol. 19(3):277-279.

Gobas, F. A. P. C., and D. C. G. Muir, D. Mackay. 1989. Dynamics of dietary bioaccumulation and faecal elimination of hydrophobic organic chemicals in fish. Chemosphere Vol. 17(5):943-962.

Godfrey, H. 1955. On the ecology of Skeena River whitefishes, *Coregonus* and *Prosopium*. Journal of the Biological Board of Canada. Vol. 12(4):499-542.

Goode, C. Brown, and Theodore Nicholas Gill. 1903. American Fishes. A popular treatise upon the Game and Food Fishes of North America with especial reference to habits and methods of capture. L. C. Page & Company, Publishers. Boston. 562pp. 1887(1903). New edition completely revised and largely extended by Theodore Gill.

Goode, G. Brown, and Tarleton H. Bean. 1879. A List of the Fishes of Essex County, including those of Massachusetts Bay according to the latest results of the work of the U.S. Fish Commission. Bulletin of the Essex Institute. Salem, Massachusetts. Vol. 11:1-37pp.

Goodrich, Edwin S. 1909. Vertebrata Craniata (1st fasc.:Cyclostomes and Fishes). Lankester's A Treatise on Zoology. Part 9: 1-518 pp.

Gordon, D., and N. A. Croll, M. E. Rau. 1978. Les parasites des animaux sauvages du Québec. 1. Les parasites des poissons et des mammifères de la région de Schefferville. Naturaliste can. Vol. 105(1):55-59.

Gore, J. A., and R. M. Bryant, Jr. 1986. Changes in fish and benthic macroinvertebrate assemblages along the impounded Arkansas River. J. Freshwater Ecol. Vol. 3(3):333-346.

Gosline, William A. 1973. Functional Morphology and Classification of Teleostean Fishes. 2nd printing. The University Press of Hawaii. Honolulu, Hawaii. 208pp.

Gould, W. R. III, and W. H. Irwin. 1962. The suitabilities and relative resistances of twelve species of fish as bioassay animals for oil-refinery effluents. Proc. Southeast. Assoc. Game Fish Commis. Vol. 16:333-348.

Gowanloch, J. N. 1951. Lake management. La. Conserv. Vol. 3(7):10-13, 20-22.

Gowanloch, J. N., and C. Gresham. 1965. Fishes and fishing in Louisiana. State Conserv. Dep. Bull. No. 23. Claitor's Book Store. Baton Rouge. 701pp.

Grande, Roger Lance. 1980. Paleontology of the Green River Formation, with a review of the fish fauna. Bulletin-Geological Survey of Wyoming. Vol. 63:1-333pp.

Grande, Roger Lance. 1984. Paleontology of the Green River Formation, with a review of the fish fauna. Second edition. Geological Survey of Wyoming. Bulletin 63. 333pp.

Grande, Roger Lance, and Joseph T. Eastman, Ted M. Cavender. 1982. *Amyzon gosiutensis*, a new catostomid fish from the Green River Formation. Copeia 1982 (3):523-532.

Greeley, J. R. 1927. Fishes of the Genesee region wtih annotated list. pp. 47-66. **IN:** A biological survey of the Genesee River system. Suppl. 16th Annu. Rep. N.Y. State Conserv. Dep. 1928.

Greeley, J. R. 1936. Fishes of the area with annotated list. pp. 45-88. **IN:** A biological survey of the Delaware and Susquehanna watershed. Suppl. 25th Annu. Rep. N.Y. State Conserv. Dep. 1935.

Greenbank, J. 1950. The length-weight relationship of some upper Mississippi River fishes. Upp. Miss. R. Conserv. Commit. 12p. m.s.

Greenbank, J. 1957. Length-weight relationship of northern redhorse (*Moxostoma aureolum*) in Upper Mississippi River (St. Paul-Dubuque). Data for Handbook of Biological Data. 2p.

Greene, C. W. 1935. The distribution of Wisconsin fishes. Wis. Conserv. Comm. 235 pp.

Greenfield, David Wayne, and Stephen T. Ross, Gary D. Deckert. 1970. Some aspects of the life history of the Santa Ana sucker, *Catostomus* (*Pantosteus*) *santaanae* (Snyder). Calif. Fish Game Vol. 56:166-179.

Fishes of El Dorado City Lake, Butler County, Kansas. Trans. Kans. Acad. Sci. Vol. 59(3):358-363.

Greger, P. D., and J. E. Deacon. 1988. Food partitioning among fishes of the Virgin River. Copeia 1988(2):314-323.

Gregory, William K. 1933. Fish Skulls. A study of the Evolution of Natural Mechanisms. Transactions of the American Philosophical Society. Vol. 23(2):75-481.

Grey, A. J., and E. G. Hayunga. 1980. Evidence for alternative site selection by *Glaridacris laruei* (Cestodea: Caryophyllidea) as a result of interspecific competition. Journal of Parasitology. Vol. 66(2):371-372.

Griffith, J. S., and T. R. Tiersch. 1989. Ecology of fishes in Redfield Canyon, Arizona, with emphasis on *Gila robusta intermedia*. Southwest Nat. Vol. 34(1):131-164.

Grimes, L. R., and G. C. Miller. 1975. Caryophyllaeid cestodes in the creek chubsucker, *Erimyzon oblongus* (Mitchill), in North Carolina. Journal of Parasitology. Vol. 61(5):973-974.

Grimes, L. R., and G. C. Miller. 1976. Seasonal periodicity of three species of caryophyllaeid cestodes in the creek chubsucker, *Erimyzon oblongus* (Mitchill), in North Carolina. Journal of Parasitology. Vol. 62(3):434-441.

Grinham, T., and D. K. Cone. 1990. A review of species of *Myxobolus* (Myxosporea) parasitizing catostomid fishes, with a redescription of *Myxobolus bibullatus* (Kudo, 1934) n. comb. and description of *Myxobolus lamellus* n. sp. from *Catostomus commersoni* in Nova Scotia. Canadian Journal of Zoology. Vol. 68:2290-2298.

Guilday, J. E., and H. W. Hamilton, E. Anderson, et al. 1978. The Baker Bluff cave deposit, Tennessee, and the late Pleistocene faunal gradient. Carnegie Mus. Nat. Hist., Bull. No. 11:67pp.

Gunning, G. E., and T. M. Berra. 1969. Fish repopulation of experimentally decimated segments in the headwaters of two streams. Transactions of the American Fisheries Society. Vol. 98:305-308.

Gunter, Gordon. 1938. Notes on invasion of fresh water by fishes of the Gulf of Mexico, with special reference to the Mississippi - Atchafalaya system. Copeia 1938(2):69-72.

Günther, Albert C. 1868. Catalogue of the Fishes in the British Museum. London. 8 vols. Vol. 7:1-512.

Günther, Albert C. 1880. An introduction to the study of fishes. Edinburgh 8 vo.:1-720pp.

Günther, Albert C. 1889. Third Contribution to our knowledge of Reptiles and Fishes from the Upper Yangtsze-kiang. Annals and Magazine of Natural History (London). Vol. 4(6):218-229.

Haas, Robert L. 1943. A list of the fishes of McHenry County, Illinois. Copeia 1943(3):160-164.

Hacker, V. A. 1977. A fine kettle of fish. Wis. Dep. Nat. Resour. Bur. Fish Mgmt. Publ. No. 17-3600(77):64pp.

Hackney, P. A., and W. M. Tatum, S. L. Spencer. 1968. Life history study of the river redhorse, *Moxostoma carinatum* (Cope), in the Cahaba River, Alabama, with notes on the management of the species as a sport fish. Proc. Southeast. Assoc. Game Fish Commnrs. Vol. 21:324-332.

Hall, A. E., and O. R. Elliott. 1954. Relationship of length of fish to incidence of sea lamprey scars on white suckers, *Catostomus commersoni*, in Lake Huron. Copeia 1954:73-74.

Hall, Gordon E. 1951. Preimpoundment fish populations of the Wister Reservoir area in the Poteau River Basin, Oklahoma. Trans. N. Amer. Wildl. Conf. Vol. 16:266-283.

Hall, Gordon E., and R. M. Jenkins. 1953. Continued fisheries investigation of Tenkiller Reservoir, Oklahoma, during its first year of impoundment, 1953. Okla. Fish. Res. Lab. Rep. Vol. 33:1-54.

Hall, Gordon E., and George A. Moore. 1954. Oklahoma lampreys: their characterization and distribution. Copeia 1954(2):127-135.

Hallam, J. C. 1959. Habitat and associated fauna of four species of fish in Ontario streams. Journal of the Fisheries Research Board of Canada. Vol. 16(2):147-173.

Halyk, Lawrence. C., and Eugene K. Balon. 1983. Structure and ecological production of the fish taxocene of a small floodplain system. Canadian Journal of Zoology. Vol. 61(11):2446-2464.

Hambrick, P. S., and R. E. Spieler. 1977. Mouthless cypriniform fishes from Louisiana and Arkansas. Southwestern Nat. Vol. 22(1):143-146.

Hamilton, S. J., and T. A. Haines. 1989. Bone characteristics and metal concentrations in white suckers (*Catostomus commersoni*) from one neutral and three acidified lakes in Maine. Can. J. Fish Aquat. Sci. Vol. 46(3):440-446.

Hamman, R. L. 1985. Induced spawning of hatchery-reared razorback sucker. Prog. Fish. Cult. Vol. 47(3):187-189.

Hamman, R. L. 1987. Survival of razorback suckers cultured in earthen ponds. Prog. Fish-Cult. Vol. 49(2):138-140.

Hancock, H. M. 1955. Age and growth of some of the principal fishes in Canton Reservoir, Oklahoma, 1951, with particular emphasis on the white crappie. Okla. Fish Game Coun. Proj. Rep., Part 2:110pp. mimeo.

Hanek, G., and K. Molnar. 1974. Parasites of freshwater and anadromous fishes from Matamek river system, Québec. Journal of the Fisheries Research Board of Canada. Vol. 31(6):1135-1139.

Hankinson, T. L. 1920. Notes on life histories of Illinois fish. Transactions of the Illinois Academy of Science. Vol. 12(1919):132-150.

Hankinson, T. L. 1923. The creek fish of western New York. Copeia 1923 (No. 115):29-34.

Hankinson, T. L. 1932. Observations on the breeding behavior and habitats of fishes in southern Michigan. Pap. Mich. Acad. Sci., Arts, Lett. Vol. 15:411-425.

Hansel, H. C., and S. D. Duke, D. T. Lofy, G. A. Gray. 1988. Use of diagnostic bones to identify and estimate original lengths of ingested prey fishes. Trans Am. Fish. Soc. Vol. 117(1):55-62.

Hansen, D. F., and Hurst H. Shoemaker. 1943. Pigment deficiency in the carp and the carp-sucker. Copeia, Ann Arbor 1943(1):54.

Hansen, D. W. 1952. Life history studies of the trout of Pathfinder Reservoir, Wyoming. M.S. Thesis. Iowa State Coll. Lib. 55pp.

Hanson, W. D., and R. S. Campbell. 1963. The effects of pool size and beaver activity on distribution and abundance of warm-water fishes in a north Missouri stream. Amer. Midl. Nat. Vol. 69(1):136-149.

Hargis, H. L. 1966. Development of improved fishing methods for use in southeastern and southcentral reservoirs. Tenn. Game Fish Comm. Dingell-Johnson Job Completion Rep., 4-5-R-1:34pp.

Harlan, J. R., and E. B. Speaker. 1956. Iowa fish and fishing. Iowa Conserv. Comm. 377pp.

Harper, F., and J. T. Nichols. 1919. Six new Fishes from Northwestern Canada. New York Bull. Amer. Mus. Vol. 41:263-270.

Harrington, Robert W., Jr. 1947. Observations on the breeding habits of the yellow perch, *Perca flavescens*. Copeia 1947(3):199-200.

Harris, Roy H. D. 1952. A study of the sturgeon sucker in Great Slave Lake, 1950-51. M.S. Thesis. University of Alberta, Edmonton. 44pp.

Harris, Roy H. D. 1962. Growth and reproduction of the longnose sucker, *Catostomus catostomus* (Forster), in Great Slave Lake. Journal of the Fisheries Research Board of Canada. Vol. 19(1):113-126.

Harris, Roy H. D. 1963. The longnose sucker in Great Slave Lake. Circulars [General Series] of the Biological Station, London, Ontario of the Fisheries Research Board of Canada. No. 6:4-12.

Harrison, H. M. 1950. The foods used by some common fish of the Des Moines River Drainage. pp. 31-44. **IN:** Biology seminar held at Des Moines, Iowa, 11 July 1950. Iowa Conserv. Div. Fish Game.

Hart, C. W., Jr., and S. L. H. Fuller. 1974. Pollution ecology of freshwater invertebrates. Academic Press, N. Y. 389pp.

Hart, J. L. 1931. The food of the whitefish, *Coregonus clupeaformis* (Mitchill), in Ontario waters, with a note on the parasites. Canad. Biol. Fish. Vol. 6(21):1-10.

Hart, J. S. 1947. Lethal temperature relations of certain fish of the Toronto region. Trans. roy. Soc. Can. (3) Vol. 41(5):57-71.

Hart, T. F., Jr., and R. G. Werner. 1987. Effects of prey density on growth and survival of white sucker, *Catostomus commersoni*, and pumpkinseed, *Lepomis gibbosus*, larvae. Environmental Biol. Fish. Vol. 18(1):41-50.

Harvey, Harold H. 1980. Widespread and diverse changes in the biota of North American lakes and rivers coincident with acidification. pp. 93-98. D. Drabl s, and A. Tollan (editors). Proc. Int. conf. ecol. impact acid precip. Norway. SNSF project. As, Norway.

Harvey, Harold H., and G. A. Fraser, J. M. McArdle. 1986. Bone concentration of manganese in white sucker (*Catostomus commersoni*) from acid circumneutral and metal-stressed lakes. Water, Air and Soil Pollution. Vol. 30(1-2):515-521.

Hathaway, R. P., and J. C. Herlevich. 1973. *Gyrodactylus stableri* sp. n., with new host and locality records for species of *Gyrodactylus*. Journal of Parasitology. Vol. 59(5):801-802.

Hauser, W. J. 1969. Life history of the mountain sucker. *Catostomus platyrhynchus* in Montana. Transactions of the American Fisheries Society. Vol. 98:209-215.

Hay, Oliver Perry. 1902. Bibliography and catalogue of the fossil Vertebrata of North America. Bull. U.S. Geol. Surv. Vol. 179:1-868.

Hay, Oliver Perry. 1927. The Pleistocene of the western region of North America and its vertebrated animals. Publ. Carnegie Instn. Wash. 322B:1-346pp.

Hay, Oliver Perry. 1929. Second Bibliography and Catalogue of the Fossil Vertebrata of North America. Vol. 1. Carnegie Institution of Washington. National Publishing Co., Washington. 916pp.

Hayes, M. L. 1955. Sucker life histories in Shadow Mountain Reservoir, Colorado. Colo. Fish. Res. Unit Quart. Rep. 2 (1+2):1-10.

Hayes, M. L. 1956. Life history studies of two species of suckers in Shadow Mountain Reservoir, Grand County, Colorado. M.S. Thesis. Colorado A.M. Coll. 126pp.

Hayunga, E. G. 1980. Two atypical lesions from white suckers *Catostomus commersoni* La Cepède infected by caryophyllid tapeworms. Journal Fish Dis. Vol. 3(2):167-172.

Hayunga, E. G. 1984. Anatomical anomalies in a leech, *Cystobranchus meyeri* (Hirundinea: Piscicolidae), infesting the white sucker, *Catostomus commersoni* La Cepède. Proc. Helminthol. Soc. Wash. Vol. 51(1):172-174.

Hayunga, E. G., and A. J. Grey. 1976. *Cystobranchus meyeri* sp.n. (Hirudinea:Piscicolidae) from *Catostomus commersoni* La Cepède in North America. Journal of Parasitology. Vol. 62(4):621-627.

Hayunga, E. G., and J. S. Mackiewicz. 1988. Comparative histology of the scolex and neck region of *Glaridacris laruei* (Lamont, 1921) Hunter, 1927 and *Glaridacris catostomi* Cooper, 1920 (Cestoidea: Caryophyllidea). Canadian Journal of Zoology. Vol. 66(4):790-805.

Hazel, P. P. 1978. Croissance en longueur et en masse des meuniers rouges *Catostomus catostomus* du basin hydrographique de La Grande Rivière, territoire de la Baie James. Annales ACFAS Vol. 45(1):176.

Heckmann, R. A., and T. Carroll. 1985. Host-parasite studies of *Trichophrya* infesting cutthroat trout *Salmo clarki* and longnose suckers *Catostomus catostomus* from Yellowstone Lake, Wyoming (USA). Great Basin Nat. Vol. 45(2):255-265.

Heckmann, R. A., and H. L. Ching. 1987. Parasites of the cuthroat trout, *Salmo clarki*, and longnose suckers, *Catostomus catostomus*, from Yellowstone Lake, Wyoming. Great Basin Nat. Vol. 47(2):259-275.

Hedges, S. B., and R. C. Ball. 1953. Production and harvest of bait fishes in Michigan. Michigan Dept. Conserv. Misc. Publ. 6:1-30.

Hedtke, S. F., and C. W. West, K. N. Allen, T. J. Norberg-King, D. I. Mount. 1986.Toxicity of pentachlorophenol to aquatic organisms under naturally varying and controlled environment conditions. Environmental Toxicol. Chem. Vol. 5(6):531-542.

Heilprin, Angelo. 1887. The geographical and geological distribution of animals. International Scientific Series, New York and London. 8 vo. 1-435pp.

Heinermann, P. H., and M. A. Ali. 1989. The photic environment and scotopic visual pigments of the creek chub, *Semotilus atromaculatus* and white sucker, *Catostomus commersoni* . J. Comp. Physiol. A. Sens. Neural Behav Physiol. Vol. 164(5):707-716.

Heit, Merrill, and Catherine S. Klusek. 1985. Trace element concentrations in the dorsal muscle of white suckers (*Catostomus commersoni*) and brown bullheads (*Ictalurus nebulosus*) from 2 acidic Adirondack lakes. (USA). Water Air Soil Pollut. Vol. 25(1):87-96.

Heit, M., and C. Schofield, C. T. Driscoll, S S. Hodgkiss. 1989.Trace element concentration in fish from three Adirondack lakes with different pH values. Water Air Soil Pollut. Vol. 44(1-2):9-30.

Helms, D. R. 1966. 1965 annual survey of the Coralville Reservoir fish population. Iowa Conserv. Comm. Quart. Biol. Rep. Vol. 18(2):27-32.

Henderson, B. A. 1986. Effect of sea lamprey (*Petromyzon marinus*) parasitism on the abundance of white suckers (*Catostomus commersoni*) in South Bay, Lake Huron, [Canada]. J. Appl. Ecol. Vol. 23(2):381-390.

Henderson, N. E., and R. E. Peter. 1969. Distribution of fishes of southern Alberta. Journal of the Fisheries Research Board of Canada. Vol. 26(2):325-338.

Hendricks, Lawrence J. 1952. Erythrocyte counts and hemoglobin determinations for two species of suckers, genus *Catostomus*, from Colorado. Copeia 1952(4):265-266.

Hendricks, Lawrence J. 1956. Growth of the smallmouth buffalo in carp ponds. Progr. Fish Cult. Vol. 18(1):45-46.

Hendricks, M. L., and J. R. Stauffer, C. H. Hocutt, Jr. A preliminary checklist of the fishes of the Youghiogheny River. Natural Hist. Misc. Chicago No. 203:1-15.

Hendrickson, G. L. 1986.Observations of the life cycle of *Ornithodiplostomum ptychocheilus* (Trematoda: Diplostomatidae). Proceedings helminth. Soc. Wash. Vol. 53(2):166-172.

Hendrix, S. S. 1973. *Plagioporus hypentelii* sp. n. (Trematoda:Opecoelidae) from the hogsucker, *Hypentelium nigricans* (Le Sueur) (Osteichthys: Catostomidae). Proceedings helminth. Soc. Wash. Vol. 40(1):144-146.

Hendrix, S. S. 1978. The life history and biology of *Plagioporus hypentelii* Hendrix 1973 (Trematoda: Opecoelidae). Journal of Parasitology. Vol. 64(4):606-612.

Hepworth, W. 1959. A study of the population dynamics of brook trout in two sub-alpine lakes in southeastern Wyoming. Wyo. Game Fish. Comm. Coop. Res. Proj. 2:69-203.

Herald, Earl S. 1967. Living Fishes of the World. The World of Nature Series. Doubleday & Company, Inc. Garden City, New York. Fifth Printing. 304pp.

Herald, Earl S. 1979. Fishes of North America. Animal Life of North America Series. Doubleday and Company, Inc., Garden City, New York. 256pp.

Herre, A. W. C. T. 1936. Notes on fishes in the zoological museum of Stanford University. IV. A new Catostomid from Mexico and a new Callionymid from Celebes and the Philippines. Proc. Biol. Soc. Washington. Vol. 49:11-13.

Hesslein, R. H., and E. Salvicek. 1984. Geochemical pathways and biological uptake of radium in small Canadian Shield lakes. Canadian Journal of Fisheries and Aquatic Sciences. Vol. 41(3):459-468.

Heuser, W. J. 1975. A hermaphroditic mountain sucker, *Catostomus platyrhynchus*. Copeia. 1975(4):775.

Hewson, L. C. 1959. A study of six winter seasons of commercial fishing on Lake Winnipeg. Journal of the Fisheries Research Board of Canada. Vol. 16(1):131-145.

Hierhorst, J. and S. D. Morley, J. Figueroa, C. Krentler, K. Lederis, D. Richter. 1989. Vasotocin and isotocin precursors from the white sucker, *Catostomus commersoni* cloning and sequence analysis of the cDNAs. Proc. Natl. Acad. Sci. USA Vol. 86(14):5242-5246.

Hildebrand, Samuel F., and William C. Schroeder. 1923. Fishes of Chesapeake Bay. Bull. United States Bur. Fish. Vol. 43(1):1-366.

Hile, R., and C. Juday. 1941. Bathymetric distribution of fish in lakes of northeastern highlands, Wisconsin. Trans. Wis. Acad. Sci., Arts, Lett. Vol. 33:147-187.

Hilgard, Theodore Charles. 1858. On the structure of the head in Vertebrata and its relation to the phyllotactic laws. Proc. Amer. Assoc. Adv. Sci. Vol. 11, Montreal 1857:81-95.

Hilgard, Theodore Charles. 1860. Comparative anatomy of Vertebrata. Trans. Acad. Sci. St. Louis. Vol. 1:678-682.

Hinks, David. 1943. The Fishes of Manitoba. The Department of Mines and Natural Resources. Winnipeg, Manitoba. 102pp.

Hinks, David. 1957. The Fishes of Manitoba. (reprinted, with supplement by J. J. Keleher and B. Kooyman.) Man. Dept. Mines Nat. Resources, Winnipeg, Man. 117 pp.

Hobe, H. 1987. Sulphate entry into soft-water fish (*Salmo gairdneri*, *Catostomus commersoni*) during low ambient pH exposure. J. Exp. Biol. Vol. 133:87-109.

Hobe, Helve, and Peter R. H. Wilkes, Richard L. Walker, Chris M. Wood, Brian R. McMahon. 1983. Acid-base balance, ionic status, and renal function in resting and acid-exposed white suckers (*Catostomus commersoni*). Canadian Journal of Zoology. Vol. 61(12):2660-2668.

Hobe, Helve, and Chris M. Wood, Brian R. McMahon. 1984. Mechanisms of acid-base and ionoregulation in white suckers (*Catostomus commersoni*) in natural soft water: 1. Acute exposure to low ambient pH. J. Comp. Physiol. B Biochem. Syst. Environ. Physiol. Vol. 154(1):35-46.

Hobe, H., and B. R. McMahon. 1988. Mechanisms of acid-base and ionoregulation in white suckers (*Catostomus commersoni*) in natural soft water 2. Exposure to a fluctuating ambient pH regime. J. Comp. Physio. B. Biochem Syst. Environ. Physiol. Vol. 158(1):67-79.

Hocutt, C. H. 1979. Drainage evolution and fish dispersal in the central Appalachians. Geol. Soc. Am. Bull. Vol. 90(2)p.I 129-I 130, II-197-II 234.

Hoese, H. Dickson, and Richard H. Moore. 1977. Fishes of the Gulf of Mexico, Texas, Louisiana, and Adjacent Waters. Texas A & M University Press. College Station, Texas. 327pp.

Hoffman, C. H., and E. W. Surber. 1948. Effects of an aerial application of wettable DDT on fish and fish-food organisms in Back Creek, West Virginia. Transactions of the American Fisheries Society. Vol. 75:48-58.

Hoffman, Glenn L. 1967. Parasites of North American Freshwater Fishes. University of California Press. Berkeley, California. 486 pp.

Hoffman, Glenn L., and Fred P. Meyer. 1974. Parasites of freshwater fishes. A Review of their control and Treatment. T. F. H. Publications, Inc. Neptune City, New Jersey. 224pp.

Hogman, W. J. 1973. The relative efficiency of nylon gill nets after transition from cotton nets in a multispecies fishery. Transactions of the American Fisheries Society. 102(4):778-785.

Hogue, J. J., Jr., and J. P. Buchanan. 1977. Larval development of spotted sucker *Minytrema melanops*. Transactions of the American Fisheries Society. Vol. 106(4):347-353.

Hogue, J. J., Jr., and J. V. Conner, V. R. Kranz. 1981. Descriptions and methods for identifying larval blue sucker *Cycleptus elongatus* (Le Sueur) Rapports P.-v. Reun. Cons. perm. int. Explor. Mer. Vol. 178:585-587.

Hokanson, Kenneth E. F. 1977.Temperature requirements of some Percids and Adaptations to the Seasonal Temperature Cycle. Journal of the Fisheries Research Board of Canada. Vol. 34(10):1524-1550.

Holden, P. B., and C. B. Stalnaker. 1975. Distribution and abundance of mainstream fishes of the middle and upper Colorado river basins, 1967-1973. Transactions of the American Fisheries Society. Vol. 104(2):217-231.

Holden, P. B., and C. B. Stalnaker. 1975. Distribution of fishes in the Dolores and Yampa River systems of the upper Colorado Basin. Southwestern Nat. Vol. 19(4):403-412.

Holey, M., and B. Hollender, M. Imhof, R. Jesien, R. Konopacky, M. Toneys, D. Coble. 1980. 'Never give a sucker an even break.' Fisheries, Bethesda.Vol. 4(1):2-6.

Hollander, E. E., and J. W. Avault, Jr. 1975. Effects of salinity on survival of buffalo fish eggs through yearlings. Progressive Fish-Culturist Vol. 37(1):47-51.

Holloway, H. L., Jr. 1978. Worms in fish? North Dakota Outdoors. Vol. 40(8):11.

Holman, J. A. 1979. New fossil vertebrate remains from Michigan. Mich. Acad. Vol. 11(4):391-396.

Hopkirk, J. D. 1973. Endemism in fishes of the Clear Lake region of central California. University Calif. Publs. Zool. Vol. 96:1-35.

Horak, D. L., and H. A. Tanner. 1964. The use of vertical gill nets in studying fish depth distribution, Horsetooth Reservoir, Colorado. Transactions of the American Fisheries Society. Vol. 93(2):137-145.

Hornshaw, T. C., and R. J. Aulerich, H. E. Johnson. 1983. Feeding Great Lakes [USA,Canada] fish to mink: Effects on mink and accumulation and elimination of polychlorinated biphenyls by mink. J. Toxicol. Environ. Health. Vol. 11(4-6):933-946.

Houser, A. 1960. A fishery survey by population estimation techniques in Lake Lawtouka. Rep. Okla. Fish. Res. Lab. Norman. Vol. 76:18pp.

Houser, A., and M. G. Bross. 1963. Average growth rates and length-weight relationships for fifteen species of fish in Oklahoma waters. Okla. Res. Lab. Rep. Vol. 85:75pp.

Houston, A. H., and K. M. Mearow, J. S. Smeda. 1976. Further observations upon the hemoglobin systems of thermally acclimated freshwater teleosts:pumpkinseed (*Lepomis gibbosus*), white sucker (*Catostomus commersoni*), carp (*Cyprinus carpio*) goldfish hybrids. Comparative Biochem. Physiol. (A). Vol. 54(2):267-273.

Howell, W. Mike, and David E. Butts. 1983. Silver staining of spermatozoa from living and preserved museum fishes: A new taxonomic approach. Copeia 1983(4):974-978.

Huang, C. T. and Cleveland P. Hickman, Jr. 1968. Binding of inorganic iodide to the plasma proteins of teleost fishes. Journal of the Fisheries Research Board of Canada. Vol. 25(8):1651-1666.

Hubbs, Carl L. 1921. An ecological study of the life-history of the freshwater atherine fish, *Labidesthes sicculus*. Ecology Vol. 2(4):262-276.

Hubbs, Carl L. 1926. A check-list of the fishes of the Great Lakes and tributary waters, with nomenclatorial notes and analytical keys. Univ. Mich. Mus. Zool. Misc. Publ. No. 15:77pp.

Materials for a revision of the Catostomid fishes of Eastern North America. Misc. Pub. Mus. Zool. Univ. Mich. Vol. 20:1-47pp.

Hubbs, Carl L. 1941. Increased number and delayed development of scales in abnormal Suckers. Pap. Mich. Acad. Sci. Vol. 26:1940(1941):229-237.

Hubbs, Carl L. 1945. Corrected distributional records for Minnesota fishes. Copeia 1945(1):13-22.

Hubbs, Carl L. 1958. Position of anal fin and length of body cavity in catostomid and cyprinid fishes. Copeia 1958(1):56.

Hubbs, Carl L., and J. D. Black. 1940. Status of the Catostomid fish, *Carpiodes carpio elongatus* Meek. Copeia, Ann Arbor. 1940 (4):226-230.

Hubbs, Carl L., and C. W. Creaser. 1924. On the growth of young suckers and the propagation of Trout. Ecology Brooklyn N. Y. Vol. 5(4):372-378.

Hubbs, Carl L., and W. I. Follett, Lillian J. Dempster. 1979. List of the Fishes of California. Occasional Papers of the California Academy of Sciences. No. 133:51pages.

Hubbs, Carl L., and Clark Hubbs. 1958. *Notropis saladonis*, a new cyprinid fish endemic in the Rio Salado of Northeastern Mexico. Copeia 1958(4):297-307.

Hubbs, Carl L., and Laura C. Hubbs. 1947. Natural hybrids between two species of Catostomid fishes. Pap. Mich. Acad. Sci. Vol. 31:147-167.

Hubbs, Carl L., and Laura C. Hubbs, R. E. Johnson. 1943. Hybridization in nature between species of Catostomid fishes. Contr. Lab. Vert. Biol. Univ. Michigan. Vol. 22:1-69.

Hubbs, Carl L., and Laura C. Hubbs, Robert Rush Miller. 1974. Hydrographic history and relict fishes of the northcentral Great Basin. California Academy of Sciences Memoirs. Vol. 7:1-259pp.

Hubbs, Carl L., and Karl F. Lagler. 1941. Guide to the Fishes of the Great Lakes and Tributary Waters. Cranbrook Institute of Science. Bulletin No. 18:1-100pp.

Hubbs, Carl L., and Karl F. Lagler. 1947. Fishes of the Great Lakes region. Bull. Cranbrook Inst. Sci. Bloomfield Hills Mich. Vol. 26:1-186 pp.

Hubbs, Carl L., and Karl F. Lagler. 1974. Fishes of the Great Lakes Region. The University of Michigan Press, Ann Arbor. 1-135 pp.

Hubbs, Carl L., and Robert Rush Miller. 1951. *Catostomus arenarius*, a great basin fish, synonymized with *C. tahoensis*. Copeia 1951 (4):299-300.

Hubbs, Carl L., and Robert Rush Miller. 1953. Hybridization in nature between the fish genera *Catostomus* and *Xyrauchen*. Pap. Mich. Acad. Sci. Vol. 38:207-234.

Hubbs, Carl L., and Leonard P. Schultz. 1932. A new Catastomid fish from the Columbia River. Univ. Washington Pub. Seattle Biol. 2(1):1-13.

Hubbs, Carl L., and A. McLaren White. 1923. A list of fishes from Cass Lake, northern Minnesota. Copeia. 1923(No. 123):103-104.

Hubbs, Clark. 1947. Mixture of marine and freshwater fishes in the Lower Salinas River, California. Copeia 1947(2):147-149.

Hubert, W. A., and F. J. Rahel. 1989. Relations of physical habitat to abundance of four nongame fishes in high-plains streams: a test of habitat suitability index models. N. Am. J. Fish. Manag. Vol. 9(3):332-340.

Hubert, W. A., and Dennis N. Schmitt. 1985. Summer and fall hoop net catches of fish in the Upper Mississippi River (USA). Iowa State J. Res. Vol. 60(1):39-50.

Huggins, Donald G., and Randall E. Moss. 1975. Fish Population structure in altered and unaltered areas of a small Kansas stream. Transactions of the Kansas AcademyVol. 77(1):18-30.

Hunn, J. B. 1972. Blood chemistry values for some fishes of the upper Mississippi River. Journal Minn. Acad. Sci. Vol. 38(1):19-21.

Huntsman, A. G. 1935. The sucker (*Catostomus commersoni*) in relation to salmon and trout. Transactions of the American Fisheries Society. Vol. 65:152-156.

Huntsman, A. G. 1942. Death of salmon and trout with high temperature. Journal of the Fisheries Research Board of Canada Vol. 5(5):485-501.

Huntsman, G. R. 1965. Paper chromatograms of body mucus of some suckers (family Catostomidae). Proc. Iowa Acad. Sci. Vol. 71:263-274.

Huntsman, G. R. 1967. Biochemical taxonomy of Catostomidae and hybridization of *Carpiodes* species. Diss. Abstr. 27B:3339.

Huntsman, G. R. 1967. Nuptial tubercles in carpsuckers (*Carpiodes*). Copeia 1967 (2):457-458.

Huntsman, G. R. 1970. Disc gel electrophoresis of blood sera and muscle extracts from some catostomid fishes. Copeia 1970:457-467.

Hussakof, Louis. 1908. Catalogue of types and figured specimens of fossil vertebrates in the American Museum of Natural History. Part I:Fishes. Bull. Amer. Mus. Nat. Hist. Vol. 25:1-103.

Hyrtl, Carl Joseph. 1862. Ueber Wirbelssynostosen und Wirbelsuturen bei Fischen. Denk. Akad. Wiss. Wien. Vol. 20:95-110.

Ichikawa, Tomoyuki, and Karl Lederis, Hideshi Kobayashi. 1984. Primary structures of multiple forms of urotensin II in the urophysis of the carp, *Cyprinus carpio*. Gen. Comp. Endocrinol. Vol. 55(1):133-141.

Isom, B. G., and R. G. Hudson. 1984. Freshwater mussels and their fish hosts: Physiological aspects. Journal of Parasitology. Vol. 70(2):318.

Iwai, Tamotsu. 1963. Taste buds on the gill rakers and gill arches of the sea catfish, *Plotosus anguillaris* (La Cepède). Copeia 1963(2):271-274.

Jackson, S. W., Jr. 1954. Rotenone survey of Black Hollow on Lower Spavinaw Lake, November, 1953. Proc. Okla. Acad. Sci. Vol. 35:10-14.

Jackson, S. W., Jr. 1957. Comparison of the age and growth of four fishes from Lower and Upper Spavinaw Lakes, Oklahoma. Proc. S-E Assn. Game Fish. Comm. Vol. 11:232-249.

Jackson, S. W., Jr. 1966. Summary of fishery management activities on Lake Eucha and Spavinaw, Oklahoma, 1951-1964. Proc. S.E. Assoc. Game Fish Comm. Vol. 19:315-343.

Jacobs, K. E., and W. D. Swink. 1983. Fish abundance and population stability in a reservoir tailwater and an unregulated headwater stream. North American Journal of Fisheries Management. Vol. 3(4):395-402.

Jaffe, R., and R. A. Hites. 1986. Anthropogenic, polyhalogenated, organic compounds in non-migratory fish from the Niagara River area and tributaries to Lake Ontario. J. Great Lakes Res. Vol. 12(1):63-71.

Jaffe, R., and E. A. Stemmler, B. D. Eitzer, R. A. Hites. 1985. Anthropogenic, polyhalogenated, organic compounds in sedentary fish from Lake Huron and Lake Superior tributaries and embayments. Journal Great Lakes Res. Vol. 11(2):156-162.

Jagoe, Charles H., and Terry A. Haines. 1985. Fluctuating asymmetry in fishes inhabiting acidified and unacidified lakes. Canadian Journal of Zoology. Vol. 63(1):130-138.

Jakle, M. D., and T. A. Gatz. 1984. Harris' hawks feeding on fish. Southwestern Nat. Vol. 29(4):506.

Jenkins, J. T., and H. A. Semken. 1972. Faunal analysis of the Lane Enclosure, Allamakee County, Iowa. Proceedings Iowa Acad. Sci. Vol. 78(3-4):76-78.

Jenkins, Robert E. 1970. Systematic studies of the catostomid fish tribe Moxostomatini. Ph.D. thesis. Cornell Univ., Ithaca, New York. 800 pp.

Jenkins, Robert E., and D. J. Jenkins. 1980. Reproductive behavior of the greater redhorse, *Moxostoma valenciennesi*, in the Thousand Islands region. Canadian Fld. Nat. Vol. 94(4):426-430.

Jenkins, Robert M. 1953a. Growth histories of the principal fishes in Grand Lake (O' the Cherokees), Oklahoma, through thirteen years of impoundment. Oklahoma Fish. Res. Lab. Rep. Vol. 34:87pp.

Jenkins, Robert M. 1953b. A report on the growth of fishes in Fort Gibson Reservoir collected in July and October, 1953-the first year of complete impoundment. Okla. Fish. Res. Lab. Rep. Vol. 32:10 p. mimeo.

Jenkins, Robert M. 1953c. A pre-impoundment survey of Fort Gibson Reservoir, Oklahoma (Summer 1952). Okla. Fish. Res. Lab. Rep. Vol. 29:1-53.

Jenkins, Robert M., and J. C. Finnell. 1957. The fishery resources of the Verdigris River in Oklahoma. Okla. Fish Res. Lab. Rep. Vol. 59:1-46.

Jenkins, Robert M., and E. M. Leonard, G. E. Hall. 1952. An investigation of the fisheries resources of the Illinois River and pre-impoundment study of Tenkiller Reservoir, Oklahoma. Okla. Fish. Res. Lab. Rep. Vol. 26:136pp. mimeo.

Jester, D. B. 1972. Life history, ecology, and management of the river carpsucker, *Carpiodes carpio* (Rafinesque), with reference to Elephant Butte Lake. N. M. State Univ. Agric. Exp. Stn. Res. Rep. No. 243. 120pp.

Jester, D. B. 1973. Life history, ecology, and management of the smallmouth buffalo, *Ictiobus bubalus* (Rafinesque), with reference to Elephant Butte Lake. N. M. State Univ. Agric. Exp. Stn. Res. Rep. No. 261:111pp.

Johnson, A., and D. Norton, B. Yake. 1988. Persistence of DDT in the Yakima River drainage, Washington. Arch. Environ. Contam. Toxicol. Vol. 17(3):289-297.

Johnson, D. W., and W. L. Minckley. 1969. Natural hybridization in buffalofishes, genus *Ictiobus* Copeia 1969:198-200.

Johnson, D. W., and W. L. Minckley. 1972. Variability in Arizona buffalofishes. Copeia 1972(1):12-17.

Johnson, F. H. 1977. Responses of walleye (*Stizostedion vitreum vitreum*) and yellow perch (*Perca flavescens*) populations to removal of white sucker (*Catostomus commersoni*) from a Minnesota lake, 1966. Journal of the Fisheries Research Board of Canada. Vol. 34(10):1633-1642.

Johnson, L. 1966. Great Bear Lake. Can. Geogr. J. Aug. pp. 58-67.

Johnson, L. 1972. Keller Lake: characteristics of a culturally unstressed salmonid community. Journal of the Fisheries Research Board of Canada. Vol. 29(6):731-740.

Johnson, L. 1975. Distribution of fish species in Great Bear Lake, Northwest Territories, with reference to Zooplankton, benthic invertebrates, and environmental conditions. Journal of the Fisheries Research Board of Canada. Vol. 32(11):1989-2004.

Johnson, L. D. 1958. Pond culture of muskellunge in Wisconsin. Wis. Conserv. Dept. Tech. Bull. Vol. 17:1-54.

Johnson, M. C. 1959. Food-fish farming in the Mississippi Delta. Progr. Fish Cult. Vol. 21(4):154-160.

Johnson, M. G. 1987. Trace element loadings to sediments of fourteen Ontario lakes and correlations with concentrations in fish. Canadian J. Fish. Aquat. Sci. Vol. 44(1):3-13.

Johnson, R. P. 1963. Studies on the life history and ecology of the bigmouth buffalo, *Ictiobus cyprinellus* (Valenciennes). Journal of the Fisheries Research Board of Canada Vol. 20(6):1397-1430.

Johnson, Sterling K. 1971. *Ergasilis wareaglei* sp. n. (Copepoda:Cyclopoida) from North American Catostomid Fishes. Journal of the Alabama Academy of Sciences. Vol. 42:243-247.

Jollie, Malcolm. 1962. Chordate Morphology. Reinhold Publishing Corporation. New York, New York. 478pp.

Jones, David T. 1929. Notes on fishes taken in the vicinity of Vinton, Iowa. Copeia 1929 (No. 171):29-34.

Jones, F. W., and F. D. Martin, J. D. Hardy, Jr. 1978. Development of fishes of the Mid-Atlantic Bight. An atlas of egg, larval and juvenile stages. Volume 1. Acipenseridae through Ictaluridae. Biological Service Program, Fish & Wildlife Service, Washington, D. C. 1-366.

Jordan, David Starr. 1876. Concerning the fishes of the Ichthyologia Ohiensis. Bull. Buffalo Soc. Nat. Hist. 1876:91-97.

Jordan, David Starr. 1877a. Contributions to North American Ichthyology. No. 2. Bull. U. S. Nat. Mus. Vol. 10:1-116.

Jordan, David Starr. 1877b. On the fishes of Northern Indiana. P. Ac. Philad. 1877:42-82.

Jordan, David Starr. 1877c. A partial synopsis of the Fishes of Upper Georgia with Supplementary Papers on Fishes of Tennessee, Kentucky, and Indiana. Ann. Lyc. N. York. Vol. 11:307-377.

Jordan, David Starr. 1878a. A catalogue of the fishes of Illinois. Illinois State Laboratory of Natural History. Bulletin 1(2):37-70.

Jordan, David Starr. 1878b. Manual of the Vertebrates of the Northern U.S. 2nd ed., revised and enlarged. Chicago. 8 Vol. pp. 407. Fishes, pp. 199-350, with addenda.antedates by a few weeks the Bull. U.S. Nat. Mus. vol. 12.

Jordan, David Starr. 1878c. A Catalogue of the Fishes of the Fresh-waters of North America. Bull. U.S. Geol. Surv. Territ., 1878. Vol. 4:407-442.

Jordan, David Starr. 1878d. Contributions to North American ichthyology, based primarily on the collections of the United States National Museum. III. B. A synopsis of the family Catostomidae. Bull. U. S. Nat. Mus. Vol. 12:97-237.

Jordan, David Starr. 1878e. Report on the collection of fishes made by Dr. Elliott Coues U.S.A. in Dakota and Montana during the season of 1873 and 1874. Bull. U.S. Geol. Surv. Terit., Vol. 4(4):777-799.

Jordan, David Starr. 1885a. Notes on the Scientific Names of the Yellow Perch, the Striped Bass, and other N. American Fishes. Proc. U. S. Nat. Mus. Vol. 8(5):72-73.

Jordan, David Starr. 1885b. Subclass II. Teleostei. Stand. Nat. Hist. Vol. 3:98-173.

Jordan, David Starr. 1886. Identification of the species of Cyprinidae and Catostomidae, described by Dr. Charles Girard in Proceedings of the Academy of Natural Science of Philadelphia, 1856. Proc. U.S. Nat. Mus. 1885(1886) Vol. 8:118-127.

Jordan, David Starr. 1889. Descriptions of fourteen species of fresh-water Fishes collected by the U.S. Fish Commission in the summer of 1888. Proc. U. S. Nat. Mus. Vol. 11:351-362.

Jordan, David Starr. 1890. Report of explorations made during the summer and autumn of in the Alleghany region of Virginia, North Carolina and Tennessee, and in western Indiana, with an account of the fishes found in each of the river basins of those regions. Bull. U.S. Fish Comm. 1888(1890). Vol. 8:97-192.

Jordan, David Starr. 1891. Report of explorations made by the U.S. Fish Commission during the summer of 1889 in Colorado and Utah, with an account of the fishes found in each river basin examined. Bull. U.S. Fish Comm. 1889 (1891). Vol. 9:1-40.

Jordan, David Starr. 1905. A Guide to the Study of Fishes. Henry Holt and Company, New York. 4 to. I. 1-624pp. Vol. II. 1-599pp.

Jordan, David Starr. 1907a. Fishes. Henry Holt and Co., New York. Amer. Nature series. 4 to. 1-789pp.

Jordan, David Starr. 1907b. The fossil fishes of California, with supplementary notes on other species of extinct fishes. Berkeley, Univ. Cal. Pub., Bull. Dept. Geol. Vol. 5:95-144.

Jordan, David Starr. 1917. Changes in names of American fishes. Copeia 1917 (No. 49):85-89.

Jordan, David Starr. 1919. The genera of fishes. Pt. II: From Agassiz to Bleeker, 1833-1858, twenty-six years, with the accepted type of each. Stanf. Univ. Publ. Univ. Ser. Vol. 62:1-284pp.

Jordan, David Starr. 1923. A classification of fishes, including families, and genera as far as known. Stanf. Univ. Publ. Univ. Ser. Biol. Sci. Vol. III(2):79-243.

Jordan, David Starr. 1929. Manual of the Vertebrate Animals of the Northeastern United States. Inclusive of Marine Species. World Book Company. Yonkers-on-Hudson, New York. 13th edition. 446pp.

Jordan, David Starr, and Alembert Winthrop Brayton. 1877. On *Lagochila*, a new genus of catostomoid fishes. Proc. Acad. Nat. Sci. Philad. 1877:280-283.

Jordan, David Starr, and Alembert Winthrop Brayton. 1878. Contributions to North American Ichthyology. Based Primarily on the Collections of the United States National Museum. III. A. On the distribution of the Fishes of the Allegheney Region of South Carolina, Georgia, and Tennessee, with Descriptions of New and Little Known Species. Bull. U.S. Nat. Mus. Vol. 12:1-95.

Jordan, David Starr, and H. E. Copeland. 1876. Check list of the fishes of the fresh waters of North America. Bull. Buffalo Soc. Nat. Hist. 1876:133-164.

Jordan, David Starr, and Barton Warren Evermann. 1896. The fishes of North and Middle America. Bull. U.S. Natl. Mus. Vol. 47(1-4):1-3313.

Jordan, David Starr, and Barton Warren Evermann. 1905. American Food and Game Fishes. Doubleday, Page & Company. New York, New York. 572pp.

Jordan, David Starr, and Barton Warren Evermann. 1917. The genera of fishes from Linnaeus to Cuvier, 1758-1833, seventy-five years with the accepted type of each. A contribution to the stability of scientific nomenclature. Stanf. Univ. Publ. Ser. 1-161.

Jordan, David Starr, and Barton Warren Evermann. 1923. American Food and Game Fishes. Doubleday, Page and Co., Garden City, N. Y. 574 pp.

Jordan, David Starr, and Charles Henry Gilbert. 1880. Notes on a Collection of Fishes from Utah Lake. P.U.S. Nat. Mus. Vol. 3:459-465.

Jordan, David Starr, and Charles Henry Gilbert. 1883. Synopsis of the fishes of North America. Bull. U. S. Nat. Mus. 1882(1883). Vol. 16:1-1018pp.

Jordan, David Starr, and Charles Henry Gilbert. 1884. Notes on the nomenclature of certain North American fishes. Proc. U.S. Nat. Mus. 1883(1884). Vol. 6:110-111.

Jordan, David Starr, and Charles Henry Gilbert. 1886. List of fishes collected in Arkansas, Indian Territory, and Texas, in September, 1884, with notes and descriptions. Proc. U. S. Natl. Mus. Vol. 9:1-25.

Jordan, David Starr, and Henry W. Henshaw. 1878. Report on the fishes collected during the years 1875, 1876 and 1877, in California and Nevada. Ann. Rept. U.S. Geogr. Surv. West 100th Meridian, 1878:187-200. Ann. Rept. Chief Engin. 1878 pt. 3:1069-1622.

Jordan, David Starr, and Seth Eugene Meek. 1885. List of fishes collected in Iowa and Missouri in August, 1884, with descriptions of three new species. Proc. U.S. Nat. Mus. Vol. 8:1-17.

Kafuku, T. 1957. Ecological and phyletic significance of anal fin between Cyprinids and Catostomid fish. Jap. J. Ichthyol. Vol. 5:163-173.

Kaiser, K. L. E. 1977. Organic contaminant residues in fishes from Nipigon Bay, Lake Superior. Journal of the Fisheries Research Board of Canada. Vol. 34(6):850-855.

Karp, C. A., and H. M. Tyus. 1990. Behavioral interactions between young Colorado squawfish and six fish species. Copeia 1990(1):25-34.

Kathrein, J. W. 1951. Growth rate of four species of fish in a section of the Missouri River between Holster Dam and Cascade, Montana. Transactions of the American Fisheries Society. Vol. 80:93-98.

Katz, M. 1954. Reproduction of fish. Data for Handbook of Biological Data. 22pp.

Kavaliers, M. 1980. Circadian activity of the white sucker, *Catostomus commersoni*: comparison of individual and shoaling fish. Canadian Journal of Zoology. Vol. 58(8):1399-1403.

Kavaliers, M. 1981. Circadian organization in white suckers *Catostomus commersoni*: the role of the pineal organ. Comparative Biochem. Physiol. (A). Vol. 68(1):127-129.

Kavaliers, M. 1982a. Seasonal and circannual rhythms in behavioural thermoregulation and their modifications by pinealectomy in the white sucker, *Catostomus commersoni*. Journal comp. Physiol. Vol. 146(2):235-243.

Kavaliers, M. 1982b. Effects of pineal shielding on the thermoregulatory behavior of the white sucker *Catostomus commersoni*. Physiological Zool. Vol. 55(2):155-161.

Kavaliers, M. 1982c. Endogenous lunar rhythms in the behavioral thermoregulation of a teleost fish, the white sucker, *Catostomus commersoni*. J. Interdiscipl. Cycle Res. Vol. 13(1):23-27.

Kavaliers, M., and M. F. Hawkins. 1981. Bombesin alters behavioral thermoregulation in fish. Life Sci. Vol. 28(12):1361-1364.

Kavaliers, M., and C. L. Ralph. 1980. Pineal involvement in the control of behavioral thermoregulation of the white sucker, *Catostomus commersoni*. Journal exp. Zool. Vol. 212(2):301-303.

Kayton, R. J., and D. C. Kritsky, R. C. Tobias. 1979. *Rhabdochona catostomi* sp.n. (Nematoda:Rhabdochonidae) from the intestine of *Catostomus* spp. (Catostomidae). Proceedings helminth. Soc. Wash. Vol. 46(2):224-227.

Keast, A. 1968. Feeding of some Great Lakes fishes at low temperatures. Journal of the Fisheries Res. Board. of Canada. Vol. 25(6):1199-1218.

Keeton, D. 1963. Growth of fishes in the Des Moines River, Iowa, with particular reference to water levels. Iowa State Univ., Ames. Ph.D. Thesis. 208 pp.

Keim, Thomas D. 1915. Notes on the fauna about the headwaters of the Allegheny, Genesee and Susquehanna Rivers in Pennsylvania. Copeia 1915 (No. 24):51-52.

Keleher, J. J. 1961a. Largest fish from Great Slave Lake. Circulars [General Series] of the Biological Station, London, Ontario of the FRB of Canada. No. 3:12-16.

Keleher, J. J. 1961b. Comparison of largest Great Slave Lake fish with North American records. Journal of the Fisheries Research Board of Canada. Vol. 18(3):417-421.

Keleher, J. J. 1963. Great Slave Lake Suckers. Circulars [General series] of the biological station, London, Ontario of the FRB of Canada. No. 6:1-4.

Keleher, J. J. 1967. The number of fisherman in relation to production in Great Slave Lake winter fishery, 1957-1963. Technical Reports of the Fisheries Research Board of Canada. No. 33. 15p.

Keleher, J. J., and B. Kooyman. 1957. Supplement to Hinks' "The Fishes of Manitoba." Manitoba Department of Mines and Natural Resources: pp. 103-117 of a new printing of the original handbook by Hinks. Studies from the Board's Establishments. No. 481.

Kelso, J. R. M. 1976. Movement of yellow perch (*Perca flavescens*) and white sucker (*Catostomus commersoni*) in a nearshore Great Lakes habitat subject to a thermal discharge. Journal of the Fisheries Research Board of Canada. Vol. 33(1):42-53.

Kelso, J. R. M., and D. S. Jeffries. 1988. Response of headwater lakes to varying atmospheric deposition in north-central Ontario 1979-85. Canadian Journal of Fisheries and Aquatic Sciences. Vol. 45(11):1905-1911.

Kelso, J. R. M., and J. K. Leslie. 1979. Entrainment of larval fish by the Douglas Point generating station, Lake Huron, in relation to seasonal succession and distribution. Journal of the Fisheries Research Board of Canada. Vol. 36(1):37-41.

Kempinger, J. 1975. Walleye fishing facts. Wis. Conserv. Bull. Vol. 40(4):19.

Kendall, William Converse. 1914. The Fishes of Maine. Proceedings of the Portland Society of Natural History. Vol. 3(Part 1.):198pp.

Kendall, William Converse. 1918. The Rangeley Lakes, Maine, with special reference to the habits of the fishes, fish culture and angling. Bull. U. S. Bur. Fish. Vol. 35 (1915-1916):487-594.

Kendall, William Converse. 1924. An annotated list of a collection of fishes made by Francis Harper in the Athabaska region in 1920, to which is appended a list of species collected by Dr. R. T. Morris in the district between Lake Winnipeg and Hudson Bay in 1905. Contributions to Canadian Biology. Vol. 1(23):419-440.

Kendall, William Converse, and W. A. Dence. 1929. The fishes of the Cranberry Lake region. Roosevelt Wildl. Bull. Vol. 5(2):219-276.

Kennedy, J. L., and P. A. Kucera. 1978. The reproductive ecology of the Tahoe sucker *Catostomus tahoensis*, in Pyramid Lake, Nevada. Great Basin Nat. Vol. 38(2):181-186.

Kennedy, W. A. 1956. The first ten years of commercial fishing on Great Slave Lake. Bulletin of the Fisheries Research Board of Canada. No. 107:1-58pp.

Kennicott, Robert. 1855. Catalogue of animals observed in Cook County, Illinois. Illinois State Agricultural Society Transactions. Vol. 1:577-595.

Kent, J. C., and D. W. Johnson. 1979a. Organochlorine residues in fish, water, and sediment of American Falls Reservoir, Idaho, 1974. Pesticides Monit. J. Vol. 13(1):28-34.

Kent, J. C., and D. W. Johnson. 1979b. Mercury, arsenic, and cadmium in fish, water, and sediment of American Falls Reservoir, Idaho, 1974. Pesticides Monit. J. Vol. 13(1):35-40.

Kernen, L. T. 1974. Fishery investigations on the lower Fox River and south Green Bay in 1973-1974. Wis. Dep. Nat. Resour. 6 pp.

Khalifa, K. A., and G. Post. 1976. Histopathological effect of *Lernaea cyprinacea* (a copepod parasite) on fish. Progressive Fish. Culturist. Vol. 38(2):110-113.

Kilgen, R. H. 1974a. Artificial spawning and hatching techniques for blacktail redhorse. Progressive Fish-Culturist Vol. 36(3):174.

Kilgen, R. H. 1974b. Mixed culture of catfish with blacktail redhorse suckers. Journal Ala. Acad. Sci. Vol. 45(2):139-143.

Kilken, R. H. 1972. Food habits and growth of fingerling blacktail redhorse, *Moxostoma poecilurum* (Jordan), in ponds. Proceedings La Acad. Sci. Vol. 35:12-20.

Kimmel, Peter G. 1975. Fishes of the Miocene-Pliocene Deer Butte Formation, Southeast Oregon. Master's thesis, December 1975, Michigan.

Kirby, G. M., and J. R. Bend, I. R. Smith, M. A. Hayes. 1990. The role of glutathione S-transferases in the hepatic metabolism of benzo[a] pyrene in white suckers (*Catostomus commersoni*) from polluted and reference sites in the Great Lakes. Comp. Biochem. Physiol. C. Comp. Pharmacol. Toxicol. Vol. 95(1):25-30.

Kirsch, Philip Henry. 1889. Notes on a Collection of Fishes obtained in the Gila River, at Fort Thomas, Arizona, by Lieut. W. L. Carpenter, U.S. Army. Proc. U.S. Nat. Mus. 1888(1889). Vol. 11:555-558.

Kirtland, Jared Potter. 1838. Report on the Zoölogy of Ohio. Columbus, 8fl. Second Annual Report. (Fishes 168-170, 190-197). Geological Survey State of Ohio. pp. 155-200.

Klaverkamp, J. F., and D. A. Duncan. 1987. Acclimation to cadium binding capacity and metal distribution in gill and liver cytosol. Environmental Toxicol. Chem. Vol. 6(4):275-289.

Klaverkamp, J. F., and D. A. Hodgins, A. Lutz. 1983. Selenite toxicity and mercury-selenium interactions in juvenile fish (*Catostomus commersoni*) Arch. Environ, Contam. Toxicol. Vol. 12(4):405-413.

Klaverkamp, J. F., and M. A. Turner, S. E. Harrison, R. H. Hesslein. 1983. Fates of metal radiotracers added to a whole lake: accumulation in slimy sculpin (*Cottus cognatus*) and white sucker (*Catostomus commersoni*). Science Tot. Environ. Vol. 28:119-128.

Klotz, P. H., and B. L. Haase. 1987. A baseline study of Jordan Creek city of Allentown, Lehigh County, Pennsylvania. Proc. Pa. Acad. Sci. Vol. 61(1):50-58.

Knapp, Leslie W., and William J. Richards, Robert Victor Muller, Neal R. Foster. 1963. Rediscovery of the percid fish *Etheostoma sellare* (Radcliffe and Welch). Copeia 1963(2):455.

Kobayashi, Yuta, and Karl Lederis, Jean Rivier, David Ko, Denis McMaster, Paule Poulin. 1986. Radioimmunoassays for fish tail neuropeptides: II. Development of a specific and sensitive assay for the occurrence of immunoreactive urotensin II in the central nervous system and blood of *Catostomus commersoni*. J. Pharmacol. Methods. Vol. 15(4):321-334.

Koch, D. L. 1973. Reproductive characteristics of the Cui-ui lakesucker (*Chasmistes cujus* Cope) and its spawning behavior in Pyramid Lake, Nevada. Transactions of the American Fisheries Society. Vol. 102(1):145-149.

Koch, D. L. 1973. Life history information on the Cui-ui lakesucker (*Chasmistes cujus* Cope, 1883) endemic to Pyramid Lake, Washoe County, Nevada. Dissertation Abstr. int. Vol. 33B(11):5576-5577.

Koch, D. L. 1976. Life history information on the Cui-ui lakesuckers (*Chasmistes cujus* Cope, 1883) in Pyramid Lake, Nevada. Occasional Pap. biol. Soc. Nevada. No. 40:1-12.

Koch, D. L., and G. P. Contreras. 1972. Swimming ability and effects on stress on the cui-ui lakesucker (*Chasmistes cujus* Cope). Occassional Pap. biol. Soc. Nevada. No. 31:1-8.

Koch, D. L., and G. P. Contreras. 1973. Hatching technique for the cui-ui lakesucker. Progressive Fish-Culturist Vol. 35(1):61-63.

Koehn, Richard K. 1966. Serum haptoglobins in some north American catostomid fishes. Comp. Biochem. Physiol. Vol. 17(1966):349-352.

Koehn, Richard K. 1968. Blood proteins in natural populations of catostomid fishes of western North America. Diss. Abstr. Vol. 28B:3104-3105.

Koehn, Richard K. 1969. Hemoglobins of fishes of the genus *Catostomus* in western North America. Copeia 1969:21-30.

Koehn, Richard K., and D. W. Johnson. 1967. Serum transferrin and serum esterase polymorphisms in an introduced population of the bigmouth buffalofish, *Ictiobus cyprinellus*. Copeia 1967:805-808.

Kononen, D. W. 1982. Saginaw Bay suckers: their dynamics and potential for increased utilization. Dissertation Abstr. int. (B). Vol. 43(2):306.

Kononen, D. W. 1989. PCB's and DDT in Saginaw Bay white suckers. Chemosphere Vol. 18(9-10):2065-2068.

Koster, William J. 1939. Some phases of the life history and relationships of the Cyprinid, *Clinostomus elongatus* (Kirtland). Copeia 1939 (4):201-208.

Koster, William J. 1957. Guide to the Fishes of New Mexico. University of New Mexico Press. Albuquerque, New Mexico. 116pp.

Kott, E., and R. E. Jenkins, G. Humphreys. 1979. Recent collections of the black redhorse, *Moxostoma duquesnei*, from Ontario. Canadian Fld. Nat. Vol. 93(1):63-66.

Kreuzer, R. O., and J. G. Sivak. 1984. Spherical aberration of the fish lens: interspecies variation and age. J. Comp. Physiol. Vol. 154A(3):415-422.

Kritsky, D. C., and R. P. Hathaway. 1969. New and previously described species of Dactylogyridae (Monogenea) from Illinois fishes. J. Parasit. Vol. 55:143-148.

Kritsky, D. C., and P. D. Leiby, M. E. Shelton. 1972. Studies on helminths of North Dakota 4. Parasites of the river carpsucker, *Carpiodes carpio*, with descriptions of three new species (Monogenea). Journ. Parasit. Vol. 58(4):723-731.

Krumholz, Louis A. 1943. A comparative study of the Weberian ossicles in North American Ostariophysine fishes. Copeia, Ann Arbor 1943 (1):33-40.

Krumholz, Louis A. 1956. Observations on the Fish Population of a Lake Contaminated by Radioactive Wastes. Bulletin of the American Museum of Natural History. Vol. 110(4):281-367.

Krygier, B. B., and R. W. Macy. 1969. *Lissorchis heterorchis* sp. n. (Trematoda: Lissorchiidae) from *Catostomus macrocheilus* Girard in Oregon. Proc. helminth. Soc. Wash. Vol. 36:136-139.

Kucera, P. A., and J. L. Kennedy. 1977. Evaluation of a sphere volume method for estimating fish fecundity. Progressive Fish-Culturist Vol. 39(3):115-117.

Kuehn, J. H. 1949. Statewide average total length in inches at each year. Minn. Fish. Res. Lab. Invest. Rep. Vol. 51(Supple.,2nd rev.)

Kuehn, J. H., and W. Niemuth, A. R. Peterson. 1961. A biological reconnaissance of the upper St. Croix River. Minn. and Wis. Conserv. Deps. 25pp.

Kurinnyi, S. A. 1984. Dynamics of malate dehydrogenase and lactate dehydrogenase activity in the early stages of embryo-larval development of *Ictiobus bubalus* (Raf.) and *Ictiobus niger* (Agassiz) and their reciprocal hybrids. Nauchnye Dokl. Vyssh. Shk. Biol. Nauki. 1984(9):57-61.

Laarman, P. W., and J. R. Ryckman. 1982. Relative size selectivity of trap nets for eight species of fish. North American Journal of Fisheries Management. American Fisheries Society. Vol. 2(1):33-37.

La Bar, G. W. 1969. *Catostomus ardens* Jordan and Gilbert, 1881, a new host record for *Neoechinorhynchus venustus* Lynch, 1936, and *N. crassus* Van Cleave, 1919, with notes on Caryophyllaeids. J. Parasit. Vol. 55:497.

La Bolle, L. D., Jr., and H. W. Li, and B. C. Mundy. 1985. Comparison of two samplers for quantitatively collecting larval fishes in upper littoral habitats. Journ. Fish Biol. Vol. 26(2):139-146.

La Cepède, Bernard Germain Étienne. 1803. Histoire naturelle des poissons. Vol. 5. Plassan, Paris. 803pp.

Lachner, E. A. 1967. Status of the catostomid fish name *Catostomus aureolus* Le Sueur. Copeia 1967:455-457.

Lacroix, Gilles L. 1985. Plasmic ionic composition of the Atlantic salmon (*Salmo salar*), white sucker (*Catostomus commersoni*), and alewife (*Alosa pseudoharengus*) in some acidic rivers of Nova Scotia [Canada]. Canadian Journal of Zoology. Vol. 63(10):2254-2261.

Lagler, Karl F. 1945. Ohio's fish program. Ohio Div. Conserv. Nat. Resources. 40pp.

Lagler, Karl F., and John E. Bardach, Robert Rush Miller. 1962. Ichthyology. John Wiley & Sons, Inc. New York, N. Y. 545pp.

Laird, Lindsay M., and Brian Stott. 1978. Chapter 4. Marking and Tagging. pp. 84-100. **IN:** Timothy Bagenal (ed.) Methods for Assessment of Fish Production in Fresh Waters. IBP Handbook No. 3. 3rd edition. Blackwell Scientific Publications Oxford, England, United Kingdom. 365pp.

Lalancette, L.-M. 1975a. The seasonal cycle in the germinal cells (testes and ovaries) of the white sucker, *Catostomus commersoni*, of Gamelin Lake, Québec. Naturaliste can. Vol. 102(6):721-736.

Lalancette, L.-M. 1975b. Studies on the growth, reproduction and diet of the white sucker, *Catostomus commersoni commersoni* (La Cepède), of Gamelin Lake, Chicoutimi, Québec. Dissertation Abstr. int. (B) Vol. 36(5):2019-2020.

Lalancette, L.-M. 1976. Annual growth and fat content of white sucker *Catostomus commersoni* in a Québec lake. Naturaliste can. Vol. 103(5):403-416.

Lalancette, L.-M. 1977. Feeding in white suckers (*Catostomus commersoni*) from Gamelin Lake, Québec, over a twelve month period. Naturaliste can. Vol. 104(4):369-376.

Lalancette, L.-M. 1981. Ellipsoidal trap for freshwater minnows and suckers. Progressive Fish-Culturist. Vol. 43(4):193-194.

Lalancette, L.-M., and E. Magnin. 1970. Croissance en longueur du Meunier de l'est, *Catostomus catostomus* (Forster), du Saguenay. Naturaliste can. Vol. 97:667-677. [Eng. summary].

Lambe, Lawrence M. 1904. The Progress of vertebrate Palæontology in Canada 1903(1904). Trans. Roy. Soc. Canada (2). Vol. 10(4):13-56.

Lambe, Lawrence M. 1906a. On *Amyzon brevipinne* Cope, from the Amyzon beds of the southern interior of British Columbia. Trans. Roy. Soc. Canada. Vol. 12(2):151-156.

Lambe, Lawrence M. 1906b. Report on vertebrate palæontology. Summ. Rep. Geol. Surv. Canada for 1906. 135-138.

Lambe, Lawrence M. 1906c. Report of vertebrate palæontologist. Summ. Rep. Geol. Surv. Canada for 1905:135-138.

Lambou, V. W. 1961. Efficiency and selectivity of flag gillnets fished in Lake Bistineau, Louisiana. Proc. S.E. Assoc. Game Fish Comm., Vol. 15:319-359.

La Monte, Francesca. 1958. North American Game Fishes. Doubleday & Company, Inc. Garden City, New York. 206pp.

Lanigan, S. H., and H. M. Tyus. 1989. Population size and status of the razorback sucker in the Green River Basin, Utah and Colorado. N. Am. J. Fish Manage. Vol. 9(1):68-73.

Lantz, A. W. 1948a. Experiments on the canning of freshwater fish. Progress Reports of the Fisheries Research Board Pacific Coast Stations. No. 74:19-21.

Lantz, A. W. 1948b. Experiments on the smoking of freshwater fish. Progress Reports of Fisheries Research Board Pacific Coast Stations. No. 75:35-39.

Lantz, A. 1962. Speciality fish products. Circulars [General Series] of the Biological Station, London, Ontario. No. 4:10-28.

Lantz, A. W. 1966. Special products from freshwater fish. Bulletins of the Fisheries Research Board of Canada. No. 151:45pp.

Lantz, A. W. 1969. Products spéciaux des poissons d' eau douce. Bulletins of the Fisheries Research Board of Canada. No. 151f: 59pp.

Lantz, A. W., and D. G. Iredale. 1966. Sweet cured freshwater fish slices. Trade News Vol. 18(10-11):8-9.

Lantz, A. W., and D. G. Iredale. 1971. A practical method for drying freshwater fish. Journal of the Fisheries Res. Board of Canada Vol. 28(7):1061-1062.

Large, T. 1903. A list of the native fishes of Illinois, with keys. Appendix to Report of the State Board of Fish Commissioners for Sept. 30, 1900 to Oct. 1, 1902. 30p.

Larimore, R. W., and P. W. Smith. 1963. The fishes of Champaign County, Illinois, as affected by 60 years of stream changes. Ill. Nat. Hist. Surv. Bull. Vol. 28(2):299-382.

La Rivers, Ira. 1962. Fishes and Fisheries of Nevada. Nevada State Fish and Game Commission, Carson City. State Printer. 782pp.

Lawler, G. H. 1964. Incidence of *Ligula intestinalis* in Heming Lake fish. Journal of the Fisheries Research Board of Canada. Vol. 21(3):549-554.

Lawler, G. H. 1965. Fin anomalies in the White Sucker, *Catostomus commersoni*, population in Hemming Lake, Manitoba. Journal of the Fisheries Research Board of Canada Vol. 22(1):219-220.

Lawler, G. H. 1969. Activity periods of some fishes in Heming Lake, Canada. Journal of the Fisheries Research Board of Canada Vol. 26(12):3266-3267.

Lawler, G. H., and G. F. M. Smith. 1963. Use of coloured tags in fish population estimates. Journal of the Fisheries Research Board of Canada. Vol. 20(6):1431-1434.

Lawler, G. H., and N. H. F. Watson. 1958. Limnological studies of Heming Lake, Manitoba, and two adjacent lakes. Journal of the Biological Board of Canada. Vol. 15(2):203-218.

Lawrence, J. L. 1970. Effects of season, host age, and sex on endohelminths of *Catostomus commersoni*. J. Parasit. Vol. 56:567-571.

Layher, W. G., and K. L. Brunson. 1986. New distributional records for some Kansas fishes. Trans. Kans. Acad. Sci. Vol. 89(1-2):124-133.

Lederis, K. 1973. Current studies on urotensions. American Zool. Vol. 13(3):771-773.

Lederis, K. 1977. Chemical properties and the physiological and pharmacological actions of urophysial peptides. American Zool. Vol. 17(4):823-832.

Lederis, K., and J. Fryer, J. Rivier, K. L. MacCannell, Y. Kobayashi, N. Woo, K. L. Wong. 1985. Neurohormones from fish tails -2. Actions of urotensin I in mammals and fishes. Recent Prog. Horm. Res. Vol. 41:553-576.

Lederis, K., and A. Letter, D. McMaster, G. Moore, D. Schlesinger. 1982. Complete amino acid sequence of urotensin I, a hypotensive and corticotropin-releasing neuropeptide from *Catostomus*. Science Vol. 218(No. 4568):162-164.

Lederis, K., and W. Vale, J. Rivier, K. L. MacCannell, D. McMaster, Y. Kobayashi, U. Suess, J. Lawrence. 1982. Urotensin 1-a novel CRF-like peptide in *Catostomus commersoni urophysis*. Proceedings West. Pharmacol. Soc. Vol. 25:223-227.

Lee, David S., and Carter R. Gilbert, Charles H. Hocutt, Robert E. Jenkins, Don E. McAllister, Jay R. Stauffer, Jr. 1980. Atlas of North American Freshwater Fishes. N.C. State Mus. Nat. Hist., Raleigh. 854pp.

Lee, Lana, and David C. Corson, Brian D. Sykes. 1985. Structural studies of calcium-binding proteins using NMR. Biophys J. Vol. 47(2 Part 1):139-142.

Lee, R. M., and S. D. Gerking, B. Jezierska. 1983. Electrolyte balance and energy mobilization in acid-stressed rainbow trout, *Salmo gairdneri*, and their relation to reproductive success. Environmental Biol. Fishes. Vol. 8(2):115-123.

Leed, J. A., and T. V. Belanger. 1981. Iron, copper and zinc in the water, sediment, and fishes of the upper St. Johns River Basin, Florida, and their relationship to watershed land use. pp. 70-79. IN: Krumholz, L. A. The warmwater streams symposium. A national symposium on fisheries aspects of warmwater streams. American Fisheries Society, Kansas. 422pp.

Legendre, Vianney. 1942. Redécouverte après un siècle et reclassification d'une espèce de Catostomidé Nat. canad. Québec. Vol. 69(1942):227-233.

Legendre, Vianney. 1943a. Un nouveau poisson pour la province de Québec. Rev. canad. Biol. Montréal Vol. 2:105-107.

Legendre, Vianney. 1943b. Reclassification d'une esp_ce de Catostomides. Ann l'Acfas Montréal. Vol. 9:124.

Leiby, P. D., and D. C. Kritsky, D. D. Bauman. 1973. Studies on helminths of North Dakota. 7. Ancyrocephalinae (Monogenea) from the gills of the blue sucker, *Cycleptus elongatus* (Le Sueur). Canadian Journal of Zoology. Vol. 51(7):777-779.

Leiby, P. D., and D. C. Kritsky, C. A. Peterson. 1972. Studies on helminths of North Dakota. 3. Parasites of the bigmouth buffalo, *Ictiobus cyprinellus* (Val.), with the description of three new species and the proposal of *Icelanochohaptor* gen. n. (Monogenea). Journal of Parasitology. Vol. 58(3):447-454.

Leidy, Joseph. 1875. On a Mouthless Fish. Proceedings of the Academy of Natural Sciences of Philadelphia. Vol. 27:125-126.

Leino, R. L. 1982. Rodlet cells in the gill and intestine of *Catostomus commersoni* and *Perca flavescens*: a comparison of their light and electron microscopic cytochemistry with that of mucous and granular cells. Canadian Journal of Zoology. Vol. 60(11):219-236.

Les, B. L. 1979. The vanishing wild-Wisconsin's endangered wildlife and its habitat. Wis. Dep. Nat. Resour. 36pp.

Leslie, J. K., and J. E. Moore. 1985. Ecology of young-of-the-year fish in Muscote Bay (Bay of Quinte), Ontario [Canada]. Can. Tech. Rep. Fish Aquat. Sci. No. 1377:1-44.

Leslie, J. K., and J. E. Moore. 1986. Changes in lengths of fixed and preserved young freshwater fish. Can. J. Fisheries Aquat. Sci. Vol. 43(5):1079-1081.

Lessman, C. A. 1981. Increase in acid phosphatase activity during fertilization of a teleost egg. Experientia Vol. 37(4):415-416.

Lessman, C. A., and C. W. Huver. 1981. Quantification of fertilization-induced gamete changes and sperm entry without egg activiation in a teleost egg. Developmental Biol. Vol. 84(1):218-224.

Lester, R. J. G., and B. A. Daniels. 1976. The eosinophilic cell of the white sucker, *Catostomus commersoni*. Journal of the Fisheries Research Board of Canada. Vol. 33(1):139-144.

Lester, R. J. G., and S. S. Desser. 1975. Cell patterns and cell movements during early development of an annual fish, *Nothobranchius neumanni*. Journal exp. Zool. Vol. 193(2):137-146.

Le Sueur, Charles Alexandre. 1817. A new genus of fishes, of the order Abdominales, proposed under the name of *Catostomus*; and the characters of this genus with its species, indicated. Academy of Natural Sciences of Philadelphia Journal. Vol. 1(5):88-96,102-111.

Leung, Siu-Yin Theresa, and Ross V. Bulkely, John J. Richard. 1981. Influence of a new impoundment on pesticide concentrations in warmwater fish, Saylorville Reservoir, Des Moines River, Iowa 1977-78. Pesticides Monit. J. Vol. 15(3):117-122.

Lewis, W. M. 1957. The fish population of a spring-fed stream system in southern Illinois. Ill. Acad. Sci. Trans. Vol. 50:23-29.

Lewis, W. M., and D. Elder. 1953. The fish population of the headwaters of a spotted bass stream in southern Illinois. Transactions of the American Fisheries Society. Vol. 82:193-202.

Li, H. W. 1973. A bioenergetic analysis of intraspecific and interspecific competition in two teleost fishes. Dissertation Abstr. Int. Vol. 34 B (4):1471.

Li, M.-M., and Arai, H. P. 1988. Electron microscopical observations on the effects of sera from two species of *Catostomus* on the tegument of *Hunterella nodulosa* (Cestoidea: Caryophyllidea). Canadian Journal of Zoology. Vol. 66(5):1191-1196.

Libosvarsky, J. 1970. Survey carried out at Lac la Martre, Northwest Territories, in summer 1969, and the entangling capacity of gill nets of different twine, color, and age when fishing for whitefish and lake trout. Technical Reports of the Fisheries Research Board of Canada. No. 180: 35 pp.

Lindberg, Georgiy Ustinovich. 1972. Krupnyye kolebaniya urovnya okeana v chetvertichnyy period; Biogeograficheskiye obosnovaniya gipotezy [Major sea-level fluctuations during the Quaternary Period; the biogeographical foundations for the hypothesis]. Akad. Nauk. SSSR, Zool. Inst. 548pp. Leningrad.

Lindeborg, R. G. 1941. Records of fishes from the Quetico Provincial Park of Ontario, with comments on the growth of the yellow pike-perch. Copeia 1941 (3):159-161.

Linder, Allan D., and Dale G. Kosluchar. 1976. A catostomid fish from Plio-Pleistocene Lake Idaho. Tebiwa Vol. 18(2):1975:75-78.

Lindsey, Casimir Charles 1956. Distribution and taxonomy of fishes in the Mackenzie drainage of British Columbia. Journal of the Biological Board of Canada. Vol. 13(6):759-789.

Lindsey, Casimir Charles 1957. Possible effects of water diversions on fish distribution in British Columbia. Journal of the Biological Board of Canada. Vol. 14(4):651-668.

Lindsey, Casimir Charles 1975. Pleomerism, the widespread tendency among related fish species for vertebral number to be correlated with maximum body length. J. Fish. Res. Board Can. Vol. 32(12):2453-2469.

Lindsey, Hague L., and James C. Randolph, John Carroll. 1983. Updated survey of the fishes of the Poteau River, Oklahoma and Arkansas (USA). Proc. Okla. Acad. Sci. Vol. 63:42-48.

Linton, Edwin. 1891. On two species of larval *Dibothria* from the Yellowstone National Park. Bull. U.S. Fish Comm. for 1889. Vol. 9(3):65-79.

Linton, T. L. 1961. A study of fishes of the Arkansas and Cimarron Rivers in the area of the proposed Keystone Reservoir. Okla. Fish. Res. Lab. Rep. Vol. 81:30pp.

Lippson, Alice J. 1976. Distinguishing Family characteristics Among Great Lakes Fish Larvae. pp. 208-216. **IN:** John Boreman (ed.) Great Lakes Fish Egg and Larvae Identification: Proceedings of a Workshop. U.S. Fish and Wildlife Service National Power Plant Team. Ann Arbor, Michigan. FWS/OBS-76/23. 220pp.

Lippson, Alice J., and R. L. Moran. 1974. Manual for identification of early developmental stages of fishes of Potomac River estuaries. Marietta Corp. Spec. Publ. PPSP-MP-13. 282pp.

Lo, Y.-I., and H.-W. Wu. 1979. Anatomical features of *Myxocyprinus asiaticus* and its systematic position. Acta Zootaxon. sin. Vol. 4(3):195-203.

Lobchenko, V. V. 1981. [Cypriniformes-Family Catostomidae]. pp. 102-104. **IN:** Ganya, I. M. (Ed.) (Animal world of Moldavia.Fishes, amphibians and reptiles). Shtiintsa, Kishinev. 1981:1-222.

Lockhart, W. L., and A. Lutz. 1976. Preliminary biochemical oberservations of fishes inhabiting an acidified lake in Ontario, Canada. USDA For. Serv. Gen. Tech. Rep. NE U.S. Northeast For. Exp. Stn. Vol. 23:545-569.

Lockhart, W. L., and A. Lutz. 1977. Preliminary biochemical observations of fishes inhabiting an acidified lake in Ontario, Canada. Water Air Soil Pollut. Vol. 7(3):317-332.

Lockhart, W. L., and D. A. Metner. 1984. Fish serum chemistry as a pathology tool. Advances envir. Sci. Technol. Vol. 16:73-85.

Lockington, William Neale. 1881. Description of a new species of *Catostomus* (*C. cypho*) from the Colorado river. Proc. Acad. Nat. Sci. Philad. 1880 (1881):237-240.

Long, Wilbur L. 1973. History and function of the teleostean periblast. Dissertation Abstr. int. Vol. 34B (5):1883.

Long, Wilbur L. 1980a. Analysis of yolk syncytium behavior in *Salmo* and *Catostomus*. Journal exp. Zool. Vol. 214(3):323-331.

Long, Wilbur L. 1980b. Proliferation, growth, and migration of nuclei in the yolk syncytium of *Salmo* and *Catosomus*. Journal exp. Zool. Vol. 214 (3):333-343.

Long, Wilbur L., and William W. Ballard. 1976. Normal embryonic stages of the white sucker, *Catostomus commersoni*. Copeia 1976(2):342-351.

Lopinot, Alvin C. 1958. How fast do Illinois fish grow? Outdoors in Illinois. Vol. 5(4):8-10.

Lopinot, Alvin C. 1960. Fish Conservation. Illinois Resource Management. Division of Conservation Education. Springfield, Illinois. 79pp.

Lopinot, Alvin C. 1965. 1965 State Conservation Lake Creel Census. Division of Fisheries Illinois Department of Conservation. Special Fisheries Report 10:1-82pp.

Lopinot, Alvin C. 1966a. Inventory of the Fishes of Four River Basins in Illinois 1965. Illinois Department of Conservation. Division of Fisheries.Special Fisheries Report 13:1-44.

Lopinot, Alvin C. 1966b. 1966 State Conservation Lake Creel Census. Illinois Department of Conservation, Division of Fisheries. Special Fisheries Report Number 15:1-80pp.

Lopinot, Alvin C. 1967. 1967 State Conservation Lake Creel Census. Illinois Department of Conservation. Division of Fisheries. Special Fisheries Report. Number 20:1-74pp.

Lopinot, Alvin C. (ed.). 1968. Inventory of the Fishes of Nine River Basins in Illinois 1967. Illinois Department of Conservation. Division of Fisheries. Special Fisheries Report Number 25. 173pp.

Lopinot, Alvin C., and Philip W. Smith. 1973. Rare and endangered fish of Illinois. Ill. Dep. Conserv. Div. Fish. 53pp.

Loranger, A. J. 1981. Late fall and early winter foods of the river otter (*Lutra canadensis*) in Massachusetts, 1976-1978. Proceedings Worldwide Furbearer Conf. Vol. 1(1):599-605.

Louder, D. E. 1961. Coastal plain lakes of Southeastern North Carolina. N.C. Wildl. Res. Comm. D-J Job Completion Rep., Proj. F5R+F6R 1:9-55.

Louder, D. E. 1962. An annotated check list of the North Carolina Bay Lakes fishes. J. Elisha Mitchell Sci. Soc. Vol. 78:68-73.

Lovett, R. J., and W. H. Glutenmann, I S. Pakkala, W. D. Youngs, D. J. Lisk, G. E. Burdick, E. J. Harris. 1972. A survey of the total cadmium content of 406 fish from 49 New York State fresh waters. Journal of the Fisheries Research Board of Canada. Vol. 29(9):1283-1290.

Low, A. P. 1896. Report on explorations in the Labrador Peninsula along the East Main, Koksoak, Hamilton, Manicuagan and portions of other rivers in 1892-93-94-95. Ann. Rept., Geol. Surv. Canada, for 1895, new ser., No. 8, rept. L:1-387.

Lowe, T. P., and T. W. May, W. G. Brumbaugh, D. A. Kane. 1985. National Contaminant Biomonitoring Program - Concentrations of 7 elements in freshwater fish, 1978-1981. Arch Environ. Contam. Toxicol. Vol. 14(3):363-388.

Lowe-McConnell, R. H. 1978. Chapter 3. Identification of Freshwater Fishes. pp. 48-83. **IN:** Timothy Bagenal (ed.) Methods for Assessment of Fish Production in Fresh Waters. IBP Handbook No. 3. 3rd edition.Blackwell Scientific Publications. Oxford, England, U.K. 365pp.

Lower, A. R. M. 1915. A report of the fish and fisheries of the west coast of James Bay. Ann. Rept. Canada Dept. Naval Serv. 1913-14. Studies Supplement Biological Board of Canada. pp. 29-67 of appendix.

Luce, W. 1933. A survey of the fishery of the Kaskaskia River. Ill. Nat. Hist. Surv. Bull. Vol. 20(2):71-123.

Lundberg, John G. 1967. Pleistocene fishes of the Good Creek formation, Texas. Copeia 1967:453-455.

Lynch, T. M., and P. A. Buscemi, D. G. Lemons. 1953. Limnological and fishery conditions of Two Buttes Reservoir, Colorado, 1950 and 1951. Colo. Game Fish Dept. Rep.:92pp.

MacCrimmon, H. R. 1979. Comparative annulus formation on anatomical structures of the white sucker, *Catostomus commersoni* (La Cepède). Fisheries Mgmt. Vol. 10(3):123-128.

Maccubbin, A. E., and P. Black, L. Trzeciak, J. J. Black. 1985. Evidence for polynuclear aromatic hydrocarbons in the diet of bottom-feeding fish. Bull. Environ. Contam. Toxicol. Vol. 34(6):876-882.

MacFarlane, G. A., and W. G. Franzin. 1978. Elevated heavy metals: a stress on a population of white suckers, *Catostomus commersoni*, in Hamell lake, Saskatchewan. Journal of the Fisheries Research Board of Canada. Vol. 35(7):963-970.

MacKay, H. H. 1963. Fishes of Ontario. Ont. Dep. Lands For., Bryant Press Limited. Toronto. 300pp.

MacKay, W. C., and D. D. Beatty. 1968a. The effect of temperature on renal function in the white sucker, *Catostomus commersoni*. Comp. Biochem. Physiol. Vol. 26:235-245.

MacKay, W. C., and D. D. Beatty. 1968b. Plasma glucose levels of the white sucker, *Catostomus commersoni*, and the northern pike, *Esox lucius*. Canadian Journal of Zoology. Vol. 46:797-803.

Mackiewicz, J. S. 1968. *Isoglaridacris hexacotyle* comb. n. (Cestoidea: Caryophillidae) from catostomid fishes in southwestern North America. Proc. Helminth. Soc. Wash. Vol. 35:193-196.

Mackiewicz, J. S. 1972. Two new species of caryophyllid tapeworms from catostomid fishes in Tennessee. Journ. Parasit. Vol. 58(6):1075-1081.

Mackiewicz, J. S. 1974. *Calentinella etnieri* gen. et sp. n. (Cestoidea: Caryophyllaeidae) from *Erimyzon oblongus* (Mitchill) (Cypriniformes: Catostomidae) in North America. Proceedings helminth.Soc. Wash. Vol. 41(1):42-45.

Mackiewicz, J. S. 1976. *Glaridacris vogei* n. sp. (Cestoidea: Caryophyllidea) from catostomid fishes in western North America. Transactions Am. microsc. Soc. Vol. 95(1):92-97.

Mackiewicz, J. S., and W. G. Deutsch. 1976. *Rowardleus* and *Janiszewskella*, new caryophyllid genera (Cestoidea: Caryophyllidae) from *Carpiodes cyprinus* (Catostomidae) in eastern North America. Proceedings helminth. Soc. Wash. Vol. 43(1):9-17.

Macphee, Craig. 1960. Postlarval development and diet of the largescale sucker, *Catostomus macrocheilus*, in Idaho. Copeia 1960(2):119-125.

Maddux, H. R., and W. G. Kepner. 1988. Spawning of bluehead sucker in Kanab Creek, Arizona (Pisces: Catostomidae). Southwest Nat. Vol. 33(3):364-365.

Madsen, James H., Jr., and W. E. Miller. 1979. The fossil vertebrates of Utah, an annotated bibliography. Brigham Young Univ., Geol. Stud. Vol. 26, Part 4. 147pp.

Magnan, P. 1988. Interactions between brook charr, *Salvelinus fontinalis*, and nonsalmonid species: ecological shift, morphological shift, and their impact on zooplankton communities. Can. J. Fish Aquat Sci. Vol. 45(6):999-1009.

Magnin, E. 1964. Premier inventaire ichtyologique du Lac et de la Riviere Waswanipi. Naturaliste Canadien. Vol. 91(11):273-308.

Magnuson, J. J., and R. M. Horral. 1977. Univ. of Wis. 1977-1978 proposal to the National Sea Grant Program for continuing Sea Grant College support. **IN:** Vol. 2. Univ. Wisc. Sea Grant Coll. Prog., Madison. 269pp.

Mahon, R., and C. B. Port. 1985. Local size related segregation of fishes in streams. Arch. Hydrobiol. Vol. 103(2):267.

Makeeva, A. P. 1980. Peculiarities of early ontogenesis in the bigmouth buffalo *Ictiobus cyprinella* (Val.) (Catostomidae). Voprosy Ikhtiol. Vol. 20(6):855-874. Translated in Journal Ichthyol. Vol. 20(6):1980(1981):73-89.

Malek, M., and G. McCallister. 1984. Incidence of the leech *Helobdella stagnalis* on the Colorado River in west central Colorado. Great Basin Nat. Vol. 44(2):361-362.

Malick, Robert W., Jr., and Wayne A. Potter. 1976. The Distribution and Relative Abundance of the Ichthyofauna of Fishing Creek, York County, Pennsylvania. Proceedings of the Pennsylvania Academy of Science. Vol. 50(1):96-100.

Mancini, E. R., and M. Busdosh, B. D. Steele. 1979. Utilization of autochthonous macroinvertebrate drift by a pool fish community in a woodland stream. Hydrobiologia. Vol. 62(3):249-256.

Manohar, S. V. 1969. Some properties of the fluorescence of fish muscle. Journal of the Fisheries Research Board of Canada Vol. 26(5):1368-1371.

Manohar, S. V. 1970. Postmortem glycolytic and other biochemical changes in white muscle of White sucker (*Catostomus commersoni*) and Northern pike (*Esox lucius*) at O C. Journal of the Fisheries Research Board of Canada Vol. 27(11):1997-2002.

Manohar, S. V. 1971. Characteristics of white muscle fluorescence in pre-rigor fish. pp. 211-215. **IN:** Kreuzer, R. (editor). Fish inspection and quality control. Fishing News. (Books) Ltd., London.

Manohar, S. V., and H. Boese. 1971. Postmortem changes in the glycogen phosporylase activity of the muscle of white sucker (*Catostomus commersoni*) and northern pike (*Esox lucius*). Journal of the Fisheries Res. Board of Canada Vol. 28(9):1325-1326.

Mansfield, P. J. 1984. Reproduction by Lake Michigan fishes in a tributary stream. Transactions of the American Fisheries Society. Vol. 113(2):231-237.

Mansueti, A. J., and J. D. Hardy. 1967. Development of fishes of the Chesapeake Bay region. An atlas of egg, larval and juvenile stages. Pt. 1. Baltimore (Univ. Maryland):1-202.

Mansueti, Romeo. 1951. Occurrence and habitat of the darter *Hololepis fusiformis erochrous* in Maryland. Copeia 1951 (4):301-302.

Mansueti, Romeo, and Harold J. Elser. 1953. Ecology, age and growth of the mud sunfish *Acantharchus pomotis*, in Maryland. Copeia 1953 (2):117-119.

Marenchin, Ginger Lee, and David M. Sever. 1981. Survey of the Fishes of the St. Joseph River Drainage in St. Joseph and Elkhart Counties, Indiana. Proceedings Indiana Academy of Science. Vol. 80:454-460.

Margaritov, N. 1988. Parasites on buffalofish: on the bigmouth buffalo *Ictiobus cyprinellus* (Val.) on the black buffalo (*I. niger* Rafinesque) and on their hybrid *Ictiobus cyprinellus* X *I. niger* in fish ponds in Bulgaria. God Sofii Univ. Biol. Fak. Vol. 18(1):95-102.

Marin, R. G., and R. S. Campbell. 1953. The small fishes of Black River and Clearwater Lake, Missouri. Univ. Missouri Studies. Vol. 26(2):45-66.

Markarian, R. K., and M. C. Matthews, L. T. Connor. 1980. Toxicity of nickel, copper, zinc and aluminium mixtures to the white sucker (*Catostomus commersoni*). Bulletin envir. Contam. Toxicol. Vol. 25(5):790-796.

Marking, L. L., and T. D. Bills. 1977. Chlorine: its toxicity to fish and detoxification of antimycin. Investigations Fish Control No. 74:1-5.

Marking, L. L., and T. D. Bills. 1985. Effects of contaminants on toxicity of the lampricides 3-trifluoromethyl-4-nitrophenol and Bayer 73 to 3 species of fish. J. Great Lakes Res. Vol. 11(2):171-178.

Marsh, Paul C. 1985. Effect of incubation temperature on survival of embryos of native Colorado River (USA) fishes. Southwest Nat. Vol. 30(1):129-140.

Marrin, D. L. 1983. Ontogenetic changes and intraspecific resource partitioning in the tahoe sucker, *Catostomus tahoensis*. Environ. Biol. Fish. Vol. 8(1):39-47.

Marrin, Donn L., and Don C. Erman, Bruce Von Dracek. 1984. Food availability, food habits, and growth of Tahoe sucker, *Catostomus tahoensis*, from a reservoir and a natural lake. Calif. Fish Game Vol. 70(1):4-10.

Marsh, P. C. 1985. Effect of incubation temperature on survival of embryos of native Colorado fishes. Southwestern Nat. Vol. 30(1):129-140.

Marsh, P. C., and J. E. Brooks. 1989. Predation by ictalurid catfishes as a deterrent to re-establishment of hatchery-reared razorback suckers. Southwestern Nat. Vol. 34(2):188-195.

Marsh, P. C., and W. L. Minckley. 1989. Observations on recruitment and ecology of razorback sucker: lower Colorado River, Arizona-California-Nevada. Great Basin Nat. Vol. 49(1):71-78.

Martin, J. D. 1985. Effects of Mount Pleasant Tungsten Mine (Canada) effluent on biota of Hatch Brook. Can Manuscr Rep Fish Aquat Sci No. 1805:1-7.

Martin, M. 1972. Morphology and variation of the modoc sucker, *Catostomus microps* Rutter, with notes on feeding adaptions. California Fish Game Vol. 58(4):277-284.

Martin, N. V. 1970. Long-term effects of diet on the biology of the lake trout and the fishery in Lake Opeongo, Ontario. Journal of the Fisheries Res. Board of Canada. Vol. 27(1):125-146.

Martin, R. E. 1964a. Growth and movement of smallmouth buffalo, *Ictiobus bubalus* (Rafinesque), in Watts Bar Reservoir, Tennessee. Diss. Abstr. Vol. 24:3030-3031.

Martin, R. E. 1964b. Age and growth of smallmouth buffalo, *Ictiobus bubalus* (Rafinesque), in Watts Bar Reservoir, Tennessee. J. Tenn. Acad. Sci. Vol. 39:72.

Martin, R. E., and S. I. Auerbach, D. J. Nelson. 1964. Growth and movement of smallmouth buffalo, *Ictiobus bubalus* (Rafinesque), in Watts Bar Reservoir, Tennessee. Ph.D. Thesis. Univ. Tenn., Oak Ridge Nat. Lab. 03530. 98pp.

Martin, R. F. 1986. Spawning behavior of the gray redhorse, *Moxostoma congestum* (Pisces: Catostomidae) in central Texas. Southwestern Nat. Vol. 31(3):399-401.

Martin, R. G., and R. S. Campbell. 1953. The small fishes of Black River and Clearwater Lake, Missouri. (pp. 45-66). **IN:** John L. Funk, et al. (eds.) The Black River studies. Univ. Missouri Stud. Vol. 26(2):1-136.

Massé, G. 1977. Répartition de suceur cuivré *Moxostoma hubbsi* (Legendre), son habitat, et son abondance relative comparée à celle des autres catostomidés, du Québec. Travaux en Cours. Rapp. Dir. gén. Faune Québ. No. 10:1-12.

Mather, Frederic. 1886. Memoranda relating to Adirondack fishes, with descriptions of new species, from researches made in 1882. State of New York Adirondack Survey from appendix to the twelfth report. (Zoology) Albany 1886:1-56.

Mathias, J. A., and J. A. Babaluk, K. D. Rowes. 1985. An analysis of the 1984 walleye, *Stizostedion vitreum vitreum*, run at Crean Lake in Prince Albert National Park, Saskatchewan [Canada] with reference to the impact of spawn-taking. Can Tech Rep Fish Aquat Sci. 0(1407):1-34.

Matthews, W. J. 1986. Diel difference in gill net and seine catches of fish in winter in a cove of Lake Texoma, Oklahoma-Texas. Texas J. Sci. Vol. 38(2):153-158.

Matthews, W. J., and L. G. Hill, S. M. Schellhaass. 1985. Depth distribution of striped bass and other fish in Lake Texoma (Oklahoma - Texas) during summer stratification. Transactions of the Am. Fish. Soc. Vol. 114(1):84-91.

Mattingly, R. 1976. Great Lakes fish cookery. Mich. State Univ. Coop. Ext. Serv. Bull. E-932, Nat. Resour. Ser. 15 pp.

Mauck, W. L., and D. W. Coble. 1971. Vulnerability of some fishes to northern pike (*Esox lucius*) predation. Journal of the Fisheries Research Board of Canada. Vol. 28(7):957-969.

Mauney, Morris, Jr. 1979. New distributional records for caryophyllid cestodes from Arkansas. Southwestern Nat. Vol. 24(4):685-686.

Maruney, Morris, Jr., and George L. Harp. 1979. The Effects of Channelization on Fish Populations of the Cache River and Bayou De View. Arkansas Academy of Science Proceedings. Vol. 33:51-54.

Maurakis, Eugene G., and William S. Woolcott. 1984. Seasonal occurrence patterns of fishes in a thermally enriched stream. Va J. Sci. Vol. 35(1):5-21.

Mavor, J. W. 1915. On the occurrence of a trypanoplasm, probably *Trypanoplasma borreli* Laveran et Mensil, in the blood of the common sucker, *Catostomus commersonii*. Journal of Parasitology. Vol. 2:1-6.

May, E. B., and C. R. Gasaway. 1967. A preliminary key to the identification of larval fishes of Oklahoma, with particular reference to Canton Reservoir, including a selected bibliography. Okla. Dep. Wildl. Conserv. Fish. Res. Lab. Bull No. 5 Norman. 32pp.

Mayhew, J. 1964. Coralville Reservoir fisheries investigation, 1963. Part II: Limnology and fish populations. Iowa Conserv. Comm. Quart. Rep. Vol. 16(1):25-31.

Mayr, Ernst. 1966. Animal Species and Evolution. The Belknap Press of Harvard University Press. Cambridge, Massachusetts. 797pp.

Mayr, Ernst. 1971. Populations, Species, and Evolution. An abridgement of Animal Species and Evolution. The Belknap Press of Harvard University Press. Cambridge, Massachusetts. 453pp.

McAda, Charles W., and Richard S. Wydoski. 1980. The razorback sucker, *Xyrauchen texanus*, in the Upper Colorado River Basin, 1974-1976. Technical Pap. U.S. Fish Wildlife Serv. No. 99:1-15.

McAda, Charles W., and Richard S. Wydoski. 1983. Maturity and fecundity of the bluehead sucker, *Catostomus discobolus* (Catostomidae), in the upper Colorado River Basin. Southwestern Nat. Vol. 28(1):120-123.

McAda, Charles W., and Richard S. Wydoski. 1985. Growth and reproduction of the flannelmouth sucker, *Catostomus latipinnis* in the upper Colorado River Basin (USA), 1975-1976. Great Basin Nat. Vol. 45(2):281-286.

McAllister, Don E. 1964. Fish collections from Eastern Hudson Bay. Canadian Field Naturalist. Vol. 78:167-178.

McAllister, Don E., and Brian W. Coad. 1974. Fishes of Canada's National Capital Region. Miscellaneous Special Publication 24. Department of the Environment Fisheries and Marine Service. Ottawa, Canada. 200pp.

McCabe, Britton C. 1943. An analysis of the distribution of fishes in the streams of western Massachusetts. Copeia 1943 (2):85-89.

McCart, P., and N. Aspinwall. 1970. Spawning habits of the Largescale sucker, *Catostomus macrocheilus*, at Stave Lake, British Columbia. Journal of the Fisheries Research Board of Canada Vol. 27(6):1154-1158.

McClane, Albert Jules. 1974. McClane's New Standard Fishing Encyclopedia and international angling guide. Enlarged and Revised Edition. Holt, Rinehart and Winston. New York, New York. 1156pp.

McCleave, James David. 1964. Movement and population of the mottled sculpin (*Cottus bairdi* Girard) in a small Montana stream. Copeia 1964(3):506-513.

McClellan, P. H. 1977. Paleontology and paleoecology of Neogene freshwater fishes from the Salt Lake Beds, northern Utah. Master's thesis, University of California, Berkeley, 243pp.

McCollum, J. L., and C. J. Quertermus. 1980. Distribution of fishes in the Dog River drainage. Georgia Journal of Science. Vol. 38(1):55-63.

McCombie, A. M., and A. H. Berst. 1969. Some effects of shape and structure of fish on selectivity of gill nets. Journal of the Fisheries Research Board of Canada. Vol. 26(10):2681-2689.

McComish, T. S. 1967. Food habits of bigmouth and smallmouth buffalo in Lewis and Clark Lake and the Missouri River. Transactions of the American Fisheries Society. Vol. 96(1):70-73.

McConnell, J. A., and J. R. Brett. 1946. Lakes of the Skeena River drainage. III. Kitwanga Lake. Progress Reports of the Fisheries Research Board Pacific Coast Stations. No. 68:55-59.

McConnell, W. J., and W. J. Clark, W. F. Sigler. 1957. Bear Lake - its fish and fishing. Utah Dept. Fish Game Publ. 76pp.

McCormick, J. H., and B. R. Jones, K. E. F. Hokanson. 1977. White sucker (*Catostomus commersoni*) embryo development, and early growth and survival at different temperatures. Journal of the Fisheries Research Board of Canada. Vol. 34(7):1019-1025.

McCraig, R. S., and J. W. Mullan, C. O. Dodge. 1960. Five-year report on the development of the fishery of a 25,000 acre domestic water supply reservoir in Massachusetts. Progr. Fish Cult. Vol. 22(1):15-23.

McCrimmon, H. R., and A. H. Berst. 1961. The native fish population and trout harvests in an Ontario farm pond. Progr. Fish Cult. Vol. 23(3):106-113.

McDonald, D. B., and P. A. Dotson. 1960. Fishery investigations of the Glen Canyon and Flaming Gorge impoundment areas. Utah St. Dept. Fish Game Info. Bull. 60-3:70pp.

McDonald, H. Gregory, and Elaine Anderson. 1975. A late Pleistocene vertebrate fauna from southeastern Idaho. Tebiwa. Vol. 18(1):19-37.

McDonald, Jerry N., and Charles S. Bartlett, Jr. 1983. An associated musk ox skeleton from Saltville, Virginia. J. Vertebr. Paleontology. Vol. 2(4):453-470.

McElman, J. F. 1983. Comparative embryonic ecomorphology and the reproductive guild classification of walleye, *Stizostedion vitreum*, white sucker, *Catostomus commersoni*. Copeia 1983(1):246-250.

McElman, J. F., and E. K. Balon. 1980. Early ontogeny of white sucker, *Catostomus commersoni*, with steps of saltatory development. Environmental Biol. Fishes. Vol. 5(3):191-224.

McFarlane, G. A., and W. G. Franzin. 1981. An examination of Cd, Cu, and Hg concentrations in livers of northern pike *Esox lucius*, and white sucker, *Catostomus commersoni* from five lakes near base metal smelter at Flin Flon, Manitoba. Canadian J. Fish. Aquat. Sci. Vol. 37(10):1573-1578.

McGeachin, R. B. 1986. Carp and buffalo. pp. 43-55. **IN:** R. R. Stickney (editor) Culture of nonsalmonid freshwater fishes. CRC Press, Boca Raton, Florida. 201pp.

McGuire, D. L. 1981. Annotated key to the larval suckers (Catostomidae) of the Missouri River drainage, Montana. Proceedings Mont. Acad. Sci. Vol. 40:1-8.

Mcinerny, M. C. and J. Witteld. 1988. Collection of young-of-the-year blue suckers (*Cycleptus elongatus*) in Navigation Pool 9 of the Upper Mississippi River. Trans. Wis. Acad. Sci. Arts Lett. Vol. 76:69-71.

McKee, J. E., and H. W. Wolf. 1963. Water Quality Criteria. Calif. St. Water Qual. Contr. Bd., Public. No. 3A. 548pp.

McKenzie, R. A. 1959. Marine and freshwater fishes of the Miramichi River and Estuary, New Brunswick. Vol. 16(6):807-833.

McKeown, B. A., and G. H. Geen, T. A. Watson, J. F. Powell, D. B. Parker. 1985. The effect of pH on plasma electrolytes, carbonic anhydrase and ATPase activities in rainbow trout (*Salmo gairdneri*) and large-scale suckers. (*Catostomus macrocheilus*) Comp. Biochem. Physiol. A. Comp. Physiol. Vol. 80(4):507-514.

McKim, J. M., and J. W. Arthur, T. W. Thorslund. 1975. Toxicity of a linear alkylate sulfonate detergent to larvae of four species of freshwater fish. Bulletin envir. Contam. Toxicol. Vol. 14(1):1-7.

McKim, J. M., and J. G. Eaton, G. W. Holcombe. 1978. Metal toxicity to embryos and larvae of eight species of freshwater fish.-2. Copper. Bulletin envir. Contam. Toxicol. Vol. 19(5):608-616.

McKinnon, G. A., and F. N. Hnytka. 1985. Fish passage assessment of culverts constructed to stimulate stream conditions on Liard River tributaries [Canada]. Can. Tech. Rep. Fish Aquat. Sci. No. 1255:1-121.

McLain, A. L., and B. R. Smith, H. H. Moore. 1965. Experimental control of sea lamprey with electricity on the south shore of Lake Superior, 1953-60. Great Lakes Fish. Comm. Tech. Rep. No. 10. 48 pp.

McMaster, D. and Y. Kobayashi, J. Rivier, K. Lederis. 1986. Characterization of the biologically and antigenically important regions of Urotensin II. Proc. West Pharmacol. Soc. Vol. 29:205-208.

McMaster, Denis, and Karl Lederis. 1983. Isolation and amino acid sequence of 2 urotensin II peptides from *Catostomus commersoni* urophyses. Peptides. Vol. 4(3):367-374.

McNally, Tom. 1970. Tom McNally's Fishermen's Bible. Follett Publishing Company. Chicago, Illinois. 321pp.

McPhail, J. D. 1987. Status of the salish sucker, *Catostomus sp.*, in Canada. Can. Field-Nat. Vol. 101(2):231-236.

McPhail, J. D., and C. C. Lindsey. 1970. Freshwater fishes of northwestern Canada and Alaska. Fish. Res. Board Canada Bull. 173:1-381.

McSwain, L. E., and R. M. Gennings. 1972. Spawning behavior of the spotted sucker *Minytrema melanops* (Rafinesque). Transactions of the American Fisheries Society. Vol. 101(4):738-740.

Meek, Alexander. 1916. The migrations of fish. Edward Arnold, publisher. London. 1-427pp.

Meek, Seth Eugene. 1891. Report of explorations made in Missouri and Arkansas during 1889, with an account of fishes observed in each of the river basins examined. Bull. U.S. Fish Comm. Vol. 9:113-141.

Meek, Seth Eugene. 1894. A catalogue of the Fishes of Arkansas. Annual Report of the Geological Society of Arkansas for 1891. Volume II. Miscellaneous Reports.:215-276.

Meek, Seth Eugene. 1902. A contribution to the Ichthyology of Mexico. Fieldiana: Zoology. Field Columbian Museum. Vol. 3:63-128.

Meek, Seth Eugene. 1904. The fresh-water Fishes of Mexico North of the Isthmus of Tehuantepec. Fieldiana: Zoology. Field Columbian Museum. Vol. 5(93):1-252.

Meek, Seth Eugene, and S. F. Hildebrand. 1910. A Synoptic List of the Fishes Known to occur within Fifty Miles of Chicago. Field Museum of Natural History. Publication 142. Zoölogical Series. Vol. 7(No. 9):223-338.

Melvill, C. D. 1915. Report on the east-coastal fisheries of James Bay. Ann. Rept. Canada Dept. Naval Serv. 1913-14, Studies Supplement. No. 119: p. 3-28 of appendix.

Mergo, J. C., Jr., and A. M. White. 1982. Two new species of Dactylogyridae (Monogenea) from the silver redhorse, *Moxostoma anisurum*. Journal of Parasitology. Vol. 68(5):946-948.

Mergo, John C., Jr., and Andrew M. White. 1984. A survey of monogeneans on the gills of catostomid fishes from Ohio, (USA)(1983). Ohio J. Sci. Vol. 84(1):33-35.

Merrill, George P. 1907. Catalogue of the types, cotypes, and figured specimens of fossil vertebrates in the department of geology, U.S. National Museum. Bull. U.S. Nat. Mus. Vol. 53, part 2:1-81.

Metcalf, A. L. 1966. Fishes of the Kansas River system in relation to zoogeography of the Great Plains. Mus. Nat. Hist., Univ. Kansas, Publ. Vol. 17(3):23-189.

Mettee, M. F. 1978. The fishes of the Birmingham-Jefferson County region of Alabama with ecologic and taxonomic notes. Bulletin geol. Surv. Ala. No. 115. 1978:1-183.

Meyer, Fred P. 1967. Chemical control of fish diseases in warm-water ponds. Proc. Fish Farming Conf., Feb. 1-2, 1967. Texas A & M University, Texas Agricultural Extension Service, College Station:35-39.

Meyer, W. H. 1961. Life history of three species of redhorse (*Moxostoma*) in the Des Moines River, Iowa. M.S. Thesis. Iowa State Univ.

Meyer, W. H. 1962. Life history of three species of redhorse (*Moxostoma*) in the Des Moines River, Iowa. Transactions of the American Fisheries Society. Vol. 91(4):412-419.

Meyers, George Sprague. 1966. Derivation of the Freshwater Fish Fauna of Central America. Copeia 1966(4):766-773.

Migdalski, E. C. 1955. Reproduction and classification of some of the better known fishes of North America. Data for Handbook of Biological Data. 42pp.

Miki, B. L. A. 1977. The histones of fish erythrocytes. Dissertation Abstr. int. (B).Vol. 37(12):6100.

Miki, B. L. A., and J. M. Neelin. 1977. Comparison of histones from fish erythrocytes. Canadian J. Biochem. Vol. 55(12):1220-1227.

Miller, N. J. 1971. Rough and detrimental fish removal-1970. Wis. Dep. Nat. Resour. 14pp.

Miller, R. B. 1947. Great Bear Lake. pp. 31-44. **IN:** Northwest Canadian fisheries surveys in 1944-45. Bull. Fish. Res. Bd. Canada Bulletin 72:1-94.

Miller, R. G. 1951. The natural history of Lake Tahoe fishes. Ph.D. Thesis. Stanford University. 160pp.

Miller, R. J., and H. W. Robison. 1973. The fishes of Oklahoma. Oklahoma State University Press, Oklahoma. 246 pp.

Miller, Robert Rush. 1946. Distributional records for North American fishes, with nomenclatorial notes on the genus *Psenes*. J. Wash. Acad. Sci. Vol. 36(6):206-212.

Miller, Robert Rush. 1955.Fish remains from archaeological sites in the Lower Colorado River basin, Arizona. Pap. Mich. Acad. Sci. Vol. 40:125-136.

Miller, Robert Rush. 1958. Origin and affinities of the Freshwater Fauna of Western North America. Chapter 9. pp. 187-222. **IN:** Carl L. Hubbs,(ed.) Zoogeography Publication No. 51. American Association for the Advancement of Science.Washington, D. C. 509pp.

Miller, Robert Rush. 1963. Distribution, variation, and ecology of *Lepidomeda vittata*, a rare cyprinid fish endemic to eastern Arizona. Copeia 1963(1):1-5.

Miller, Robert Rush. 1965. Quaternary freshwater fishes of North America. pp. 569-581. **IN:** H. E. Wright, Jr., and David G. Frey (eds.) The Quaternary of the United States: A review for the VII Congress of the International Association for Quaternary research. Princeton University Press. Princeton. 922pp.

Miller, Robert Rush. 1966. Geographical Distribution of Central American Freshwater Fishes. Copeia 1966(4):773-802.

Miller, Robert Rush. 1968. Records of some native freshwater fishes transplanted into various waters of California, Baja California, and Nevada. Calif. Fish Game Vol. 54:170-179.

Miller, Robert Rush. 1972. Threatened freshwater fishes of the United States. Transactions of the American Fisheries Society. Vol. 101(2):239-252.

Miller, Robert Rush. 1973. Two new fishes, *Gila bicolor snyderi* and *Catostomus fumeiventris*, from the Owens River Basin, California. Occassional Pap. Mus. Zool. Univ. Mich. No. 667:1-19.

Miller, Robert Rush. 1981. Chapter 3. Coevolution of Deserts and Pupfishes (Genus Cyprinodon in the American Southwest. pp. 39-94. **IN:** Robert J. Naiman and David L. Soltz (eds.) Fishes in North American Deserts. John Wiley & Sons. N.Y., N.Y. 552pp.

Miller, Robert Rush, and Ralph G. Miller. 1948. The contribution of the Columbia river system to the fish fauna of Nevada: five species unrecorded from the State. Copeia, Ann Arbor. 1948(3):174-187.

Miller, Robert Rush, and Gerald R. Smith. 1967. New fossil fishes from Plio-Pleistocene Lake Idaho. Occ. Pap. Mus. Zool. Univ. Mich. No. 654:1-24.

Miller, Robert Rush, and Gerald R. Smith. 1981. Distribution and evolution of *Chasmistes* (Pisces:Catostomidae) in western North America. Occasional Pap. Mus. Zool. Univ. Mich. No. 696:1-46.

Miller, Robert Rush, and H. E. Winn. 1951. Additions to the known fish fauna of Mexico: three species and one subspecies from Sonora. J. Wash. Acad. Sci. Vol. 41:83-84.

Miller, Rudolph J., and H. E. Evans. 1965. External morphology of the brain and lips in catostomid fishes. Copeia 1965(4):467-487.

Miller, Rudolph J., and Henry W. Robinson. 1973. The fishes of Oklahoma. Okla. State Univ. Press, Stillwater, Oklahoma. 246 pp.

Mills, Harlow B., and William C. Starrett, Frank C. Belrose. 1966. Man's Effect on the Fish and Wildlife of the Illinois River. Illinois Natural History Survey. Biological Notes No. 57:1-24.

Mills, K. H., and S. M. Chalanchuk, L. C. Mohr, I. J. Davies. 1987. Responses of fish populations in Lake 223 to 8 years of experimental acidification. Canadian Journal of Fisheries and Aquatic Sciences. Vol. 44(Supplement 1):114-125.

Mills, Paul A., Jr., and Charles H. Hocutt, Jay R. Stauffer, Jr. 1978. The pre-impoundment fish fauna of Big River (Meramec Drainage, Missouri). Transactions, Missouri Academy of Science. Vol. 12:25-35.

Minckley, C. O. 1973. A new record of the quillback carpsucker *Carpiodes cyprinus* (Le Seuer) from the Kansas River Basin. Transactions Kans. Acad. Sci. Vol. 72(1):108.

Minckley, C. O., and S. W. Carothers. 1979. Recent collections of the Colorado River squawfish and razorback sucker from the San Juan and Colorado rivers in New Mexico and Arizona. Southwestern Nat. Vol. 24(4):686-687.

Minckley, W. L. 1959. Fishes of the Big Blue River Basin, Kansas. Univ. Kans. Publ. Mus. nat. Hist. Vol. 11(7):401-442.

Minckley, W. L. 1963. The ecology of a spring stream, Doe Run, Meade County, Kentucky. Wildl. Monogr. Vol. 11:1-124.

Minckley, W. L. 1969. Investigations of commercial fisheries potentials in reservoirs. Final Rep. - P. L. 88-309. Res. Ariz. Game Fish Dep., Ariz. State Univ., Tempe. (mimeo).

Minckley, W. L. 1983. Status of the razorback sucker, *Xyrauchen texanus* (Abbott), in the lower Colorado River Basin. Southwestern Nat. Vol. 28(2):165-187.

Minckley, W. L., and Frank B. Cross. 1960. Taxonomic status of the shorthead redhorse, *Moxostoma aureolum* (Le Sueur) from the Kansas river basin, Kansas. Trans. Kansas Acad. Sci. Vol. 63:35-40.

Minckley, W. L., and R. H. Goodyear, J. E. Craddock. 1964. Incidence of aberrant scalation in catostomid fishes from Doe Run, Meade County, Kentucky. Transactions of the American Fisheries Society. Vol. 93(2):202-203.

Minckley, W. L., and E. S. Gustafson. 1982. Early development of the razorback sucker, *Xyrauchen texanus* (Abbott). Great Basin Nat. Vol. 42(4):553-561.

Minckley, W. L., and Dean A. Hendrickson, Carl E. Bond. 1986. Chapter 15. Geography of Western North American Freshwater Fishes: Description and Relationships to Intracontinental Tectonism. pp. 519-613. **IN:** Charles H. Hocutt and E. O. Wiley (eds.) The Zoogeography of North American Freshwater Fishes. John Wiley and Sons. New York, New York. 1985(1986). 866pp.

Minckley, W. L., and J. E. Johnson, J. N. Rinne, S. E. Willoughby. 1970. Foods of Buffalofishes, genus *Ictiobus*, in central Arizona reservoirs. Transactions of the American Fisheries Society. Vol. 99:333-342.

Mitchell, L. G. 1978. Myxosporidian infections in some fishes of Iowa. Journal Protozool. Vol. 25(1):100-105.

Mitchell, Patricia, and Ellie Prepas. 1990. Atlas of Alberta Lakes. University of Alberta Press. Edmonton, Alberta. 675 pp.

Mitchill, Samuel Latham. 1815. The fishes of New York, described and arranged. Literary and Philosophical Society of New York. Transactions. Vol. 1(5):355-492.

Mitzner, L. 1966. Age and growth of bigmouth buffalo in Coralville Reservoir. Iowa Conserv. Comm. Quart. Biol. Rep. Vol. 18(4):66-74.

Mitzner, L. 1971. Movement of bigmouth buffalo in Coralville reservoir, Iowa. Proceedings Iowa Acad. Sci. Vol. 78(1-2):34-35.

Moen, T. E. 1954. Food of the bigmouth buffalo, *Ictiobus cyprinellus* (Valenciennes), in Northwest Iowa Lakes. Proc. Iowa Acad. Sci. Vol. 61:561-569.

Moen, T. E. 1960. Length-weight tables for fishes from northwest Iowa lakes. typewritten ms.

Moen, T. E. 1970. The occurrence of Black Buffalo, *Ictiobus niger* (Rafinesque), in Lake Mitchell, South Dakota. Proc. S. Dak. Acad. Sci. Vol. 49:42-45.

Moen, T. E. 1974. Population trends, growth and movement of bigmouth buffalo, *Ictiobus cyprinellus*, in Lake Oahe, 1963-70. Technical Pap. Bur. Sport. Fish. Widl. No. 78:1-20.

Mohr, Lloyd C., and Sandra M. Chalanchuk. 1985. The effect of pH on sperm motility of white suckers, *Catostomus commersoni*, in the Experimental Lakes area [Canada]. Environ. Biol. Fishes. Vol. 14(4):309-314.

Molnar, K., and G. L. Chan, C. H. Fernando. 1982. Some remarks on the occurrence and development of philometrid nematodes infecting the white sucker, *Catostomus commersoni* La Cepède (Pisces: Catostomidae), in Ontario. Canadian Journal of Zoology. Vol. 60(3):443-451.

Molnar, K., and G. Hanek. 1974. Seven new *Eimeria* spp. (Protozoa, Coccidia) from freshwater fishes of Canada. Journal Protozool. Vol. 21(4):489-493.

Molnar, K., and G. Hanek, C. H. Fernando. 1974. Parasites of fishes from Laurel Creek, Ontario. Journal of Fish Biology. Vol 6(6):717-728.

Molya, S. P., and P. D. Arikov. 1988. A comparative study of the development of the reproductive system of three species of buffalo fish in ponds of Moldavia. Gos Nauchno - Issled Inst. Ozern Rechn Rybn Khoz Sb. Nauchn Tr. No. 288:41-42.

Mongeau, J. -R., and P. Dumont, L. Cloutier. 1986. La biologie du suceur cuivre, *Moxostoma hubbsi*, une espece rare et endemique a la region de Montreal, Quebec, Canada. Rapport techn. Gouv. Quebec Minist. Loisir Chasse Peche Nos. 06-39:1-137.

Mongeau, J. -R., and P. Dumont, L. Cloutier, A.-M. Clement. 1988. Le statut de suceur cuivre, *Moxostoma hubbsi*, au Canada. Can. Field-Nat. Vol. 102(1):132-139.

Montgomery, W. L., and S. D. McCormick, R. J. Naiman, F. G. Whoriskey, Jr., G. A. Black. 1983. Spring migratory synchrony of salmonid, catostomid, and cyprinid fishes in Riviere a la Truite, Québec. Canadian Journal of Zoology. Vol. 61(11):2495-2502.

Moody, H. L. 1957. A fisheries study of Lake Panasoffkee, Florida. Quart. J. Florida Acad. Sci. Vol. 20(1):21-88.

Moore, G. A., and Frank B. Cross. 1950. Additional Oklahoma fishes with validation of *Poecilichthys parvipinnis* (Gilbert and Swain). Copeia 1950(2):139-148.

Moore, G., and A. Letter, M. Tesanovic, K. Lederis. 1975. Studies on molecular weights of two peptide hormones from the urophysis of white sucker (*Catostomus commersoni*) Canadian. J. Biochem. Vol. 53(2):242-247.

Moore, K. A., and D. D. Williams. 1990. Novel strategies in the complex defense repertoire of a stonefly (*Pteronarcys dorsata*) nymph. Oikos Vol. 57(1):49-56.

Moore, R. A. 1948. Morphology of the kidneys of Ohio fishes. Contr. Fr. T. Stone Lab. Ohio St. Univ. No. 5 1933:1-34.

Morgan, R. P., II, and R. E. Smith, Jr., J. R. Stauffer, Jr. 1983. Electrophoretic separation of larval silver redhorse (*Moxostoma anisurum*) and golden redhorse (*Moxostoma erythrurum*). Comp. Biochem. Physiol. B. Comp. Biochem. Vol. 76(4):721-722.

Moring, John R., and Paul D. Eiler, Mary T. Negus, Elizabeth Gibbs. 1986. Ecological importance of submerged pulpwood logs in a Maine reservoir. Transactions of the American Fisheries Society. Vol. 115(2):335-342.

Morley, S. D., and C. Schonrock, J. Heierhorst, J. Figueroa, K. Lederis, D. Richter. 1990. Vasotocin genes of the teleost fish *Catostomus commersoni*:gene structure, exonintron boundary, and hormone precursor organization. Biochemistry Vol. 29(10):2505-2511.

Morris, L. A. 1965. Age and growth of the river carpsucker *Carpiodes carpio* in the Missouri River. American Midland Naturalist. Vol. 73:423-429.

Morris, M. A., and Brooks M. Burr. 1982. Breeding tubercles in *Ictiobus cyprinellus* (Pisces: Catostomidae) American Midl. Nat. Vol. 107(1):199-201.

Morrison, K. A., and N. Therien, B. Coupal. 1985. Simulating fish redistribution in the LG-2 reservoir after flooding. Ecol. Model. Vol. 28(1/2):97-112.

Morrow, James E. 1980. The Freshwater Fishes of Alaska Alaska Northwest Publishing Company. Anchorage, Alaska. 248pp.

Moss, R. E., and J. W. Scanlan, C. S. Anderson. 1983. Observations on the natural history of the blue sucker (*Cycleptus elongatus* (Le Sueur)) in the Neosho River. American Midl. Nat. Vol. 109(1):15-22.

Moyle, J. B. 1975. The uncommon ones. Minn. Dep. Nat. Resour. 32pp.

Moyle, J. B., and C. R. Burrows. 1954. Manual of instructions for lake survey. Minn. Bur. Fish. Fish Res. Unit Spec. Publ. 1:70pp.

Moyle, Peter B. 1969. Ecology of the fishes of a Minnesota lake with special reference to the cyprinidae. Univ. Minn., Minneapolis. Ph.D. Thesis. 169pp.

Moyle, Peter B. 1976. Inland fishes of California. University of California Press, Berkeley, Los Angeles & London. 1-405pp.

Moyle, Peter B. 1977. Are Coarse Fish a Curse? Fly Fisherman. Vol. 8(5):35-39.

Moyle, Peter B., and Donald M. Baltz. 1985. Microhabitat use by an assemblage of California (USA) stream fishes: Developing criteria for instream flow determinations. Transactions of the American Fisheries Society. Vol. 114(5):695-704.

Moyle, Peter B., and Joseph J. Cech, Jr. 1982. Fishes: An Introduction to Ichthyology. Prentice-Hall, Inc. Englewood Cliffs, New Jersey. 593pp.

Moyle, Peter B., and Robert A. Daniels, Bruce Herbold, Donald M. Baltz. 1986. Patterns in distribution and abundance of a noncoevolved assemblage of estuarine fishes in California. U.S. Natl. Mar. Fish Serv. Fish Bull. Vol. 84(1):105-118.

Moyle, Peter B., and A. Marciochi. 1975. Biology of the Modoc sucker, *Catostomus microps*, in northeastern California. Copeia 1975(3):556-560.

Moyle, Peter B., and B. Vondracek. 1983. Responses of fish populations in the North Fork of the Feather River, California, to treatments with fish toxicants. North American Journal of Fisheries Management. American Fisheries Society. Vol. 3(1):48-60.

Moyle, Peter B., and Bruce Vondracek. 1985. Persistence and structure of the fish assemblage in a small California (USA) stream. Ecology Vol. 66(1):1-13.

Mpoame, M., and J. N. Rinne. 1983. Parasites of some fishes native to Arizona and New Mexico. Southwestern Nat. Vol. 28(4):399-405.

Mudry, D. R., and H. P. Arai. 1973a. The life cycle of *Hunterella nodulosa* Mackiewicz and McCrae, 1962. (Cestoidea: Caryophyllidea) in Alberta. Canadian Journal of Zoology. Vol. 51(7):781-786.

Mudry, D. R., and H. P. Arai. 1973b. Population dynamics of *Hunterella nodulosa* (Cestoidea: Caryophyllidea) in Alberta. Canadian Journal of Zoology. Vol. 51(7):787-792.

Mueller, G. 1989. Observations of spawning razorback sucker (*Xyrauchen texanus*) utilizing riverine habitat in the lower Colorado River, Arizona-Nevada Southwest. Nat. Vol. 34(1):147-149.

Muench, B. 1963. Length-weight relationship of eighteen species of fish in northeastern Illinois. N.E. Area Fish. HQ, Rt. 2, Box 51, Marengo, Ill. Typed ms.

Munkittrick, K. R., and D. G. Dixon. 1989. Use of a white sucker (*Catostomus commersoni*) populations to assess the health of aquatic ecosystems exposed to low-level contaminated stress. Canadian Journal of Fisheries and Aquatic Sciences. Vol. 46(8):1455-1462.

Munro, J. A., and W. A. Clemens. 1937. The American merganser in British Columbia and its relation to the fish population. Bulletins of the Biological Board of Canada. 55:50pp.

Munthe, Jens. 1980. Catalog of fossil type and figured specimens in the Milwaukee Public Museum Contrib. Biol. Geol. 39:1-27pp.

Muzzal, P. M. 1979a. Studies on the population biology, host-parasite relationships, and community diversity of several endohelminths infecting the white sucker, *Catostomus commersoni* (La Cepède), from the Bellamy and Oyster Rivers, New Hampshire. Dissertation Abstr. int. (B) Vol 39(11):5277.

Muzzall, P. M. 1979b. The occurrence of *Cryptobia catostomi* (Protozoa: Cryptobiidae). Transactions Am. Microsc. Soc. Vol. 98(3):472-473.

Muzzall, P. M. 1980a. Seasonal distribution and ecology of three caryophyllaeid cestode species infecting white suckers in SE New Hampshire. Journal of Parasitology. Vol. 66(3):542-550.

Muzzall, P. M. 1980b. Population biology and host-parasite relationships of *Triganodistomum attenuatum* (Trematoda: Lissorchiidae) infecting the white sucker, *Catostomus commersoni* (La Cepède). Journal of Parasitology. Vol. 66(2):293-298.

Muzzall, P. M. 1980c. Ecology and seasonal abundance of three acanthocephalan species infecting white suckers in SE New Hampshire. Journal of Parasitology. Vol. 66(1):127-133.

Muzzall, P. M. 1982a. Metazoan parasites of fish from Red Cedar River, Ingham County, Michigan. Proceedings helminth. Soc. Wash. Vol. 49(1):93-98.

Muzzall, P. M. 1982b. Comparison of the parasite communities of the white sucker (*Catostomus commersoni*) from two rivers in New Hampshire. Journal of Parasitology. Vol. 68(2):300-305.

Muzzall, P. M., and F. C. Rabalais. 1975. Studies on *Acanthocephalus jacksoni* Bullock, 1962. (Acanthocephala: Echinorhynchidae). 1. Seasonal periodicity and new host records. Proceedings helminth. Soc. Wash. Vol. 42(1):31-34.

Myers, George Sprague. 1949. Usage of anadromous, catadromous and allied terms for migratory fishes. Copeia 1949 (2):89-97.

Naiman, Robert J. 1981. Chapter 16. An Ecosytem Overview: Desert Fishes and Their Habitats. pp. 493-533. **IN:** Robert J. Naiman and David L. Soltz (eds.) Fishes in North American Deserts. John Wiley & Sons. New York, N.Y. 552pp.

Nall, G. H. 1930. The life of sea trout. Seeley, Service and Co., London. 335pp.

Nash, R. D. M., and Y. Sun, C. S. Clay. 1987. High resolution acoustic structure of fish. J. Cons. Cons. Int. Explor. Mer. Vol. 44(1):23-31.

Nasini, S. K. 1973. Growth of carpsuckers, *Carpiodes spp.* as indicated by RNA/DNA ratios. Dissertation Abstr. int. Vol. 33B(8):4045.

Neave, F., and A. Bajkov. 1929. Reports of the Jasper Park lakes investigations, 1926-28. V. Food and growth of Jasper Park fishes. Contr. Canad. Biol. Fish. Vol. 4:199-217.

Neff, Nancy A. 1975. Fishes of the Kanoplis local fauna (Pleistocene) of Ellsworth County, Kansas. pp. 39-48. **IN:** Smith, G. R., and N. E. Friedland. (editors). Studies on Cenozoic paleontology and stratigraphy in honour of Claude W. Hibbard. Papers on Paleontology, (Claude W. Hibbard memorial Vol. 3).Mus. Paleontol. Univ. Mich. 12:1-143.

Negus, M. T., and J. M. Aho, C. S. Anderson. 1987. Influence of acclimation temperature and developmental stage on behavioural responses of lake chubsuckers to temperature gradients. Am. Fish Soc. Symp. No. 2:157-163.

Nei Menggu Zizhi Qu Dizhi Ju, and Dongbei Dizhi Kexue Yanjiusuo. [Geological Bureau of the Inner Mongolia Autonomous Zone and the Northwest Institute of Geological Science.]. 1976. Hua bei diqu gushengwu tuce: Nei Menggu fence. [Fossils of Inner Mongolia.][Geological picture of the Northern China Area:Inner Mongolia Border.] Volume 2. [Mesozoic & Neozoic]. Dizhi Chuban She [Geological Publishing Co.], Peking. 261pp.

Neilands, J. B. 1947. Thiaminase in aquatic animals of Nova Scotia. Journal of the Biological Board of Canada. Vol. 7(2):94-99.

Nelson, Edward M. 1948. The comparative morphology of the Weberian apparatus of the Catostomidae and its significance in systematics. J. Morph. Philad. Vol. 83(2):225-252.

Nelson, Edward M. 1949. The opercular series of the Catostomidae. J. Morph., Philadelphia. Vol. 85(3):559-567.

Nelson, Edward M. 1955. The 2-3 intervertebral joint in the fish genus *Catostomus*. Copeia 1955(2):151-152.

Nelson, Edward M. 1959. The embryology of the swim bladder in the common sucker *Catostomus commersoni* (La Cepède). Amer. midl. Nat. Vol. 61:245-252.

Nelson, Edward M. 1961. The comparative morphology of the definitive swim bladder in the Catostomidae. Amer. midl. Nat. Vol. 65:101-110.

Nelson, Edward M. 1976. Some notes on the Chinese sucker *Myxocyprinus*. Copeia. 1976(3):594-595.

Nelson, E. W. 1876. A partial catalogue of the fishes of Illinois. Illinois Museum of Natural History Bulletin. Vol. 1(1):33-52.

Nelson, E. W. 1878. Chapter II.-Fisheries of Chicago and Vicinity. pp. 783-800. **IN:** Part IV. Report of the Commissioner for 1875-1876. United States Commission of Fish and Fisheries. Washington, D.C.

Nelson, Joseph S. 1965. Effects of fish introductions and hydroelectric development on fishes in the Kananaskis River System, Alberta. Journal of the Fisheries Research Board of Canada. Vol. 22(3):721-753.

Nelson, Joseph S. 1966. Hybridization and isolating mechanisms in *Catostomus commersonii* and *Catostomus macrocheilus* (Pisces:Catosomidae). Diss. Abstr. 27B:1331.

Nelson, Joseph S. 1968. Hybridization and isolating mechanisms between *Catostomus commersonii* and *C. macrocheilus* (Pisces:Catostomidae). Journal of the Fisheries Research Board of Canada. Vol. 25(1):101-150.

Nelson, Joseph S. 1973. Occurrence of hybrids between longnose sucker (*Catostomus catostomus*) and white sucker (*C. commersoni*) in upper Kananaskis Reservoir, Alberta. Journal of the Fisheries Research Board of Canada. Vol. 30(4):557-560.

Nelson, Joseph S. 1974. Hybridization between *Catosomus commersoni* (white sucker) and *Catostomus macrocheilus* (largescale sucker) in Williston Reservoir, British Columbia, with notes on other fishes. Syesis. Vol. 7:187-194.

Nelson, Joseph S. 1976. Fishes of the World. John Wiley & Sons. New York. 416pp.

Nelson, Joseph S. 1977. The Postglacial Invasion of Fishes into Alberta. Alberta Naturalist. Vol. 7(2):129-135.

Nelson, Joseph S. 1984. Fishes of the World. 2nd edition. John Wiley & Sons. New York. 523pp.

Nelson, W. R. 1961a. Report of fisheries investigations during the sixth year of impoundment of Gavins Point Reservoir, South Dakota, 1960. S.D. Dingell-Johnson Proj., F-1-R-10 (Jobs 2-4):59pp.

Nelson, W. R. 1961b. Report of fisheries investigations during the eighth year of impoundment of Fort Randall Reservoir, South Dakota, 1960. S.D. Dept. Game Fish Parks. 30pp. mimeo.

Nelson, W. R. 1962. Report of fisheries investigations during the seventh year of impoundment of Gavins Point Reservoir, South Dakota, 1961. S.D. Dingell-Johnson Proj., F-1-R-11 (Jobs 1-3,7):40pp.

Nelson, W. R. 1980. Ecology of larval fishes in Lake Oahe, South Dakota. Technical Pap. U. S. Fish. Wildl. Serv. No. 101:1-18.

Nester, R. T., and T. P. Poe. 1984. Predation on lake whitefish eggs by longnose suckers. Journal Gt. Lakes Res. Vol. 10(3):327-328.

Newton, S. H., and C. J. Haskins, J. M. Martin. 1981. Polyculture of buffalo hybrids with channel catfish. Proceedings a. Conf. SEast. Ass. Game Fish Wildl. Agencies. Vol. 35: 562-565.

Ney, J. J., and J. H. van Hassel. 1983. Sources of variability in accumulation of heavy metals by fishes in a roadside stream. Archives envir. Contam. Toxicol. Vol. 12(3):701-706.

Nichols, John Treadwell. 1911. Notes on Teleostean fishes from the Eastern United States. New York, N. Y. Bull. Amer. Mus. Nat. Hist. Vol. 30:275-278.

Nichols, John Treadwell. 1925. Some Chinese fresh-water fishes. I. Loaches of the genus *Botia* in the Yangtze Basin. II. A new Minnow-like Carp from Szechwan. III. The Chinese Sucker, *Myxocyprinus*. Amer. Mus. Novit. New York. Vol. 177:1-9.

Nichols, John Treadwell. 1928. Chinese freshwater fishes in the American Musueum of Natural History's Collections. Bul. Amer. Mus. Nat. Hist. N. Y. Vol. 58(1928):1-62.

Nichols, John Treadwell. 1930. Speculation on the history of the Ostariophysi. Copeia 1930 (4):148-151.

Nichols, John Treadwell. 1943. The Fresh-Water Fishes of China. Natural History of Central Asia. Volume 9. American Museum of Natural History. New York, New York. 322pp.

Nichols, John Treadwell, and William K. Gregory. 1918. Fishes of the Vicinity of New York City. American Museum of Natural History. Handbook Series No. 7. New York. 122pp.

Nickol, B. b., and N. Samuel. 1983. Geographical distribution of Acanthocephala in Nebraska fishes. Trans. Nebr. Acad. Sci. Vol. 11:31-52.

Niculescu-Duvaz, M., and R. Giurca, V. Popovici. 1979. Data concerning the reproduction and breeding of the species *Ictiobus cyprinellus*, *Ictiobus bubalus* and *Ictiobus niger* (Catostomidae) newly brought into the waters of our country. Buletinul Cerc. pisc. (N.S.) Vol. 32(1-2):56-67.

Nigrelli, R. F. 1948. Prickle cell hypoplasia in the snout of the Redhorse Sucker (*Moxostoma aureolum*) associated with an infection by the myxosporidian *Myxobolus moxostomi sp. nov.* Zoologica, New York. Vol. 33:43-46.

Niimi, A. J. 1975. Relationship of body surface area to weight in fishes. Canadian Journal of Zoology. Vol. 53(8):1192-1194.

Niimi, A. J. 1983. Biological and toxicological effects of environmental contaminants in fish and their eggs. Canadian J. Fish. aquat. Sci. Vol. 40(3):306-312.

Nikolsky, G. V. 1961. [Special Ichthyology.] 2nd ed. (In Russian; English translation by Israel Program for Sci. Translations, Jerusalem, 1961.) 538pp.

Nikonova, R. S., and T. V. Solomatina. 1981. [An experiment in rearing the big mouth buffalo in conditions of the Volga Delta] Rybnoe Khoz., Mosk. 1981(12):26-28.

Noland, W. E. 1951. The hydrography, fish, and turtle populations of Lake Wingra. Trans. Wis. Acad. Sci., Arts, Lett. Vol. 40(2):5-58.

Nord, R. C. 1967. A compendium of fishery information on the upper Mississippi River. Upper Misc. R. Conserv. Com. 238pp.

Northcote, T. G., and G. F. Hartman. 1959. A case of "schooling" behavior in the prickly sculpin, *Cottus asper* Richardson. Copeia 1959(2):156-158.

Novacek, Michael J., and Larry G. Marshall. 1976. Early Biogeographic History of Ostariophysan Fishes. Copeia 1976(1):1-12.

Novikov, A. S., and E. A. Streletskaya. 1966. On the biology of *Catostomus catostomus rostratus* (Tilesius). Byull. mosk. Obshch. Ispyt. Prir. Vol. 71(1):133-136.

Novokshonov, Yu. D. 1981. Winter-hardiness of large-mouth buffalo in water bodies of (Suskan) Fish Farm. Sbornik nauch. Trud. gos. nauchno-issled. Inst. ozern. rechn. rybn. Khozyaist No. 170:58-63.

Novokshonov, Yu. D., and Yu. N. Dyakonov. 1980. [Daily dynamics of feeding in fingerlings of *Saccopharynx* and carp.] Rybokhozyaistvennoe Izuch. vnutr. Vod. Vol. 25:42-50.

Nurnberger, P. K. 1928. A list of the plant and animal food of some fishes of Jay Cooke Park. Transactions of the American Fisheries Society. Vol. 58:175-177.

Nurnberger, P. K. 1930. The plant and animal food of the fishes of Big Sandy Lake. Transactions of the American Fisheries Society. Vol. 60:253-259.

Nursall, J. R. 1963. The hypurapophysis, an important element of the caudal skeleton. Copeia 1963(2):458-459.

Obraztsov, A. N., and O. B. Semenova. 1982. Sperm characteristics in males of redside sucker. Sbornik nauch. Trud. gos. nauchno-issled. Inst. ozern. rechn. rybn. Khozyaist. No. 178:134-137.

Obruchev, D. V. (ed.) 1967. Volume 11. Agnatha, Pisces. **IN:** Yu. A. Orlov, et al. (ed.) Fundamentals of Paleontology. (Osnovy paleontologii). Izdatel 'stvo "Nauka" Moskva 1964. Translated from Russian. Israel Program for Scientific Translations. Jerusalem, Israel. 825pp.

O'Donnell, D. J. 1935. Annotated list of the fishes of Illinois. Illinois Natural History Survey Bulletin. Vol. 20(5):473-500.

Odum, Howard T., and David K. Caldwell. 1955. Fish respiration in the natural oxygen gradient of an anaerobic spring in Florida. Copeia 1955(2):104-106.

Okawara, Y., and S. D. Morley, L. O. Burzio, H. Zwiers, K. Lederis, D. Richter. 1988. Cloning and sequence analysis of CDNA for corticotropin-releasing factor precursor from the teleost fish *Catostomus commersoni*. Proc. Natl. Acad. Sci. Vol. 85(22):8439-8443.

Olson, D. E., and W. J. Scidmore. 1963. Homing tendency of spawning white suckers in Many Point Lake, Minnesota. Transactions of the American Fisheries Society. Vol. 92:13-16.

Ommanney, Francis Downes. 1969. The Fishes. Life Nature Library. Time-Life Books. New York, N. Y. 192pp.

Ono, R. Dana, and James D. Williams, Anne Wagner. 1983. Vanishing Fishes of North America. Stone Wall Press, Inc. Washington, D. C. 257pp.

Opinion 1582. *Ictiobus* Rafinesque, 1820 (Osteicthyes, Cypriniformes): conserved. Bull. Zool. Nomencl. Vol. 47(1):77-78.

Orr, O. E. 1958. The populations of fishes and limnological conditions of Heyburn Reservoir with reference to productivity. Ph.D. Thesis. Oklahoma State Univ. 68pp.

Orr, William N., and Elizabeth L. Orr. 1981. Handbook of Oregon Plant and Animal Fossils. Pan Typesetters, Eugene, Oregon. 285pp.

Osborn, H. F., and W. B. Scott, Francis Speir, Jr. 1878. Palæontological report of the Princeton scientific expedition of 1877. Contrib. Mus. Geol. and Arch., Princeton College. no. 1:1-107, followed by systematic catalogue of the Eocene vertebrates of Wyoming, pp. 131-146.

Osburn, Raymond Carroll. 1901. The fishes of Ohio; an authenticated list, with especial reference to occurrence and distribution. Ohio State Acad. Sci. Special Papers, No. 4:1-105.

Oseid, D. M. 1977. Control of fungus growth on fish eggs by *Asellus militaris* and *Gammarus pseudolimnaeus*. Transactions of the American Fisheries Society. Vol. 106(2):192-195.

Ostland, v. E., and B. D. Hicks, J. G. Daly. 1987. Furunculosis in faitfish and its transmission to salmonids. Dis. Aquat. Org. (2):163-166.

Ostrow, M. E. 1979. Aquatic sowbugs protect fish eggs from fungal attack. Tropical Fish Hobby. Vol. 27(12):87-95.

Otnes, M. A. 1973. Discovery of the northern hog sucker in the Ottertail River. Journal Minn. Acad. Sci. Vol. 39:8-9.

Ovchynnyk, M. M. 1965. On age determination with scales and bones of the white sucker, *Catostomus commersoni* (La Cepède). Zool. Anz. Vol. 175:325-345.

Paetz, Martin J., and Joseph S. Nelson. 1970. The fishes of Alberta. The Queen's Printer, Edmonton, Alberta. 282pp.

Page, Lawrence M. 1982. Blacknose and Pugnose Shiners in Hickory Creek, Will and Cook Counties, Illinois. Report to Illinois Department of Transportation, Springfield. September 15, 1982. 8pp. typewritten.

Page, L. M., and C. E. Johnston. 1990. Spawning in the creek chubsucker, *Erimyzon oblongus*, with a review of spawning behavior in suckers (Catostomidae). Environ. Biol. Fishes. Vol. 27(4):265-272.

Pallai, Peter V., and Massimo Mabilia, Murray Goodman, Wylie Vale, Jean Rivier. 1983. Structural homology of corticotropin-releasing factor, sauvagine, and urotensin 1: circular dichroism and prediction studies. Proceedings natn. Acad. Sci. USA (biol. Sci.) Vol. 80 (22):6770-6774.

Palmieri, J., and R. Heckmann. 1976. Potential biological control of diplostomatosis (*Diplostomum spathaceum*) in fishes by hyperparasitism. Proceedings Utah Acad. Sci. Arts Letters Vol. 53(1):17-19.

Paragamian, V. L. 1976. Vulnerability of three species of forage fish to predation by smallmouth bass in a hatchery trough. Progressive Fish-Culturist. Vol. 38(2):86-87.

Parker, B., and P. McKee. 1984a. Status of the spotted sucker, *Minytrema melanops*, in Canada. Can. Field Natur. Vol. 98(1):104-109.

Parker, B., and P. McKee. 1984b. Status of the river redhorse, *Moxostoma carinatum*, in Canada. Can. Field Natur. Vol. 98(1):110-114.

Parker, B. J. 1988. Updated status of the river redhorse, *Moxostoma carinatum*, in Canada. Can. Field-Nat. Vol. 102(1):140-146.

Parker, R. A. 1958. Some effects of thinning on a population of fishes. Ecology Vol. 39(2):304-317.

Patriarche, M. H. 1953. The fishery in Lake Wappapello, a flood-control reservoir on the St. Francis River, Missouri. Transactions of the American Fisheries Society. Vol. 82:242-254.

Patriarche, M. H., and R. S. Campbell. 1958. The development of the fish population in a new flood-control reservoir in Missouri, 1948-1954. Transactions of the American Fisheries Society. Vol. 87:240-258.

Patrick, R., and J. Cairns, S. S. Roback. 1966. An ecosystematic study of the fauna and flora of the Savannah River. Proc. Acad. nat. Sci. Philad. Vol. 118:109-407.

Patten, Benjamin G. 1960. A high incidence of the hybrid *Acrocheilus alutaceum* **X** *Ptychocheilus oregonense*. Copeia. 1960(1):71-73.

Pearson, William D., and Louis A. Krumholz 1984. Distribution and Status of Ohio River Fishes. National Technical Information Service. U.S. Department of Commerce. DE 84 007922 400pp.

Penhallow, D. P. 1908. Report on Tertiary Plants of British Columbia collected by Lawrence M. Lambe in 1906, together with a discussion of previously recorded Tertiary floras. Geol. Surv. Can., Ottawa.167pp.

Perry, W. G. 1976. Black and bigmouth buffalo spawn in brackish water ponds. Progressive Fish-Culturist Vol. 38(2):81.

Perry, W. G., Jr., and J. W. Avault, Jr. 1976. Polyculture studies with channel catfish and buffalo.Proceedings a. Conf. SEast. Ass. Game Fish Commis. Vol 29. 1975(1976):91-98.

Personius, Robert Giles, and Samuel Eddy. 1955. Fishes of the Little Missouri River. Copeia 1955(1):41-43.

Peters, J. C. (ed.) 1964. Summary of calculated growth data on Montana fishes, 1948-1961. Montana Fish and Game Dept. Fisheries Division. D.-J. Job Completion Rep., F-23-R-6 (Jobs I-II):76pp. mimeo.

Peterson, E. J., and E. W. Steucke, Jr., W. H. Lynch. 1966. Disease treatment at Gavins Point Aquarium. The Dorsal Fin. Vol. 6(1):18-19.

Peterson, P. H., and d. J. Martin-Robichaud. 1986. Perivitelline and vitelline potentials in teleost eggs as influenced by ambient ionic strength, natal salinity, and electrode electrolyte; and the influence of these potentials on cadium dynamics within the egg. Canadian J. Fish. Aquat. Sci. Vol. 43(7):1445-1450.

Pfeiffer, Roman A. 1955. Studies on the life history of the rosyface shiner, Notropis rubellus. Copeia 1955(2):95-104.

Pfeiffer, W. 1963. Vergleichende Untersuchungen über die Schreckreaktion und den Schreckstoff der Ostariophysen. Z. vergl. Physiol. Vol. 47:111-147.

Pflieger, William L. 1971. A Distributional Study of Missouri Fishes. University of Kansas Publications Museum of Natural History Vol. 20(3):225-570.

Pflieger, William L. 1975. The Fishes of Missouri. Missouri Department of Conservation. Western Publishing Co. 343pp.

Phillips, G. L. 1971. Distribution and variation of the Catostomidae of Minnesota. Occassional Pap. Bell. Mus. nat Hist. Univ. Minn. No. 10:1-45.

Phillips, Gary L., and William D. Schmid, James C. Underhill. 1982. Fishes of the Minnesota Region. University of Minnesota Press. Minneapolis, Minnesota. 248pp.

Phillips, Gary L., and James C. Underhill. 1971. Distribution and variation of the Catostomidae of Minnesota. Occas. Pap. Bell Mus. Nat. Hist. Univ. Minn. No. 10. 45pp.

Phillips, R. J., and Henry Weed Fowler. 1913. Fishes in the water-supply of Wilmington, Delaware. Copeia 1913 (No. 1):3-4.

Pickens, A. L. 1928. Fishes of upper South Carolina. Copeia 1928 (No. 167):29-32.

Pigg, J. 1982. Noteworthy distribution and habitat records for four Oklahoma fishes. Proceedings Okla. Acad. Sci. Vol. 62:93-94.

Pigg, J. 1987. Survey of fishes in the Oklahoma Panhandle and Harper county, northwestern Oklahoma. Proc. Okla. Acad. Sci. Vol. 67:45-59.

Pippy, J. H. C. 1970. Fish mortalities in the Northwest Miramichi River in 1969. Technical Reports of the Fisheries Research Board of Canada. No. 226:7 pp.

Pippy, J. H. C., and G. M. Hare. 1969. Relationship of river pollution to bacterial infection in salmon (*Salmo salar*) and suckers (*Catostomus commersoni*). Transactions of the American Fisheries Society. Vol. 98:685-690.

Pister, Edwin P. 1981. Chapter 13. The Conservation of Desert Fishes. pp. 411-446. **IN:** Robert J. Naiman and David L. Soltz (eds.)   Fishes in North American Deserts. John Wiley & Sons. New York, N.Y. 552pp.

Platt, D. R., and Frank B. Cross, D. Distler, O. S. Fent, E. R. Hall, M. Terman, J. Zimmerman, J. Walstrom. 1973. Rare, endangered and extirpated species in Kansas. Trans. Kans. Acad. Sci. Vol. 76(2):97-105.

Platts, W. S., and F. E. Partridge. 1983. Inventory of salmon, steelhead trout, and bull trout: South Fork Salmon River, Idaho. United States Dep. Agric. For. Serv. Res. Note INT No. 324:1-9.

Polovova, T. P. 1970. Primary informations on feeding some fishes in the middle current of Kolima basin. Izv. tikhookean. nauchno-issled. Inst. ryÔb. Khoz. Okeanogr. Vol. 71:249-257. [In Russian].

Porter, T. R., and D. M. Rosenberg, D. K. McGowan. 1974. Winter studies of the effects of a highway crossing on the fish and benthos of the Martin River, N.W.T. Technical Rep. Ser. Resour. Mgmt. Brch. Fish. mar. Serv. Can. 1974(3):1-50.

Pot, W., and D. L. G. Noakes, M. M. Ferguson, G. Coker. 1984. Quantitative sampling of fishes in a simple system: Failure of conventional methods. Hydrobiologia. Vol. 114(3):249-254.

Potter, Wayne A., and Robert W. Malick, Jr., Janet L. Polk. 1976. The Composition and Distribution of Fishes of the Swatara Creek Drainage, Pennsylvania. Proceedings of the Pennsylvania Academy of Science. Vol. 50:136-140.

Powers, D. A. 1972. Hemoglobin adaptation for fast and slow water habitats in sympatric catostomid fishes. Science, N.Y. Vol. 177(4046):360-362.

Powers, D. A., and A. B. Edmundson. 1972. Multiple hemoglobins of catostomid fish. 1. Isolation and characterization of the isohemoglobins from *Catostomus clarkii*. Journal Biol. Chem. Vol. 247(20):(1972):6686-6693.

Powers, D. A., and A. B. Edmundson. 1973. Multiple hemoglobins of catostomid fish. 2. The amino acid sequence of the major **a** chain from *Catostomus clarkii* hemoglobins. Journal Biol. Chem. Vol. 247(20):6694-6707.

Priegel, G. R. 1967. A list of the fishes of Lake Winnebago. Wis. Conserv. Dep. Res. Rep. No. 27:6pp.

Priegel, G. R. 1976. Age and growth of the white sucker in Lake Winnebago. Transactions Wis. Acad. Sci. Arts Lett. Vol. 64:132-143.

Prieto, A., and M. Vinjoy, E. Fajer. 1988. Enfermedades parasitarias de carpas chinas (Cyprinidae) y peces bufalo (Catostomidae) durante su aclimatacion en Cuba. Rev. Salud. Anim. Vol. 10(1):20-26.

Principe, P. A. 1977. A late Pliocene (Ringold Formation) fish fauna from South-central Washington and its distributional significance to the Columbia-Snake drainage system. Master's thesis. Univ. of Massachusetts, Amherst, Mass. 97 pp.

Proffitt, M. A., and R. S. Benda. 1971. Growth and movement of fishes, and distribution of invertebrates, related to a heated discharge into the White River at Petersburg, Indiana. Indiana Univ. Water Resour. Invest. Rep. 5:94 pp.

Propst, David L., and Clarence A. Carlson. 1986. The distribution and status of warmwater fishes in the Platte River drainage, Colorado. Southwest. Nat. Vol. 31(2):149-168.

Pugachev, O. N. 1980. Parasite fauna of the sucker (*Catostomus catostomus*) from the Kolyma River. Parazitologiya. Vol. 14(6):511-513.

Purkett, C. A., Jr. 1958. Growth of the fishes in the Salt River, Missouri. Transactions of the American Fisheries Society. Vol. 87:116-131.

Purkett, C. A., Jr. 1958. Growth rates of Missouri stream fishes. Missouri Cons. Comm.,, Fish and Game Div., D-J Ser. Vol. 1:1-46.

Pyefinch, K. A. 1964. Salmon and freshwater fisheries research. Fish. Scot. Rep., 1964. 25p. extract.

Quanwei, Xiong, and Xia Shenglin. 1985. A study of isozymes in *Myxocyprinus asiaticus* (Bleeker). Acta Zool. Sinica. Vol. 31(1):20-27.

Quinn, Stephen P., and Michael R. Ross. 1985. Non-annual spawning in the white sucker, *Catostomus commersoni*. Copeia 1985(3):613-618.

Quinn, T. P., and R. F. Tallman. 1987. Seasonal environmental predictability and homing in riverine fishes. Environmental Biol. Fishes. Vol. 18(2):155-159.

Rabb, L., and L. A. McDermott. 1962. Bacteriological studies of freshwater fish. II. Furunculosis in Ontario fish in natural waters. Journal of the Fisheries Research Board of Canada. Vol 19(6):989-995.

Rabeni, C. F., and J. G. Stanley. 1979. Operational spraying of acephate to suppress spruce budworm has minor effects on stream fishes and invertebrates. Bulletin envir. Contam. Toxicol. Vol. 23(3):327-334.

Raciunas, L. 1985a. The effect of flibol preparation on vitality and structure of zooplankton. Acta hydrobiol. lituan. Vol. 5:15-20.

Raciunas, L. 1985b. Nature of feeding and the results of rearing of two-year-old bighead and silver carp hybrids and big-mouthed buffaloes in a fertilized pond. Acta hydrobiol. lituan. Vol. 5:74-79.

Rafinesque, Constantine Samuel. 1818a. Description of three genera of fluviatile fish, *Pomoxis*, *Sarchirus*, and *Exoglossum*. Academy of Natural Sciences of Philadelphia Journal 1:417-422.

Rafinesque, Constantine Samuel. 1818b. Discoveries in natural history, made during a Journey through the Western Region of the United States, by Constantine Samuel Rafinesque, Esq. Addressed to Samuel L. Mitchill, President and the other Members of the Lyceum of Natural History, in a letter dated at Louisville, Falls of Ohio, 20th July, 1818. The American Monthly Magazine and Critical Review. Vol. 3(5):354-356.

Rafinesque, Constantine Samuel. 1819. Prodrome De 70 nouveaux Generes d'Animaux découverts dans l'inté_rieur des États-Unis d'Amérique, durant l'année 1818. Journal de Physique, de Chimie, d'Histoire naturelle et des Arts, Vol. 88:417-429.

Rafinesque, Constantine Samuel. 1820a. Fishes of the River Ohio. Western Rev. and Misc. Mag. Vol. 2:48-57, 169-177, 235-242, 299-307.

Rafinesque, Constantine Samuel. 1820b. Ichthyologia Ohiensis or Natural History of the Fishes Inhabiting the River Ohio and its Tributary Streams. W. G. Hunt Publisher. Lexington, Kentucky. 90pp.

Rahel, F. J. 1986. Biogeographic influences on fish species composition of northern Wisconsin lakes with applications for lake acidification studies. Can. J. Fisheries Aquat. Sci. Vol. 43(1):124-134.

Ramamoorthy, S., and J. W. Moore, L. George. 1985. Partitioning of mercury in the North Saskatchewan River (Canada). Chemosphere. Vol. 14(10):1455-1468.

Ramaswami, L. S. 1955a. Skeleton of cyprinid fishes in relation to phylogenetic studies. 6. The skull and Weberian apparatus in the subfamily Gobioninae (Cyprinidae). Acta Zoologica. Vol. 36:127-158.

Ramaswami, L. S. 1955b. Skeleton of cyprinoid fishes in relation to phylogenetic studies. 7. The skull and Weberian apparatus of Cyprininae. (Cyprinidae). Acta Zoologica. Vol. 36:199-242.

Ramaswami, L. S. 1957. Skeleton of cyprinoid fishes in relation to phylogenetic studies. 8. The skull and weberian ossicles of catostomidae. Proc. Zool. Soc. (Calcutta) Mookerjee Mem. 1957:293-303.

Raney, Edward C. 1939. The breeding habits of *Ichthyomyzon greeleyi* Hubbs and Trautman. Copeia 1939(2):111-112.

Raney, Edward C. 1940. *Rhinichthys bowersi* from West Virginia a hybrid, *Rhinichthys cataractae* **X** *Nocomis micropogon*. Copeia 1940(4):270-271.

Raney, Edward C. 1943. Unusual spawning habitat for the common white sucker *Catostomus c. commersonii*. Copeia, Ann Arbor. 1943:256.

Raney, Edward C. 1952. A new lamprey, *Ichthyomyzon hubbsi*, from the upper Tennesee River system. Copeia 1952(2):93-99.

Raney, Edward C., and Ernest A. Lachner. 1939. Observations on the life history of the spotted darter, *Poecilichthys maculatus* (Kirtland). Copeia 1939 (3):157-165.

Raney, Edward C., and Ernest A. Lachner. 1946a. *Thoburnia hamiltoni*, a new sucker from the Upper Roanoke river system in Virginia. Copeia, Ann Arbor. 1946 (4):218-226.

Raney, Edward C., and Ernest A. Lachner. 1946b. Age, growth and habits of the hog sucker, *Hypentelium nigricans* (Le Sueur), in New York. Amer. Midl. Nat., Notre Dame. Vol. 36(1):76-86.

Raney, Edward C., and Ernest A. Lachner. 1946c. Age and growth of the rustyside sucker, *Thoburnia rhothoeca* (Thoburn). Amer. Midl. Nat., Notre Dame. Vol. 36(3):675-681.

Raney, Edward C., and Ernest A. Lachner. 1947. *Hypentelium roanokense*, a new Catostomid fish from the Roanoke river in Virginia. Amer. Mus. Nov. No. 1333:1-15.

Raney, Edward C., and Robert M. Roecker. 1947. Food and growth of two species of watersnakes from western New York. Copeia 1947(3):171-174.

Raney, Edward C., and D. A. Webster. 1942. The spring migration of the common white sucker, *Catostomus c. commersonnii* (La Cepède), in Skaneateles Lake Inlet, New York. Copeia, Ann Arbor. 1942 (3):139-148.

Rankin, Edward T. 1986. Habitat selection by smallmouth bass (*Micropterus dolomieui*) in response to physical characteristics in a natural stream. Transactions of the American Fisheries Society. Vol. 115(2):322-334.

Rasmussen, J. L., editor. 1979. A compendium of fishery information on the upper Mississippi River. 2nd ed. Proc. 35th Annu. Meet. Upper Miss. R. Conserv. Com. Spec. Publ. 259pp.

Rauther, M. 1913. Fische. Pisces. Handwöterbuch der Naturwissenschaften (Gustav Fischer, Jena). Vol. 3:1055-1107.

Rawson, D. S. 1951. Studies of the fish of Great Slave Lake. Journal of the Fisheries Research Board of Canada. Vol. 8(4):207-240.

Rawson, D. S. 1957. Limnology and fisheries of five lakes in the Upper Churchill drainage, Saskatchewan. Sask. Dept. Nat. Res. Fish. Rep. 3:61pp.

Rawson, D. S. 1960. Five lakes on the Churchill River near Stanley, Saskatchewan. Sask. Dept. Nat. Res. Fish. Rep. Vol. 5:1-38pp.

Rawson, D. S., and C. A. Elsey. 1950. Reduction in the longnose sucker population of Pyramid Lake, Alberta, in an attempt to improve angling. Transactions of the American Fisheries Society. Vol. 78(1948):13-31.

Reece, M. 1963. Fish and fishing. Meredith Press, N. Y. 224pp.

Reed, E. B. 1962. Limnology and fisheries of the Saskatchewan River in Saskatchewan. Saskatchewan Dept. Nat. Res. Fish. Rep. 6. 48pp.

Reed, Roger J. 1957. The prolonged spawning of the rosyface shiner, *Notropis rubellus* (Agassiz), in northwestern Pennsylvania. Copeia 1957(3):250.

Reed, Roger J. 1959. Age, growth and food of the longnose dace, *Rhinichthys cataractae*. Copeia 1959(2):160-162.

Regan, Charles Tate. 1907. Pisces. Biol. Centr. Amer., London:33-168.

Regan, Charles Tate. 1911. The classification of the teleostean fishes of the order Ostariophysi. I. Cyprinoidea. Ann. Mag. Nat. Hist. Vol. 8(8):13-32.

Regan, Charles Tate. 1922. The distribution of the fishes of the order Ostariophysi. Bijdr. Dierk. Amsterdam. Vol. 22(Feestnum. Max Weber):203-208.

Rehnberg, B. G., and C. B. Schreck. 1987. Chemosensory detection of predators by coho salmon (*Oncorhynchus kisutch*): behavioral reaction and the physiological stress response. Canadian Journal of Zoology. Vol. 65(3):481-485.

Reickhow, K. H., and R. W. Black, T. B. Stockton, Jr., J. D. Vogt, J. G. Wood. 1987. Empirical models of fish response to lake acidification. Can. J. Fish Aquat. Sci. Vol. 44(8):1432-1442.

Reid, George K., Jr. 1950. Notes on the Centrarchid fish *Mesogonistius chaetodon elizabethae* in Peninsular Florida. Copeia 1950 (3):239-240.

Reighard, Jacob E. 1915. An ecological reconnaissance of the fishes of Douglas Lake, Cheboygan County, Michigan, in midsummer. Bull. U.S. Comm. Fish. Vol. 33:215-249.

Reighard, Jacob E. 1920. The breeding behavior of the Suckers and Minnows. I. The Suckers. Biol. Bull. Wood's Hole Mass. Vol. 38:1-37.

Reigle, N. J., Jr. 1969a. Bottom trawl explorations in Green Bay of Lake Michigan, 1963-1965. U. S. Fish Wildl. Serv. Bur. Commer. Fish. Circ. 297. 14pp.

Reigle, N. J., Jr. 1969b. Bottom trawl explorations in northern Lake Michigan, 1963-1965. U.S. Fish Wildl. Serv. Bur. Commer. Fish. Circ. 301. 35pp.

Reinking, L. N. 1983. Aldosterdone response to renin, angiotensin, ACTH, hemorrhage and sodium depletion in a freshwater teleost, *Catostomus macrocheilus*. Comparative Biochem. Physiol. (A). Vol. 74(4):873-880.

Rendahl, H. 1932. Die Fischfauna der Chinesischen Provinz Szetschwan. Ark. Zool. Stockholm. Vol. 24A(16):1-134.

Reynolds, W. W., and M. E. Casterlin. 1978. Behavioural thermoregulation and diel activity in white sucker (*Catostomus commersoni*). Comparative Biochem. Physiol. (A). Vol. 59(3):261-262.

Ribble, D. O., and M. H. Smith. 1983. Relative intestine length and feeding ecology of freshwater fishes. Growth. Vol. 47(3):292-300.

Richardson, John R. 1823. Account of some fishes observed during Captain Franklin's and Dr. Richardson's journey to the Polar Sea. Mem. Wern. Nat. Hist. Soc. Edinburgh, 1823-24. Vol. 5:509-522.

Richardson, John R. 1836. Fauna Boreali-Americana: or the zoology of the northern parts of British America, containing descriptions of the objects of natural history collected on the late northern land expeditions under the command of Sir John Franklin, R. N. Pt. 3, The Fish. Richard Bentley. London. 327pp.

Richardson, Laurence R. 1938. A note on variation in squamation of the cheek operculum in two Etheostomid fishes from Québec. Copeia 1938 (3):126-128.

Richardson, Laurence R. 1942. The occurrence of nuptial tubercles on the female of *Osmerus mordax* (Mitchill). Copeia 1942 (1):27-29.

Richardson, Laurence R. 1944. Brief record of fishes from central northern Québec. Copeia 1944 (4):205-208.

Richardson, R. E. 1913. Observations on the breeding habits at Havana, Illinois, 1910 and 1911. Bull. Ill. St. Lab. Nat. Hist. Vol. 9:405-416.

Ricker, W. E. 1945. Abundance, exploitation and mortality of the fishes in two lakes. Invest. Ind. Lakes Streams. Vol. 2(17):345-448.

Ricker, W. E. 1962. Productive capacity of Canadian fisheries. Circulars [General Series] of the Biological Station, Nanaimo, B. C. of the FRB of Canada. No. 64:79pp.

Riggs, C. D., and G. A. Moore. 1963. A new record of *Moxostoma macrolepidotum pisolabrum*, and a range extension for *Percina shumardi*, in the Red River, Oklahoma and Texas. Copeia 1963(2):451-452.

Riley, D. M. 1978. Parasites of grass carp and native fishes in Florida. Transactions Am. Fish. Soc. Vol. 107(1):207-212.

Rimsky-Korsakoff, V. N. 1930. The food of certain fishes of the Lake Champlain watershed. pp. 88-104. **IN:** A biological survey of the Champlain watershed. Suppl. 19th Annu. Rep. (1929). N. Y. State Conserv. Dep.

Rinne, J. N. 1985a. Livestock grazing effects on southwestern streams: a complex research problem. U. S. For. Serv. Gen. Tech. Rep. R. M. No. 120:295-299.

Rinne, J. N. 1985b. Physical habitat evaluation of small stream fishes: point vs. transect, observation vs. capture methodologies. Journal freshwat. Ecol. Vol. 3(1):121-131.

Rinne, J. N. 1988. Grazing effects on stream habitat and fishes: research design considerations. N. Am. J. Fish Manage. Vol. 8(2):240-247.

Ritson, Philip C., and Janet L. Polk, Robert W. Malick, Jr. 1977. Fishes of the Conewago Creek Drainage, York and Adams Counties, Pennsylvania. Proceedings of the Pennsylvania Academy of Science. Vol. 51:59-66.

Roach, L. S. 1948a. Common sucker. Ohio Conserv. Bull. Vol. 12(5):13.

Roach, L. S. 1948b. Golden mullet. Ohio Conserv. Bull. Vol. 12(11):13.

Roberto, Julis, C. and K. Lederis. 1988. Relationship between urotensin II - and somatostatin - immunoreactive spinal cord neurons of *Catostomus commersoni* and *Oncorhynchus kisutch* (Teleostei). Cell Tissue Res. Vol. 254(3):539-542.

Roberts, J. R. 1967. The fecundity of the spotted sucker in Pine Creek, Center Hill Reservoir. J. Tenn. Acad. Sci. Vol. 42(1967):78[abstract].

Roberts, J. R., and A. S. W. De Frietas, M. A. J. Gidney. 1977. Influence of lipid pool size on bioaccumulation of the insecticide chlordane by northern redhorse suckers (*Moxostoma macrolepidotum*). Journal of the Fisheries Research Board of Canada. Vol. 34(1):89-97.

Roberts, Tyson R. 1973. Interrelationships of ostariophysans. pp. 373-395. **IN:** Greenwood, P. H., and R. S. Miles, Colin Patterson. (eds.) Interrelationships of Fishes. Supplement No. 1 to the Zoological Journal of the Linnean Society. Vol. 53. Academic Press, Inc. New York, New York. 536pp.

Roberts, Wayne Emerson. 1975. Food and Space Utilization by the Piscivorous Fishes of Cold Lake with Emphasis on Introduced Coho Salmon. M.Sc. Thesis. Department of Zoology. Edmonton, Alberta, Canada. 145pp.

Robins, C. Richard. 1961. Two new cottid fishes from the fresh waters of eastern United States. Copeia 1961(3):305-315.

Robins, C. Richard, and Reeve M. Bailey, Carl E. Bond, James R. Brooker, Ernest A. Lachner, Robert N. Lea, W. B. Scott. 1980. A List of Common and Scientific Names of Fishes from the United States and Canada. Fourth Edition. American Fisheries Society Special Publication No. 12. Bethesda, Maryland. 174pp.

Robins, C. Richards, and Edward C. Raney. 1956. Studies of the catostomid fishes of the genus *Moxostoma*, with descriptions of two new species. Mem. Cornell Univ. Agri. exp. Sta. No. 343:1-56.

Robins, C. Richards, and Edward C. Raney. 1957a. Distributional and nomenclatorial notes on the suckers of the genus *Moxostoma*. Copeia 1957(2):154-155.

Robins, C. Richards, and Edward C. Raney. 1957b. The systematic study of the suckers of the genus *Moxostoma* from Texas, New Mexico and Mexico. Tulane Stud. Zool. Vol. 5:291-318.

Robinson, Dorthea Trevino. 1959. The ichthyofauna of the lower Rio Grande, Texas and Mexico. Copeia 1959(3):253-256.

Robinson, G. L., and L. A. Jahn. 1980. Some observations of fish parasites in Pool 20, Mississippi River. Transactions Am. Microsco. Soc. 99(2):206-212.

Robinson, H. W., and T. M. Buchanan. 1988. Fishes of Arkansas. Univeristy of Arkansas Press. Fayetteville, Arkansas. 536 pp.

Rogers, I. H., and H. W. Mahood. 1982. Environmental monitoring of the Fraser River at Prince George. Chemical analysis of fish, sediment, municipal sewage and bleached kraft wastewater samples. Canadian tech. Rep. Fish. Aquatic. Sci. No. 1135:1-15.

Rogers, Wilmer A. 1967.Studies on Dactylogyrinae (Monogenea) with descriptions of 24 new species of *Dactylogyrus*, 5 new species of *Pellucidhaptor* and the proposal of *Aplodiscus* gen. n. J. Parasit. Vol. 53:501-524.

Rogers, Wilmer A. 1968. Eight new species of *Gyrodactylus* (Monogenea) from the southeastern U.S. with redescriptions of *G. fairporti* Van Cleave, 1921 and *G. cyprini* Diarova, 1964. Journal of Parasitology. Vol. 54(3):490-495.

Rogers, Wilmer A. 1969. Two new species of *Pseudomurraytrema* from gills of Alabama catostomid fishes. J. Parasit. Vol. 55:321-323.

Rogers, Wilmer A., and J. D. Mizelle. 1966. New species of Dactylogyrinae from Alabama fishes. J. Parasit. Vol. 52:707-712.

Roland, J. V., and K. B. Cumming. 1973. The effect of water quality alteration on the growth rate of white sucker. Proceedings a. Conf. S. East. Ass. Game Fish Commnrs. Vol. 23 1970:332-352.

Romer, Alfred Sherwood. 1966. Vertebrate Paleontology. 3rd edition. University of Chicago Press. Chicago. 468pp.

Roosa, D. M. 1977. Endangered and threatened fish of Iowa. Iowa State Preserves Advis. Board, Des Moines. Spec. Rep. No. 1. 25pp.

Rosenthal, H. L., and M. M. Eves, O. A. Cochran. 1970. Common strontium concentration of mineralized tissues from marine and sweet water animals. Comp. Biochem. Physiol. Vol. 32:445-450.

Rostlund, Erhard. 1951. Three early historical reports of North American freshwater fishes. Copeia 1951 (4):295-296.

Roth, R. R. 1972. Some factors contributing to the development of fungus infection in freshwater fish. Journal Wildl. Dis. Vol. 8(1):24-28.

Roussow, G. 1954. La ligulose des catostomes du lac Lauzon. Ann. ACFAS Vol. 20:85-90.

Ruggles, C. P., and W. D. Watt. 1975. Ecological changes due to hydroelectric development on the Saint John River. Journal of the Fisheries Research Board of Canada Vol. 32(1):161-170.

Rupprecht, R. J., and L. A. Jahn. 1980. Biological notes on blue suckers in the Mississippi River. Transactions of the American Fisheries Society. Vol. 109(3):323-326.

Rutherford, D. A., and A. A. Echelle, O. E. Maughan. 1985. An addition to the fish fauna of Oklahoma - *Erimyzon succeta* (Catostomidae). Southwest Naturalist. Vol. 30(2):305.

Rutter, Cloudsley M. 1904. Notes on Fishes from Streams and Lakes of Northeastern California not tributary to the Sacramento Basin. Bull. U.S. Fish. Comm. Vol. 22:143-148.

Rutter, Cloudsley M. 1908. The fishes of the Sacramento - San Joaquin basin with a study of their distribution and variation. Washington, D. C. Dept. Comm. Lab., Bull. Bur. Fish. Vol. 27(1907)1908:103-152.

Sagemehl, M. 1884. Beiträge zur vergleichenden Anatomie der Fische. III. Das Cranium der Chariciniden nebst allgemeinen Bemerkungen über die mit einem Weber'-schen Apparat versehenen Physostomenfamilien. Morpholog. Jahrbuch. Vol. 10:1-119.

Sagemehl, M. 1891. Beiträge zur vergleichenden Anatomie der Fische. 4. Das Cranium der Cyprinoiden. Morph. Jahrb. Vol. 17:489-595.

Salki, A., and M. Turner, K. Patalas, J. Rudd, D. Findlay. 1985. The influence of fish-zooplankton-phytoplankton interactions on the results of selenium toxicity experiments within large enclosures. Can. J. Fisheries Aquat. Sci. Vol. 42(6):1132-1143.

Sanderson, A. E., Jr. 1958. Smallmouth bass management in the Potomac River basin. Trans. N. Amer. Wildl. Conf. Vol. 23:248-262.

Sandoz, O. 1960. A pre-impoundment study of Arbuckle Reservoir, Rock Creek, Murray County, Oklahoma. Okla. Fish. Res. Lab. Rep. Vol. 77:28pp.

Sather, L. M., and C. W. Threinen. 1968. Surface water resources of Sawyer County. Wis. Dep. Nat. Resour. Lake and Strm. Classifi. Proj. 213pp.

Saunders, Richard L. 1961. The irrigation of the gills in fishes. I. Studies of the mechanism of branchial irrigation. Canadian Journal of Zoology. Vol. 39(5):637-653.

Saunders, Richard L. 1962. The irrigation of the gills in fishes. II. Efficiency of oxygen uptake in relation to respiratory flow activity and concentrations of oxygen and carbon dioxide. Canadian Journal of Zoology. Vol. 40(5):817-862.

Savage, Jay M. 1970. On the Trail of the Golden Frog: with Warszewicz and Gabb in Central America. Proceedings of the California Academy of Sciences. 4th Series. Vol. 38(14):273-288.

Savan, M., and J. Budd, P. W. Reno, S. Darley. 1979. A study of two species of fish inoculated with spruce budworm nuclear polyhedrosis virus. Journal Wildl. Dis. Vol. 15(2):331-334.

Savitz, J. 1987. The first record of the smallmouth buffalo, *Ictiobus bubalus* (Rafinesque), in Illinois waters of Lake Michigan. Transactions of the Illinois Academy of Science. Vol. 80(3-4):347-348.

Savitz, J., and L. G. Bardygula, L. Scoma. 1989. The first record of the quillback carpsucker (*Carpiodes cyprinus*) in Illinois waters of Lake Michigan. Transactions of the Illinois Academy of Science. Vol. 82(3-4):191.

Sayigh, L., and R. Morin. 1986. Summer diet and daily consumption of periphyton of the longnose sucker, *Catostomus catostomus* in the Lower Matamek River, Quebec. Nat. Can. (Que.) Vol. 113(4):361-368

Scarola, J. F. 1973. Freshwater fishes of New Hampshire. N. H. Fish Game Dep. Div. Inland and Mar. Fish. 131pp.

Scharff, R. F. 1911. Distribution and origin of life in America. 8 vo. 1-497 pp.

Schell, S. C. 1973. The life history of *Neopaleorchis catostomi* gen. et sp. n. (Trematoda: Monorchiidae), an intestinal parasite of the coarsescale sucker, *Catostomus macrocheilus* Girard. Journal of Parasitology. Vol. 59(3):463-468.

Schlaikjer, E. M. 1937. New fishes from the continental Tertiary of Alaska. Bull. Amer. Mus. Nat. Hist. Vol. 74(1):1-23.

Schlosser, Isaac J. 1985. Flow regime, juvenile abundance, and the assemblage structure of stream fishes. Ecology. Vol. 66(5):1484-1490.

Schlosser, I. J. 1987. The role of preation in age- and size-related habitat use by stream fishes. Ecology Vol. 68(3):651-659.

Schlosser, Max. 1917. Zeitliche und räumliche Verbreitung und Stammesgeschicte der fossilen Fische. Sitz.-Ber. Akad. Wiss. München 1917:131-150.

Schmidt, P. J. 1949. Analyses of freshwater fishes from Canadian interior provinces. Industrial Memoranda of the Technological Station, Vancouver, B. C. No. 12:10 pp.

Schmidt, P. J. 1950. Analyses of freshwater fishes from Canadian interior provinces. Industrial Memoranda of the Technological Station, Vancouver, B. C. No. 13:1-8pp.

Schmitt, Christopher J., and F. James Dwyer, Susan E. Finger. 1984. Bioavailability of lead and zinc from mine tailings as indicated by erythrocyte δ-aminolevulinic acid dehydratase (ALA-D) activity in suckers (Pisces:Catostomidae). Can. J. Fish Aquat. Sci. Vol. 41(7):1030-1040.

Schmitt, C. J., and S. E. Finger. 1987. The effects of sample preparation on measured concentrations of eight elements in edible tissues of fish from streams contaminated by lead mining. Archives envir. Contam. Toxicol. Vol. 16(2):185-207.

Schmitt, Christopher J., and J. L. Zajicek, M. A. Ribick. 1985. National pesticide monitoring program- Residues of organochlorine chemicals in freshwater fish, 1980-81. Arch Environ. Contam. Toxicol. Vol. 14(2):225-260.

Schneberger, E. 1972. The white sucker, its life history, ecology and management. Wisc. Dep. Nat. Resour. Publi. No. 245-72. 18pp.

Schneidervin, Roger W., and Wayne A. Hubert. 1986. A Rapid Technique for Otolith Removal from Salmonids and Catostomids. North American Journal of Fisheries Management. Vol. 6(2):287.

Schneidervin, R. W., and W. A. Hubert. 1987. Diet overlap among zooplanktophagous fishes in Flaming Gorge Reservoir, Wyoming-Utah. N. Am. J. Fish Manage. Vol. 7(3):379-385.

Schoenthal, N. D. 1964. Some effects of DDT on cold water fish and fish-food organisms. Proc. Mont. Acad. Sci. Vol. 23:63-95.

Schoffman, R. J. 1943. Age and growth of the gourdhead buffalo in Reelfoot Lake. J. Tenn. Acad. Sci. Vol. 18(1):36-46.

Schoffman, R. J. 1944. Age and growth of the smallmouth buffalo in Reelfoot Lake. J. Tenn. Acad. Sci. Vol. 19:3-9.

Schoonover, R., and W. H. Thompson. 1954. A post-impoundment study of the fisheries resources of Fall River Reservoir, Kansas. Trans. Kans. Acad. Sci. Vol. 57(2):172-179.

Schultz, Leonard P. 1936. Keys to the Fishes of Washington, Oregon and Closely adjoining Regions. University of Washington Publications in Biology. Vol. 2(4):103-228.

Schultz, Leonard P. 1947. A fine-scaled sucker, *Catostomus*, from Lake Cushman, Washington State. Copeia, Ann Arbor. 1947(3):202.

Schultz, Leonard P. 1952. Fishing in Pacific Coast Streams. pp. 81-101. **IN:** John Oliver La Gorce (ed.) The Book of Fishes. National Geographic Society. Washington, D.C. 339pp.

Schultz, Leonard P., and R. J. Thompson. 1936. *Catostomus syncheilus palouseanus*, a new subspecies of a Catostomid fish from the Palouse River (Columbia R. system). Proc. Biol. Soc. Washington Vol. 49:71-76.

Schwalme, Karl, and William C. MacKay, Dieter Lindner. 1985. Suitability of vertical slot and denil fishways for passing north-temperate, nonsalmonid fish. Can. J. Fish Aquat. Sci. Vol. 42(11):1815-1822.

Schwartz, T. R., and D. L. Stalling. 1987. Are polychlorinated biphenyl residues adequately described by arocolor mixture equivalents? Isomer-specific principal components analysis of such residues in fish and turtles. Environmental Sci. Technol. Vol. 21(1):72-76.

Scidmore, W. J. 1953. Use of pectoral fin rays to determine age of the white sucker. Progressive Fish-Culturist. Vol. 15:114-115.

Scidmore, W. J., and D. E. Woods. 1960. Some observations on competition between several species of fish for summer foods in four southern Minnesota lakes in 1955, 1956 and 1957. Minn. Fish Game Invest. Fish. Ser. 2:13-24.

Scoppettone, G. G. 1988. Growth and longevity of the cui-ui and longevity of other catostomids and cyprinids in western North America. Trans. Am. Fish Soc. Vol. 117(3):301-307.

Scoppettone, G. Gary, and Mark Coleman, Gary A. Wedemeyer. 1986. Life history and Status of the Endangered Cui-ui of Pyramid Lake, Nevada. U.S. Department of the Interior Fish and Wildlife Service.Fish and Wildlife Research 1:1-23.

Scoppettone, G. Gary, and Gary A. Wedemeyer, Mark Coleman, Howard Burge. 1983. Reproduction by the endangered cui-ui in the lower Truckee River. Transactions of the Am. Fish. Soc. Vol. 112(6):788-793.

Scott, A. P., and Duncan S. MacKenzie, Norman E. Stacey. 1984. Endocrine changes during natural spawning in the white sucker, *Catostomus commersoni*: 2. Steroid hormones. Gen. Comp. Endocrinol. Vol. 56(3):349-359.

Scott Cone, R., and K. Barbour, M. Russell, S. K. Simonet. 1986. The effects of flooding on the growth rates of fishes in Lake Texoma. Proceedings Okla. Acad. Sci. Vol. 66:21-25.

Scott, Donald C. 1951. Sampling Fish Populations in the Coosa River, Alabama. Transactions of the American Fisheries Society. Vol. 80(1950):28-40.

Scott, D. M. 1955. Additional records of two fishes, *Erimyzon succetta kennerlyi* and *Hadropterus copelandi*, from Southern Ontario, Canada. Copeia 1955(2):151.

Scott, D. P. 1974. Mercury concentration of white muscle in relation to age, growth, and condition in four species of fishes from Clay Lake, Ontario. Journal of the Fisheries Research Board of Canada Vol. 31(11):1723-1729.

Scott, D. P., and F. A. J. Armstrong. 1972. Mercury concentration in relation to size in several species of freshwater fishes from Manitoba and northwestern Ontario. Journal of the Fisheries Research Board of Canada. Vol. 29(12):1685-1690.

Scott, W. B. 1952. Records of the western lake Chubsucker, *Erimyzon sucetta kennerleyi*, from Ontario, Canada. Copeia 1952(3):203.

Scott, W. B. 1954. Freshwater Fishes of Eastern Canada. University of Toronto Press. Toronto, Ontario, Canada. 128pp.

Scott, W. B. 1957. Distributional records of fishes in Western Canada. Copeia 1957:160-161.

Scott, W. B. 1958. A Checklist of the Freshwater Fishes of Canada and Alaska. Royal Ontario Museum. Division of Zoology and Palaeontology. 30pp.

Scott, W. B. 1967. Freshwater Fishes of Eastern Canada. Second edition. Toronto, Univ. of Toronto Press. 1-137pp.

Scott, W. B., and E. J. Crossman. 1969. Checklist of Canadian Freshwater Fishes with Keys for Identification. Royal Ontario Museum Publications in Life Sciences. Toronto, Canada. 104pp.

Scott, W. B., and E. J. Crossman. 1973. Freshwater fishes of Canada. Bulletin Fish. Res. Bd. Canada. Vol. 184:1-966.

Scruton, D. A. 1984. A survey of selected lakes in Labrador (Canada), with an assessment of lake status and sensitivity in relation to acid precipitation. Can. Tech. Rep. Fish Aquat. Sci. No. 1296:1-115.

Seaman, E. A. 1950. Notes on the effect of flash flood on stream fish in West Virginia. Copeia 1950(4):320.

Sebastien, R. J., and R. A. Brust, D. M. Rosenberg. 1989. Impact of methoxychlor on selected nontarget organisms in a riffle of the Souris River, Manitoba. Can. J. Fish Aquat. Sci. Vol. 46(6):1047-1061.

Seegert, G. L. 1973. The effects of lethal heating on plasma potassium levels, hematocrit and cardiac activity in the alewife (*Alosa pseudoharengus*) compared with three other teleosts. Proceedings Conf. Gt. Lakes Res. Vol. 16:154-162.

Seegert, Greg. 1986. Rediscovery of the Greater Redhorse (*Moxostoma valenciennesi* Jordan) (Cypriniformes: Catostomidae) in Illinois. Transactions of the Illinois Academy of Science. Vol. 79(3-4):293-294.

Semmens,.K. J. 1985. Induced spawning of the blue sucker, (*Cycleptus elongatus*). Progressive Fish-culturist. Vol. 47(2);119-120.

Shaklee, J. B., and M. J. Champion, Gregory S. Whitt. 1974. Developmental genetics of teleosts: a biochemical analysis of lake chubsucker ontogeny. Developmental Biol. Vol. 38(2):356-382.

Shchukin, G. P., and N. N. Mirgorodchenko, M. Kh. Bulatov, M. Kh. Abdullin, A. N. Salakhutdinov, A. A. Shchukina. 1982. Food supply in fish ponds of Ulyanov Nursery Farm (Kuibyshev Reservoir) and its utilization with fish fry. Sbornik nauch. Trud. gos. nauchno-issled. Inst. ozern. rechn. rybn. Khozyaist. No. 180:69-86.

Sheldon, Andrew L. 1968. Species Diversity and Longitudinal Succession in Stream Fishes. Ecology. Vol. 49(2):193-198.

Shelford, Victor E. 1911a. Ecological Succession. I. Stream Fishes and the Method of Physiographic Analysis. Biological Bulletin. Vol. 21(1):9-35.

Shelford, Victor E. 1911b. Ecological Succession. II. Pond Fishes. Biological Bulletin. Vol. 21(3):127-151.

Shelford, Victor E. 1937. Chapter 6. Animal Communities of Streams. pp. 86-123. **IN:** Victor E. Shelford. Animal Communities in Temperate America As Illustrated in the Chicago Region. The Geographic Society of Chicago. Bulletin No. 5. University of Chicago Press. Chicago, Illinois.

Shields, J. T. 1955a. Report of fisheries investigations during the second year of impoundment of Fort Randall Reservoir, South Dakota, 1954. S. D. Dept. Game Fish Parks. 100pp. mimeo.

Shields, J. T. 1955b. Report of fisheries investigations during the second year of impoundment of Fort Randall Reservoir, South Dakota, 1954. South Dakota Dept. Game Fish Parks, Dingell-Johnson Proj. 1470 102pp.

Shields, J. T. 1956. Report of fisheries investigations during the third year of impoundment of Fort Randall Reservoir, South Dakota, 1955. S. D. Dept. Game Fish Parks Dingell-Johnson Proj., F-1-R-5:91pp.

Shields, J. T. 1957a. Report of fisheries investigations during the second year of impoundment of Gavins Point Reservoir, South Dakota, 1956. S. D. Dept. Game Fish Parks Dingell-Johnson Proj., F-1-R-6:34pp. mimeo.

Shields, J. T. 1957b. Report of fisheries investigations during the fourth year of impoundment of Fort Randall Reservoir, South Dakota, 1956. S. D. Dept. Game Fish Parks Dingell-Johnson Proj., F-1-R-6:1-60pp.

Shields, J. T. 1958a. Report of fisheries investigations during the third year of impoundment of Gavins Point Reservoir, South Dakota, 1957. S. D. Dept. Game Fish Parks Dingell-Johnson Proj., F-1-R-7:1-48.

Shields, J. T. 1958b. Experimental control of carp reproduction through water drawdowns in Fort Randall Reservoir, South Dakota. Transactions of the American Fisheries Society. Vol. 87:23-33.

Shih, M. C., and W. A. Rogers. 1970. Four new species of monogenetic trematodes, genus *Pellucidhaptor*, from fishes of the southeastern U.S. J. Parasit. Vol. 56:480-485.

Shilenko, Yu. V. and V. G. Krasnikov, N. V. Shilenko. 1986. Residues of herbicide "Saturn" in fish and in aquatic invertebrates. Gidrobiol. Zh. Vol. 22(5):75-77.

Shilin, Yu A. 1973. Reproduction of chukuchana *Catostomus catostomus rostratus* (Tilesius) in the Kolyma River. Izvestiya tikhookean. nauchno-issled. Inst. ryb. Khoz. Okeanogr. Vol. 86:131-133. [in Russian, with English summary].

Shireman, J. V., and R. L. Stetler, D. E. Colle. 1978. Possible use of the lake chubsucker as a baitfish. Progressive Fish-Culturist. Vol. 40(1):33-34.

Shumkov, M. A. 1985. Effect of vegetation on the intensity of the comsumption of mosquito larvac and pupae by young commercial fishes. Meditsinskaya Parazitol. Parazit. Bolezni. Vol. 54(5):71-74.

Sibley, C. K. 1929. The food of certain fishes of the Lake Erie drainage basin. pp. 180-188. IN: A biological survey of the Erie-Niagara system. New York Cons. Dept., Suppl. to 18th Annual Rep. (1928): 244pp.

Siddiqi, M. N. 1981. Helminth parasites of fishes of northern Colorado. Biologia, Lahore. Vol. 27(1):75-79.

Siebert, Darrell J., and W. L. Minckley. 1986. Two new catostomid fishes (Cypriniformes) from the Northern Sierra Madre occidental of Mexico. Am. Mus. Novit. Number 2849:1-17.

Siefert, R. E. 1972. First food of larval yellow perch, white sucker, bluegill, emerald shiner, and rainbow smelt. Transactions of the American Fisheries Society. Vol. 101(2):219-225.

Siefert, R. E., and W. A. Spoor. 1974. Effects of reduced oxygen on embryos and larvae of the white sucker, coho salmon, brook trout, and walleye. pp. 487-495. IN: Blaxter, J. H. S. [Ed.]. The early life history of fish. Springer Verlag, Berlin. 1-765pp.

Sigler, W. F., and S. Vigg, M. Bres. 1985. Life history of the cui-ui. *Chasmistes cujus* Cope, in Pyramid Lake, Nevada: a review. Great Basin Nat. Vol. 45(4):571-603.

Simon, James R. 1946. Wyoming Fishes. Bulletin No. 4. Wyoming Game and Fish Department. Cheyenne, Wyoming. 129pp.

Simpson, James C., and Richard L. Wallace. 1982. Fishes of Idaho. University Press of Idaho. Moscow, Idaho. 238pp.

Sipponen, M. 1978. Tolerance of water acidification by fish. Luonnon Tutk. Vol. 82(4):97-99.

Sivak, J. G. 1973. Interrelation of feeding behaviour and accomodative lens movements in some species of North American freshwater fishes. Journal of the Fisheries Research Board of Canada. Vol. 30(8):1141-1146.

Skea, J. C., and H. A. Simonin, H. J. Dean, J. R. Colquhoun, J. J. Spagnoli, G. D. Veith. 1979. Bioaccumulation of Aroclor 1016 in Hudson River Fish. Bulletin envir. Contam. Toxicol. Vol. 22(3):332-336.

Slastenenko, E. P. 1957. A list of natural fish hybrids of the world. Hidrobiologi, Istanbul Vol. 4:76-97.

Slastenenko, E. P. 1958. The Freshwater Fishes of Canada. Kiev Printers. Toronto, Ontario. 1-388.

Sloley, B. D. 1988. Noradrenaline, dopamine, 5-hydroxytryptamine and tryptophan concentrations in the brains of four cohabiting species of fish. Comp. Biochem. Physiol. C. Comp. Pharmacol. Vol. 89(2):197-199.

Smith, C. G. 1977. The biology of three species of *Moxostoma* (Pisces: Catostomidae) in Clear Creek, Hocking and Fairfield Counties, Ohio, with emphasis on the golden redhorse, *M. erythrurum* (Rafinesque). Dissertation Abstr. int. Vol. 38(2):549-550.

Smith, C. G., and W. M. Lewis, H. M. Kaplan. 1952. A comparative morphologic and physiologic study of fish blood. Progr. Fish Cult. Vol. 14(4):169-172.

Smith, C. Lavett. 1954. Pleistocene fishes of the Berends fauna of Beaver County, Oklahoma. Copeia 1954(4):282-289.

Smith, C. Lavett. 1958. Additional Pleistocene fishes from Kansas and Oklahoma. Copeia 1958(3):176-180.

Smith, C. Lavett. 1962. Some Pliocene fishes from Kansas, Oklahoma, and Nebraska. Copeia 1962(3):505-520.

Smith, C. Lavett. 1986. The Inland Fishes of New York State. New York State department of Environmental Conservation, 1985. Albany, New York. 522pp.

Smith, Gerald R. 1963. A late Illinoian fish fauna from southwestern Kansas and its climatic significance. Copeia 1963(2):278-285.

Smith, Gerald R. 1965. Distribution and evolution of the North American fishes of the subgenus *Pantosteus*. Diss. Abstr. Vol. 26:3549.

Smith, Gerald R. 1966. Distribution and evolution of the North American catostomid fishes of the subgenus *Pantosteus*, genus *Catostomus*. Miscellaneous Publications Museum of Zoology, University of Michigan. No. 129:5-133.

Smith, Gerald R. 1975. Fishes of the Pliocene Glenns Ferry Formation, Southwest Idaho: Papers on Paleontology, No. 14(Claude W. Hibbard memorial volume 5). pp. 1-68.

Smith, Gerald R. 1981a. Chapter 5. Effects of Habitat Size on Species Richness and Adult Body Sizes of Desert Fishes. pp. 125-171. **IN:** Robert J. Naiman and David L. Soltz (eds.) Fishes in North American Deserts. John Wiley and Sons. New York, N.Y. 552pp.

Smith, Gerald R. 1981b. Late Cenozoic Freshwater Fishes of North America. Annual Review of Ecology and Systematics. Vol. 12(4191):163-193.

Smith, Gerald R. 1985. The archaeology of Hidden Cave, Nevada. Chapter 12. Anthropological Pap. Am. Mus. nat. Hist. Vol. 61(1):171-178.

Smith, Gerald R. 1987. Key to native and introduced fishes of the Great Basin. pp. 75-93. **IN:** Sigler, W. F., and J. W. Sigler. Fishes of the Great Basin. A natural history. University of Nevada Press. Reno, Nevada. 425 pp.

Smith, Gerald R., and J. G. Hall, R. K. Koehn, D. J. Innes. 1983. Taxonomic relationships of the Zuni Mountain sucker, *Catostomus discobolus yarrowi*. Copeia 1983(1):37-48.

Smith, Gerald R., and J. G. Lundberg. 1972. The Sand Draw fish fauna. Amer. Mus. Natur. Hist., Bull. Vol. 148(1):40-54.

Smith, Gerald R., and W. L. Stokes, K. F. Horn. 1968. Some Late Pleistocene fishes of Lake Bonneville. Copeia. 1968(4):807-816.

Smith, Hugh M. 1893. Report on a collection of fishes from the Albelmarle Region of North Carolina for 1891 (1893). Bull. U. S. Fish Commission. Vol. 11:185-200.

Smith, Hugh M., and William Converse Kendall. 1921. Fishes of the Yellowstone National Park with description of the Park Waters and Notes on Fishing. Appendix 3 to the Report of the U.S. Commissioner of Fisheries for 1921. Bureau of Fisheries Document No. 904. 30pp.

Smith, I. R., and K. W. Baker, M. A. Hayes, H. W. Ferguson. 1989. Ultrastructure of Malpighian and inflammatory cells in epidermal papillomas of white sucker *Catostomus commersoni*. Dis. Aquat. Org. Vol. 6(1):17-26.

Smith, I. R., and H. W. Ferguson, M. A. Hayes,. 1989. Histopathology and prevalence of epidermal papillomas epidemic in brown bullhead *Ictalurus nebulosus* (Le Sueur), and white sucker, *Catostomus commersoni* (La Cepède), populations from Ontario, Canada. J. Fish Dis. Vol. 12(4):373-388.

Smith, I. R., and B. A. Zajdlik. 1987. Regression and development of epidermal papillomas affecting white suckers, *Catostomus commersoni* (La Cepède), from Lake Ontario, Canada. J. Fish. Dis. Vol. 10(6):487-494.

Smith, John B., and Wayne A. Hubert. 1989. Use of a Tributary by Fishes in a Great Plains River System. Prairie Nat. Vol. 21(1):27-38.

Smith, L. L., Jr., and N. L. Moe (compilers). 1944. Minnesota fish facts. Minn. Dept. Conserv. Bull. Vol. 7:1-31.

Smith, L. L., Jr., and D. M. Oseid. 1974. Effect of hydrogen sulfide on development and survival of eight freshwater fish species. pp. 417-430. **IN:** J. H. S. Blaxter (Ed.) The Early Life History of Fish. Springer-Verlag, Berlin. 1-765pp.

Smith, Michael L. 1981. Chapter 2. Late Cenozoic Fishes in the Warm Deserts of North America: A Reinterpretation of Desert Adaptations. pp. 11-38. **IN:** Robert J. Naiman and David L. Soltz (eds.) Fishes in North American Deserts. John Wiley & Sons. New York, N.Y. 552pp.

Smith, Michael L., and Ted M. Cavender, Robert R. Miller. 1975. Climatic and biogeographic significance of a fiah fauna from the late Pliocene-early Pleistocene of the Lake Chapala Basin (Jalisco, Mexico). pp. 29-38. **IN:** Gerald R. Smith, <F 2>et al.<F> (editors). Studies on Cenozoic paleontology and stratigraphy in honor of Claude W. Hibbard. Papers on Paleontology. No. 12 (Claude W. Hibbard memorial volume 3).

Smith, M. W. 1935. A preliminary note on the fish population of Lake Jesse, Nova Scotia. Transactions of the American Fisheries Society. Vol. 65:297-299.

Smith, M. W. 1937. Fish production in three Nova Scotia lakes. Progress Reports of Fisheries Research Board Atlantic Coast Stations. No. 20:6-7.

Smith, M. W. 1938. A preliminary account of the fish populations in certain Nova Scotian Lakes. Transactions of the American Fisheries Society for 1937. Vol. 67:178-183.

Smith, M. W. 1939. The fish population of Lake Jesse, Nova Scotia. Proceedings of the Nova Scotian Institute of Science [for 1937-1938]. Vol. 19(Pt. 4):389-427.

Smith, M. W. 1952. Limnology and trout angling in Charlotte County lakes, New Brunswick. Journal of the Fisheries Research Board of Canada Vol. 8(6):383-452.

Smith, M. W. 1961. A limnological reconnaissance of a Nova Scotian brown-water lake. Journal of the Fisheries Research Board of Canada Vol. 18(3):463-478.

Smith, Philip W. 1963. A study of seasonal distribution of fishes in the Kaskaskia River Ditch, a highly modified stream in eastern Illinois. Copeia 1963(2):251-259.

Smith, Philip W. 1965. A preliminary annotated list of the lampreys and fishes of Illinois. Illinois Natural History Survey. Biological Notes No. 54:12 pp.

Smith, Philip W. 1968. An assessment of changes in the fish fauna of two Illinois Rivers and its bearing on their future. Transactions Illinois State Academy of Science. Vol. 61(1):31-45.

Smith, Philip W. 1971. Illinois Streams: A Classification Based on Their Fishes and an Analysis of Factors Responsible for Disappearance of Native Species. Illinois Natural History Survey. Biological Notes No. 76:1-14.

Smith, Philip W. 1973. A Key to the Fishes of Illinois. Dept. of Conservation, Division of Fisheries. Springfield, Illinois. Fishery Bulletin no. 6:1-43pp.

Smith, Philip W. 1979. The Fishes of Illinois. University of Illinois Press, Urbana. Chicago and London. 1-314pp.

Smith, Philip W., and A. C. Lopinot, W. L. Pflieger. 1971. A distributional atlas of upper Mississippi River fishes. Ill. Nat. Hist. Surv. Biol. Notes No. 73:20pp.

Smith, S. H. 1968. Species succession and fishery exploitation in the Great Lakes. Journal of the Fisheries Research Board of Canada. Vol. 25(4):667-693.

Snyder, D. E. 1975. Passage of fish eggs and young through a pumped storage generating station. Journal of the Fisheries Research Board of Canada. Vol. 32(8):1259-1266.

Snyder, D. E. 1983. Identification of catostomical larvae in Pyramid Lake and the Truckee River, Nevada. Transactions of the American Fisheries Society. Vol. 112(2B):333-348.

Snyder, Darrel E., and Robert T. Muth. 1990. Descriptions and identification of razorback, flannelmouth, white, Utah, bluehead, and mountain sucker larvae and early juveniles. Colorado Division of Wildlife. Technical Public. No. 38:1-152 pp.

Snyder, John Otterbein. 1908a. Description of *Pantosteus santa-anae*, a new species of fish from the Santa Ana River, California. Washington, D.C., Smithsonian Inst., U.S. Nation. Mus., Proc. Vol. 34:33-34.

Snyder, John Otterbein. 1908b. Relationships of the fish fauna of the lakes of south-eastern Oregon. Washington, D. C., Dept. Comm. Lab., Bull. Bur. Fish. Vol. 27 1907(1908):69-102.

Snyder, John Otterbein. 1908c. The fishes of the coastal streams of Oregon and northern California. Washington, D. C., Dept. Comm. Lab., Bull. Bur. Fish. Vol. 27 1907(1908):153-189.

Snyder, John Otterbein. 1913. The fishes of the streams tributary to Monterey Bay, California. Washington Bull. U.S. Bur. Fish. Vol. 32 1912(1913):47-52.

Snyder, John Otterbein. 1916. Notes on a collection of Fishes made by Dr. Edgar A. Mearns from rivers tributary to the Gulf of California. Washington. Smithsonian Inst. National Mus. Proc. Vol. 49:573-586.

Snyder, John Otterbein. 1917. The fishes of the Lahontan system of Nevada and northern California. Bull. U.S. Bur. Fish. Vol. 35(1915-1916):31-86.

Snyder, John Otterbein. 1924. Notes on certain Catostomids of the Bonnerville System, including the type of *Pantosteus virescens* Cope. Proc. U.S. Nat. Mus. Washington. Vol. 64(18):1-6.

Snyder, Richard C. 1949. Vertebral counts in four species of suckers (Catostomidae). Copeia, Ann Arbor. 1949(1):62-65.

Soltz, David L., and Robert J. Naiman. 1978. The natural history of native fishes in the Death Valley system. Science Ser. nat. Hist. Mus. Los Ang. City. no. 30:1-76.

Sonnevil, G. M. 1978. Restoration status of the cui-ui. CAL-NEVA Wildl.:18-22.

Sonstegard, R. A., and L. A. McDermott, K. S. Sonstegard. 1972. Isolation of infectious pancreatic necrosis virus from white suckers (*Catostomus commersoni*) Nature, Lond. Vol. 236(5343):174-175.

Souter, B. W., and R. A. Sonstegard, L. A. McDermott. 1976. Enteric bacteria in carp (*Cyprinus carpio*) and white suckers (*Catostomus commersoni*) Journal of the Fisheries Research Board of Canada. Vol. 33(6):1401-1403.

Sparks, Richard E., and William C. Starrett. 1975. An Electrofishing Survey of the Illinois River, 1959-1974. Illinois Natural History Survey Bulletin. Vol. 31(8):317-380.

Spence, J. A., and B. N. Hynes. 1971. Differences in fish populations upstream and downstream of a mainstream impoundment. Journal of the Fisheries Research Board of Canada. Vol. 28(1):45-46.

Spoor, W. A. 1935. On the sexual dimorphism of *Catostomus commersonnii* (La Cepède). Copeia, Ann Arbor, Michigan. 1935(4):167-171.

Spoor, W. A. 1938. Age and growth of the sucker *Catostomus commersonnii* (La Cepède), in Muskellunge Lake, Vilas County, Wisconsin. Trans. Wisc. Acad. Sci. Arts. Lett. Vol. 31:457-505.

Spoor, W. A., and C. L. Schloemer. 1939. Diurnal activity of the common sucker, *Catostomus commersonii*, and rock bass, *Ambloplites rupestris*, in Muskellunge Lake. Transactions of the American Fisheries Society. Vol. 68:211-220.

Sprague, J. W. 1959a. Report of fisheries investigations during the fourth year of impoundment of Gavins Point Reservoir, South Dakota, 1958. S. D. Dept. Game Fish Parks. 42pp. mimeo.

Sprague, J. W. 1959b. Report of fisheries investigations during the sixth year of impoundment of Fort Randall Reservoir, South Dakota. S. D. Dept. Game Fish Parks, Dingell-Johnson Proj., F-1-R-8:32pp.

Sprague, J. W. 1961. Report of fisheries investigations during the seventh year of impoundment of Fort Randall Reservoir, South Dakota, 1959. S. D. Dept. Game Fish Parks, Dingell-Johnson Proj., F-1-R-9 (Jobs 5-8):49pp.

Sprules, W. M., and K. H. Doan. 1947. Records of the mooneye (*Hiodon tergisus*) and the quill-back sucker (*Carpiodes cyprinus*) from Saskatchewan. Copeia, Ann Arbor. 1947(3):196-197.

Srivastava, V. M. 1971. Fish of the Gulf of St. Lawrence, an unabridged bibliography. Technical Reports of the Fisheries Research Board of Canada. No. 261. 141 pp.

Stacey, Norman E., and Duncan S. MacKenzie, Tracy A. Marchant, Ann L. Kyle, Richard E. Peter. 1984. Endocrine changes during natural spawning in the white sucker, *Catostomus commersoni*: 1. Gonadotropin, growth hormone and thyroid hormones. Gen. Comp. Endocrinol. Vol. 56(3):333-348.

Stanley, D. R. 1988. Sexual dimorphism of pelvic fin shape in four species of Catostomidae. Transactions of the American Fisheries Society Vol. 117(6):600-602.

Stanley, J. G., and J. B. Jones. 1976. Feeding algae to fish. Aquaculture. Vol. 7(3):219-223.

Stannius, H. 1854. Handbuch der Zootomie von Siebold und Stannius. Zweiter Theil. Die Wirbelthiere von Hermann Stannius. Erstes Buch. Die Fische. Zweite Auflage, Berlin. pp. 1-279.

Stark, B. J., and M. E. Eberle, G. W. Ernsting, T. L. Wenke. 1987. Distributional records of some Kansas fishes. Trans. Kans. Acad. Sci. Vol. 90:153-156.

Starks, Edwin C. 1907. **IN:** David Starr Jordan. The fossil fishes of California; with supplementary notes on other species of extinct fishes. Bull. Dept. Geol., Univ. of Calif. Vol. 5:95-145.

Starnes, L. B. 1984. Faunal changes in a small east Tennessee reservoir following remedial reclamation of coal surface mine drainage. Journal Tenn. Acad. Sci. Vol. 59(3):33-38.

Starostka, V. J., and R. L. Applegate. 1970. Food selectivity of Bigmouth buffalo, *Ictiobus cyprinellus*, in Lake Poinsett, South Dakota. Transactions of the American Fisheries Society. Vol. 99:571-576.

Starrett, William C. 1958. Fishery values of a restored Illinois river bottomland lake. Transactions of the Illinois Academy of Science. Vol. 50:41-48.

Starrett, William C., and William J. Harth, Philip W. Smith. 1960. Parasitic lampreys of the genus *Ichthyomyzon* in the rivers of Illinois. Copeia 1960(4):337-346.

Stenton, J. E. 1951. Eastern brook trout eggs taken by longnose suckers in Banff National Park, Canada. Copeia 1951(2):171-173.

Sterba, Günther. 1983. The Aquarium Encyclopedia. MIT Press, Cambridge, Massachusetts. 607pp.

Stevens, E. D., and F. E. J. Fry. 1974. Heat transfer and body temperatures in non-thermoregulatory teleosts. Canadian Journal of Zoology. Vol. 52(9):1137-1143.

Stevenson, H. M. 1976. <u>Vertebrates</u> <u>of</u> <u>Florida</u>. University Presses of Florida. Gainesville, Florida. 607pp.

Stevenson, J. H. 1964. Fish farming experimental station. U.S. Fish Wildl. Serv. Circ.178:79-100.

Stewart, Kenneth W., and Iain M. Suthers, Kelly Leavesley. 1985. New fish distribution records in Manitoba [Canada] and the role of a man-made interconnection between two drainages as an avenue of dispersal. Can Field-Nat. Vol. 99(3):317-326.

Stewart, N. H. 1927. Development, growth and food habits of the White Sucker, (*Catostomus commersonii*). Bul. Bur. Fish. Washington. Vol. 42:1926(1927):147-184.

Stiles, R. A., and D. A. Etnier. 1971. Fishes of the Conasauga River drainage, Polk and Bradley Counties, Tennessee. J. Tenn. Acad. Sci. Vol. 46(1):12-16.

Stone, U. B. 1947. A study of the deep-water cisco fishery of Lake Ontario with particular reference to the bloater, *Leucichthys hoyi* (Gill). Transactions of the American Fisheries Society. Vol. 74(1944):230-249.

Storer, David Humphreys. 1867. A History of the Fishes of Massachusetts. Memoirs of the American Academy of Arts and Sciences. 287pp.

Strawn, K. 1958. Optimum and extreme temperatures for growth and survival: various fishes. For Handbook of Biological Data. 1 p. table.

Stuber, R. J. 1985. Trout habitat, abundance, and fishing opportunities in fenced vs. unfenced riparian habitat along Sheep Creek, Colorado. U. S. For. Serv. Gen. Tech. Rep. R. M. No. 120:310-314.

Suess, Ursula, and Jane Laurence, David Ko, Karl Lederis. 1986. Radioimmunoassays for fish tail neuropeptides: I. Development of assay and measurement of immunoreactive urotensin I in *Catostomus commersoni* brain, pituitary, and plasma. J. Pharmacol. Methods. Vol. 15(4):335-346.

Sule, Michael J., and Thomas M. Skelly. 1985. The Life History of the Shorthead Redhorse, *Moxostoma macrolepidotum*, in the Kankakee River Drainage, Illinois. Illinois Natural History Survey. Biological Notes No. 123:1-16.

Summerfelt, R. C., and P. E. Mauck, G. Mensinger. 1972. Food habits of river carpsucker and freshwater drum in four Oklahoma reservoirs. Proceedings Okla. Acad. Sci. Vol. 52:19-26.

Sun, J. and Harold H. Harvey. 1986. Population dynamics of yellow perch (*Perca flavescens*) and pumpkinseed (*Lepomis gibbosus*) in two acid-stressed lakes. Water Air Soil Pollut. Vol. 30(3-4):611-617.

Sun, Ying, and Richard Nash, C. S. Clay. 1985. Acoustic measurements of the anatomy of fish at 220 kiloherz. J. Acoust. Soc. Am. Vol. 78(5):1772-1776.

Surber, T. 1940. Propagation of minnows. Minn. Dept. Conserv. 22pp.

Swanson, Stella M. 1983. Levels of radium-226, lead-210 and uranium in fish near a Saskatchewan [Canada] uranium mine and mill. Health Phys. Vol. 45(1):67-80.

Swift, Camm, and Ralph W. Yerger, Patrick R. Parrish. 1977. Distribution and natural history of the fresh and brackish water fishes of the Ochlockonee River, Florida and Georgia. Bulletin of Tall Timbers Research Station. No. 20:1-111pp.

Swingle, H. S. 1956. A repressive factor controlling reproduction in fishes. Oceanog. Zool. Proc. Eighth Pacif. Sci. Cong. IIIA (1953):865-871.

Swingle, H. S. 1957. Revised procedures for commercial production of bigmouth buffalo fish in ponds in the southeast. Proc. Southeast. Assoc. Game Fish Commrs. Vol. 10: 1956(1957):162-165.

Swingle, W. E. 1965. Length-weight relationships of Alabama fishes. Auburn Univ. Agric. Exp. Sta. Zool.- Ent. Ser. Fish. Vol. 3:87pp.

Swink, W. D., and K. E. Jacobs. 1983. Influence of a Kentucky flood-control reservoir on the tailwater and headwater fish populations. N. A. J. Fisheries Management. Vol. 3(2):197-203.

Swofford, D. L., and S. H. Berlocher. 1987. Inferring evolutionary trees from gene frequency data under the principle of maximum parsimony. Syst. Zool. Vol. 36(3):293-325.

Sychevskaya, E. K. 1984. [Fishes of the Early Palaeogene from Zajsan Hollow.] pp. 51-61. **IN:** L. K. Gabuniya. (Editor). [Flora and fauna of Zajsan Hollow.] Metsniereba, Tbilisi. pp. 1-166. [In Russian].

Sytchevskaya, E. K. 1986. Palaeogene freshwater fish fauna of the USSR and Mongolia. Trudy sovm. sov.-mongol. paleont. Eksped. No. 29. pp. 1-154.

Szalai, A. J., and T. A. Dick. 1987. Parasites of quillback, *Carpiodes cyprinus* (Le Sueur), from Dauphin Lake, Manitoba, Canada.. J. Parasitol. Vol. 73(2):446-447.

Szalai, A. J., and T. A. Dick. 1987. Intestinal pathology and site specificity of the acanthocephalan *Neoechinorhynchus carpiodi* Dechtiar, 1968, in quillback, *Carpiodes cyprinus* (Le Sueur). Journal of Parasitology. Vol. 73(3):467-475.

Szalai, A. J., and G. V. Danell, T. A. Dick. 1988. Intestinal leakage and precipitating antibodies in the serum of quillback, *Carpiodes cyprinus* (Le Sueur), infected with (Acanthocephala: Neoechinorhynchidae). Journal of Parasitology. Vol. 74(3):415-420.

Tanner, V. M. 1932. A description of *Notolepidomyzon utahensis*, a new Catostomid from Utah. Copeia 1932:135-136.

Tanner, V. M. 1942. A review of the genus *Notolepidomyzon* with a description of a new species (Pisces, Catostomidae). Gtr. Basin Nat. Provo Utah. Vol. 3:27-32.

Tao, S.-K. 1973. Investigations of the use of gonadotrophins to induce spawning in the white sucker *Catostomus commersoni* (La Cepède) in North Dakota. Report Inst. Fish. Biol., Taipei. Vol. 3(1):173-186.

Tarr, H. L. A. 1952. Cause of the browning of certain heat-processed fish products. Progress Reports of Fisheries Research Board Pacific Coast Stations. No. 92:23-24.

Tatum, W. M., and P. A. Hackney. 1973. Age and growth of river redhorse, *Moxostoma carinatum* (Cope) from the Cahaba River, Alabama. Proceedings a. Conf. SEast. Ass. Game Fish Commnrs. Vol. 23: 1970:255-261.

Taylor, Dwight W., and Gerald R. Smith. 1981. Pliocene molluscs and fishes from northeastern California and northwestern Nevada. Contrib. Mus. Paleontol. Univ. Mich. Vol. 25(18):339-413.

Taylor, W. R. 1954. Records of fishes in the John N. Lowe collection from the Upper Peninsula of Michigan. Univ. Mich. Mus. Zool. Publ. No. 87:50pp.

Teller-Marshall, Susan, and David Bardack. 1978. Post-glacial fishes from a Lake Michigan drainage in Milwaukee, Wisconsin. Milw. Public Mus., Contrib. Biol. Geol. No. 15:19pp.

Tchang, T.-L. 1929. Description de Cyprinidés nouveaux de Chine. Bull. Mus. Hist. nat. Paris. Vol. 1(1929):239-243.

Thomas, M. L. H. 1966. Benthos of four Lake Superior bays. Can. Field-Natur. Vol. 80:200-212.

Thompson, Peter. 1980. The Game Fishes of New England and Southeastern Canada. Down East. Camden, Maine. 296pp.

Thompson, W. H. 1950. Investigations of the fisheries resources of Grand Lake. Okla. Game Fish Dept. Fish Mgmt. Rep. Vol. 18:1-46.

Threinen, C. W., and W. T. Helm. 1952. Composition of the fish population and carrying capacity of Spauldings Pond, Rock County, as determined by rotenone treatment. Wis. Conserv. Dep. Invest. Rep. No. 656. 19pp.

Threlfall, W. 1974. New and previously described species of monogenetic trematodes from Labrador catostomids and cyprinids. Folia Parasit. Praha. Vol. 21 (3): 205-214.

Threlfall, W., and G. Hanek. 1970. Metazoan parasites, excluding Monogea, from Longnose and White suckers. Journal of the Fisheries Research Board of Canada Vol. 27(7):1317-1319.

Tilesius von Tilenau, Wilhelm Gottlieb. 1813.Iconum et descriptionum piscium Kamtschaticorum continuatio, tentamen monographiæ generis Agoni blochiani sistens. Mém. Acad. Sci. St. Pétersb. Vol. 4:406-478.

Timmons, T. J., and J. S. Ramsey. 1983. Life history and habitat of the blackfin sucker, *Moxostoma atripinne* (Osteichthyes: Catostomidae). Copeia 1983(1):538-541.

Timmons, T. J., and W. A. Rogers. 1977. *Dactylogyrus atripinnei* sp. n. from the blackfin sucker in Tennessee. Journal of Parasitology. Vol. 63(2):238-239.

Tökés, L. 1970. Nuclear-magnetic-resonance and mass-spectral examination of the principal bile alcohol from *Catostomus commersoni* and its anhydro derivative. Biochem. J., Tokyo. Vol. 116:585-587.

Toner, G. C. 1933. Annotated list of fishes of Georgian Bay. Copeia 1933(3):133-140.

Torrans, E. L., and H. P. Clemens. 1981. Commercial polyculture of bigmouth buffalo and channel catfish in Oklahoma Proceedings a. Conf. SEast Ass. Game Fish Widl. Agencies. Vol. 35:554-561.

Torrans, L., and F. Lowell, H. Clemens. 1986. Evaluation of a fin ray scarring technique for individually marking fish. Arkansas Acad. Sci. Proc. Vol. 40:96-97.

Trautman, Milton B. 1956. *Carpiodes cyprinus hinei*, a new subspecies of carpsucker from the Ohio and Upper Mississippi River systems. Ohio J. Sci. Vol. 56:33-40.

Trautman, Milton B. 1957. The Fishes of Ohio. Ohio State Univ. Press, Columbus. 683pp.

Trautman, Milton B. 1981. The Fishes of Ohio. Ohio State University Press, Columbus, Ohio. Revised edition. 782pp.

Trautman, Milton B., and R. G. Martin. 1951. *Moxostoma aureolum pisolabrum*, a new subspecies of sucker from the Ozarkian Streams of the Mississippi River system. Occ. Pap. Mus. Zool. Univ. Mich. No. 534:1-10.

Tremblay, L. 1962. Température de l'eau d'un lac et la migration de frai du Catostome, *Catostomus c. commersoni*. Nat. Canad. Vol. 89:119-128.

Trembley, F. J. 1960. Research project on effect of condenser discharge water on aquatic life. Inst. Res. Lehigh Univ. Progr. Rep. 1956-1959.

Trippel, Edward A., and Harold H. Harvey. 1987. Reproductive responses of five white sucker (*Catostomus commersoni*) populations in relation to lake acidity. Canadian Journal of Fisheries and Aquatic Sciences. Vol. 44(5):1018-1023.

Trippel, Edward A., and Harold H. Harvey. 1987. Abundance, growth, and food supply of white suckers (*Catostomus commersoni*) in relation to lake morphometry and pH. Canadian Journal of Zoology. Vol. 65(3):558-564.

Trippel, Edward A., and Harold H. Harvey. 1989. Missing opportunities to reproduce: an energy dependent or fecundity gaining strategy in white sucker (*Catostomus commersoni*)? Canadian Journal of Zoology. Vol. 67(9):2180-2188.

Trippel, Edward A., and Harold H. Harvey. 1990. Ovarian atresia and sex ratio imbalance in white sucker *Catostomus commersoni*. J. Fish Biol. Vol. 36:231-239.

Trojnar, J. R. 1977. Egg and larval survival of white suckers (*Catostomus commersoni*) at low pH. Journal of the Fisheries Research Board of Canada. Vol. 34(2):262-266.

Trombitsky, I. D. 1984. Changes in the blood parameters of big-mouthed buffalo, *Ictiobus cyprinellus* during its infection with *Ichthyophthirius multifiliis* (Ciliata, Ophryoglenidae). Parazitologiya (Leningr.). Vol. 18(5):342-348.

Trombitsky, I. D. 1987. Blood pattern of *Hypophthalmichthys molitrix*, *Aristichthys nobilis* and *Ictiobus cyprinellus* infected with metacercariae of the genus *Diplostomum* (Trematoda, Diplostomidae). Parazitologiya (Leningr.) Vol. 21(1):43-49.

Truhlar, J. F., and L. A. Reed. 1976. Occurrence of pesticide residues in four streams draining different land use areas in Pennsylvania. 1969-71. Pesticides Monit. J. Vol. 10(3):101-110.

Tsoi, S. C. M., and S.-C. Lee, W.-C. Chao. 1989. Duplicate gene expression and diploidization in an Asian tetraploid catostomid, *Myxocyprinus asiaticus* (Cypriniformes, Catostomidae). Comp. Biochem. Vol. 93(1):27-32.

Tsuyuki, H., and E. Roberts, R. H. Kerr, J. F. Uthe, L. W. Clarke. 1967. Comparative electropherograms of the family Castomidae. Journal of the Fisheries Research Board of Canada Vol. 24(2):299-304.

Turner, Michael A., and John W. M. Rudd. 1983. The English-Wabigoon River [Ontario, Canada] system: 3. Selenium in lake enclosures: Its geochemistry, bioaccumulation and ability to reduce mercury bioaccumulation. Canadian Journal of Fisheries and Aquatic Sciences. Vol. 40(12):2228-2240.

Tuten, J. S., and J. W. Avault, Jr. 1981. Growing red swamp crayfish (*Procambarus clarkii*) and several North American fish species together. Progressive Fish-Culturist. Vol. 43(2):1981:99.

Twomey, Katie. 1984. Habitat suitability index models and instream flow suitability curves: redear sunfish. Washington, D. C., Western Energy and Land Use Team, Division of Biological Services, Research and Development, Fish & Wildlife Service, U. S. Dept. of the Interior. 29p.

Twomey, Katie, and Kathryn L. Williamson, Patrick Nelson. 1984. Habitat suitability index models and instream flow suitability curves: white sucker. Washington, D. C., Western Energy and Land Use Team, Division of Biological Services, Research and Development, Fish & Wildlife Service, U. S. Dept. of the Interior. 56p.

Tyus, H. M. 1987. Distribution, reproduction, and habitat use of the razorback sucker in the Green River, Utah, 1979-1986. Transactions of the American Fisheries Society Vol. 116(1):111-116.

Tyus, H. M. 1988. Long-term retention of implanted transmitters in Colorado squawfish and razorback sucker. N. Am. J. Fish. Manage.. Vol. 8(2):264-267.

Tyus, H. M., and C. A. Karp. 1989. Habitat use and streamflow needs of rare and endangered fishes, Yampe River, Colorado. U.S. Fish Wildl. Surv. Biol. Rep. Vol. 89(14):1-27.

Tyus, H. M., and W. L. Minckley. 1988. Migrating mormon crickets, *Anabrus simplex* (Orthoptera: Tettigoniidae), as food for stream fishes. Great Basin Nat. Vol. 48(1):25-30.

Ueno, K., and A. Nagase, J.-J. Ye. 1988. Tetraploid origin of the karyotype of the Asian sucker, *Myxocyprinus asiaticus*. Japanese Journal of Ichthyology. Vol. 34(4):512-514.

Uglem, G. L. 1972. The life cycle of *Neoechinorhynchus cristatus* Lynch, 1936 (Acanthocephala) with notes on the hatching of eggs. Journal of Parasitology. Vol. 58(6):1071-1074.

Uglem, G. L., and S. M. Beck. 1972. Habitat specificity and correlated aminopeptidase activity in the acanthocephalans *Neoechinorhynchus cristatus* and *N. crassus*. Journal of Parasitology. Vol. 58(5):911-920.

Uhazy, L. S. 1976. *Philometroides huronensis* n. sp. (Nematoda: Drancunculoidea) of the common white sucker (*Catostomus commersoni*) from Lake Huron, Ontario. Canadian Journal of Zoology. Vol. 54(3):369-376.

Uhazy, L. S. 1977a. Development of *Philometroides huronensis* (Nematoda: Dracunculoidea) in the intermediate and definitive hosts. Canadian Journal of Zoology. Vol. 55(2):265-273.

Uhazy, L. S. 1977b. Biology of *Philometroides huronensis* (Nematoda: Dracunculoidea) in the white sucker (*Catostomus commersoni*). Canadian Journal of Zoology. Vol. 55(9):1430-1441.

Uhazy, L. S. 1977c. Biology of *Philometroides huronensis* n. sp. (Nematoda: Dracunculoidea) of common white sucker (*Catostomus commersoni*). Dissertation Abstr. int. (B) Vol. 37(9):4361-4362.

Uhazy, L. S. 1978. Lesions associated with *Philometroides huronensis* (Nematoda: Philometridae) in the white sucker (*Catostomus commersoni*) Journal Wildl. Dis. Vol. 14(4):401-408.

Underhill, A. H. 1941. Estimation of a breeding population of chub suckers. Trans. 5th North Amer. Wildl. Conf. pp. 251-256.

Underhill, James C. 1957. The distribution of Minnesota minnows and darters in relation to Pleistocene glaciation. Occ. Pap. Minn. Mus. nat. Hist. No. 7:1-45.

Uthe, J. F. 1965. A new method of identifying various species of fish. Circulars of the Fisheries Research Board of Canada. Freshwater Institute. Vol. 7:16-20.

Uyeno, Teruya. 1972. Concerning the Cretaceous and Tertiary fish fossils from the Hidaka and Yubari Districts: Mem. Natl. Sci. Mus. (Tokyo), 5:223-226. (Japanese, incl. English summ.), Eng. summ. title: On Cretaceous and Tertiary fish remains from the Hidaka and Yubari Districts in Hokkaido, Japan. Vol. title: Natural History of the Hidaka Mountains and the neighbouring districts (11).

Uyeno, Teruya, and Robert Rush Miller. 1962. Late Pleistocene fishes from a Trinity River Terrace, Texas. Copeia 1962(2):338-345.

Uyeno, Teruya, and Robert Rush Miller. 1963. Summary of Late Cenozoic Freshwater Fish Records for North America. Occasional Papers of the Museum of Zoology. University of Michigan. Number 631:1-34.

Uyeno, Teruya, and Gerald R. Smith. 1972. Tetraploid origin of the karyotype of catostomid fishes. Science, N. Y. Vol. 175(4022):644-646.

Valenciennes, Achille. 1844. *Sclerognathus cyprinella* p. 477. **IN:** Cuvier, Georges and Achille Valenciennes. Histoire naturelle des poissons. Paris. Vol. 17:1-497.

Van Coillie, R., and A. Rousseau. 1974. Composition minerale des écailles du *Catostomus commersoni* issu de deux milieux differents: étude par microscopie électronique analytique. Journal of the Fisheries Research Board of Canada. Vol. 31(1):63-66.

Van Coillie, R., and A. Rousseau. 1975. Distribution minérale dans les écailles des poissons d'eau douce et ses relations avec le milieu aquatique. Verhandlungen int. Verein. theor. angew. Limnol. Vol. 19(3):2440-2447.

Van Coillle, R., and A. Rousseau, M. Ouellet. 1976. Examen des divers métaux incorporés dans des structures ostéoides: étude par microscopie électronique analytique. Annales Histochim. Vol. 21(3):179-187.

van Deventer, J. S., and W. S. Platts. 1985. A computer software system for entering, managing, and analyzing fish capture data from streams. United States Dep. Agric. For. Serv. Res. Pap. Int. No. 352:1-12.

Van Duzen, Evelyn M. 1939. Observations on the breeding habits of the cut-lips minnow, *Exoglossum maxillingua*. Copeia 1939(2):65-75.

Vanicek, D. 1961. Life history of the quillback and highfin carpsuckers in the Des Moines River. Proc. Iowa Acad. Sci. Vol. 68:238-246.

Van Oosten, J., and H. J. Deason. 1939. Age, growth and condition of the walleyed pike, yellow perch, and goldeye of Lower Red Lake, Beltrami and Clearwater Counties, Minnesota. Paper given Midw. Wildl. Conf., 1939. Typewritten.

Velichko, A. M., and S. B. Podushka. 1985. Type of spawning in Siberian red side sucker *Catostomus catostomus rostratus* (Tilesius). Gos. Nauchno Issled. Inst. Ozern Rechn. Rybn. Khoz. Sb. Nauchn. Tr. No. 230:70-74.

Velichko, A. M., and B. B. Voloshenko, D. P. Bulanov, A. A. Salazkin. 1979. Results of collecting and transportation of the Kobyma redside sucker eggs and rearing of its fingerlings in water bodies of Leningrad District. Sbornik nauch. Trud. gos. nauchno-issled. Inst. ozern. rechn. rybn. Khozyaist. No. 147:47-53.

Verdon, R., and G. Codin-Blumer, E. Magnin. 1978. Croissance en longueur et en masse des meuniers noirs, *Catostomus commersoni*, du bassin hydrographiques de La Grande Rivière, territoire de la Baie James. Annales ACFAS Vol. 45(1):177.

Verdon, R., and E. Magnin. 1977a. Croissance en longueur du meunier noir *Catostomus commersoni commersoni* (La Cepède) du lac Croche dans les Laurentides, Québec. Naturaliste can. Vol. 104(3):187-195.

Verdon, R., and E. Magnin. 1977b. Dynamique de la population de meuniers noirs *Catostomus commersoni commersoni* (La Cepède) du lac Croche dans les Laurentides, Québec. Naturaliste Can. Vol. 104(3):197-206.

Verigina, I. A. 1976. The structure of the digestive tract in the American suckers of the genus *Ictiobus* (Cypriniformes, Catostomidae) 1. The bigmouth buffalo *Ictiobus cyprinella* (Cuv. et Val.) Voprosy Ikhtiol. Vol. 16(1):99-107. Translated in: Journal Ichthyol. Vol. 16(1):88-95.

Verigina, I. A. 1983. Peculiarities in the structure of the alimentary canal in Catostomidae and Cyprinidae and generic considerations between these families. Sbornik Trud. zool. Muz. MGU Vol. 20:187-205.

Vessel, M. F., and S. Eddy. 1941. A preliminary study of the egg production of certain Minnesota fishes. Minn. Dep. Conserv. Fish. Res. Invest. Rep.No. 26. 26pp.

Victor, R., and G. L. Chan, C. H. Fernando. 1979. Notes on the recovery of live ostracodes from the gut of the white sucker (*Catostomus commersoni* (La Cepède, 1808)) (Pisces: Catostomidae). Canadian Journal of Zoology. Vol. 57(9):1745-1747.

Vigg, S. 1978. Vertical distribution of adult fish in Pyramid Lake, Nevada. Great Basin Nat. Vol. 38(4):417-428.

Vigg, S. 1980. Seasonal benthic distribution of adult fish in Pyramid Lake, Nevada. California Fish Game. Vol. 66(1):49-58.

Villa, Nick A. 1985. Life history of the sacramento sucker, *Catostomus occidentalis*, in Thomes Creek, Tehama County, California [USA]. Calif. Fish Game. Vol. 71(2):88-106.

Villar, José Alvarez del. 1970. *Peces mexicanos* (claves). Comisión nacional consultiva de pesca. México. 166pp.

Viosca, Percy, Jr. 1936. A new rock bass from Louisiana and Mississippi. Copeia 1936(1):37-45.

Viosca, Percy, Jr. 1937. A tentative revision of the genus *Necturus* with descriptions of three new species from the southern Gulf drainage area. Copeia 1937(2):120-138.

Viosca, Percy, Jr. 1952. Eleventh report to International Paper Company, August 5, 1952. 21p. typewritten. (Most of data also given in a paper at Amer. Fish. Soc., Dallas, Texas, Sept. 1952).

Vladykov, Vadim D. 1933. Biological and oceanographic conditions in Hudson Bay. 9. Fishes from the Hudson Bay region (except the Coregonidae). Contributions to Canadian Biology and Fisheries (New Series). Series A. General Papers. Vol. 8(2):13-61.

Vladykov, Vadim D. 1934. Geographical variation in the number of rows of pharyngeal teeth in the cyprinid genera. Copeia 1934(3):134-136.

Vladykov, Vadim D. 1942. Two freshwater fishes new to Québec. Copeia Ann Arbor. 1942(3):193-194.

Voloshenko, B. B., and A. M. Velichko. 1979. Redside sucker *Catostomus catostomus rostratus* (Tilesius) and prospects for its utilization as an item for artificial reproduction. Sbornik nauch. Trud. gos. nauchno-issled. Inst. Ozern. rechn. rybn. Khozyaist. No. 147:3-15.

Vondracek, B. C. 1977. Life history characteristics of suckers from Green Bay and Lake Michigan with special reference to the white sucker. Univ. Wis., Madison. M.S. Thesis. 79pp.

Vondracek, B. C. 1982. The energetics of the Tahoe sucker, *Catostomus tahoensis*, in cyclic and constant temperatures. Dissertation Abstr. int. (B). Vol. 42(8):3108.

Vondracek, B. C., and L. R. Brown, J. J. Cech, Jr. 1982. Comparison of age, growth and feeding of the Tahoe sucker from Sierra Nevada streams and a reservoir. California Fish Game. Vol. 68(1):36-46.

Vondracek, B. C., and J. J. Cech, Jr. 1980. A preliminary study of stream fish respiration in cycling temperatures and its potential influence on growth rates. CAL-NEVA Wildl. 1980:22-26.

Vondracek, B., and J. J. Cech, Jr., R. K. Buddington. 1989. Growth, growth efficiency, and assimilation efficiency of the Tahoe sucker in cyclic and constant temperature. Environ. Biol. Fishes. Vol. 24(2):151-156.

Vondracek, B. C., and J. J. Cech, Jr., D. Longanecker. 1982. Effect of cycling and constant temperatures on the respiratory metabolism of the Tahoe sucker *Catostomus tahoensis* (Pisces: Catostomidae). Comparative Biochem. Physiol. (A) Vol. 73(1):11-14.

Voth, D. R., and O. R. Larson. 1968. Metazoan parasites of some fishes from Goose River, North Dakota. American Midland Naturalist. Vol. 79:216-224.

Wagner, Charles C., and Edwin L. Cooper. 1963. Population density, growth and fecundity of the creek chubsucker, *Erimyzon oblongus*. Copeia 1963(2):350-357.

Wagner, G. 1908. Notes on the fish fauna of Lake Pepin. Trans. Wis. Acad. Sci., Arts, Lett. Vol. 16(1):23-37.

Waiwood, K. G., and P. H. Johansen. 1974. Oxygen consumption and activity of the white sucker (*Catostomus commersoni*), in lethal and non lethal levels of the organo-chlorine insecticide, methoxychlor. Water Res. Vol. 8(7):401-406.

Walburg, C. H. 1964. Fish population studies, Lewis and Clark Lake, Missouri River, 1956 to 1962. Spec. Sci. Rep., U.S. Fish Wildl. Serv. Vol. 482:1-27.

Walburg, C. H. 1976. Changes in the fish populations of Lewis and Clark Lake, 1956-74, and their relation to water management and the environment. U. S. Fish Wildl. Serv. Res. Rep. 79:34pp.

Walburg, C. H., and W. R. Nelson. 1966. Carp, river carpsucker, smallmouth buffalo, and bigmouth buffalo in Lewis and Clark Lake, Missouri River. Res. Rep. U. S. Fish. Wildl. Serv. No. 69:(1966):1-30.

Walden, Howard T., 2d. 1964. Familiar Freshwater Fishes of America. Harper & Row Publishers. New York, N. Y. 324pp.

Walker, Chris M. Wood, and Brian R. McMahon. 1983. Acid-base balance, ionic status, and renal function in resting and acid-exposed white suckers (*Catostomus commersoni*). Canadian Journal of Zoology. Vol. 61(12):2660-2668.

Walker, G. W. 1951. A fish population study of an artificial lake in southern Illinois. M.S. Thesis. South. Ill. Univ. 33pp.

Walker, R. L., and P. R. H. Wilkes, C. M. Wood. 1989. The effects of hypersaline exposure on oxygen-affinity of the blood of the freshwater teleost *Catostomus commersoni*. J. Exp. Biol. Vol. 142:125-142.

Walker, M. C., and P. T. Frank. 1952. The propagation of buffalo. Progr. Fish Cult. Vol. 14(3):129-130.

Wallace, R. G. 1976. About Bait-Fish in Ontario. Ministry of Natural Resources. Ontario, Canada. 55pp.

Wallace, Ron R., and Peter J. McCart. 1984. The Fish and Fisheries of the Athabasca River Basin Their Status and Environmental Requirements. Planning Division, Alberta Environment. Water Resources. Edmonton, Alberta. 269pp.

Walters, Vladimir. 1953. The fishes collected by the Canadian Arctic Expedition, 1913-1918, with additional notes on the ichthyofauna, of western Arctic Canada. Bull. Natl. Mus. Canada. No. 128:257-274.

Walters, V. 1955. Fishes of western arctic America and eastern arctic Siberia. Bull. Am. Museum Nat. Hist. Vol. 106(5):255-368.

Walton, B. D. 1980. The reproductive biology, early life history and growth of white suckers (*Catostomus commersoni*), and longnose suckers, (*C. catostomus*), in the Willow Creek, Chain Lakes System, Alberta. Alberta Department of Energy and Natural Resources. Fisheries Research Report No. 23:1-180pp.

Wang, Johnson C. S., and Ronnie J. Kernehan. 1979. Fishes of the Delaware estuaries-a guide to the early life histories. EA Communications, Towson, Maryland:1-410.

Ward, C. M. 1960. A survey of the fishes of Nolichacky River. Tenn. Game Fish Comm. 30pp. mimeo.

Ward, H. C. 1949. A study of fish populations, with special reference to the white bass, *Lepibema chrysops* (Rafinesque), in Lake Duncan, Oklahoma. Master's Thesis. Univ. Okla. 44pp. typewritten.

Watson, T. G. 1981. *Metorchis conjunctus* (Cabbold, 1860) Looss, 1899 (Trematoda:Opisthorchiidae): isolation of metacercariae from fish hosts. Canadian Journal of Zoology. Vol. 59(10):2010-2013.

Waxman, J. B. 1975. The locomotor behavior of fish in response to a subacute concentration of copper alone, and in combination with other environmental factors. Dissertation Abstr. int. (B). Vol. 35(8):3752.

Webster, Dwight A. 1942. The life histories of some Connecticut fishes. A fishery survey of important Connecticut lakes. Bull. Geol. Nat. Hist. surv. Conn. Vol. 63:122-227.

Webster, Dwight A. 1944. Notes on the food of the smallmouth bass (*Micropterus dolomieu*) in Columbia Lake, Connecticut. Copeia 1944(2):125-126.

Webster, Dwight A. 1954. A survival experiment and an example of selective sampling of brook trout (*Salvelinus fontinalis*) by angling and rotenone in an Adirondack pond. N.Y. Fish Game J. Vol. 1(2):214-219.

Weed, Alfred Cleveland. 1921. Fishes from southern Wisconsin. Copeia 1921(No. 99):69-72.

Weigel, R. D., and J. A. Holman, A. A. Paloumpis. 1974. Vertebrates from Russell Cave. pp. 81-85. **IN:** Investigations in Russell Cave; Russell Cave National Monument, Alabama (Griffin, J. W.) U.S. Natl. Park Serv., Publ. Archeol. Vol. 13.

Weiner, J. G., and R. A. Jacobson, P. S. Schmidt, P. R. Heine. 1985. Serum calcium concentrations in white sucker, *Catostomus commersoni* La Cepède, and bluegill, *Lepomis macrochirus* Rafinesque, in northern Wisconsin lakes: relation to pH and waterborne calcium. Journal Fish. Biol. Vol. 27(6):699-709.

Weisel, G. F. 1957. Fish Guide for inter-mountain Montana. Mont. State Univ. Press. Missoula. 88pp.

Weisel, George F. 1958. The comparative effects of fresh-water and marine teleost pituitary on the water balance of frogs. Copeia 1958(2):86-91.

Weisel, George F. 1960. The osteocranium of the catostomid fish, *Catostomus macrocheilus*. A study in adaptation and natural relationship. J. Morph. Vol. 106(1):109-129.

Weisel, George F. 1962. Comparative study of the digestive tract of a sucker, *Catostomus catostomus*, and a predaceous minnow, *Ptychocheilus oregonense*. Amer. Midl. Nat. Vol. 68:334-346.

Weisel, George F. 1967a. The pharyngeal teeth of larval and juvenile suckers (*Catostomus*). Copeia 1967:50-54.

Weisel, George F. 1967b. Early ossification in the skeleton of the sucker *Catostomus macrocheilus* and the guppy *Poecilia reticulata*. J. Morph. Vol. 121(1):1-18.

Weisel, George F., and Eldon L. McLaury. 1964. Blind catfish (*Ictalurus nebulosus*) from Dog Lake, Oregon. Copeia 1964(4):687-690.

Weisel, George F., Jr., and H. William Newman. 1951. Breeding habits, development and early life history of *Richardsonius balteatus*, a northwestern minnow. Copeia 1951(3):187-194.

Welch, K. J., and D. W. Khuehl, E. N. Leonard, G. D. Veith, N. D. Schoenthal. 1981. Background hydrocarbon residues in fishes from the Great Lakes and eastern Montana. Bulletin envir. Contam. Toxicol. Vol. 26(6):724-728.

Wells, La Rue, and A. L. McLain. 1973. Lake Michigan. Man's effects on native fish stocks and other biota. Technical Rep. Gt. Lakes Fish. Commn. No. 20 1973:1-55.

Welsh, W. W. 1916. Notes on the fishes of the Peedee River Basin, North and South Carolina. Copeia 1916 (No. 33):54-56.

Welter, Wilfred A. 1938. A list of the fishes of the Licking River drainage in eastern Kentucky. Copeia 1938(2):64-68.

Wenzel, L. E., and T. H. Leik. 1956. A fish management study of Guernsey Reservoir and the adjacent portion of North Platte River. Wyo. Game Fish. Comm. Fish. Tech. Rep. Vol. 5:41pp.

Werner, Robert G. 1976a. Current Level of Taxonomic Information on Great Lakes Fish Eggs and Larvae. pp. 6-18. **IN:** John Boreman (ed.) Great Lakes Fish Egg and Larvae Identification: Proceedings of a Workshop. U.S. Fish and Wildlife Service National Power Plant Team. Ann Arbor, Michigan FWS/OBS-76/23 220pp.

Werner, Robert G. 1976b. A preliminary annotated bibliography of the literature relevant to descriptions of eggs and larval stages of fishes of the Great Lakes. Appendix I. pp. 107-200. **IN:** John Boreman (ed.) Great Lakes Fish Egg and Larvae Identification: Proceedings of a Workshop. U.S. Fish and Wildlife Service National Power Plant Team. Ann Arbor, Michigan. FWS/OBS-76/23. 220pp.

Werner, Robert G. 1979. Homing mechanism of spawning white suckers in Wolf Lake, New York. New York Fish Game J. Vol. 26(1):48-58.

Werner, Robert G. 1980. Freshwater fishes of New York State. Syracuse University Press, Syracuse, New York. 1-186pp.

Whitaker, J. O., Jr., and R. A. Schlueter. 1975. Occurrence of the crustacean parasite, *Lernaea cyprinacea*, on fishes from the White River at Petersburg, Indiana. American Midl. Nat. Vol. 93(2):446-450.

Whitaker, J. O., and D. C. Wallace. 1966. Fishes of Vigo County, Indiana. Proc. Indiana Acad. Sci. Vol. 75:279 (Abstract).

White, A. M., and Milton B. Trautman. 1981. Discovery of the river redhorse, *Moxostoma carinatum*, in the Grand River, an Ohio tributary of Lake Erie. Ohio J. Sci. Vol. 81(1):45-46.

White, D. S. 1975. The biology of *Minytrema melanops* (Rafinesque), the spotted sucker. Dissertation Abstr. int. (B) Vol. 36(2):546-547.

White, D. S. 1977. Early development and pattern of scale formation in the spotted sucker, *Minytrema melanops* (Catostomidae). Copeia 1977(2):400-403.

White, D. S., and K. H. Haag. 1977. Foods and feeding habits of the spotted sucker, *Minytrema melanops* (Rafinesque). American Midl. Nat. Vol. 98(1):137-146.

White, G. E. 1974. Parasites of the common white sucker (*Catostomus commersoni*) from the Kentucky River drainage. Transactions Am. Microsc. Soc. Vol. 93(2):280-282.

White, G. E., and J. P. Harley. 1973. Helminth parasites of the white sucker, *Catostomus commersoni*, from Lake Wilgreen in Kentucky. Transactions Ky. Acad. Sci. Vol. 34(3-4):53-54.

White, G., and J. P. Harley. 1974. Helminth parasites of the white sucker (Pisces: Catostomidae) in the Kentucky River Drainage. Transactions Ky. Acad. Sci. Vol. 35(1-2):24-26.

White, W. J., and R. J. Beamish. 1972. A simple fish tag suitable for long-term marking experiments. Journal of the Fisheries Research Board of Canada. Vol. 29(3):339-341.

Whitehouse, Francis C. 1946. <u>Sport</u> <u>Fishes</u> <u>of</u> <u>Western</u> <u>Canada</u>, <u>and</u> <u>Some</u> <u>Others</u>. McClelland & Stewart Limited. Toronto, Canada. 129pp.

Whitfield, Robert Parr. 1890. Observations on a fossil fish from the Eocene beds of Wyoming. Bull. Amer. Mus. Nat. Hist., 1890. Vol. 3:117-120.

Whitworth, W. R., and P. L. Berrien, W. T. Keller. 1968. Freshwater fishes of Connecticut. Bull. State Geol. Nat. Hist. Surv. Conn. 101:134pp.

Wickliff, Edward L., and Milton B. Trautman. 1934. List of the fishes of Ohio. Ohio Dept. Agric., Div. of Cons., Bur. Sci. Research. Bull. 1, Jan.:1-3 mimeo.

Wiener, J. G., and J. P. Giesy, Jr. 1979. Concentration of Cd, Cu, Mn, Pb, and Zn in fishes in a highly organic softwater pond. Journal of the Fisheries Research Board of Canada. Vol. 36(3):270-279.

Wiener, J. G., and R. A. Jacobson, P. S. Schmidt, P. R. Heine. 1985. Serum calcium concentrations in white sucker, *Catostomus commersoni* and bluegill, *Lepomis macrochirus*, in northern Wisconsin [USA] lakes: Relation to pH and waterborne calcium. J. Fish Biol. Vol. 27(6):699-710.

Wier, W., and L. F. Mayberry, H. G. Kinzer, P. R. Turner. 1983. Parasites of fishes in the Gila River drainage in southwestern New Mexico. Journal Wildl. Dis. Vol. 19(1):59-60.

Wigley, R. L. 1959. Life history of the sea lamprey of Cayuga Lake (N.Y.). Fish. Bull. U.S. Vol. 59(No. 154):561-617.

Wiles, M., and D. K. Cone. 1987. A species of *Trichophrya* (Suctoria: Dendrosomidae) from *Catostomus commersoni* La Cepède in Nova Scotia. Proc. N. S. Inst. Sci. Halifax. Vol. 37(1):9-12.

Wilkes, P. R. H., and B. R. McMahon. 1986a. Responses of a stenohaline freshwater teleost (*Catostomus commersoni*) to hypersaline exposure: I. The dependence of plasma pH and bicarbonate concentration on electrolyte regulation. J. Exp. Biol. Vol. 121(0):77-94.

Wilkes, P. R. H., and B. R. McMahon. 1986b. Responses of a stenohaline freshwater teleost (*Catostomus commersoni*) to hypersaline exposure. II. Transepithelial flux of sodium, chloride and "acidic equivalents". J. Exp. Biol. 121(0):95-114.

Wilkes, P. R. H., and R. L. Walker, D. G. McDonald, C. M. Wood. 1981. Respiratory, ventilatory, acid-base and ionoregulatory physiology of the white sucker *Catostomus commersoni* the influence of hyperoxia. Journal exp. Biol. Vol. 91:239-254.

Williams, C. D., and J. E. Williams. 1982. Summer food habits of fishes from two springs in east-central Nevada. Southwestern Nat. Vol. 27(4):437-445.

Williams, D. D. 1977a. A key to caryophyllaeid cestodes of Wisconsin fishes. Iowa St. J. Res. Vol. 51(4):471-477.

Williams, D. D. 1977b. *Isoglaridacris chetekensis* sp. n. and *I. wisconsinensis* sp.n. (Cestoda: Caryophyllaeidae) from Red Cedar River, Wisconsin catostomid fishes. Proceedings helminth. soc. Wash. Vol. 44(1):91-95.

Williams, D. D. 1978a. *Biacetabulum oregoni* sp.n. (Cestoda:Caryophyllaeidae) from *Catostomus macrocheilus*. Iowa St. J. Res. Vol. 52(4):397-400.

Williams, D. D. 1978b.A key to caryophyllidean cestodes. Iowa St. J. Res. Vol. 52(4): 401-409.

Williams, D. D. 1979. *Lissorchis hypentelii* (Trematoda: Lissorchiidae) from Red Cedar River, Wisconsin, catostomid fishes. Proceedings helminth. Soc. Wash. Vol. 46(1):150-151.

Williams, D. D. 1980. Procercoid development of *Isoglaridacris wisconsinensis* (Cestoda: Caryophyllaeidae). Proceedings helminth. Soc. Wash. Vol. 47(1):138-139.

Williams, D. D. 1980. Fish hosts and distribution of caryophyllidean cestodes in North America. Univ. Wis. Mus. Nat. Hist. Rep. Fauna Flora Wis. No. 17:1-14.

Williams, D. D. 1980. Caryophyllaeid cestodes of *Moxostoma macrolepidotum* in northwestern Wisconsin. Univ. Wis. Mus. Nat. Hist. Rep. Fauna Flora Wis. No. 17:15-17.

Williams, D. D. 1980. Morphological variation of *Glaridacris laruei* from catostomid fishes in northwestern Wisconsin and synonymy of *G. oligorchis*. Univ. Wis. Mus. Nat. Hist. Rep. Fauna Flora Wis. No. 17:18-20.

Williams, D. D. 1980. Anomalous morphology of the caryophyllaeid, *Isoglaridacris wisconsinensis* Univ. Wis. Mus. Nat. Hist. Rep. Fauna Flora Wis. No. 17:23-24.

Williams, D. D., and M. J. Ulmer. 1970. Caryophyllaeid cestodes from four species of *Carpiodes* (Teleostei: Catostomidae). Proc. Iowa Acad. Sci. Vol. 77:185-195.

Williams, D. D., and M. J. Ulmer. 1980. Host and locality records for *Plagioporus sinitsini* (Trematoda: Opecoelidae). Proceedings helminth. Soc. Wash. Vol. 47(2):263.

Williams, E. H., Jr. 1974. Two new species of *Monobothrium* (Cestoda: Carophyllaeidae) from Catostomid fishes of the southeastern United States. Transactions of the American Fisheries Society. Vol. 103(3):610-615.

Williams, E. H., Jr. 1978. *Dieffluvium unipapillatum* n.g., n. sp. (Cestoda: Caryophyllaeidae) from the river redhorse *Moxostoma carinatum* (Cope) from the southeastern United States. Transactions Am. Microsc. Soc. Vol. 97(4):601-605.

Williams, E. H., Jr. 1979., *Penarchigetes fessus* sp. n. from the lake chubsucker, *Erimyzon sucetta* (La Cepède) in the southeastern United States. Proceedings helminth. Soc. Wash. Vol. 46(1):84-87.

Williams, E. H., Jr. 1980. *Rogersus rogersi* gen. et sp. n. (Cestoda: Caryophyllaeidae) from the blacktail redhorse, *Moxostoma poecilurum* (Jordan) (Osteichthyes) in the southeastern United States. Journal of Parasitology. Vol. 66(3):564-568.

Williams, E. H., Jr., and W. A. Rogers. 1972. *Isoglaridacris agminis* sp. n. (Cestoda: Caryophyllaeidae) from the lake chubsucker, *Erimyzon sucetta* (La Cepède). Journal of Parasitology. Vol. 58(6):1082-1084.

Williams, E. H., Jr., and W. A. Rogers. 1982. New host records for Acanthocephala of some Alabama freshwater fishes. Proceedings helminth. Soc. Wash. Vol. 49(1):140-142.

Williams, E. H., Jr., and W. A. Rogers. 1984. *Pomphorhynchus lucyi* sp. n. (Acanthocephala) from fresh and brackish water fishes of the southeastern U.S. gulf coast. Journal of Parasitology. Vol. 70(4):580-583.

Williamson, J., and R. O. Smitherman. 1976. Food habits of hybrid buffalofish, *Tilapia*, Israeli carp and channel catfish in polyculture. Proceedings a. Conf. SEast Ass. Game Fish Commnrs. Vol. 29:1975(1976):86-91.

Willis, David W. 1979. The buffalo in Lake Sakakawea. North Dakota Outdoors. Vol. 41(11):16-17.

Willis, David W., and Lanny D. Jones. 1986. Fish standing crops in wooded and nonwooded coves of Kansas reservoirs. Am. J. Fish Manage. Vol. 6(1):105-108.

Willis, David W., and J. B. Owen. 1978. Decline of the year-class strength of buffalo fishes in Lake Sakakawea, North Dakota. Prairie Nat. Vol. 10(3):89-91.

Willock, T. A. 1969. Distributional list of fishes in the Missouri drainage of Canada. Journal of the Fisheries Research Board of Canada. Vol. 26(6):1439-1449.

Wilson, Mark Vincent Hardman. 1974. Fossil Fishes of the Tertiary of British Columbia. Ph.D. Thesis. University of Toronto. Geology Department. 375pp. + 110 pp. appendices.

Wilson, Mark Vincent Hardman. 1977a. Fossil fishes of the Tertiary of British Columbia. Doctoral thesis, 1974, Univ. of Toronto, Toronto, Ont., Canada. Dissertation Abstr. int. (B) Vol. 37(12)Part 1.:6034-6035.

Wilson, Mark Vincent Hardman. 1977b. Paleoecology of Eocene lacustrine varves at Horsefly, British Columbia. Can. J. Earth Sci. Vol. 14(5):953-962.

Wilson, Mark Vincent Hardman. 1977c. Middle Eocene freshwater fishes from British Columbia Life Sci. Contr. R. Ont. Mus. No. 113:1-61.

Wilson, Mark Vincent Hardman. 1978. *Eohiodon woodruffi* n. sp. (Teleostei, Hiodontidae), from the middle Eocene Klondike Mountain Formation near Republic, Washington. Can. J. Earth Sci. Vol. 15(5):679-686.

Wilson, Mark Vincent Hardman. 1979. A second species of *Libotonius* (Pisces: Percopsidae) from the Eocene of Washington State. Copeia. 1979(3):400-405.

Wilson, Mark Vincent Hardman. 1980. Eocene lake environments depth and distance from shore variation in fish, insect, and plant assemblages. Palaeogeogr., Palaeoclimatol., Palaeoecol. Vol. 32(No. 1-2):21-44.

Wilson, Mark Vincent Hardman. 1984. Year classes and sexual dimorphism in the Eocene Catostomid Fish *Amyzon aggregatum*. Journal of Vertebrate Paleontology. Vol. 3(3):137-142.

Wilson, R. L. 1968. Systematics and faunal analysis of a Lower Pliocene vertebrate assemblage from Trego County, Kansas. Contr. Mus. Paleont. Univ. Mich. Vol. 22:75-126.

Wiltz, J. W. 1984. Developmental stages of the highfin carpsucker (*Carpiodes velifer*), and its separation from other catostomids of the Altamaha River, Georgia. Georgia Journal of Science. Vol. 42(4):97-108.

Wiltz, J. W. 1986. Description of the mesolarva and metalarva Alabama hog sucker (*Hypentelium etowanum*) from Georgia. Georgia Journal of Science. Vol. 44(3):81-89.

Winger, P. V., and J. K. Andreasen. 1985. Contaminants residues in fish and sediments from lakes in the Atchafalaya River Basin (Louisiana). Arch. Environ. Contam. Toxicol. Vol. 14(5):579-586.

Winger, P. V., and D. P. Schultz, W. W. Johnson. (Undated). Contamination from battey salvage operations on the Chipola River, Florida. Proc. Annu. conf. Southeast Assoc. Fish Wildl. Agencies. Vol. 39:139-145.

Winn, H. E., and Robert Rush Miller. 1954. Native postlarval fishes of the lower Colorado River basin, with a key to their identification. Calif. Fish Game. Vol. 40: 273-285.

Wisdom, J. L. A. 1972. Acceptability of flavor and aroma of smallmouth buffalo, river carpsucker, and carp from Elephant Butte Lake, New Mexico. N. M. State Univ., Las Cruces. M.S. Thesis. 26pp.

Withler, F. C. 1948. Lakes of the Skeena River Drainage. VIII. Lakes of the Lac-da-dah Basin. No. 74:9-12.

Withler, F. C., and J. A. McConnell, V. H. McMahon. 1949. Lakes of the Skeena River Drainage. IX. Babine Lake. Progress Reports of Fisheries Research Board of Canada Pacific Coast Stations. No. 78:6-10.

Witt, Arthur, Jr. and Richard C. Marzolf. 1954. Spawning and behavior of the longear sunfish, *Lepomis megalotis megalotis*. Copeia 1954(3):188-190.

Wobeser, G., and F. M. Atton. 1973. An outbreak of columnaris disease in white suckers (*Catostomus commersoni*) in Saskatchewan. Journal of the Fisheries Research Board of Canada. Vol. 30(5):681-683.

Wobeser, G., and N. O. Nielsen, R. H. Dunlop, F. M. Atton. 1970. Mercury concentrations in tissues of fish from the Saskatchewan River. Journal of the Fisheries Research Board of Canada. Vol. 27(4):830-834.

Woo, Patrick T. K., and Geoff A. Black. 1984. Host specificity and hosts effect on morphometrics. Journal of Parasitology. Vol. 70(5):788-793.

Woodbury, L. A. 1941. A sudden mortality of fishes accompanying a super saturation of oxygen in Lake Waubesa, Wisconsin. Transactions of the American Fisheries Society. Vol. 71:112-117.

Wooding, Frederick H. 1959. The Book of Canadian Fishes. McGraw-Hill Ryerson Limited. Toronto. 303pp.

Woodling, J. 1985. Colorado's little fish. A guide to the minnows and other lesser known fishes in the State of Colorado. Colorado Division of Wildlife, Denver. 77 pp.

Woods, A. E., and R. F. Carlton, M. E. Casto, G. I. Gleason. 1979. Environmental bromine in freshwater and freshwater organisms: factors affecting bioaccumulation. Bulletin envir. Contam. Toxicol. Vol. 23(1-2):179-185.

Woods, Loren P. 1959. A survey of Fishes in an Illinois Stream. Chicago Natural History Museum Bulletin. January 1959:6-7.

Woodward, A. Smith. 1901. Catalogue of the fossil fishes in the British Museum. Part IV: Containing the actinopterygian Teleostomi of the suborders Isospondyli (in part), Ostariophysi, Apodes, Percesoces, Hemibranchii, Acanthopterygii, and Anacanthini. 8 vo. 1-636 pp.

Woodward, R. L., and T. E. Wissing. 1976. Age, growth and fecundity of the quillback (*Carpiodes cyprinus*) and highfin (*C. velifer*) carpsuckers in an Ohio stream. Transactions of the American Fisheries Society. Vol. 105(3):411-415.

Wrenn, W. B., and B. G. Grinstead. 1968. Larval development of the smallmouth buffalo, *Ictiobus bubalus*. J. Tenn. Acad. Sci. Vol. 46:117-120.

Wu, H.-w., and J. L. Lo, J. T. Lin. 1979. Phylogenetic relationship and systematic position of *Gyrinocheilus* (Gyrinocheilidae, Pisces). Acta zootaxon. sin. Vol. 4(4):307-311.

Wyatt, E. J. 1979. *Facieplatycauda pratti* gen. n., sp. n. and two new species of *Myxobolus* (Myxosporida). Journal Protozool. Vol. 26(1):47-51.

Wydoski, Richard S., and Richard R. Whitney. 1979. Inland fishes of Washington. University of Washington Press, Seattle and London. 1-220pp.

Wynne-Edwards, V. C. 1952. Freshwater vertebrates of the Arctic and Subarctic. Bulletins of the Fisheries Research Board of Canada. No. 94:28pp.

Xiong Quanimo. 1988. Phosphoglucose isomerase in *Moxostoma*. Acta Genet. Sin. Vol. 15(3):201-206.

Yashouv, A. 1958. Report on the growth of the buffalo fish (*Megastomatobus cyprinella*). Bamidgeh Vol. 10(4):81-84.

Yeager, Bruce L., and Kenneth J. Semmens. 1987. Early Development of the Blue Sucker, *Cycleptus elongatus.*. Copeia. 1987(2):312-316.

Yeager, Lee E. 1936. An observation on spawning Buffalofish in Mississippi. Copeia Ann Arbor. 1936(4):238-239.

Yerger, R. W., and R. D. Suttkus. 1962. Records of freshwater fishes in Florida. Tulane Stud. Zool. Vol. 9:323-330.

Ying, Sun, and, R. Nash, C. S. Clay. 1985. Acoustic measurements of the anatomy of fish at 220 KHz. Journal Acoust. Soc. Am. Vol. 78(5):1772-1776.

Yoder, Chris O., and Raymond A. Beaumier. 1986. The occurrence and distribution of river redhorse, *Moxostoma carinatum* and greater redhorse, *Moxostoma valenciennesi*, in the Sandusky River, Ohio. Ohio J. Sci. Vol. 86(1):18-21.

Young, Leah Bendell, and Harold H. Harvey. 1989. Concentrations and distribution of Fe, Zn and Cu in tissues of the white sucker (*Catostomus commersoni*) in relation to elevated levels of metals and low pH. Hydrobiologica Vol. 176/177:349-354.

Yu, Z., and Z. Deng, M. Cai, X. Deng, H. Jiang, J. Yi, J. Tian. 1988.Preliminary report on reproductive biology and artificial propagation of the Chinese sucker (*Myxocyprinus asiaticus*) in the downstreams of Gezhouba hydroelectric project. Acta Hydrobiol. Sin. Vol. 12(1):87-89.

Yulis, Carlos Roberto, and Karl Lederis. 1986. The distribution of "extraurophysial" urotensin I-immunoreactiviity in the central nervous system of *Catostomus commersoni* after urophysectomy. Neurosci. Lett. Vol. 70(1):75-80.

Yulis, Carlos Roberto, and Karl Lederis. 1986. Extraurophyseal distribution of urotensin II immunoreactive neuronal perikarya and their processes. Proc. Natl. Acad. Sci. U.S.A. Vol. 83(18):7079-7083.

Yulis, C. R., and K. Lederis. 1987. Co-localization of the immunoreactivities of the pituitary system of the teleost *Catostomus commersoni*. Cell Tissue Res. Vol. 247(2):267-273.

Yulis, C. R., and K. Lederis. 1988. Occurrence of an anterior spinal, cerebrospinal fluid-contacting, urotensin II neuronal system in various fish species. Gen. Comp. Endocrinol. Vol. 70(2):301-311.

Yulis, Carlos Roberto, and Karl Lederis, Kar-Lit Wong, Anthony W. F. Fisher. 1986. Localization of urotensin I- and corticotropin- releasing factor-like immunoreactivity in the central nervous system of *Catostomus commersoni*. Peptides Vol. 7(1):79-86.

Yurawecz, M. P., and J.-Y. Chen, B. J. Puma. 1986. Identification of cis-and trans-1,1,2,3,4,-pentachloro- 4-[1-methylethoxyl]-1,3-butadiene residues in Mississippi River fish. Journal Ass. of Analyt. Chem. Vol. 69(4):586-591.

Yurkevich, N. V. 1978. [The rearing of two year old big mouth buffaloes in a monoculture in the experimental fish farm 'Nivka'.]. Rybnol Khoz., Kiev. No. 27:50-52.

Zabik, M. E., and B. Olson, T. M. Johnson. 1978. Dieldrin, DDT, PCB's and mercury levels in freshwater mullet from the upper Great Lakes. Pesticides Monit. J. Vol. 12(1):36-39.

Zalewski, M. 1983. The influence of fish community structure on the efficiency of electrofishing. Fish Manage. Vol. 14(4):177-186.

Zittel, Karl A. von. 1932. Text-Book of Palaeontology. Vol. 2. (2nd English edition revised, with additions, by Sir Arthur Smith Woodward). Macmillan and Co., Limited. London, U.K. 464pp.

Zuckerman, L. D., and E. P. Bergersen. 1986. Aquatic ecology and management of wilderness streams in the Great sand dunes National Monument, Colorado. United States Dep. Agric. For. Serv. gen. tech. Rep. INT. No. 212:221-231.

INDEX TO MASTER OF SCIENCE THESES

Al-Rawi, T. R. (1964), Bassett, H. N. (1957), Beers, G. D. (1955), Behmer, D. J. (1965a), Bernhardt, R. W. (1957), Bowman, M. L. (1954), Campbell, R. S. (1935), Carnes, W. C., Jr. (1958), Davis, J. T. (1955), Dorkin, John L., Jr. (1980), Elsey, C. A. (1946), Geen, G. H. (1958), Gerlack, Jim. (1973), Hansen, D. W. (1952), Harris, Roy H. D. (1952), Hayes, M. L. (1956), Kimmel, Peter G. (1975), McClellan, P. H. (1977), Meyer, W. H. (1961), Principe, P. A. (1977), Walker, G. W. (1951), Ward, H. C. (1949),

INDEX TO DOCTORAL DISSERTATIONS

Andreasen, J. K. (1976), Baker, J. P. (1981), Barclay, L. A., Jr. (1974), Beamish, R. J. (1972b), Beecher, H. A. (1979b), Behmer, D. J. (1966), Bowman, M. L. (1959), Bussjaeger, C. E. (1973), Buth, Donald G. (1978), Chan, G.-L. (1981), Curry, Kevin D. (1980), Deacon, James Everett. (1960), Jenkins, Robert E. (1970), Keeton, D. (1963), Koch, D. L. (1973b), Koehn, Richard K. (1968), Kononen, D. W. (1982), Long, Wilbur L. (1973), Martin, R. E. (1964a), Miki, B. L. A. (1977), Miller, R. G. (1951), Moyle, Peter B. (1969), Muzzall, P. M. (1979a), Nasini, S. K. (1973), Nelson, Joseph S. (1966), Orr, O. E. (1958), Smith, C. G. (1977), Smith, Gerald R. (1965), Uhazy, L. S. (1977c), Vondracek, B. C. (1982), White, D. S. (1975),

INDEX TO COMMON NAMES

Alabama hog sucker.
see *Hypentelium etowanum* (Jordan, 1877).

Allegheny red horse.
see *Moxostoma duquesnii* (Le Sueur, 1817).

bigeye jumprock.
see *Moxostoma ariommum* Robins and Raney, 1956.

bigmouth buffalo, also known as red-mouthed buffalo, red mouth buffalo fish, common buffalo fish.
see *Ictiobus cyprinellus* (Valenciennes, 1844, **IN:** Cuvier and Valenciennes, 1844).

big-mouth sucker.
see *Catostomus megastomus* Rafinesque, 1820.

black buffalo.
see *Ictiobus niger* (Rafinesque, 1820).

black buffalo-fish.
see *Catostomus niger* Rafinesque, 1820.

black horse.
see *Cycleptus* Rafinesque, 1819.

black jumprock.
>   see *Moxostoma cervinum* (Cope, 1868).

black redhorse.
>   see *Moxostoma duquesni* (Le Sueur, 1817).

black redhorse.
>   see *Moxostoma duquesnii duquesnii* (Le Sueur, 1817).

black redhorse, also known as **common redhorse, mullet, Allegheny red horse.**
>   see *Moxostoma duquesnei* (Le Sueur, 1817).

black suckerel.
>   see *Cycleptus nigrescens* Rafinesque, 1819.

black-back sucker, also known as **black sucker, blue sucker.**
>   see *Catostomus melanotus*

black-face sucker.
>   see *Cotostomus melanops.*

blackfin sucker.
>   see *Moxostoma (Thoburnia) atripinne* Bailey, 1959.

blacktail redhorse.
>   see *Moxostoma pœcilurum* (Jordan, 1877).

blue mullet.
>   see *Moxostoma coregonus* (Cope).

blue sucker, also known as **gourd-seed sucker, suckerel, Missouri sucker, black-horse.**
>   see *Cycleptus elongatus* (Le Sueur, 1817).

bluehead sucker.
>   see *Catostomus discobolus* Cope, 1872.

blueheaded sucker.
>   see *Pantosteus delphinus* (Cope, 1872).

blunt-nosed river carp.
>   see *Carpiodes difformis* Cope, 1870.

bridgelip sucker.
>   see *Pantosteus columbianus* Eigenmann and Smith, 1893.

bridgelip sucker.
>   see *Catostomus columbianus* (Eigenmann and Eigenmann, 1893).

brown buffalo-fish.
>   see *Catostomus bubalus* (Rafinesque, 1818).

buffalo carp sucker, also known as **buffalo carp, buffalo perch, buffalo sucker, white buffalo-fish.**
>   see *Cotostomus anisopterus.*

buffalo fishes.
      see *Ictiobus* Rafinesque, 1820.

central quillback carpsucker.
      see *Carpiodes cyprinus* hinei Trautman, 1956.

chub-sucker, also known as **sweet sucker, creek-fish.**
      see *Erimyzon sucetta oblongus* (Mitchill, 1815).

chub suckers.
      see *Erimyzon* Jordan, 1876.

common red-horse, also known as **mullet, white sucker, large-scaled sucker.**
      see *Moxostoma aureolum* (Le Sueur, 1817).

common sucker, also known as **white sucker.**
      see *Catostomus teres* (Mitchill, 1815).

common sucker, also known as **fine-scaled sucker, white sucker, brook sucker.**
      see *Catostomus commersonii* (La Cepède, 1803).

common sucker, also known as **white sucker.**
      see *Catostomus commersonnii* (La Cepède, 1803).

common white sucker.
      see *Catostomus commersoni commersoni* (La Cepède, 1803).

copper redhorse.
      see *Moxostoma hubbsi* Legendre, 1952.

creek chubsucker.
      see *Erimyzon oblongus* (Mitchill, 1815).

cui-ui, also known as **couia.**
      see *Chasmistes cujus* Cope, 1883.

dwarf white sucker.
      see *Catostomus commersoni utawana* Mather, 1890.

dwarf white sucker.
      see *Catostomus commersonnii utawana* Mather, 1890.

desert sucker.
      see *Catostomus clarki* Baird and Girard, 1854.

eastern longnose sucker.
      see *Catostomus catostomus catostomus* (Forster, 1773).

Eastern quillback carpsucker.
      see *Carpiodes cyprinus cyprinus* (Le Sueur).

fine-scaled suckers.
      see *Catostomus* Le Sueur, 1817.

flannelmouth sucker, also known as **flannel-mouthed sucker.**

see *Catostomus latipinnis* Baird and Girard, 1854.

golden mullet.
see *Moxostoma crassilabre* (Cope, 1870).

golden redhorse.
see *Moxostoma erythrurum* (Rafinesque, 1818).

gourdhead buffalo, also known as **red-mouth buffalo, bigmouth buffalo.**
see *Megastomatobus cyprinella* (Valenciennes, 1844).

gray redhorse, also known as **Texas red horse.**
see *Moxostoma congestum* (Baird and Girard, 1855).

greater jumprock.
see *Moxostoma lachneri* Robins and Raney, 1956.

greater redhorse.
see *Moxostoma valenciennesi* Jordan, 1885.

harelip sucker.
see *Quassilabia lacera* (Jordan and Brayton, 1877).

harelip sucker, also known as **hare-lip sucker, split-mouth sucker, May sucker, pea-lip sucker, rabbit-mouth sucker, cutlips.**
see *Lagochila lacera* Jordan and Brayton, 1877.

highfin carpsucker, also known as **quillback, silver carp, spearfish, sailfish, skimback.**
see *Carpiodes velifer* (Rafinesque, 1820).

hogsucker, also known as **hogmolly, stone-roller, stone toter, hog molly, mullet, stone lugger, hammer head, crawl-a-bottom, toter.**
see *Catostomus nigricans* Le Sueur, 1817.

huo-shao-pien.
see *Myxocyprinus asiaticus chinensis* (Dabry de Thiersant, 1872).

jumprocks, also known as **jumping mullet.**
see *Scartomyzon cervinus* (Cope).

June sucker.
see *Chasmistes liorus mictus* Miller and Smith, 1981.

June sucker, also known as **June sucker of Utah Lake.**
see *Chasmistes liorus* Jordan, 1878.

Kentucky sucker.
see *Catostomus flexuosus* Rafinesque, 1820.

Klamath largescale sucker.
see *Catostomus snyderi* Gilbert, 1898.

Klamath smallscale sucker.
see *Catostomus rimiculus* Gilbert and Snyder **IN:** Gilbert, 1898.

lake carp.
      see *Carpiodes thompsoni* Agassiz, 1855.

lake chubsucker, also known as **sweet sucker, creek fish, chub sucker.**
      see *Erimyzon sucetta* (La Cepède, 1803).

largescale sucker, also known as **Columbia river sucker.**
      see *Catostomus macrocheilus* Girard, 1856.

long sucker, also known as **brown sucker.**
      see *Catostomus elongatus* Le Sueur, 1817.

longnose sucker, also known as **long-nosed sucker, northern sucker, red sucker.**
      see *Catostomus catostomus* (Forster, 1773).

Lost river sucker.
      see *Catostomus luxatus* (Cope, 1879).

modoc sucker.
      see *Catostomus microps* Rutter, 1908.

mountain sucker, also known as **northern mountain sucker.**
      see *Catostomus platyrhynchus* (Cope, 1874).

mountain sucker.
      see *Pantosteus generosus* (Girard, 1856).

mountain suckers.
      see *Pantosteus* Cope, 1875.

mud sucker.
      see *Catostomus xanthopus* Rafinesque, 1820.

northern hog sucker, also known as **hog sucker, stone lugger, stone toter, hammerhead, crawl-a-bottom, hog mullet.**
      see *Hypentelium nigricans* (Le Sueur, 1817).

northern mountain sucker.
      see *Pantosteus platyrhynchus* (Cope, 1874).

northern river carpsucker.
      see *Carpiodes carpio carpio* (Rafinesque, 1820).

northern shorthead redhorse.
      see *Moxostoma macrolepidotum macrolepidotum* (Le Sueur, 1817).

Ohio carp sucker.
      see *Catostomus anisurus* Rafinesque, 1820.

Ohio shorthead redhorse.
      see *Moxostoma macrolepidotum breviceps* (Cope, 1870).

olive carp sucker. Two different species described under the same name.
      see *Catostomus carpio* Rafinesque, 1820; and, *Catostomus* carpio Valenciennes, 1844.

Owens sucker.
>   see *Catostomus fumeiventris* Miller, 1973.

pavement-toothed red-horse.
>   see *Placopharynx duquesnei* (Le Sueur, 1817).

Pittsburgh sucker, also known as **white sucker.**
>   see *Catostomus duquesni* Le Sueur, 1817.

quillback, also known as **eastern carp sucker, skimback.**
>   see *Carpiodes cyprinus* (Le Sueur, 1817).

quill-back, also known as **skim-back, carp sucker.**
>   see *Ictiobus velifer* (Rafinesque, 1820).

razorback sucker, also known as **humpback sucker.**
>   see *Xyrauchen texanus* (Abbott, 1861).

razor-back sucker, also known as **hump-backed sucker.**
>   see *Xyrauchen cypho* (Lockington, 1881).

razor-backed buffalo, also known as **mongrel buffalo, round buffalo.**
>   see *Ictiobus urus* (Agassiz, 1854).

red horse.
>   see *Moxostoma* Rafinesque, 1820.

red-mouth buffalo, also known as **big-mouth buffalo.**
>   see *Ictiobus cyprinella* (Valenciennes, 1844, **IN:** Cuvier and Valenciennes, 1844).

red-tail sucker, also known as **red-horse, horse-fish, horse-sucker.**
>   see *Catostomus erythrurus* Rafinesque, 1818.

Rio Grande sucker.
>   see *Catostomus plebeius* Baird and Girard, 1854.

Rio Grande sucker.
>   see *Catostomus plebejus* Baird and Girard, 1854.

Rio Grande sucker.
>   see *Catostomus plebius* Baird and Girard, 1854.

river carpsucker, also known as **carp sucker, common river carp.**
>   see *Carpiodes carpio* (Rafinesque, 1820)

river redhorse.
>   see *Moxostoma carinatum* (Cope, 1870).

Roanoke hog sucker.
>   see *Hypentelium roanokense* Raney and Lachner, 1947.

rough-head sucker, also known as **pike sucker, striped sucker.**
>   see *Catostomus fasciolaris* Rafinesque, 1820.

rustyside sucker.

see *Moxostoma hamiltoni* (Raney and Lachner, 1946).

Sacramento sucker.
see *Catostomus occidentalis* Ayres, 1854.

sailing sucker.
see *Catostomus velifer* Rafinesque, 1820.

Santa Ana sucker.
see *Catostomus santaanae* (Snyder, 1908).

sharpfin chubsucker.
see *Erimyzon tenuis* (Agassiz, 1855).

shortnose sucker.
see *Chasmistes brevirostris* Cope, 1879.

shorthead redhorse, also known as **eastern red horse, white sucker.**
see *Moxostoma macrolepidotum* (Le Sueur, 1817).

short-headed red-Horse.
see *Moxostoma breviceps* (Cope, 1870).

silver redhorse, also known as **white-nosed sucker.**
see *Moxostoma anisurum* (Rafinesque, 1820).

smallfin redhorse.
see *Moxostoma robustum* (Cope, 1870)

smallmouth buffalo, also known as **small-mouthed buffalo, sucker-mouthed buffalo, small-mouth buffalo, razor-backed buffalo, quillback buffalo.**
see *Ictiobus bubalus* (Rafinesque, 1818).

small-mouthed red horse.
see *Moxostoma collapsum* (Cope, 1870).

Snake river sucker.
see *Chasmistes muriei* Miller and Smith, 1981.

Sonora sucker.
see *Catostomus insignis* Baird and Girard, 1854.

spotted suckers.
see *Minytrema* Jordan, 1878.

spotted sucker, also known as **winter sucker, striped sucker.**
see *Moxostoma melanops* (Rafinesque, 1820).

spotted sucker, also known as **winter sucker, striped sucker.**
see *Minytrema melanops* (Rafinesque, 1820).

striped jumprock, also known as **jump-rocks.**
see *Moxostoma rupiscartes* Jordan and Jenkins **IN:** Jordan, 1889.

suckermouth redhorse, also known as **V-lip redhorse, white mullet.**

see *Moxostoma pappillosum* (Cope, 1870).

Tahoe sucker.
see *Catostomus tahoensis* Gill and Jordan **IN:** Jordan, 1878.

torrent sucker.
see *Moxostoma rhothoecum* (Thoburn **IN:** Jordan and Evermann, 1896).

Utah sucker, also known as **mullet of Utah lake.**
see *Catostomus ardens* Jordan and Gilbert, 1880.

Warner sucker.
see *Catostomus warnerensis* Snyder, 1908.

webug sucker.
see *Catostomus fecundus* Cope and Yarrow, 1875.

west Mexican redhorse.
see *Moxostoma austrinum* (Bean, 1879).

western creek chubsucker.
see *Erimyzon oblongus claviformis* (Girard).

western lake chubsucker.
see *Erimyzon sucetta kennerlyi* (Girard).

white sucker, also known as **common sucker, fine-scaled sucker.**
see *Catostomus commersoni* (La Cepède, 1803).

Yaqui sucker.
see *Catostomus bernardini* Girard, 1856.

zuni mountain sucker.
see *Catostomus discobolus yarrowi* (Jordan and Copeland, 1876).

INDEX TO SCIENTIFIC NAMES

CATOSTOMIDAE
Amin, O. M. (1987), Andreasen, J. K. (1976), Anonymous. (1973), Arai, Hisao P., and R. H. Kussat. (1967), Arldt, Th. (1907), Arldt, Th. (1912), Arldt, Th. (1923), Behnke, Robert J., and Ralph M. Wetzel. (1960), Berg, Leo Simonovich. (1912), Berg, Leo Simonovich. (1932), Berg, Leo Simonovich. (1940), Berg, Leo Simonovich. (1949), Berg, Leo Simonovich. (1964), Berkman, Hilary E., and Charles F. Rabeni, Terence P. Boyle. (1986), Blackwelder, Richard E. (1972), Boulenger, G. A. (1904), Branson, Branley A., and George A. Moore. (1962), Buchanon, T. M. (1973), Bussjaeger, C. E. (1973), Bussjaeger, C. E., and T. Briggs. (1978), Buth, Donald G. (1978), Buth, Donald G. (1979a), Buth, Donald G. (1984), Buynak, G. L., and H. W. Mohr, Jr. (1980), Casteel, Richard W., and D. P. Adam. (1977), Chadwick, James W., and Steven P. Canton. (1983), Cockerell, T. D. A. (1913), Cockerell, T. D. A., and Edith M. Allison. (1909), Comiskey, C. E., and D. A. Etnier. (1972), Cope, Edward Drinker. (1872a), Curry, Kevin D. (1980), Curry, Kevin D., and Anne Spacie. (1980), Denison, Samuel G., and Carl R. Carlson, John L. Dorkin, Jr., Cecil Lue-Hing. (1978), Denoncourt, R. F. (1975), Dunham, A. E., and Gerald R. Smith, J. N. Taylor. (1979), Dymond, J. R. (1947), Eastman, Joseph T. (1977), Eaton, T. H., Jr. (1935), Edwards, L. F. (1926), Emery, Alan R. (1973), Eschmeyer, William N. (1990), Fedoruk, A.

N. (1971), Ferris, Stephen D. (1983), Ferris, Stephen D., and S. L. Portnoy, Gregory S. Whitt. (1979), Ferris, Stephen D., and Gregory S. Whitt. (1980), Fowden, M. (1980), Frick, H. C. (1965), Fuiman, L. A., and L. Corazza. (1979), Gammon, J. R. (1977), Geen, G. H., and T. G. Northcote. (1968), Gill, Theodore Nicholas. (1861), Gill, Theodore Nicholas. (1872), Gill, Theodore Nicholas. (1875), Gill, Theodore Nicholas. (1885), Gill, Theodore Nicholas. (1893), Gill, Theodore Nicholas. (1905), Goodrich, Edwin S. (1909), Gosline, William A. (1973), Gregory, William K. (1933), Günther, Albert C. (1868), Günther, Albert C. (1880), Hacker, V. A. (1977), Hay, Oliver Perry. (1929), Herald, Earl S. (1967), Herald, Earl S. (1979), Hocutt, C. H. (1979), Hoffman, Glenn L., and Fred P. Meyer. (1974), Hornshaw, T. C., and R. J. Aulerich, H. E. Johnson. (1983), Hubbs, Carl L. (1958), Huntsman, G. R. (1965), Huntsman, G. R. (1967a), Huntsman, G. R. (1970), Jones, F. W., and F. D. Martin, J. D. Hardy, Jr. (1978), Jordan, David Starr. (1885b), Jordan, David Starr. (1886), Jordan, David Starr. (1905), Jordan, David Starr. (1907a), Jordan, David Starr. (1923), Jordan, David Starr. (1929), Jordan, David Starr, and Alembert Winthrop Brayton. (1877), Jordan, David Starr, and Barton Warren Evermann. (1896), Kafuku, T. (1957), Krumholz, Louis A. (1943), Lagler, Karl F., and John E. Bardach, Robert Rush Miller. (1962), Laird, Lindsay M., and Brian Stott. (1978), Lee, David S., and Carter R. Gilbert, Charles H. Hocutt, Robert E. Jenkins, Don E. McAllister, Jay R. Stauffer, Jr. (1980), Lindberg, Georgiy Ustinovich. (1972), Lindsey, Casimir Charles. (1975), Lippson, Alice J. (1976), Loranger, A. J. (1981), Lowe-McConnell, R. H. (1978), Mackiewicz, J. S. (1968), McAllister, Don E., and Brian W. Coad. (1974), McDonald, H. Gregory, and Elaine Anderson. (1975), McDonald, Jerry N., and Charles S. Bartlett, Jr. (1983), McGuire, D. L. (1981), McKee, J. E., and H. W. Wolf. (1963), McNally, Tom. (1970), McPhail, J. D., and C. C. Lindsey. (1970), Mettee, M. F. (1978), Meyers, George Sprague. (1966), Miller, R. J., and H. W. Robison. (1973), Miller, Robert Rush. (1955), Miller, Robert Rush. (1958), Miller, Robert Rush. (1972), Molnar, K., and G. Hanek, C. H. Fernando. (1974), Moore, R. A. (1948), Moyle, Peter B. (1976), Moyle, Peter B. (1977), Moyle, Peter B., and Joseph J. Cech, Jr. (1982), Moyle, Peter B., and Bruce Vondracek. (1985), Munthe, Jens. (1980), Nelson, Edward M. (1961), Nelson, Joseph S. (1976), ~~1190~~. Novacek, Michael J., and [*Nelson, Joseph S. (1984)*] Larry G. Marshall. (1976), Obruchev, D. V. (ed.) (1967), Ommanney, Francis Downes. (1969), Patrick, R., and J. Cairns, S. S. Roback. (1966), Pfeiffer, W. (1963), Pflieger, William L. (1971), Phillips, G. L. (1971), Phillips, Gary L., and William D. Schmid, James C. Underhill. (1982), Pister, Edwin P. (1981), Principe, P. A. (1977), Ramaswami, L. S. (1955a), Ramaswami, L. S. (1955b), Ramaswami, L. S. (1957), Rauther, M. (1913), Regan, Charles Tate. (1911), Regan, Charles Tate. (1922), Ricker, W. E. (1962), Roberts, Tyson R. (1973), Robinson, H. W., and T. M. Buchanan. (1988), Romer, Alfred Sherwood. (1966), Sagemehl, M. (1891), Scoppettone, G. G. (1988), Shchukin, G. P., and N. N. Mirgorodchenko, M. Kh. Bulatov, M. Kh. Abdullin, A. N. Salakhutdinov, A. A. Shchukina. (1982), Slastenenko, E. P. (1957), Slastenenko, E. P. (1958), Smith, C. Lavett. (1962), Smith, Gerald R. (1981b), Smith, Gerald R. (1987), Stevenson, H. M. (1976), Swanson, Stella M. (1983), Teller-Marshall, Susan, and David Bardack. (1978), Trautman, Milton B. (1981), Underhill, James C. (1957), Uyeno, Teruya. (1972), Uyeno, Teruya, and Robert Rush Miller. (1962), Uyeno, Teruya, and Gerald R. Smith. (1972), van Deventer, J. S., and W. S. Platts. (1985), Verigina, I. A. (1983), Vladykov, Vadim D. (1934), White, G., and J. P. Harley. (1974), Wigley, R. L. (1959), Williams, D. D. (1977a), Williams, D. D. (1978b), Williams, D. D. (1980b), Williams, D. D., and M. J. Ulmer. (1970), Wiltz, J. W. (1984), Winn, H. E., and Robert Rush Miller. (1954), Woodling, J. (1985), Woods, Loren P. (1959), Wu, H.-w., and J. L. Lo, J. T. Lin. (1979),

Acomus Girard, 1856.
Eschmeyer, William N. (1990), Girard, C. F. (1857), Jordan, David Starr. (1923), Jordan, David Starr, and Barton Warren Evermann. (1896),

Acomus forsterianus Girard, 1857.
Girard, C. F. (1857), Jordan, David Starr, and Barton Warren Evermann. (1896),

Acomus generosus (Girard, 1856).
  Smith, Gerald R. (1966),

Acomus guzmaniensis (Girard, 1857).
  Girard, C. F. (1857), Smith, Gerald R. (1966),

Acomus latipinis (Baird and Girard, 1854).
  Günther, Albert C. (1868), 1739,

Amblodon Rafinesque, 1818.
  Bailey, R. M., and W. N. Eschmeyer. (1988), Eschmeyer, William N. (1990), Fowler,
  Henry Weed. (1914a), Opinion 1582. (1990),.

Amblodon bubalus Rafinesque, 1818.
  Forbes, Stephen Alfred., and Robert Earl Richardson. (1920), Jordan, David Starr, and
  Barton Warren Evermann. (1896), Rafinesque, Constantine Samuel. (1818a), Rafinesque,
  Constantine Samuel. (1820b), Smith, Philip W. (1979),

Amblodon niger Rafinesque, 1819.
  Jordan, David Starr, and Barton Warren Evermann. (1896), Rafinesque, Constantine
  Samuel. (1819),

Amyzon Cope, 1872.
  Arldt, Th. (1907), Arldt, Th. (1923), Cavender, Ted M. (1968), Cavender, Ted M. (1986),
  Cockerell, T. D. A. (1906), Cockerell, T. D. A. (1908), Cockerell, T. D. A. (1914), Cope,
  Edward Drinker. (1872b), Cope, Edward Drinker. (1873), Cope, Edward Drinker. (1885),
  Cross, Frank B., and Richard L. Mayden, J. D. Stewart. (1986), Dawson, George Mercer.
  (1896), Drew, Wayland, and Don Baldwin, Alan Emery, Wayne McLaren, Robert Collins.
  (1974), Eastman, Charles Rochester. (1917), Eastman, Joseph T. (1980), Grande, Roger
  Lance. (1980), Hay, Oliver Perry. (1902), Hay, Oliver Perry. (1929), Jordan, David Starr.
  (1923), Meek, Alexander. (1916), Miller, Robert Rush. (1958), Minckley, W. L., and Dean
  A. Hendrickson, Carl E. Bond. (1986), Nelson, Edward M. (1948), Nelson, Edward M.
  (1949), Nelson, Joseph S. (1984), Obruchev, D. V. (ed.) (1967), Orr, William N., and
  Elizabeth L. Orr. (1981), Penhallow, D. P. (1908), Regan, Charles Tate. (1922), Romer,
  Alfred Sherwood. (1966), Schlosser, Max. (1917), Smith, Gerald R. (1966), Uyeno, Teruya,
  and Robert Rush Miller. (1962), Vladykov, Vadim D. (1934), Wilson, Mark Vincent
  Hardman. (1974), Wilson, Mark Vincent Hardman. (1977a), Wilson, Mark Vincent
  Hardman. (1977b), Wilson, Mark Vincent Hardman. (1977c), Wilson, Mark Vincent
  Hardman. (1978), Wilson, Mark Vincent Hardman. (1979), Wilson, Mark Vincent Hardman.
  (1984), Woodward, A. Smith. (1901), Zittel, Karl A. von. (1932),

Amyzon aggregatum Wilson, 1977.
  Wilson, Mark Vincent Hardman. (1974), Wilson, Mark Vincent Hardman. (1977a), Wilson,
  Mark Vincent Hardman. (1977c), Wilson, Mark Vincent Hardman. (1980), Wilson, Mark
  Vincent Hardman. (1984),

Amyzon brevipinne Cope, 1894.
  Cockerell, T. D. A. (1908), Cope, Edward Drinker. (1894), Eastman, Charles Rochester.
  (1917), Hay, Oliver Perry. (1902), Hay, Oliver Perry. (1929), Lambe, Lawrence M. (1904),
  Lambe, Lawrence M. (1906a), Lambe, Lawrence M. (1906b), Lambe, Lawrence M.
  (1906c), Penhallow, D. P. (1908), Wilson, Mark Vincent Hardman. (1974), Wilson, Mark
  Vincent Hardman. (1977a), Wilson, Mark Vincent Hardman. (1977c), Wilson, Mark
  Vincent Hardman. (1980), Wilson, Mark Vincent Hardman. (1984), Woodward, A. Smith.
  (1901),

Amyzon brevipinnis Cope, 1894.
  Uyeno, Teruya, and Robert Rush Miller. (1963),

Amyzon commune Cope, 1874.
  Cockerell, T. D. A. (1908), Cope, Edward Drinker. (1874a), Cope, Edward Drinker. (1874b), Cope, Edward Drinker. (1875), Cope, Edward Drinker. (1885), Hay, Oliver Perry. (1902), Hay, Oliver Perry. (1929), Lambe, Lawrence M. (1906a), Lambe, Lawrence M. (1906b), Lambe, Lawrence M. (1906c), Merrill, George P. (1907), Osborn, H. F., and W. B. Scott, Francis Speir, Jr. (1878), Penhallow, D. P. (1908), Wilson, Mark Vincent Hardman. (1974), Wilson, Mark Vincent Hardman. (1977a), Wilson, Mark Vincent Hardman. (1977c), Wilson, Mark Vincent Hardman. (1984), Woodward, A. Smith. (1901),

Amyzon fusiforme Cope, 1875.
  Cockerell, T. D. A. (1908), Cope, Edward Drinker. (1875), Cope, Edward Drinker. (1885), Hay, Oliver Perry. (1902), Hay, Oliver Perry. (1929), Wilson, Mark Vincent Hardman. (1974), Wilson, Mark Vincent Hardman. (1977a), Wilson, Mark Vincent Hardman. (1977c), Woodward, A. Smith. (1901),

Amyzon gosiutensis Grande, Eastman and Cavender, 1982. Grande, Roger Lance. (1984), Grande, Roger Lance, and Joseph T. Eastman, Ted M. Cavender. (1982),

Amyzon interruptus Sytchevskaya, 1986.
  Sytchevskaya, E. K. (1986),

Amyzon mentale Cope, 1872.
  Cockerell, T. D. A. (1908), Cope, Edward Drinker. (1872b), Cope, Edward Drinker. (1872c), Cope, Edward Drinker. (1873), Cope, Edward Drinker. (1885), Hay, Oliver Perry. (1902), Hay, Oliver Perry. (1929), Merrill, George P. (1907), Wilson, Mark Vincent Hardman. (1974), Wilson, Mark Vincent Hardman. (1977a), Wilson, Mark Vincent Hardman. (1977c), Woodward, A. Smith. (1901),

Amyzon mentalis Cope, 1872.
  La Rivers, Ira. (1962), Uyeno, Teruya, and Robert Rush Miller. (1963),

Amyzon pandatum Cope, 1875.
  Cockerell, T. D. A. (1908), Cope, Edward Drinker. (1875), Cope, Edward Drinker. (1885), Hay, Oliver Perry. (1902), Hay, Oliver Perry. (1929), Wilson, Mark Vincent Hardman. (1974), Wilson, Mark Vincent Hardman. (1977a), Wilson, Mark Vincent Hardman. (1977c), Woodward, A. Smith. (1901),

Bubalichthys Agassiz, 1855.
  Eschmeyer, William N. (1990), Jordan, David Starr. (1923), Jordan, David Starr, and Barton Warren Evermann. (1896), Jordan, David Starr, and Charles Henry Gilbert. (1884),

Bubalichthys altus Nelson, 1877.
  IN: Jordan, 1877. Forbes, Stephen Alfred., and Robert Earl Richardson. (1920), Goode, C. Brown, and Theodore Nicholas Gill. (1903), Jordan, David Starr. (1877b), Jordan, David Starr, and Barton Warren Evermann. (1896), Jordan, David Starr, and Charles Henry Gilbert. (1883),

Bubalichthys bonasus Agassiz, 1855.
  Agassiz, John Louis Rodolphe. (1855), Jordan, David Starr, and Barton Warren Evermann. (1896),

Bubalichthys bubalinus Jordan, 1877.
    Jordan, David Starr. (1878b), Jordan, David Starr, and Barton Warren Evermann. (1896),

Bubalichthys bubalus (Rafinesque, 1818).
    Agassiz, John Louis Rodolphe. (1855), Jordan, David Starr. (1878d), Jordan, David Starr, and Barton Warren Evermann. (1896), Nelson, E. W. (1878),

Bubalichthys cyanellus.
    Forbes, Stephen Alfred., and Robert Earl Richardson. (1920), Smith, Philip W. (1979),

Bubalichthys niger Agassiz, 1855.
    Agassiz, John Louis Rodolphe. (1855), Forbes, Stephen Alfred., and Robert Earl Richardson. (1920), Jordan, David Starr, and Barton Warren Evermann. (1896),

Bubalichthys urus (Agassiz, 1854).
    Agassiz, John Louis Rodolphe. (1855), Goode, C. Brown, and Theodore Nicholas Gill. (1903), Jordan, David Starr. (1878d), Jordan, David Starr, and Barton Warren Evermann. (1896), Jordan, David Starr, and Charles Henry Gilbert. (1884), Smith, Philip W. (1979),

Carpiodes Rafinesque, 1820.
    Carp Suckers.
    Beecher, H. A. (1979b), Berner, Lester M. (1948), Clay, W. M. (1975), Drew, Wayland, and Don Baldwin, Alan Emery, Wayne McLaren, Robert Collins. (1974), Eastman, Joseph T. (1977), Eschmeyer, William N. (1990), Gregory, William K. (1933), Günther, Albert C. (1868),.Hoffman, Glenn L. (1967), Huntsman, G. R. (1967a), Jordan, David Starr. (1923), Jordan, David Starr, and Barton Warren Evermann. (1896), Jordan, David Starr, and Charles Henry Gilbert. (1884), Jordan, David Starr, and Seth Eugene Meek. (1885), Lopinot, Alvin C. (ed.). (1968), Miller, Robert Rush. (1958), Moyle, Peter B., and Joseph J. Cech, Jr. (1982), Nasini, S. K. (1973), Nelson, Edward M. (1948), Nelson, Edward M. (1949), Nelson, Joseph S. (1976), Rafinesque, Constantine Samuel. (1820b), Ramaswami, L. S. (1957), Romer, Alfred Sherwood. (1966), Smith, Gerald R. (1966), Stark, B. J., and M. E. Eberle, G. W. Ernsting, T. L. Wenke. (1987), Uyeno, Teruya, and Robert Rush Miller. (1962), Whitaker, J. O., Jr., and R. A. Schlueter. (1975), Yeager, Bruce L., and Kenneth J. Semmens. (1987),

Carpiodes asiaticus Bleeker, 1864.
    Bleeker, P. (1864), Günther, Albert C. (1868),

Carpiodes bison Agassiz, 1854.
    Agassiz, John Louis Rodolphe. (1854), Günther, Albert C. (1868), Jordan, David Starr, and Barton Warren Evermann. (1896), Jordan, David Starr, and Seth Eugene Meek. (1885), Smith, Philip W. (1979),

Carpiodes brevidens Sytchevskaya, 1986.
    Sytchevskaya, E. K. (1986),

Carpiodes bubalis (Rafinesque, 1818).
    Jordan, David Starr, and Seth Eugene Meek. (1885),

Carpiodes carpio (Rafinesque, 1820).
    River carpsucker, Carp Sucker, Common River Carp. Al-Rawi, T. R. (1964), Anonymous. (1961), Anonymous. (1965a), Anonymous. (1965b), Arruda, J. A., and M. S. Cringar, D. Gilliland, S. G. Haslouer, J. E. Fry, R. Broxterman, K. L. Brunson. (1987), Bailey, Reeve M., and John E. Fitch, Earl S. Herald, Ernest A. Lachner, C. C. Lindsey, C. Richard Robins, W. B. Scott. (1970), Bailey, Reeve M., and Ernest A. Lachner, C. C.

136

Lindsey, C. Richard Robins, Phil M. Roedel, W. B. Scott, Loren P. Woods. (1966), Barnhart, M. C., and E. C. Powell. (1979), Barnickol, P. G., and W. C. Starrett. (1951), Bass, J. C., and C. D. Riggs. (1959), Baxter, George T., and James R. Simon. (1970), Becker, George C. (1983), Behmer, D. J. (1965a), Behmer, D. J. (1965b), Behmer, D. J. (1966), Behmer, D. J. (1969a), Behmer, D. J. (1969b), Bennett, G. W., and W. F. Childers. (1966), Blatchley, W. S. (1938), Boschung, Herbert T., Jr., and James D. Williams, Daniel W. Gotshall, David K. Caldwell, Melba C. Caldwell, Carol Nehring, Jordan Verner. (1983), Bosley, T. R., and J. V. Conner. (1984), Branson, Branley A., and Donald L. Batch. (1974), Brezner, J. (1956), Brezner, J. (1958), Briggs, T., and C. Bussjaeger. (1972), Brown, C. J. D. (1971), Buck, D. H., and Frank B. Cross. (1952), Bulkley, R. V., and S.-Y. T. Leung, J. J. Richard. (1981), Carlander, Kenneth D. (1949), Carlander, Kenneth D. (1969), Carlander, Kenneth D., and R. B. Moorman. (1949), Chien, Shin Ming, and Wilmer A. Rogers. (1970), Christenson, L. M., and L. L. Smith. (1965), Clay, W. M. (1975), Cooper, Edwin Lavern. (1983), Cornelius, R. R. (1966), Cross, Frank B. (1967), Cross, Frank B., and Joseph T. Collins. (1975), Curry, Kevin D., and Anne Spacie. (1979), Cvancara, V. A., and S. F. Stieber, B. A. Cvancara. (1977), Dalquest, Walter W. (1962), Davis, Kenneth B., and Nick C. Parker. (1986), Deacon, James Everett. (1960), Deacon, James Everett. (1961), Dechtiar, A. O. (1968), Dietz, E. M. C., and K. C. Jurgens. (1963), Douglas, Neil H. (1974), Eastman, Joseph T. (1977), Eddy, Samuel. (1957), Eddy, Samuel. (1969), Eddy, Samuel, and James C. Underhill. (1974), Elkin, R. E., Jr. (1954), Elrod, J. H., and T. J. Hassler. (1971), Emery, Lee. (1976), Eschmeyer, R. W., and R. H. Stroud, A. M. Jones. (1944), Ferris, Stephen D., and Gregory S. Whitt. (1978), Finnell, Joe C. (1955), Fogle, N. E. (1961a), Fogle, N. E. (1961b), Fogle, N. E. (1963a), Fogle, N. E. (1963b), Forbes, Stephen Alfred. (1884), Forbes, Stephen Alfred., and Robert Earl Richardson. (1908), Forbes, Stephen Alfred., and Robert Earl Richardson. (1920), Fowler, Henry Weed. (1919), Fowler, Henry Weed. (1945), Funk, J. L., and R. S. Campbell. (1953), Goode, C. Brown, and Theodore Nicholas Gill. (1903), Hall, Gordon E., and R. M. Jenkins. (1953), Hancock, H. M. (1955), Hansen, D. F., and Hurst H. Shoemaker. (1943), Hanson, W. D., and R. S. Campbell. (1963), Hargis, H. L. (1966), Harlan, J. R., and E. B. Speaker. (1956), Harrison, H. M. (1950), Hoese, H. Dickson, and Richard H. Moore. (1977),.Hoffman, Glenn L. (1967), Houser, A. (1960), Houser, A., and M. G. Bross. (1963), Huggins, Donald G., and Randall E. Moss. (1975), Huntsman, G. R. (1967b), Jackson, S. W., Jr. (1966), Jenkins, Robert M. (1953a), Jenkins, Robert M. (1953c), Jenkins, Robert M., and J. C. Finnell. (1957), Jenkins, Robert M., and E. M. Leonard, G. E. Hall. (1952), Jester, D. B. (1972), Jordan, David Starr. (1878a), Jordan, David Starr. (1929), Jordan, David Starr, and Barton Warren Evermann. (1896), Jordan, David Starr, and Barton Warren Evermann. (1905), Jordan, David Starr, and Charles Henry Gilbert. (1883), Jordan, David Starr, and Charles Henry Gilbert. (1886), Jordan, David Starr, and Seth Eugene Meek. (1885), Keeton, D. (1963), Koster, William J. (1957), Kritsky, D. C., and P. D. Leiby, M. E. Shelton. (1972), Lambou, V. W. (1961), Large, T. (1903), Layher, W. G., and K. L. Brunson. (1986), Lee, David S., and Carter R. Gilbert, Charles H. Hocutt, Robert E. Jenkins, Don E. McAllister, Jay R. Stauffer, Jr. (1980), Leung, Siu-Yin Theresa, and Ross V. Bulkely, John J. Richard. (1981), Linton, T. L. (1961), Lopinot, Alvin C. (1966a), Lundberg, John G. (1967), Martin, R. E., and S. I. Auerbach, D. J. Nelson. (1964), Martin, R. G., and R. S. Campbell. (1953), Matthews, W. J. (1986), Matthews, W. J., and L. G. Hill, S. M. Schellhaass. (1985), May, E. B., and C. R. Gasaway. (1967), Miller, Rudolph J., and H. E. Evans. (1965), Miller, Rudolph J., and Henry W. Robinson. (1973), Mills, Paul A., Jr., and Charles H. Hocutt, Jay R. Stauffer, Jr. (1978), Minckley, W. L. (1959), Minckley, W. L., and R. H. Goodyear, J. E. Craddock. (1964), Morris, L. A. (1965), Nelson, E. W. (1876), Nelson, W. R. (1961a), Nelson, W. R. (1961b), Nelson, W. R. (1962), Nickol, B. B., and N. Samuel. (1983), O'Donnell, D. J. (1935), Orr, O. E. (1958), Page, Lawrence M. (1982), Pearson, William D., and Louis A. Krumholz (1984), Pflieger, William L. (1971), Pflieger, William L. (1975), Phillips, Gary L., and William D. Schmid, James C. Underhill. (1982), Proffitt, M. A., and R. S. Benda. (1971), Purkett, C. A., Jr. (1958a), Purkett, C. A., Jr. (1958b), Robins, C. Richard, and Reeve M. Bailey, Carl E. Bond, James R. Brooker, Ernest

A. Lachner, Robert N. Lea, W. B. Scott. (1980), Robinson, G. L., and L. A. Jahn. (1980), Sandoz, O. (1960), Shields, J. T. (1955a), Shields, J. T. (1955b), Shields, J. T. (1956), Shields, J. T. (1957a), Shields, J. T. (1957b), Shields, J. T. (1958a), Shields, J. T. (1958b), Shih, M. C., and W. A. Rogers. (1970), Smith, C. Lavett. (1986), Smith, Gerald R. (1981b), Smith, John B., and Wayne A. Hubert. (1989), Smith, Philip W. (1965), Smith, Philip W. (1971), Smith, Philip W. (1973), Smith, Philip W. (1979), Sparks, Richard E., and William C. Starrett. (1975), Sprague, J. W. (1959a), Sprague, J. W. (1959b), Sprague, J. W. (1961), Stone, U. B. (1947), Summerfelt, R. C., and P. E. Mauck, G. Mensinger. (1972), Swingle, W. E. (1965), Thompson, W. H. (1950), Trautman, Milton B. (1957), Uyeno, Teruya, and Robert Rush Miller. (1963), Walburg, C. H. (1964), Walburg, C. H. (1976), Walburg, C. H., and W. R. Nelson. (1966), Ward, H. C. (1949), Werner, Robert G. (1976a), Werner, Robert G. (1976b), Whitaker, J. O., and D. C. Wallace. (1966), Willis, David W., and Lanny D. Jones. (1986), Wisdom, J. L. A. (1972),

Carpiodes carpio carpio (Rafinesque, 1820).
Northern River carpsucker.
Bailey, Reeve M., and Marvin O. Allum. (1962), Berner, Lester M. (1948), Buchanon, T. M. (1973), Cross, Frank B., and G. A. Moore. (1952), Davis, J. T. (1955), Hansen, D. F., and Hurst H. Shoemaker. (1943), Hubbs, Carl L. (1945), Hubbs, Carl L., and J. D. Black. (1940), Hubbs, Carl L., and Karl F. Lagler. (1941), Hubbs, Carl L., and Karl F. Lagler. (1947), Hubbs, Carl L., and Karl F. Lagler. (1974), Krumholz, Louis A. (1943), Nelson, Edward M. (1948), Personius, Robert Giles, and Samuel Eddy. (1955), Simon, James R. (1946), Smith, Philip W. (1979), Trautman, Milton B. (1957), Trautman, Milton B. (1981), Welter, Wilfred A. (1938),

Carpiodes carpio elongatus Meek.
Hubbs, Carl L., and J. D. Black. (1940), Lee, David S., and Carter R. Gilbert, Charles H. Hocutt, Robert E. Jenkins, Don E. McAllister, Jay R. Stauffer, Jr. (1980), Nelson, Edward M. (1948), Villar, José Alvarez del. (1970),

Carpiodes cutisanserinus Cope, 1870.
Cope, Edward Drinker. (1870), Forbes, Stephen Alfred., and Robert Earl Richardson. (1920), Jordan, David Starr, and Barton Warren Evermann. (1896), Jordan, David Starr, and Seth Eugene Meek. (1885), Smith, Philip W. (1979), Trautman, Milton B. (1981),

Carpiodes cyprinus (Le Sueur, 1817).
Quillback, Eastern Carp Sucker, Skimback.
Amin, Omar M., and Ernest H. Williams, Jr. (1983), Bailey, Reeve M., and Marvin O. Allum. (1962), Bailey, Reeve M., and John E. Fitch, Earl S. Herald, Ernest A. Lachner, C. C. Lindsey, C. Richard Robins, W. B. Scott. (1970), Bailey, Reeve M., and Ernest A. Lachner, C. C. Lindsey, C. Richard Robins, Phil M. Roedel, W. B. Scott, Loren P. Woods. (1966), Bailey, Reeve M., and Gerald R. Smith. (1981), (1954), Barnickol, P. G., and W. C. Starrett. (1951), Bauer, Bruce H., and Branley A. Branson, Strant T. Colwell. (1978), Baxter, George T., and James R. Simon. (1970), Becker, George C. (1964a), Becker, George C. (1983), Beecher, H. A. (1979a), Beecher, H. A. (1980), Berner, Lester M. (1948), Beverly-Burton, Mary. (1984), Boschung, Herbert T., Jr., and James D. Williams, Daniel W. Gotshall, David K. Caldwell, Melba C. Caldwell, Carol Nehring, Jordan Verner. (1983), Breder, C. M., Jr., and D. E. Rosen. (1966), Buth, Donald G. (1983), Cahn, A. R. (1927), Call, M. W. (1960), Carlander, Kenneth D. (1944b), Carlander, Kenneth D. (1949), Carlander, Kenneth D. (1969), Carlander, Kenneth D., and R. B. Moorman. (1949), Carlander, Kenneth D., and J. W. Parsons. (1949), Chien, Shin Ming, and Wilmer A. Rogers. (1970), Clark, C. F. (1960), Clay, W. M. (1975), Cooper, Edwin Lavern. (1983), Cornelius, R. R. (1966), Cross, Frank B. (1967), Cross, Frank B., and Joseph T. Collins. (1975), Curry, Kevin D., and Anne Spacie. (1979), Dechtiar, A. O. (1972b), Dechtiar, A. O., and W. A. Dillon. (1974), Denison, Samuel G., and Carl R. Carlson, John L. Dorkin,

Jr., Cecil Lue-Hing. (1978), Deutsch, W. G. (1978), Dorkin, John L., Jr. (1980), Douglas, Neil H. (1974), Eastman, Joseph T. (1977), Eastman, Joseph T. (1980), Eddy, Samuel. (1957), Eddy, Samuel. (1969), Eddy, Samuel, and Roy C. Tasker, James C. Underhill. (1972), Eddy, Samuel, and James C. Underhill. (1974), Elser, H. J. (1961), Emery, Lee. (1976), Eschmeyer, R. W., and R. H. Stroud, A. M. Jones. (1944), Fago, Don. (1984b), Fernholz, W. B. (1966), Fernholz, W. B. (1971), Fernholz, W. B. (1972), Fernholz, W. B., and V. E. Crawley. (1976), Fernholz, W. B., and V. E. Crawley. (1977), Ferris, Stephen D., and Gregory S. Whitt. (1978), Fish, M. P. (1932), Forbes, Stephen Alfred. (1884), Forbes, Stephen Alfred. (1890), Forbes, Stephen Alfred., and Robert Earl Richardson. (1908), Fry, J. P. (1962), Fuiman, Lee A. (1979), Gammon, J. R. (1973), Gammon, J. R. (1977), Gerking, Shelby D. (1945), Gerlack, Jim. (1973), Goode, C. Brown, and Theodore Nicholas Gill. (1903), Grinham, T., and D. K. Cone. (1990), Haas, Robert L. (1943), Hanson, W. D., and R. S. Campbell. (1963), Harlan, J. R., and E. B. Speaker. (1956), Henderson, N. E., and R. E. Peter. (1969), Herald, Earl S. (1967), Herald, Earl S. (1979), Hinks, David. (1943),.Hoffman, Glenn L. (1967), Hubbs, Carl L. (1930), Hubbs, Carl L., and J. D. Black. (1940), Hubbs, Carl L., and Karl F. Lagler. (1941), Hubbs, Carl L., and Karl F. Lagler. (1947), Hubbs, Carl L., and Karl F. Lagler. (1974), Hubert, Wayne A., and Dennis N. Schmitt. (1985), Huntsman, G. R. (1967b), Jones, David T. (1929), Jordan, David Starr. (1878a), Jordan, David Starr. (1929), Jordan, David Starr, and Barton Warren Evermann. (1896), Jordan, David Starr, and Barton Warren Evermann. (1905), Jordan, David Starr, and Charles Henry Gilbert. (1883), Jordan, David Starr, and Seth Eugene Meek. (1885), Keleher, J. J., and B. Kooyman. (1957), Kritsky, D. C., and R. P. Hathaway. (1969), Krumholz, Louis A. (1943), Large, T. (1903), Lee, David S., and Carter R. Gilbert, Charles H. Hocutt, Robert E. Jenkins, Don E. McAllister, Jay R. Stauffer, Jr. (1980), Le Sueur, Charles Alexandre. (1817), Lippson, Alice J., and R. L. Moran. (1974), Lopinot, Alvin C. (1966a), Mackiewicz, J. S., and W. G. Deutsch. (1976), Malick, Robert W., Jr., and Wayne A. Potter. (1976), Mansueti, A. J., and J. D. Hardy. (1967), Massé, G. (1977), Mayhew, J. (1964), McAllister, Don E., and Brian W. Coad. (1974), Miller, Rudolph J., and H. E. Evans. (1965), Mills, Paul A., Jr., and Charles H. Hocutt, Jay R. Stauffer, Jr. (1978), Minckley, C. O. (1973), Nelson, Edward M. (1948), Nelson, E. W. (1876), Nelson, Joseph S. (1976), Nelson, Joseph S. (1984), Nickol, B. B., and N. Samuel. (1983), O'Donnell, D. J. (1935), Paetz, Martin J., and Joseph S. Nelson. (1970), Pearson, William D., and Louis A. Krumholz (1984), Pflieger, William L. (1971), Pflieger, William L. (1975), Phillips, Gary L., and William D. Schmid, James C. Underhill. (1982), Potter, Wayne A., and Robert W. Malick, Jr., Janet L. Polk. (1976), Priegel, G. R. (1967), Propst, David L., and Clarence A. Carlson. (1986), Richardson, Laurence R. (1938), Robins, C. Richard, and Reeve M. Bailey, Carl E. Bond, James R. Brooker, Ernest A. Lachner, Robert N. Lea, W. B. Scott. (1980), Robinson, G. L., and L. A. Jahn. (1980), Savitz, J., and L. G. Bardygula, L. Scoma. (1989), Scott, W. B. (1954), Scott, W. B. (1958), Scott, W. B. (1967), Scott, W. B., and E. J. Crossman. (1969), Scott, W. B., and E. J. Crossman. (1973), Smith, C. Lavett. (1986), Smith, Philip W. (1965), Smith, Philip W. (1973), Smith, Philip W. (1979), Snyder, D. E. (1975), Sparks, Richard E., and William C. Starrett. (1975), Sprules, W. M., and K. H. Doan. (1947), Sterba, Günther. (1983), Stewart, Kenneth W., and Iain M. Suthers, Kelly Leavesley. (1985), Swingle, W. E. (1965), Szalai, A. J., and G. V. Danell, T. A. Dick. (1988), Szalai, A. J., and T. A. Dick. (1987a), Szalai, A. J., and T. A. Dick. (1987b), Thompson, Peter. (1980), Trautman, Milton B. (1957), Vanicek, D. (1961), Walden, Howard T., 2d. (1964), Welter, Wilfred A. (1938), Werner, Robert G. (1976a), Werner, Robert G. (1976b), Werner, Robert G. (1980), Williams, D. D., and M. J. Ulmer. (1970), Wooding, Frederick H. (1959), Woodward, R. L., and T. E. Wissing. (1976),

Carpiodes cyprinus cyprinus (Le Sueur).
Eastern quillback carpsucker.
Clay, W. M. (1975), Hubbs, Carl L., and Karl F. Lagler. (1947), Hubbs, Carl L., and Karl F. Lagler. (1974), Trautman, Milton B. (1957), Trautman, Milton B. (1981),

Carpiodes cyprinus hinei Trautman, 1956.
   Central Quillback Carpsucker.
   Clay, W. M. (1975), Hubbs, Carl L., and Karl F. Lagler. (1974), Larimore, R. W., and P.
   W. Smith. (1963), Lee, David S., and Carter R. Gilbert, Charles H. Hocutt, Robert E.
   Jenkins, Don E. McAllister, Jay R. Stauffer, Jr. (1980), Smith, Philip W. (1979), Trautman,
   Milton B. (1956), Trautman, Milton B. (1957), Trautman, Milton B. (1981),

Carpiodes cyprinus thompsoni.
   Carlander, Kenneth D. (1948), Hubbs, Carl L. (1945), Trautman, Milton B. (1981),
   Wickliff, Edward L., and Milton B. Trautman. (1934),

Carpiodes damalis Girard, 1856.
   Girard, C. F. (1857), Hubbs, Carl L., and J. D. Black. (1940), Jordan, David Starr, and
   Barton Warren Evermann. (1896), Jordan, David Starr, and Seth Eugene Meek. (1885),
   Meek, Seth Eugene. (1894),

Carpiodes difformis Cope, 1870.
   Blunt-Nosed River Carp.
   Blatchley, W. S. (1938), Cope, Edward Drinker. (1870), Forbes, Stephen Alfred., and
   Robert Earl Richardson. (1920), Fowler, Henry Weed. (1945), Grinham, T., and D. K.
   Cone. (1990),.Hoffman, Glenn L. (1967), Jones, David T. (1929), Jordan, David Starr.
   (1878d), Jordan, David Starr. (1929), Jordan, David Starr, and Barton Warren Evermann.
   (1896), Jordan, David Starr, and Charles Henry Gilbert. (1883), Jordan, David Starr, and
   Seth Eugene Meek. (1885), Larimore, R. W., and P. W. Smith. (1963), Meek, Seth Eugene,
   and S. F. Hildebrand. (1910), Smith, Philip W. (1979), Trautman, Milton B. (1981),

Carpiodes elongatus Meek.
   Hubbs, Carl L., and J. D. Black. (1940), Meek, Seth Eugene. (1904),

Carpiodes forbesi Hubbs.
   Bailey, Reeve M., and Ernest A. Lachner, C. C. Lindsey, C. Richard Robins, Phil M.
   Roedel, W. B. Scott, Loren P. Woods. (1966), Berner, Lester M. (1948), Eddy, Samuel.
   (1969), Gerking, Shelby D. (1955), Hubbs, Carl L. (1930), Hubbs, Carl L. (1945),
   Minckley, W. L. (1959), Nelson, Edward M. (1948), Simon, James R. (1946), Smith, Philip
   W. (1979), Trautman, Milton B. (1981), Williams, D. D., and M. J. Ulmer. (1970),

Carpiodes grayi Cope, 1870.
   Cope, Edward Drinker. (1870), Fowler, Henry Weed. (1904), Hubbs, Carl L., and J. D.
   Black. (1940), Jordan, David Starr, and Barton Warren Evermann. (1896), Jordan, David
   Starr, and Seth Eugene Meek. (1885),

Carpiodes labiosus Meek, 1904.
   Meek, Seth Eugene. (1904),

Carpiodes meridonalis.
   Nelson, Edward M. (1948),

Carpiodes microstomus Meek.
   Hubbs, Carl L., and J. D. Black. (1940), Meek, Seth Eugene. (1904),

Carpiodes nummifer Cope, 1870.
   Cope, Edward Drinker. (1870),

Carpiodes selene Cope, 1870.

Cope, Edward Drinker. (1870), Jordan, David Starr, and Barton Warren Evermann. (1896), Jordan, David Starr, and Seth Eugene Meek. (1885), Smith, Philip W. (1979),

Carpiodes taurus Agassiz, 1854.
Agassiz, John Louis Rodolphe. (1854), Günther, Albert C. (1868), Jordan, David Starr, and Barton Warren Evermann. (1896),

Carpiodes thomsoni Agassiz, 1855.
Jordan, David Starr, and Seth Eugene Meek. (1885),

Carpiodes thompsoni Agassiz, 1855.
Lake Carp.
Agassiz, John Louis Rodolphe. (1855), Forbes, Stephen Alfred., and Robert Earl Richardson. (1920), Günther, Albert C. (1868), Hubbs, Carl L. (1930), Jordan, David Starr. (1878d), Jordan, David Starr, and Barton Warren Evermann. (1896), Jordan, David Starr, and Barton Warren Evermann. (1905), Jordan, David Starr, and Charles Henry Gilbert. (1883), Smith, Philip W. (1979), Trautman, Milton B. (1981),

Carpiodes timidus Baird and Girard, 1854.
Jordan, David Starr, and Seth Eugene Meek. (1885),

Carpiodes tumidum Baird and Girard, 1854.
Clay, W. M. (1975),

Carpiodes tumidus Baird and Girard, 1854.
Hubbs, Carl L., and J. D. Black. (1940), Jordan, David Starr, and Barton Warren Evermann. (1896), Nelson, Edward M. (1948),

Carpiodes urus Agassiz, 1854.
Agassiz, John Louis Rodolphe. (1854), Günther, Albert C. (1868), Jordan, David Starr, and Barton Warren Evermann. (1896),

Carpiodes vaca Agassiz, 1854.
Agassiz, John Louis Rodolphe. (1854), Günther, Albert C. (1868), Jordan, David Starr, and Barton Warren Evermann. (1896),

Carpiodes velifer (Rafinesque, 1820).
Highfin carpsucker, Quillback, Silver Carp, Spearfish, Sailfish, Skimback.
Bailey, Reeve M., and John E. Fitch, Earl S. Herald, Ernest A. Lachner, C. C. Lindsey, C. Richard Robins, W. B. Scott. (1970), Bailey, Reeve M., and Ernest A. Lachner, C. C. Lindsey, C. Richard Robins, Phil M. Roedel, W. B. Scott, Loren P. Woods. (1966), Bailey, Reeve M., and Howard E. Winn, C. Lavett Smith. (1954), Barnickol, P. G., and W. C. Starrett. (1951), Bauer, Bruce H., and Branley A. Branson, Strant T. Colwell. (1978), Becker, George C. (1976), Becker, George C. (1983), Beecher, H. A. (1980), Berner, Lester M. (1948), Blatchley, W. S. (1938), Boschung, Herbert T., Jr., and James D. Williams, Daniel W. Gotshall, David K. Caldwell, Melba C. Caldwell, Carol Nehring, Jordan Verner. (1983), Branson, Branley A., and Donald L. Batch. (1974), Breder, C. M., Jr., and D. E. Rosen. (1966), Bur, M. T. (1976), Cahn, A. R. (1927), Carlander, Kenneth D. (1969), Chien, Shin Ming, and Wilmer A. Rogers. (1970), Clay, W. M. (1975), Cleary, R. E. (1956), Cooper, Edwin Lavern. (1983), Cornelius, R. R. (1966), Cross, Frank B. (1967), Cross, Frank B., and Joseph T. Collins. (1975), Curry, Kevin D., and Anne Spacie. (1979), Deacon, James Everett. (1960), Deacon, James Everett. (1961), Douglas, Neil H. (1974), Eastman, Joseph T. (1977), Eddy, Samuel. (1957), Eddy, Samuel. (1969), Eddy, Samuel, and James C. Underhill. (1974), Ferris, Stephen D., and Gregory S. Whitt. (1978), Forbes, Stephen Alfred. (1884), Forbes, Stephen Alfred., and Robert Earl Richardson. (1908),

Forbes, Stephen Alfred., and Robert Earl Richardson. (1920), Goode, C. Brown, and Theodore Nicholas Gill. (1903), Günther, Albert C. (1868), Hall, Gordon E., and R. M. Jenkins. (1953), Harlan, J. R., and E. B. Speaker. (1956), Harrison, H. M. (1950),.Hoffman, Glenn L. (1967), Hubbs, Carl L. (1926), Hubbs, Carl L., and Karl F. Lagler. (1974), Jenkins, Robert M. (1953b), Jenkins, Robert M., and E. M. Leonard, G. E. Hall. (1952), Jones, David T. (1929), Jordan, David Starr. (1878a), Jordan, David Starr, and Barton Warren Evermann. (1896), Jordan, David Starr, and Barton Warren Evermann. (1905), Jordan, David Starr, and Seth Eugene Meek. (1885), Krumholz, Louis A. (1943), Lagler, Karl F., and John E. Bardach, Robert Rush Miller. (1962), Large, T. (1903), Larimore, R. W., and P. W. Smith. (1963), Lee, David S., and Carter R. Gilbert, Charles H. Hocutt, Robert E. Jenkins, Don E. McAllister, Jay R. Stauffer, Jr. (1980), Lopinot, Alvin C. (1966a), Meek, Seth Eugene, and S. F. Hildebrand. (1910), Miller, Rudolph J., and H. E. Evans. (1965), Miller, Rudolph J., and Henry W. Robinson. (1973), Mills, Paul A., Jr., and Charles H. Hocutt, Jay R. Stauffer, Jr. (1978), Nelson, Edward M. (1948), Nelson, E. W. (1876), O'Donnell, D. J. (1935), Pearson, William D., and Louis A. Krumholz (1984), Pflieger, William L. (1971), Pflieger, William L. (1975), Phillips, Gary L., and William D. Schmid, James C. Underhill. (1982), Proffitt, M. A., and R. S. Benda. (1971), Robins, C. Richard, and Reeve M. Bailey, Carl E. Bond, James R. Brooker, Ernest A. Lachner, Robert N. Lea, W. B. Scott. (1980), Rogers, Wilmer A. (1967), Smith, Philip W. (1965), Smith, Philip W. (1971), Smith, Philip W. (1973), Smith, Philip W. (1979), Smith, Philip W., and A. C. Lopinot, W. L. Pflieger. (1971), Swingle, W. E. (1965), Trautman, Milton B. (1957), Trautman, Milton B. (1981), Vanicek, D. (1961), Ward, C. M. (1960), Werner, Robert G. (1976a), Werner, Robert G. (1976b), Williams, D. D., and M. J. Ulmer. (1970), Williams, E. H., Jr., and W. A. Rogers. (1984), Wiltz, J. W. (1984), Woodward, R. L., and T. E. Wissing. (1976),

Carpiodes velifer tumidus.
Hubbs, Carl L., and J. D. Black. (1940),

Carpiodes vitulus Agassiz, 1854.
Agassiz, John Louis Rodolphe. (1854), Günther, Albert C. (1868), Jordan, David Starr, and Barton Warren Evermann. (1896),

Castostomus sonorensis Meek.
Villar, José Alvarez del. (1970),

Catastoma psephotum Cope, 1875.
Savage, Jay M. (1970),

Catastomus
Stannius, H. (1854),

Catastomus commersoni
Grinham, T., and D. K. Cone. (1990),

Catostomis bostonensis Le Sueur, 1817.
Jordan, David Starr, and Barton Warren Evermann. (1896), Le Sueur, Charles Alexandre. (1817),

Catostomites Schlaikjer, 1937.
Nelson, Edward M. (1948), Nelson, Edward M. (1949), Obruchev, D. V. (ed.) (1967),

Catostomites alaskensis Schlaikjer, 1937.
Schlaikjer, E. M. (1937), Uyeno, Teruya, and Robert Rush Miller. (1962),

142

Catostomus Le Sueur, 1817.
  Fine-Scaled Suckers.
  Allis, Edward Phelps. (1909), Allis, Edward Phelps. (1919), Andreasen, J. K. (1976), Arldt, Th. (1907), Beamish, R. J., and H. Tsuyuki. (1972), Beck, R. V. (1952), Boschung, Herbert T., Jr., and James D. Williams, Daniel W. Gotshall, David K. Caldwell, Melba C. Caldwell, Carol Nehring, Jordan Verner. (1983), Cockerell, T. D. A. (1910), Cockerell, T. D. A. (1911), Cockerell, T. D. A. (1913), Cockerell, T. D. A., and Edith M. Allison. (1909), Dawson, L. E., and K. L. Uebersax, M. A. Uebersax. (1978), Duméril, A. M. Constant. (1856), Dunham, A. E., and Gerald R. Smith, J. N. Taylor. (1979), Eaton, T. H., Jr. (1935), Edwards, L. F. (1926), Erman, D. C. (1973), Erman, D. C. (1986), Eschmeyer, William N. (1990), Gregory, William K. (1933), Griffith, J. S., and T. R. Tiersch. (1989), Günther, Albert C. (1868), Hansel, H. C., and S. D. Duke, D. T. Lofy, G. A. Gray. (1988), Hay, Oliver Perry. (1902), Hay, Oliver Perry. (1929), Heilprin, Angelo. (1887), Hilgard, Theodore Charles. (1858), Hilgard, Theodore Charles. (1860),.Hoffman, Glenn L. (1967), Hogman, W. J. (1973), Holey, M., and B. Hollender, M. Imhof, R. Jesien, R. Konopacky, M. Toneys, D. Coble. (1980), Hubbs, Carl L., and W. I. Follett, Lillian J. Dempster. (1979), Hubbs, Carl L., and Laura C. Hubbs, R. E. Johnson. (1943), Hubbs, Carl L., and Laura C. Hubbs, Robert Rush Miller. (1974), Hyrtl, Carl Joseph. (1862), Iwai, Tamotsu. (1963), Jollie, Malcolm. (1962), Jordan, David Starr. (1885b), Jordan, David Starr. (1923), Jordan, David Starr, and Barton Warren Evermann. (1917), Jordan, David Starr, and Barton Warren Evermann. (1896), Jordan, David Starr, and Charles Henry Gilbert. (1883), Kayton, R. J., and D. C. Kritsky, R. C. Tobias. (1979), Kimmel, Peter G. (1975), Koehn, Richard K. (1968), Koehn, Richard K. (1969), Lagler, Karl F., and John E. Bardach, Robert Rush Miller. (1962), Mackiewicz, J. S. (1976), Madsen, James H., Jr., and W. E. Miller. (1979), McClellan, P. H. (1977), McMaster, D. and Y. Kobayashi, J. Rivier, K. Lederis. (1986), McPhail, J. D. (1987), Meek, Seth Eugene. (1894), Miller, Robert Rush. (1958), Miller, Robert Rush. (1981), Minckley, W. L., and Dean A. Hendrickson, Carl E. Bond. (1986), Moyle, Peter B., and Joseph J. Cech, Jr. (1982), Nei Menggu Zizhi Qu Dizhi Ju, and Dongbei Dizhi Kexue Yanjiusuo. (1976), Nelson, Edward M. (1948), Nelson, Edward M. (1949), Nelson, Joseph S. (1976), Nelson, Joseph S. (1984), Orr, William N., and Elizabeth L. Orr. (1981), Pister, Edwin P. (1981), Platts, W. S., and F. E. Partridge. (1983), Ramaswami, L. S. (1957), Regan, Charles Tate. (1922), Richardson, Laurence R. (1942), Romer, Alfred Sherwood. (1966), Sagemehl, M. (1884), Sagemehl, M. (1891), Scharff, R. F. (1911), Schneidervin, Roger W., and Wayne A. Hubert. (1986), Smith, Gerald R. (1965), Smith, Gerald R. (1966), Smith, Gerald R. (1981a), Smith, Gerald R. (1981b), Smith, S. H. (1968), Uyeno, Teruya, and Robert Rush Miller. (1962), Weisel, George F. (1967a), Wells, La Rue, and A. L. McLain. (1973), White, W. J., and R. J. Beamish. (1972), Woodward, A. Smith. (1901), Wydoski, Richard S., and Richard R. Whitney. (1979),

Catostomus alticolus Cope, 1874.
  Cope, Edward Drinker. (1874c), Cope, Edward Drinker, and H. C. Yarrow. (1875), Jordan, David Starr, and Barton Warren Evermann. (1896),

Catostomus anisurus Rafinesque, 1820.
  Ohio Carp sucker.
  Jordan, David Starr, and Barton Warren Evermann. (1896), Rafinesque, Constantine Samuel. (1820b), Smith, Philip W. (1979),

Catostomus arœopus Jordan, 1878.
  Gilbert, Charles Henry. (1893), Jordan, David Starr. (1878d), Jordan, David Starr, and Barton Warren Evermann. (1896), Jordan, David Starr, and Charles Henry Gilbert. (1883), Jordan, David Starr, and Henry W. Henshaw. (1878), Smith, Gerald R. (1966),

Catostomus ardens Jordan and Gilbert, 1880.

Utah Sucker, Mullet of Utah Lake.
Andreasen, J. K., and J. R. Barnes. (1975), Bailey, Reeve M., and John E. Fitch, Earl S. Herald, Ernest A. Lachner, C. C. Lindsey, C. Richard Robins, W. B. Scott. (1970), Bailey, Reeve M., and Ernest A. Lachner, C. C. Lindsey, C. Richard Robins, Phil M. Roedel, W. B. Scott, Loren P. Woods. (1966), Baxter, George T., and James R. Simon. (1970), Carlander, Kenneth D. (1969), Dunham, A. E., and Gerald R. Smith, J. N. Taylor. (1979), Eddy, Samuel. (1957), Eddy, Samuel. (1969), Evans, R. S., and R. A. Heckmann, J. Palmieri. (1976), Goode, C. Brown, and Theodore Nicholas Gill. (1903),.Hoffman, Glenn L. (1967), Jordan, David Starr, and Barton Warren Evermann. (1896), Jordan, David Starr, and Barton Warren Evermann. (1905), Jordan, David Starr, and Charles Henry Gilbert. (1880), Jordan, David Starr, and Charles Henry Gilbert. (1883), Kayton, R. J., and D. C. Kritsky, R. C. Tobias. (1979), Kent, J. C., and D. W. Johnson. (1979a), Kent, J. C., and D. W. Johnson. (1979b), La Bar, G. W. (1969), La Rivers, Ira. (1962), Lee, David S., and Carter R. Gilbert, Charles H. Hocutt, Robert E. Jenkins, Don E. McAllister, Jay R. Stauffer, Jr. (1980), Linton, Edwin. (1891), McConnell, W. J., and W. J. Clark, W. F. Sigler. (1957), Minckley, W. L., and Dean A. Hendrickson, Carl E. Bond. (1986), Nelson, Edward M. (1948), Palmieri, J., and R. Heckmann. (1976), Robins, C. Richard, and Reeve M. Bailey, Carl E. Bond, James R. Brooker, Ernest A. Lachner, Robert N. Lea, W. B. Scott. (1980), Simpson, James C., and Richard L. Wallace. (1982), Smith, Gerald R. (1966), Smith, Gerald R. (1981a), Smith, Gerald R., and W. L. Stokes, K. F. Horn. (1968), Smith, Hugh M., and William Converse Kendall. (1921), Snyder, Darrel E., and Robert T. Muth. (1990), Walden, Howard T., 2d. (1964),

Catostomus arenarius Snyder.
Hubbs, Carl L., and Robert Rush Miller. (1951),

Catostomus arenatus Miller and Smith, 1967.
Lee, David S., and Carter R. Gilbert, Charles H. Hocutt, Robert E. Jenkins, Don E. McAllister, Jay R. Stauffer, Jr. (1980), Miller, Robert Rush, and Gerald R. Smith. (1967), Smith, Gerald R. (1975),

Catostomus arizonæ (Gilbert and Scofield, 1898).
Gilbert, Charles Henry, and N. B. Scofield. (1898),

Catostomus aureolus Le Sueur, 1817.
DeKay, James Ellsworth. (1842), Günther, Albert C. (1868), Jordan, David Starr, and Barton Warren Evermann. (1896), Lachner, E. A. (1967), Le Sueur, Charles Alexandre. (1817), Rafinesque, Constantine Samuel. (1820b), Smith, Philip W. (1979),

Catostomus aurora Agassiz, 1850.
Agassiz, John Louis Rodolphe. (1850), Günther, Albert C. (1868), Jordan, David Starr, and Barton Warren Evermann. (1896),

Catostomus batrachops Cope, 1883.
Cope, Edward Drinker. (1883), Cope, Edward Drinker. (1889a), Cope, Edward Drinker. (1889b), Hay, Oliver Perry. (1927), Hussakof, Louis. (1908),

Catostomus bernardini Girard, 1857.
Yaqui sucker.
Günther, Albert C. (1868), Hubbs, Carl L., and Robert Rush Miller. (1951), Jordan, David Starr, and Barton Warren Evermann. (1896), Jordan, David Starr, and Charles Henry Gilbert. (1883), Lee, David S., and Carter R. Gilbert, Charles H. Hocutt, Robert E. Jenkins, Don E. McAllister, Jay R. Stauffer, Jr. (1980), Minckley, W. L., and Dean A. Hendrickson, Carl E. Bond. (1986), Robins, C. Richard, and Reeve M. Bailey, Carl E. Bond, James R.

Brooker, Ernest A. Lachner, Robert N. Lea, W. B. Scott. (1980), Villar, José Alvarez del. (1970),

Catostomus bostoniensis Le Sueur, 1817.
Rafinesque, Constantine Samuel. (1820b),

Catostomus brevirostris (Cope, 1879).
Andreasen, J. K. (1976), Jordan, David Starr, and Barton Warren Evermann. (1896), Lee, David S., and Carter R. Gilbert, Charles H. Hocutt, Robert E. Jenkins, Don E. McAllister, Jay R. Stauffer, Jr. (1980),

Catostomus bubalus (Rafinesque, 1818).
Brown Buffalo-Fish.
Bailey, R. M., and W. N. Eschmeyer. (1988), Günther, Albert C. (1868), Jordan, David Starr, and Barton Warren Evermann. (1896), Kirtland, Jared Potter. (1838), Leidy, Joseph. (1875), Opinion 1582. (1990),.Rafinesque, Constantine Samuel. (1820b), Trautman, Milton B. (1981),

Catostomus cahita Siebert and Minckley, 1986.
Siebert, Darrell J., and W. L. Minckley. (1986),

Catostomus carpio Rafinesque, 1820; and, Valenciennes, 1844. Two different species described under the same name.
Olive Carp sucker.
Forbes, Stephen Alfred., and Robert Earl Richardson. (1920), Günther, Albert C. (1868), Jordan, David Starr. (1885a), Rafinesque, Constantine Samuel. (1820b), Smith, Philip W. (1979), Trautman, Milton B. (1981), Valenciennes, Achille. (1844),

Catostomus catostomi. Rabeni, C. F., and J. G. Stanley. (1979),

Catostomus catostomus (Forster, 1773).
Longnose sucker, Long-Nosed Sucker, Northern sucker, Red Sucker.
Anderson, E. D., and L. L. Smith, Jr. (1971), Anonymous. (1964), Bailey, B. E., and A. W. Lantz, P. J. Schmidt. (1951), Bailey, M. M. (1969), Bailey, Reeve M., and Marvin O. Allum. (1962), Bailey, Reeve M., and John E. Fitch, Earl S. Herald, Ernest A. Lachner, C. C. Lindsey, C. Richard Robins, W. B. Scott. (1970), Bailey, Reeve M., and Ernest A. Lachner, C. C. Lindsey, C. Richard Robins, Phil M. Roedel, W. B. Scott, Loren P. Woods. (1966), Bailey, Reeve M., and Gerald R. Smith. (1981), (1954), Bangham, Ralph V., and James R. Adams. (1954), Barton, B. A. (1980), Barton, B. A., and B. F. Bidgood. (1980), Bassett, H. N. (1957), Baxter, George T., and James R. Simon. (1970), Beamish, R. J., and H. Tsuyuki. (1972), Becker, George C. (1983), Bennett, G. W., and W. F. Childers. (1966), Bensley, B. A. (1915), Beverly-Burton, Mary. (1984), Birt, T. P., and R. E. Dillinger, Jr., J. M. Green, W. S. Davidson. (1990), Black, Edgar C. (1953), Black, Edgar C. (1955), Bligh, E. G. (1970), Bligh, E. G. (1971), Boschung, Herbert T., Jr., and James D. Williams, Daniel W. Gotshall, David K. Caldwell, Melba C. Caldwell, Carol Nehring, Jordan Verner. (1983), Boucher, R., and R. Schetagne, E. Magnin. (1985), Breder, C. M., Jr., and D. E. Rosen. (1966), Brett, J. R., and A. L. Pritchard. (1946b), Brown, C. J. D. (1971), Brown, C. J. D., and R. J. Graham. (1954), Cameron, J. N. (1974), Cameron, J. N. (1975), Canton, S. P., and L. D. Cline, R. A. Short, J. V. Ward. (1984), Carl, G. Clifford, and Wilbert Amie Clemens, Casimir Charles Lindsey. (1977), Carlander, Kenneth D. (1944b), Carlander, Kenneth D. (1969), Clemens, W. A. (1939), Clemens, W. A., and J. R. Dymond, N. K. Bigelow. (1923), Clemens, W. A., and J. R. Dymond, N. K. Bigelow, F. B. Adamstone, W. J. K. Harkness. (1923), Clemens, W. A., and D. S. Rawson, J. L. McHugh. (1939), Coble, Daniel W. (1966), Cooper, Edwin Lavern. (1983), Cope, O. B. (1969), Cumbra, Stephen L., and Don E. McAllister, Richard E. Morlan. (1981), Curtis, M. A., and

M. E. Rau. (1980), Dechtiar, A. O. (1969), Dechtiar, A. O. (1972a), Dechtiar, A. O., and W. A. Dillon. (1974), Dryer, W. R. (1966), Dunbar, M. J., and H. H. Hildebrand. (1952), Dunham, A. E., and Gerald R. Smith, J. N. Taylor. (1979), Dwyer, W. P., and C. E. Smith. (1989), Dymond, J. R. (1936), Eastman, Joseph T. (1977), Eddy, Samuel. (1957), Eddy, Samuel. (1969), Eddy, Samuel, and Kenneth D. Carlander. (1942), Eddy, Samuel, and T. Surber. (1947), Eddy, Samuel, and Roy C. Tasker, James C. Underhill. (1972), Eddy, Samuel, and James C. Underhill. (1974), Eder, S., and C. A. Carlson. (1977), Elsey, C. A. (1946), Emery, Lee. (1976), Ergens, R. and R. A. Kudentsova, Iu. A. Strelkov. (1980), Everhart, W. H., and W. R. Seaman. (1971), Evermann, Barton Warren, and E. L. Goldsborough. (1907), Ferris, Stephen D., and Gregory S. Whitt. (1978), Foerster, R. E. (1937), Forbes, Stephen Alfred., and Robert Earl Richardson. (1908), Forbes, Stephen Alfred., and Robert Earl Richardson. (1920), Forster, J. R. (1773), Fredeen, F. J. H., and J. G. Saha, L. M. Royer. (1971), Fujihara, M. P. and F. P. Hungate. (1972), Fuiman, Lee A., and D. C. Witman. (1979), Gadd, Ben. (1986), Geen, G. H., and T. G. Northcote, G. F. Hartman, C. C. Lindsey. (1966), Girard, C. F. (1857), Godfrey, H. (1955), Goode, C. Brown, and Theodore Nicholas Gill. (1903), Gordon, D., and N. A. Croll, M. E. Rau. (1978), Greene, C. W. (1935), Grinham, T., and D. K. Cone. (1990), Hanek, G., and K. Molnar. (1974), Hansen, D. W. (1952), Harris, Roy H. D. (1952), Harris, Roy H. D. (1962), Harris, Roy H. D. (1963), Hart, J. L. (1931), Hathaway, R. P., and J. C. Herlevich. (1973), Hayes, M. L. (1955), Hayes, M. L. (1956), Hazel, P. P. (1978), Heckmann, R. A., and T. Carroll. (1985), Henderson, N. E., and R. E. Peter. (1969), Hendricks, M. L., and J. R. Stauffer, C. H. Hocutt, Jr., C. R. Gilbert. (1979), Hepworth, W. (1959), Hewson, L. C. (1959), Hinks, David. (1943), Hinks, David. (1957),.Hoffman, Glenn L. (1967), Hubbs, Carl L., and Karl F. Lagler. (1974), Hubbs, Carl L., and Leonard P. Schultz. (1932), Johnson, L. (1972), Johnson, L. (1975), Jordan, David Starr. (1878a), Jordan, David Starr. (1929), Jordan, David Starr, and Barton Warren Evermann. (1896), Jordan, David Starr, and Barton Warren Evermann. (1905), Kaiser, K. L. E. (1977), Kathrein, J. W. (1951), Kayton, R. J., and D. C. Kritsky, R. C. Tobias. (1979), Keleher, J. J. (1961a), Keleher, J. J. (1961b), Keleher, J. J. (1963), Keleher, J. J. (1967), Kendall, William Converse. (1914), Kendall, William Converse. (1918), Kendall, William Converse. (1924), Kendall, William Converse, and W. A. Dence. (1929), Kennedy, W. A. (1956), Lagler, Karl F., and John E. Bardach, Robert Rush Miller. (1962), Lalancette, L.-M., and E. Magnin. (1970), Large, T. (1903), Lee, David S., and Carter R. Gilbert, Charles H. Hocutt, Robert E. Jenkins, Don E. McAllister, Jay R. Stauffer, Jr. (1980), Li, M.-M., and Arai, H. P. (1988), Libosvarsky, J. (1970), Lindsey, Casimir Charles. (1956), Lindsey, Casimir Charles. (1957), Magnin, E. (1964), Mayr, Ernst. (1966), Mayr, Ernst. (1971), McAllister, Don E. (1964), McAllister, Don E., and Brian W. Coad. (1974), McClane, Albert Jules. (1974), McConnell, J. A., and J. R. Brett. (1946), McPhail, J. D., and C. C. Lindsey. (1970), Meek, Alexander. (1916), Meek, Seth Eugene, and S. F. Hildebrand. (1910), Miller, R. B. (1947), Miller, Robert Rush. (1958), Miller, Rudolph J., and H. E. Evans. (1965), Minckley, W. L., and Dean A. Hendrickson, Carl E. Bond. (1986), Mitchell, Patricia, and Ellie Prepas. (1990), Montgomery, W. L., and S. D. McCormick, R. J. Naiman, F. G. Whoriskey, Jr., G. A. Black. (1983), Moring, John R., and Paul D. Eiler, Mary T. Negus, Elizabeth Gibbs. (1986), Morrison, K. A., and N. Therien, B. Coupal. (1985), Morrow, James E. (1980), Munro, J. A., and W. A. Clemens. (1937), Nall, G. H. (1930), Neave, F., and A. Bajkov. (1929), Nelson, Edward M. (1948), Nelson, Joseph S. (1965), Nelson, Joseph S. (1973), Nelson, Joseph S. (1976), Nelson, Joseph S. (1984), Nester, R. T., and T. P. Poe. (1984), Nichols, John Treadwell. (1943), Nikolsky, G. V. (1961), Novokshonov, Yu. D., and Yu. N. Dyakonov. (1980), O'Donnell, D. J. (1935), Paetz, Martin J., and Joseph S. Nelson. (1970), Peters, J. C. (ed.) (1964), Phillips, Gary L., and William D. Schmid, James C. Underhill. (1982), Porter, T. R., and D. M. Rosenberg, D. K. McGowan. (1974), Pugachev, O. N. (1980), Ramamoorthy, S., and J. W. Moore, L. George. (1985), Rawson, D. S. (1951), Rawson, D. S. (1957), Rawson, D. S. (1960), Rawson, D. S., and C. A. Elsey. (1950), Reigle, N. J., Jr. (1969b), Richardson, John R. (1836), Roberts, Wayne Emerson. (1975), Robins, C. Richard, and Reeve M. Bailey, Carl E. Bond, James R. Brooker, Ernest

A. Lachner, Robert N. Lea, W. B. Scott. (1980), Sayigh, L., and R. Morin. (1986), Schmidt, P. J. (1949), Schoenthal, N. D. (1964), Schwalme, Karl, and William C. MacKay, Dieter Lindner. (1985), Scoppettone, G. Gary, and Mark Coleman, Gary A. Wedemeyer. (1986), Scott, W. B. (1954), Scott, W. B. (1958), Scott, W. B. (1967), Scott, W. B., and E. J. Crossman. (1969), Scott, W. B., and E. J. Crossman. (1973), Scruton, D. A. (1984), Siddiqi, M. N. (1981), Simpson, James C., and Richard L. Wallace. (1982), Sloley, B. D. (1988), Smith, C. Lavett. (1986), Smith, Gerald R. (1966), Smith, Gerald R. (1981b), Smith, Hugh M., and William Converse Kendall. (1921), Smith, John B., and Wayne A. Hubert. (1989), Smith, Philip W. (1965), Smith, Philip W. (1973), Smith, Philip W. (1979), Snyder, Darrel E., and Robert T. Muth. (1990), Spence, J. A., and B. N. Hynes. (1971), Srivastava, V. M. (1971), Stanley, D. R. (1988), Stenton, J. E. (1951), Sterba, Günther. (1983), Stuber, R. J. (1985), Threlfall, W. (1974), Threlfall, W., and G. Hanek. (1970), Tsuyuki, H., and E. Roberts, R. H. Kerr, J. F. Uthe, L. W. Clarke. (1967), Uthe, J. F. (1965), Vladykov, Vadim D. (1933), Walden, Howard T., 2d. (1964), Wallace, Ron R., and Peter J. McCart. (1984), Walton, B. D. (1980), Watson, T. G. (1981), Weisel, George F. (1957), Weisel, George F. (1962), Weisel, George F. (1967a), Wenzel, L. E., and T. H. Leik. (1956), Werner, Robert G. (1976a), Werner, Robert G. (1976b), Werner, Robert G. (1980), Whitehouse, Francis C. (1946), Willock, T. A. (1969), Withler, F. C. (1948), Wobeser, G., and N. O. Nielsen, R. H. Dunlop, F. M. Atton. (1970), Wooding, Frederick H. (1959), Wydoski, Richard S., and Richard R. Whitney. (1979), Wynne-Edwards, V. C. (1952), Yeager, Bruce L., and Kenneth J. Semmens. (1987), Zabik, M. E., and B. Olson, T. M. Johnson. (1978),

Catostomus catostomus camersoni.
Ramaswami, L. S. (1957),

Catostomus catostomus catostomus (Forster, 1773).
Eastern Longnose Sucker.
Backus, Richard H. (1957), Behnke, Robert J., and Ralph M. Wetzel. (1960), Carlander, Kenneth D. (1948), Dymond, J. R. (1937), Dymond, J. R. (1964), Dymond, J. R., and W. B. Scott. (1941), Eastman, Joseph T. (1980), Hubbs, Carl L., and Karl F. Lagler. (1941), Hubbs, Carl L., and Karl F. Lagler. (1947), Hubbs, Carl L., and Karl F. Lagler. (1974), McCabe, Britton C. (1943), Nelson, Edward M. (1955), Nichols, John Treadwell. (1930), Simon, James R. (1946), Smith, Philip W. (1979), Snyder, Richard C. (1949), Stenton, J. E. (1951), Toner, G. C. (1933), Trautman, Milton B. (1981), Weisel, George F. (1958), Weisel, George F., Jr., and H. William Newman. (1951),

Catostomus catostomus griseus Girard.
Eddy, Samuel. (1969), Hendricks, Lawrence J. (1952), Schultz, Leonard P. (1936), Schultz, Leonard P. (1947), Simon, James R. (1946), Smith, Gerald R. (1966),

Catostomus catostomus lacustris Bajkov, 1927.
Bajkov, A. (1927), Hubbs, Carl L., and Leonard P. Schultz. (1932),

Catostomus catostomus nannomyzon Mather.
Behnke, Robert J., and Ralph M. Wetzel. (1960), Hubbs, Carl L., and Karl F. Lagler. (1941), Hubbs, Carl L., and Karl F. Lagler. (1947), Hubbs, Carl L., and Karl F. Lagler. (1974), McCabe, Britton C. (1943), Smith, C. Lavett. (1986),

Catostomus catostomus rostratus (Tilesius, 1813).
Berg, Leo Simonovich. (1936), Chranilov, Ivar N. S. (1926), Nelson, Edward M. (1948), Novikov, A. S., and E. A. Streletskaya. (1966), Obraztsov, A. N., and O. B. Semenova. (1982), Polovova, T. P. (1970), Shilin, Yu A. (1973), Tilesius von Tilenau, Wilhelm Gottlieb. (1813), Velichko, A. M., and S. B. Podushka. (1985), Velichko, A. M., and B. B.

Voloshenko, D. P. Bulanov, A. A. Salazkin. (1979), Voloshenko, B. B., and A. M. Velichko. (1979), Walters, V. (1955),

Catostomus chloropteron Abbott, 1861.
Abbott, Charles Conrad. (1861), Günther, Albert C. (1868), Jordan, David Starr, and Barton Warren Evermann. (1896),

Catostomus (Pantosteus) clarii.
Powers, D. A. (1972),

Catostomus clarki Baird and Girard, 1854.
Desert sucker. Clarkson, R. W., and W. L. Minckley. (1988), Crabtree, C. B., and Donald G. Buth. (1987), Cross, Jeffrey N. (1985), Deacon, J. E., and P. B. Schumann, E. L. Stuenkel. (1987), Eddy, Samuel. (1969), Greger, P. D., and J. E. Deacon. (1988), Lee, David S., and Carter R. Gilbert, Charles H. Hocutt, Robert E. Jenkins, Don E. McAllister, Jay R. Stauffer, Jr. (1980), Minckley, W. L., and Dean A. Hendrickson, Carl E. Bond. (1986), Mpoame, M., and J. N. Rinne. (1983), Rinne, J. N. (1985b), Robins, C. Richard, and Reeve M. Bailey, Carl E. Bond, James R. Brooker, Ernest A. Lachner, Robert N. Lea, W. B. Scott. (1980), Smith, Gerald R. (1965), Smith, Gerald R. (1966), Wier, W., and L. F. Mayberry, H. G. Kinzer, P. R. Turner. (1983),

Catostomus clarki intermedius.
Williams, C. D., and J. E. Williams. (1982),

Catostomus clarki **X** *Catostomus insignis.*
Clarkson, R. W., and W. L. Minckley. (1988), Smith, Gerald R. (1966),

Catostomus clarkii Baird and Girard, 1854.
Amin, Omar M. (1968), Bailey, Reeve M., and John E. Fitch, Earl S. Herald, Ernest A. Lachner, C. C. Lindsey, C. Richard Robins, W. B. Scott. (1970), Fisher, S. G., and D. E. Busch, N. B. Grimm. (1981), Powers, D. A., and A. B. Edmundson. (1972), Powers, D. A., and A. B. Edmundson. (1973), Smith, Gerald R. (1966),

Catostomus columbianus (Eigenmann and Eigenmann, 1893).
Bridgelip Sucker.
Bailey, Reeve M., and John E. Fitch, Earl S. Herald, Ernest A. Lachner, C. C. Lindsey, C. Richard Robins, W. B. Scott. (1970), Bailey, Reeve M., and Ernest A. Lachner, C. C. Lindsey, C. Richard Robins, Phil M. Roedel, W. B. Scott, Loren P. Woods. (1966), Carl, G. Clifford, and Wilbert Amie Clemens, Casimir Charles Lindsey. (1977), Dauble, Dennis D. (1980), Dauble, Dennis D. (1986), Dauble, Dennis D., and R. L. Buschbom. (1981), Dunham, A. E., and Gerald R. Smith, J. N. Taylor. (1979), Eddy, Samuel. (1969), Ferris, Stephen D., and Gregory S. Whitt. (1978),.Hoffman, Glenn L. (1967), Hubbs, Carl L., and Robert Rush Miller. (1951), Johnson, A., and D. Norton, B. Yake. (1988), La Rivers, Ira. (1962), Lee, David S., and Carter R. Gilbert, Charles H. Hocutt, Robert E. Jenkins, Don E. McAllister, Jay R. Stauffer, Jr. (1980), Lindsey, Casimir Charles. (1957), Miller, Robert Rush, and Ralph G. Miller. (1948), Miller, Rudolph J., and H. E. Evans. (1965), Minckley, W. L., and Dean A. Hendrickson, Carl E. Bond. (1986), Nelson, Edward M. (1955), Robins, C. Richard, and Reeve M. Bailey, Carl E. Bond, James R. Brooker, Ernest A. Lachner, Robert N. Lea, W. B. Scott. (1980), Rogers, I. H., and H. W. Mahood. (1982), Scott, W. B. (1958), Scott, W. B., and E. J. Crossman. (1969), Scott, W. B., and E. J. Crossman. (1973), Simpson, James C., and Richard L. Wallace. (1982), Smith, Gerald R. (1965), Smith, Gerald R. (1966), Smith, Gerald R. (1981a), Wydoski, Richard S., and Richard R. Whitney. (1979),

Catostomus columbianus columbianus.
   Dunham, A. E., and Gerald R. Smith, J. N. Taylor. (1979), Smith, Gerald R. (1966),

Catostomus columbianus hubbsi Smith, 1966.
   Dunham, A. E., and Gerald R. Smith, J. N. Taylor. (1979), Smith, Gerald R. (1966),

Catostomus columbianus palouseanus Schultz and Thompson, 1936.
   Miller, Robert Rush, and Ralph G. Miller. (1948), Smith, Gerald R. (1966),

Catostomus columnaris Sytchevskaya, 1986.
   Sytchevskaya, E. K. (1986),

Catostomus comersoni.
   Bennett, D. K. (1979),

Catostomus commersoni (La Cepède, 1803).
   White Sucker, Common Sucker, Fine-scaled sucker.
   Aadland, L. P., and J.J. Peterka. (1981), Adams, C. C., and T. L. Hankinson. (1928),
   Adelman, I. R. (1980), Agassiz, John Louis Rodolphe. (1854), Ahlgren, M. O. (1990a),
   Ahlgren, M. O. (1990b), Amedjo, S. D., and John C. Holmes. (1990), Amin, Omar M.
   (1974), Amin, Omar M. (1975), Amin, Omar M. (1977a), Amin, Omar M. (1977b), Amin,
   O. M. (1981), Amin, O. M. (1984), Amin, Omar M. (1986a), Amin, Omar M. (1986b),
   Anderson, I. G., and G. A. D. Haslewood. (1970), Andrews, C. W. (1946), Anonymous.
   (1958b), Anonymous. (1964), Anonymous. (1965a), Anonymous. (1972), Anonymous.
   (1978), Anonymous. (1981), Bailey, Reeve M., and Marvin O. Allum. (1962), Bailey,
   Reeve M., and John E. Fitch, Earl S. Herald, Ernest A. Lachner, C. C. Lindsey, C. Richard
   Robins, W. B. Scott. (1970), Bailey, Reeve M., and Ernest A. Lachner, C. C. Lindsey, C.
   Richard Robins, Phil M. Roedel, W. B. Scott, Loren P. Woods. (1966), Bailey, Reeve M.,
   and Gerald R. Smith. (1981), (1954), Baker, J. P. (1981), Ball, R. C. (1949), Ballard, W.
   W. (1982), Bangham, Ralph V., and James R. Adams. (1954), Barber, D. L., and J. E.
   Mills Westermann. (1975a), Barber, D. L., and J. E. Mills Westermann. (1975b), Barber, D.
   L., and J. E. Mills Westermann. (1983), Barber, D. L., and J. E. Mills Westermann. (1985),
   Barber, D. L., and J. E. Mills Westermann. (1986), Barclay, L. A., Jr. (1974), Barnhart, R.
   (1955), Barton, B. A. (1980), Bassett, H. N. (1957), Basu, Satyendra Prasanna. (1959),
   Bauer, Bruce H., and Branley A. Branson, Strant T. Colwell. (1978), Baumann, Paul C.
   (1984), Baxter, George T., and James R. Simon. (1970), Beamish, R. J. (1972a), Beamish,
   R. J. (1972b), Beamish, R. J. (1973), Beamish, R. J. (1974), Beamish, R. J., and E. J.
   Crossman. (1977), Beamish, R. J., and H. H. Harvey. (1969), Beamish, R. J., and H. H.
   Harvey. (1972), Beamish, R. J., and W. L. Lockhart, J. C. Van Loon, Harold H. Harvey.
   (1975), Beamish, R. J., and G. A. McFarlane. (1983), Beamish, R. J., and H. Tsuyuki.
   (1972), Bean, L. S. (1936), Beatty, S. A. (1937), Becker, George C. (1959), Becker, George
   C. (1983), Bell, D. A., and Mary Beverly-Burton. (1980), Bendell-Young, Leah I., and
   Harold H. Harvey. (1986a), Bendell-Young, Leah I., and Harold H. Harvey. (1986b),
   Bendell-Young, Leah I., and Harold H. Harvey. (1989), Bendell-Young, Leah I., and
   Harold H. Harvey, Jeffrey F. Young. (1986), Bennett, D. H., and O. E. Maughan, D. B.
   Jester, Jr. (1985), Bensley, B. A. (1915), Bernhardt, R. W. (1957), Bernstein, J. W., and S.
   M. Swanson. (1989), Berst, A. H. (1961), Beverly-Burton, Mary. (1984), Birkenholz, D.,
   and A. W. Fritz. (1956), Black, G. A., and J. M. Fraser. (1984), Black, J. J. (1984), Black,
   J. J., and M. Holmes, P. P. Dymerski, W. F. Zapisek. (1979), Blouin, E. F., and A. D.
   Johnson, D. G. Dunlap, D. K. Spiegel. (1984), Borgmann, Uwe, and Karen M. Ralph.
   (1986a), Borgmann, Uwe, and Karen M. Ralph. (1986b), Boschung, Herbert T., Jr., and
   James D. Williams, Daniel W. Gotshall, David K. Caldwell, Melba C. Caldwell, Carol
   Nehring, Jordan Verner. (1983), Bower, S. M., and P. T. K. Woo. (1977a), Bower, S. M.,
   and P. T. K. Woo. (1977b), Bower, S. M., and P. T. K. Woo. (1979), Bradley, R. W., and
   J. R. Morris. (1986), Branson, Branley A., and Donald L. Batch. (1974), Breder, C. M., Jr.,

and D. E. Rosen. (1966), Brett, J. R. (1944), Brett, J. R. (1956), Brothers, E. B. (1984), Brousseau, R. A. (1976), Brown, C. J. D. (1971), Brown, E. H., Jr. (1960), Brynildson, C., and J. Truog. (1958), Buth, Donald G. (1983), Buynak, G. L., and H. W. Mohr, Jr. (1978a), Call, R. E. (1887), Campbell, K. P. (1974), Campbell, R. S. (1935), Canton, S. P., and L. D. Cline, R. A. Short, J. V. Ward. (1984), Carbine, W. F., and V. C. Applegate. (1948), Carl, G. Clifford, and Wilbert Amie Clemens, Casimir Charles Lindsey. (1977), Carlander, Kenneth D. (1942), Carlander, Kenneth D. (1943), Carlander, Kenneth D. (1944a), Carlander, Kenneth D. (1944b), Carlander, Kenneth D. (1949), Carlander, Kenneth D. (1955), Carlander, Kenneth D. (1969), Carlander, Kenneth D., and L. E. Hiner. (1943a), Carlander, Kenneth D., and L. E. Hiner. (1943b), Carlander, Kenneth D., and J. W. Parsons. (1949), Chalanchuk, S. M. (1985), Chan, G.-L. (1981), Chan, D. K. O., and R. Gunther, H. A. Bern. (1978), Chapman, D. W. (1978), Chew, Robert D., and Martin A. Hamilton. (1985), Chau, Y. K., and P. T. S. Wong, G. A. Bengert, J. L. Dunn, B. Glen. (1985), Chovelon, A., and L. George, C. Gulayets, Y. Hoyano, E. McGuinness, J. Moore, S. Ramamoorthy, S. Ramammoorthy, P. Singer, K. Smiley, A. Wheatley. (1984), Christensen, G. M. (1972), Ciepielewski, W. (1985), Cincotta, Dan A., and J. R. Stauffer, Jr. (1984), Cincotta, Dan A., and J. R. Stauffer, Jr., C. H. Hocutt. (1982), Cincotta, Dan A., and J. R. Stauffer, Jr., C. H. Hocutt. (1984), Clay, W. M. (1975), Clifford, H. F. (1972), Clifford, T. J., and S. Facciana. (1972), Coble, Daniel W. (1966), Coble, Daniel W. (1967), Cochran, P. A. (1985), Cole, H., and D. Barry, D. E. H. Frear, A. Bradford. (1967), Cone, D. K. (1983), Cone, D. K., and M. Wiles. (1985), Cooper, Edwin Lavern. (1983), Cooper, G. P., and R. N. Schafer. (1954), Corbett, B. W., and P. M. Powles. (1983), Corbett, B. W., and P. M. Powles. (1986), Cross, Frank B. (1967), Cross, Frank B., and Joseph T. Collins. (1975), Crossman, E. J. (1976), Curry, Kevin D., and Anne Spacie. (1979), Curry, Kevin D., and Anne Spacie. (1984), Curtis, M. A., and M. E. Rau. (1980), Dahl, F. H., and R. B. McDonald. (1980), Dawe, C. J., and M. F. Stanton, F. J. Schwartz. (1964), Dechtiar, A. O. (1969), Dechtiar, A. O. (1972a), Dechtiar, A. O. (1972b), Denison, Samuel G., and Carl R. Carlson, John L. Dorkin, Jr., Cecil Lue-Hing. (1978), Desser, S. S., and R. Lester. (1975), Deutsch, M., and V. E. Engelbert. (1970), Deutsch, W. G. (1978), Devault, D. S. (1985), Devine, A., and E. Stevens. (1985), Dobie, J. (1952), Dobie, J. (1962), Dobie, J. (1966), Dobie, J. R., and O. L. Meehean, S. F. Snieszko, F. N. Washburn. (1956), Dobie, J., and J. B. Moyle. (1956), Donahue, J., and R. Stuckenrath, J. M. Adovasio, et al. (1978), Dorkin, John L., Jr. (1980), Driscoll, C. T., Jr., and J. P. Baker, J. J. Bisogni, Jr., C. L. Schofield. (1980), Dunham, A. E., and Gerald R. Smith, J. N. Taylor. (1979), Duru, C., and A. D. Johnson, E. Blouin. (1981), Eastman, Joseph T. (1977), Eastman, Joseph T. (1980), Eaton, J., and J. Arthur, Hermanutz, R. Kiefer, L. Mueller, R. Anderson, R. Erickson, B. Nordling, J. Rogers, H. Pritchard. (1985), Eaton, J. G., and J. M. McKim, G. W. Holcombe. (1978), Eddy, Samuel. (1957), Eddy, Samuel. (1969), Eddy, Samuel, and Kenneth D. Carlander. (1940), Eddy, Samuel, and Kenneth D. Carlander. (1942), Eddy, Samuel, and T. Surber. (1947), Eddy, Samuel, and Roy C. Tasker, James C. Underhill. (1972), Eddy, Samuel, and James C. Underhill. (1974), Embody, G. C. (1915), Emery, Lee. (1976), Engstrom-Heg, R., and R. T. Colesante, G. A. Stillings. (1988), Everhart, W. H. (1958), Evermann, Barton Warren, and W. C. Kendall. (1895), Faber, D. J. (1967), Fago, Don. (1984b), Farmer, G. J., and F. W. H. Beamish, P. F. Lett. (1977), Ferris, Stephen D., and Gregory S. Whitt. (1978), Figueroa, J. and S. D. Morley, J. Heierhorst, C. Krentler, K. Lederis, D. Richter. (1989), Fischthal, J. H., and D. O. Carson, R. S. Vaught. (1982), Fish, M. P. (1929), Fish, M. P. (1932), Fisher, A. W. F., and K. Wong, V. Gill, K. Lederis. (1984), Fisher, H. J. (1962), Flemer, D. A., and W. S. Woolcott. (1966), Flick, W. A., and D. A. Webster. (1961), Forbes, Stephen Alfred. (1884), Forbes, Stephen Alfred., and Robert Earl Richardson. (1908), Forney, J. L. (1957a), Forney, J. L. (1957b), Fowler, Henry Weed. (1948a), Franke, E. D., and S. MacKiewicz. (1982), Franzin, W. G. (1984), Franzin, W. G., and G. A. McFarlane. (1981), Franzin, W. G., and G. A. McFarlane. (1987), Fraser, G. A., and Harold H. Harvey. (1982), Fraser, D. F., and T. N. Mottolese. (1984), Fraser, Grant A., and Harold H. Harvey. (1984), Frederick, L. L. (1975), Fried, B., and J. G. Kitchen. (1966), 565, Fried, B., and R. S. Koplin. (1967), Fuiman, Lee A. (1979), Fuiman, Lee A.

(1983), Fuiman, Lee A. (1984), Fuiman, Lee A., and J. R. Trojnar. (1980), Fujihara, M. P. and F. P. Hungate. (1972), Gadd, Ben. (1986), Geen, G. H. (1958), Geen, G. H., and T. G. Northcote, G. F. Hartman, C. C. Lindsey. (1966), Gilbert, Charles Henry. (1891), Gill, V. E., and G. D. Burford, K. Lederis, E. A. Zimmerman. (1977), Glass, N. R. (1969), Godfrey, H. (1955), Goode, C. Brown, and Theodore Nicholas Gill. (1903), Gordon, D., and N. A. Croll, M. E. Rau. (1978), Gore, J. A., and R. M. Bryant, Jr. (1986), Grey, A. J., and E. G. Hayunga. (1980), Grinham, T., and D. K. Cone. (1990), Guilday, J. E., and H. W. Hamilton, E. Anderson, et al. (1978), Hall, A. E., and O. R. Elliott. (1954), Halyk, Lawrence. C., and Eugene K. Balon. (1983), Hamilton, S. J., and T. A. Haines. (1989), Hankinson, T. L. (1920), Hansen, D. W. (1952), Hanson, W. D., and R. S. Campbell. (1963), Hart, C. W., Jr., and S. L. H. Fuller. (1974), Hart, T. F., Jr., and R. G. Werner. (1987), Harvey, Harold H. (1980), Harvey, Harold H., and G. A. Fraser, J. M. McArdle. (1986), Hayes, M. L. (1955), Hayes, M. L. (1956), Hayunga, E. G. (1980), Hayunga, E. G. (1984), Hayunga, E. G., and A. J. Grey. (1976), Hayunga, E. G., and J. S. Mackiewicz. (1988), Heckmann, R. A., and H. L. Ching. (1987), Hedges, S. B., and R. C. Ball. (1953), Hedtke, S. F., and C. W. West, K. N. Allen, T. J. Norberg-King, D. I. Mount. (1986), Heierhorst, J. and S. D. Morley, J. Figueroa, C. Krentler, K. Lederis, D. Richter. (1989), Heinermann, P. H., and M. A. Ali. (1989), Heit, Merrill, and Catherine S. Klusek. (1985), Heit, M., and C. Schofield, C. T. Driscoll, S S. Hodgkiss. (1989), Henderson, B. A. (1986), Henderson, N. E., and R. E. Peter. (1969), Hendrickson, G. L. (1986), Hesslein, R. H., and E. Salvicek. (1984), Hile, R., and C. Juday. (1941), Hobe, H. (1987), Hobe, H., and B. R. McMahon. (1988), Hobe, Helve, and Peter R. H. Wilkes, Richard L. Walker, Chris M. Wood, Brian R. McMahon. (1983), Hobe, Helve, and Chris M. Wood, Brian R. McMahon. (1984),.Hoffman, Glenn L. (1967), Hoffman, C. H., and E. W. Surber. (1948), Hokanson, Kenneth E. F. (1977), Holman, J. A. (1979), Horak, D. L., and H. A. Tanner. (1964), Houston, A. H., and K. M. Mearow, J. S. Smeda. (1976), Huang, C. T. and Cleveland P. Hickman, Jr. (1968), Hubert, W. A., and F. J. Rahel. (1989), Huggins, Donald G., and Randall E. Moss. (1975), Huntsman, A. G. (1935), Huntsman, A. G. (1942), Ichikawa, Tomoyuki, and Karl Lederis, Hideshi Kobayashi. (1984), Jackson, S. W., Jr. (1966), Jaffe, R., and R. A. Hites. (1986), Jaffe, R., and E. A. Stemmler, B. D. Eitzer, R. A. Hites. (1985), Jagoe, Charles H., and Terry A. Haines. (1985), Jenkins, Robert M. (1953b), Johnson, F. H. (1977), Johnson, L. D. (1958), Johnson, L. (1966), Johnson, M. G. (1987), Jordan, David Starr. (1878a), Kaiser, K. L. E. (1977), Kathrein, J. W. (1951), Kavaliers, M. (1980), Kavaliers, M. (1981), Kavaliers, M. (1982a), Kavaliers, M. (1982b), Kavaliers, M. (1982c), Kavaliers, M., and M. F. Hawkins. (1981), Kavaliers, M., and C. L. Ralph. (1980), Keast, A. (1968), Keleher, J. J. (1967), Kelso, J. R. M. (1976), Kelso, J. R. M., and, D. S. Jeffries. (1988), Kelso, J. R. M., and J. K. Leslie. (1979), Kempinger, J. (1975), Kendall, William Converse. (1924), Khalifa, K. A., and G. Post. (1976), Kirby, G. M., and J. R. Bend, I. R. Smith, M. A. Hayes. (1990), Klaverkamp, J. F., and D. A. Duncan. (1987), Klaverkamp, J. F., and D. A. Hodgins, A. Lutz. (1983), Klaverkamp, J. F., and M. A. Turner, S. E. Harrison, R. H. Hesslein. (1983), Klotz, P. H., and B. L. Haase. (1987), Kobayashi, Yuta, and Karl Lederis, Jean Rivier, David Ko, Denis McMaster, Paule Poulin. (1986), Kononen, D. W. (1982), Kononen, D. W. (1989), Koster, William J. (1957), Kreuzer, R. O., and J. G. Sivak. (1984), Kuehn, J. H. (1949), Laarman, P. W., and J. R. Ryckman. (1982), La Cepède, Bernard Germain Étienne. (1803), Lacroix, Gilles L. (1985), Lagler, Karl F. (1945), Lagler, Karl F., and John E. Bardach, Robert Rush Miller. (1962), Lalancette, L.-M. (1975a), Lalancette, L.-M. (1976), Lalancette, L.-M. (1977), Lalancette, L.-M. (1981), Lantz, A. W. (1966), Lantz, A. W. (1969), Lantz, A. W., and D. G. Iredale. (1966), Lantz, A. W., and D. G. Iredale. (1971), Large, T. (1903), Lawler, G. H. (1965), Lawler, G. H. (1969), Lawrence, J. L. (1970), Lederis, K. (1973), Lederis, K. (1977), Lederis, K., and J. Fryer, J. Rivier, K. L. MacCannell, Y. Kobayashi, N. Woo, K. L. Wong. (1985), Lederis, K., and A. Letter, D. McMaster, G. Moore, D. Schlesinger. (1982), Lederis, K., and W. Vale, J. Rivier, K. L. MacCannell, D. McMaster, Y. Kobayashi, U. Suess, J. Lawrence. (1982), Lee, David S., and Carter R. Gilbert, Charles H. Hocutt, Robert E. Jenkins, Don E. McAllister, Jay R. Stauffer, Jr. (1980), Lee, R. M., and S. D. Gerking,

B. Jezierska. (1983), Leino, R. L. (1982), Leslie, J. K., and J. E. Moore. (1985), Leslie, J. K., and J. E. Moore. (1986), Lessman, C. A. (1981), Lessman, C. A., and C. W. Huver. (1981), Lester, R. J. G., and B. A. Daniels. (1976), Lester, R. J. G., and S. S. Desser. (1975), Lewis, W. M., and D. Elder. (1953), Li, M.-M., and Arai, H. P. (1988), Lindsey, Casimir Charles. (1957), Lippson, Alice J., and R. L. Moran. (1974), Lockhart, W. L., and A. Lutz. (1976), Lockhart, W. L., and A. Lutz. (1977), Lockhart, W. L., and D. A. Metner. (1984), Long, Wilbur L. (1973), Long, Wilbur L. (1980a), Long, Wilbur L. (1980b), Long, Wilbur L., and William W. Ballard. (1976), Lopinot, Alvin C. (1958), Lopinot, Alvin C. (1965), Lopinot, Alvin C. (1966a), Lopinot, Alvin C. (1966b), Lopinot, Alvin C. (ed.). (1968), Lovett, R. J., and W. H. Glutenmann, I S. Pakkala, W. D. Youngs, D. J. Lisk, G. E. Burdick, E. J. Harris. (1972), Lowe, T. P., and T. W. May, W. G. Brumbaugh, D. A. Kane. (1985), MacCrimmon, H. R. (1979), Maccubbin, A. E., and P. Black, L. Trzeciak, J. J. Black. (1985), MacFarlane, G. A., and W. G. Franzin. (1978), MacKay, H. H. (1963), Magnan, P. (1988), Magnin, E. (1964), Magnuson, J. J., and R. M. Horral. (1977), Mahon, R., and C. B. Port. (1985), Malick, Robert W., Jr., and Wayne A. Potter. (1976), Mancini, E. R., and M. Busdosh, B. D. Steele. (1979), Manohar, S. V. (1969), Manohar, S. V. (1970), Manohar, S. V. (1971), Manohar, S. V., and H. Boese. (1971), Mansfield, P. J. (1984), Mansueti, A. J., and J. D. Hardy. (1967), Marenchin, Ginger Lee, and David M. Sever. (1981), Markarian, R. K., and M. C. Matthews, L. T. Connor. (1980), Marking, L. L., and T. D. Bills. (1977), Marking, L. L., and T. D. Bills. (1985), Martin, J. D. (1985), Martin, N. V. (1970), Mathias, J. A., and J. A. Babaluk, K. D. Rowes. (1985), Mattingly, R. (1976), Mauck, W. L., and D. W. Coble. (1971), Maurakis, Eugene G., and William S. Woolcott. (1984), Mayr, Ernst. (1966), Mayr, Ernst. (1971), McClane, Albert Jules. (1974), McCombie, A. M., and A. H. Berst. (1969), McCormick, J. H., and B. R. Jones, K. E. F. Hokanson. (1977), McCraig, R. S., and J. W. Mullan, C. O. Dodge. (1960), McCrimmon, H. R., and A. H. Berst. (1961), McElman, J. F. (1983), McElman, J. F., and E. K. Balon. (1980), McFarlane, G. A., and W. G. Franzin. (1981), McKim, J. M., and J. W. Arthur, T. W. Thorslund. (1975), McKim, J. M., and J. G. Eaton, G. W. Holcombe. (1978), McKinnon, G. A., and F. N. Hnytka. (1985), McMaster, Denis, and Karl Lederis. (1983), McPhail, J. D., and C. C. Lindsey. (1970), Meek, Seth Eugene. (1891), Mergo,John C., Jr., and Andrew M. White. (1984), Metcalf, A. L. (1966), Miki, B. L. A. (1977), Miki, B. L. A., and J. M. Neelin. (1977), Miller, N. J. (1971), Miller, Rudolph J., and Henry W. Robinson. (1973), Mills, K. H., and S. M. Chalanchuk, L. C. Mohr, I. J. Davies. (1987), Mills, Paul A., Jr., and Charles H. Hocutt, Jay R. Stauffer, Jr. (1978), Minckley, W. L. (1959), Minckley, W. L. (1963), Minckley, W. L., and R. H. Goodyear, J. E. Craddock. (1964), Minckley, W. L., and Dean A. Hendrickson, Carl E. Bond. (1986), Mitchell, L. G. (1978), Mitchell, Patricia, and Ellie Prepas. (1990), Mohr, Lloyd C., and Sandra M. Chalanchuk. (1985), Molnar, K., and G. L. Chan, C. H. Fernando. (1982), Molnar, K., and G. Hanek. (1974), Montgomery, W. L., and S. D. McCormick, R. J. Naiman, F. G. Whoriskey, Jr., G. A. Black. (1983), Moore, G., and A. Letter, M. Tesanovic, K. Lederis. (1975), Moore, K. A., and D. D. Williams. (1990), Morley, S. D., and C. Schonrock, J. Heierhorst, J. Figueroa, K. Lederis, D. Richter. (1990), Moring, John R., and Paul D. Eiler, Mary T. Negus, Elizabeth Gibbs. (1986), Moyle, J. B., and C. R. Burrows. (1954), Moyle, Peter B. (1969), Mudry, D. R., and H. P. Arai. (1973a), Mudry, D. R., and H. P. Arai. (1973b), Muench, B. (1963), Munkittrick, K. R., and D. G. Dixon. (1989), Muzzall, P. M. (1979a), Muzzall, P. M. (1979b), Muzzall, P. M. (1980a), Muzzall, P. M. (1980b), Muzzall, P. M. (1980c), Muzzall, P. M. (1982b), Neilands, J. B. (1947), Nelson, Edward M. (1959), Nelson, E. W. (1876), Nelson, Joseph S. (1973), Nelson, Joseph S. (1974), Nelson, Joseph S. (1976), Nelson, Joseph S. (1977), Nelson, Joseph S. (1984), Ney, J. J., and J. H. van Hassel. (1983), Nickol, B. B., and N. Samuel. (1983), Niimi, A. J. (1975), Niimi, A. J. (1983), Nurnberger, P. K. (1928), Nurnberger, P. K. (1930), Okawara, Y., and S. D. Morley, L. O. Burzio, H. Zwiers, K. Lederis, D. Richter. (1988), Olson, D. E., and W. J. Scidmore. (1963), Ommanney, Francis Downes. (1969), Ostland, V. E., and B. D. Hicks, J. G. Daly. (1987), Ostrow, M. E. (1979), Ovchynnyk, M. M. (1965), Paetz, Martin J., and Joseph S. Nelson. (1970), Page, Lawrence M. (1982), Pallai, Peter V., and Massimo

Mabilia, Murray Goodman, Wylie Vale, Jean Rivier. (1983), Paragamian, V. L. (1976), Parker, R. A. (1958), Pearson, William D., and Louis A. Krumholz (1984), Peters, J. C. (ed.) (1964), Peterson, P. H., and D. J. Martin-Robichaud. (1986), Pflieger, William L. (1971), Pflieger, William L. (1975), Phillips, Gary L., and William D. Schmid, James C. Underhill. (1982), Pippy, J. H. C. (1970), Pippy, J. H. C., and G. M. Hare. (1969), Pot, W., and D. L. G. Noakes, M. M. Ferguson, G. Coker. (1984), Potter, Wayne A., and Robert W. Malick, Jr., Janet L. Polk. (1976), Priegel, G. R. (1976), Purkett, C. A., Jr. (1958a), Quinn, Stephen P., and Michael R. Ross. (1985), Quinn, T. P., and R. F. Tallman. (1987), Rabeni, C. F., and J. G. Stanley. (1979), Rahel, F. J. (1986), Rawson, D. S. (1951), Rawson, D. S. (1957), Reckhow, K. H., and R. W. Black, T. B. Stockton, Jr., J. D. Vogt, J. G. Wood. (1987), Reece, M. (1963), Reighard, Jacob E. (1915), Reigle, N. J., Jr. (1969a), Reynolds, W. W., and M. E. Casterlin. (1978), Ritson, Philip C., and Janet L. Polk, Robert W. Malick, Jr. (1977), Roach, L. S. (1948a), Roberto Julis, C. and K. Lederis. (1988), Roberts, Wayne Emerson. (1975), Robins, C. Richard, and Reeve M. Bailey, Carl E. Bond, James R. Brooker, Ernest A. Lachner, Robert N. Lea, W. B. Scott. (1980), Roland, J. V., and K. B. Cumming. (1973), Roussow, G. (1954), Ruggles, C. P., and W. D. Watt. (1975), Salki, A., and M. Turner, K. Patalas, J. Rudd, D. Findlay. (1985), Savan, M., and J. Budd, P. W. Reno, S. Darley. (1979), Schlosser, Isaac J. (1985), Schlosser, I. J. (1987), Schmitt, Christopher J., and J. L. Zajicek, M. A. Ribick. (1985), Schneberger, E. (1972), Schneidervin, Roger W., and Wayne A. Hubert. (1987), Schwalme, Karl, and William C. MacKay, Dieter Lindner. (1985), Scidmore, W. J. (1953), Scidmore, W. J., and D. E. Woods. (1960), Scoppettone, G. Gary, and Mark Coleman, Gary A. Wedemeyer. (1986), Scott, A. P., and Duncan S. MacKenzie, Norman E. Stacey. (1984), Scott, D. P. (1974), Scott, D. P., and F. A. J. Armstrong. (1972), Scott, W. B. (1958), Scott, W. B. (1967), Scott, W. B., and E. J. Crossman. (1969), Scott, W. B., and E. J. Crossman. (1973), Scruton, D. A. (1984), Sebastien, R. J., and R. A. Brust, D. M. Rosenberg. (1989), Seegert, G. L. (1973), Sheldon, Andrew L. (1968), Siddiqi, M. N. (1981), Siefert, R. E. (1972), Siefert, R. E., and W. A. Spoor. (1974), Sipponen, M. (1978), Sivak, J. G. (1973), Sloley, B. D. (1988), Smith, C. Lavett. (1954), Smith, C. Lavett. (1986), Smith, Gerald R. (1963), Smith, Gerald R. (1966), Smith, Gerald R. (1981b), Smith, I. R., and K. W. Baker, M. A. Hayes, H. W. Ferguson. (1989), Smith, I. R., and H. W. Ferguson, M. A. Hayes,. (1989), Smith, I. R., and B. A. Zajdlik. (1987), Smith, John B., and Wayne A. Hubert. (1989), Smith, L. L., Jr., and N. L. Moe (compilers). (1944), Smith, L. L., Jr., and D. M. Oseid. (1974), Smith, M. W. (1952), Smith, M. W. (1961), Smith, Philip W. (1965), Smith, Philip W. (1973), Smith, Philip W. (1979), Snyder, Darrel E., and Robert T. Muth. (1990), Sonstegard, R. A., and L. A. McDermott, K. S. Sonstegard. (1972), Souter, B. W., and R. A. Sonstegard, L. A. McDermott. (1976), Spoor, W. A., and C. L. Schloemer. (1939), Sprague, J. W. (1961), Srivastava, V. M. (1971), Stacey, Norman E., and Duncan S. MacKenzie, Tracy A. Marchant, Ann L. Kyle, Richard E. Peter. (1984), Starnes, L. B. (1984), Stevens, E. D., and F. E. J. Fry. (1974), Strawn, K. (1958), Suess, Ursula, and Jane Laurence, David Ko, Karl Lederis. (1986), Sun, J. and Harold H. Harvey. (1986), Surber, T. (1940), Tao, S.-K. (1973), Thomas, M. L. H. (1966), Thompson, Peter. (1980), Threinen, C. W., and W. T. Helm. (1952), Threlfall, W. (1974), Threlfall, W., and G. Hanek. (1970), Tökés, L. (1970), Trautman, Milton B. (1957), Trembley, F. J. (1960), Trippel, Edward A., and Harold H. Harvey. (1987a), Trippel, Edward A., and Harold H. Harvey. (1987b), Trippel, Edward A., and Harold H. Harvey. (1989), Trippel, Edward A., and Harold H. Harvey. (1990), Trojnar, J. R. (1977), Truhlar, J. F., and L. A. Reed. (1976), Tsuyuki, H., and E. Roberts, R. H. Kerr, J. F. Uthe, L. W. Clarke. (1967), Turner, Michael A., and John W. M. Rudd. (1983), Twomey, Katie. (1984), Twomey, Katie, and Kathryn L. Williamson, Patrick Nelson. (1984), Uhazy, L. S. (1976), Uhazy, L. S. (1977a), Uhazy, L. S. (1977b), Uhazy, L. S. (1977c), Uhazy, L. S. (1978), Uthe, J. F. (1965), Uyeno, Teruya, and Robert Rush Miller. (1963), Van Coillie, R., and A. Rousseau. (1974), Van Coillie, R., and A. Rousseau. (1975), Van Coillle, R., and A. Rousseau, M. Ouellet. (1976), Van Oosten, J., and H. J. Deason. (1939), Verdon, R., and G. Codin-Blumer, E. Magnin. (1978), Vessel, M. F., and S. Eddy. (1941), Victor, R., and G. L. Chan, C. H. Fernando. (1979),

Vondracek, B. C. (1977), Waiwood, K. G., and P. H. Johansen. (1974), Walker, R. L., and P. R. H. Wilkes, C. M. Wood. (1989), Walburg, C. H. (1964), Walden, Howard T., 2d. (1964), Walker, Chris M. Wood, and Brian R. McMahon. (1983), Wallace, R. G. (1976), Wallace, Ron R., and Peter J. McCart. (1984), Walters, V. (1955), Walton, B. D. (1980), Wang, Johnson C. S., and Ronnie J. Kernehan. (1979), Watson, T. G. (1981), Webster, Dwight A. (1942), Webster, Dwight A. (1954), Weiner, J. G., and R. A. Jacobson, P. S. Schmidt, P. R. Heine. (1985), Wells, La Rue, and A. L. McLain. (1973), Wenzel, L. E., and T. H. Leik. (1956), Werner, Robert G. (1976a), Werner, Robert G. (1976b), Werner, Robert G. (1979), Werner, Robert G. (1980), White, G. E. (1974), White, G. E., and J. P. Harley. (1973), White, G. E., and J. P. Harley. (1974), Whitworth, W. R., and P. L. Berrien, W. T. Keller. (1968), Wiener, J. G., and R. A. Jacobson, P. S. Schmidt, P. R. Heine. (1985), Wiles, M., and D. K. Cone. (1987), Wilkes, P. R. H., and B. R. McMahon. (1986a), Wilkes, P. R. H., and B. R. McMahon. (1986b), Wilkes, P. R. H., and R. L. Walker, D. G. McDonald, C. M. Wood. (1981), Williams, D. D. (1980c), Williams, D. D., and M. J. Ulmer. (1980), Willock, T. A. (1969), Wobeser, G., and F. M. Atton. (1973), Wobeser, G., and N. O. Nielsen, R. H. Dunlop, F. M. Atton. (1970), Woo, Patrick T. K., and Geoff A. Black. (1984), Woodbury, L. A. (1941), Wooding, Frederick H. (1959), Woods, Loren P. (1959), Yeager, Bruce L., and Kenneth J. Semmens. (1987), Young, Leah Bendell, and Harold H. Harvey. (1989), Yulis, Carlos Roberto, and Karl Lederis. (1986a), Yulis, Carlos Roberto, and Karl Lederis. (1986b), Yulis, C. R., and K. Lederis. (1987), Yulis, C. R., and K. Lederis. (1988), Yulis, Carlos Roberto, and Karl Lederis, Kar-Lit Wong, Anthony W. F. Fisher. (1986), Zabik, M. E., and B. Olson, T. M. Johnson. (1978), Zalewski, M. (1983),

Catostomus commersoni commersoni (La Cepède, 1803).
Common White Sucker.
Backus, Richard H. (1957), Behnke, Robert J., and Ralph M. Wetzel. (1960), Carbine, W. F. (1943), Dobie, J. (1969), Eastman, Joseph T. (1980), Gee, R. J. (1989), Knapp, Leslie W., and William J. Richards, Robert Victor Muller, Neal R. Foster. (1963), Lalancette, L.-M. (1975b), Larimore, R. W., and P. W. Smith. (1963), Macphee, Craig. (1960), McCleave, James David. (1964), Nelson, Edward M. (1955), Oseid, D. M. (1977), Personius, Robert Giles, and Samuel Eddy. (1955), Pfeiffer, Roman A. (1955), Reed, Roger J. (1959), Roth, R. R. (1972), Smith, C. Lavett. (1958), Smith, Gerald R. (1963), Smith, Philip W. (1963), Trautman, Milton B. (1981), Tremblay, L. (1962), Verdon, R., and E. Magnin. (1977a), Verdon, R., and E. Magnin. (1977b), Waxman, J. B. (1975),

Catostomus commersoni suckleyi.
Eastman, Joseph T. (1980), Smith, Philip W. (1979),

Catostomus commersoni sucklii.
Simon, James R. (1946),

Catostomus commersoni utawana Mather, 1890.
Dwarf white sucker.
Beamish, R. J., and E. J. Crossman. (1977), Eastman, Joseph T. (1980), Smith, C. Lavett. (1986),

Catostomus commersonii (La Cepède, 1803).
Common Sucker, Fine-Scaled Sucker, White Sucker, Brook Sucker.
Berst, A. H., and A. M. McCombie. (1963), Bigelow, N. K. (1923), Blatchley, W. S. (1938), Crawford, D. R. (1923), Culbertson, G. (1904), Dugal, L. C. (1962), Dunbar, M. J., and H. H. Hildebrand. (1952), Evermann, Barton Warren, and U. O. Cox. (1894), Forbes, Stephen Alfred., and Robert Earl Richardson. (1920), Foskett, D. R. (1947), Fraser, D. I., and A. Mannan, W. J. Dyer. (1962), Hallam, J. C. (1959), Hart, J. S. (1947), Hildebrand, Samuel F., and William C. Schroeder. (1923), Hinks, David. (1943), Hubbs, Carl L., and C.

W. Creaser. (1924), Jordan, David Starr, and Barton Warren Evermann. (1896), Jordan, David Starr, and Barton Warren Evermann. (1905), Jordan, David Starr, and Charles Henry Gilbert. (1883), Keleher, J. J. (1961a), Keleher, J. J. (1963), Kendall, William Converse. (1914), Kennedy, W. A. (1956), La Monte, Francesca. (1958), Lantz, A. (1962), Lawler, G. H. (1964), Lawler, G. H., and G. F. M. Smith. (1963), Lawler, G. H., and N. H. F. Watson. (1958), Lindsey, Casimir Charles. (1956), Lower, A. R. M. (1915), MacKay, William C., and D. D. Beatty. (1968a), MacKay, William C., and D. D. Beatty. (1968b), Mavor, J. W. (1915), McAllister, Don E., and Brian W. Coad. (1974), McConnell, J. A., and J. R. Brett. (1946), McKenzie, R. A. (1959), Meek, Seth Eugene, and S. F. Hildebrand. (1910), Melvill, C. D. (1915), Miller, Rudolph J., and H. E. Evans. (1965), Nelson, E. W. (1878), Nelson, Joseph S. (1966), Nelson, Joseph S. (1968), Nichols, John Treadwell, and William K. Gregory. (1918), Phillips, R. J., and Henry Weed Fowler. (1913), Rabb, L., and L. A. McDermott. (1962), Reighard, Jacob E. (1920), Saunders, Richard L. (1961), Saunders, Richard L. (1962), Schmidt, P. J. (1949), Schwartz, T. R., and D. L. Stalling. (1987), Shelford, Victor E. (1937), Smith, M. W. (1935), Smith, M. W. (1937), Smith, M. W. (1938), Smith, M. W. (1939), Stewart, N. H. (1927), Voth, D. R., and O. R. Larson. (1968), Withler, F. C., and J. A. McConnell, V. H. McMahon. (1949), Wynne-Edwards, V. C. (1952),

Catostomus commersonii commersonii.
Dobie, J. R., and O. L. Meehean, G. N. Washburn. (1948), Fowler, Henry Weed. (1945), Hubbs, Carl L. (1941), Hubbs, Carl L., and Karl F. Lagler. (1941), Hubbs, Carl L., and Karl F. Lagler. (1947), Hubbs, Carl L., and Karl F. Lagler. (1974), Raney, Edward C. (1943),

Catostomus commersonni (La Cepède, 1803).
Fowler, Henry Weed. (1918), Krumholz, Louis A. (1956), Richardson, Laurence R. (1944),

Catostomus commersonnii (La Cepède, 1803).
Common Sucker, White Sucker.
Carlander, Kenneth D. (1948), Carlander, Kenneth D., and Lloyd L. Smith, Jr. (1945), Dence, Wilford A. (1940), Dymond, J. R. (1937), Dymond, J. R., and W. B. Scott. (1941), Ellis, Max M., and G. C. Roe. (1917), Evermann, Barton Warren. (1916), Fowler, Henry Weed. (1914b), Fowler, Henry Weed. (1914c), Fowler, Henry Weed. (1916b), Fowler, Henry Weed. (1917), Fowler, Henry Weed. (1921), Fowler, Henry Weed. (1925), Friedrich, George W. (1933), Geen, G. H., and T. G. Northcote, G. F. Hartman, C. C. Lindsey. (1966), Gerking, Shelby D. (1947), Haas, Robert L. (1943), Hankinson, T. L. (1923), Hubbs, Carl L., and Karl F. Lagler. (1974), Hubbs, Carl L., and A. McLaren White. (1923), Jones, David T. (1929), Jordan, David Starr. (1929), Keim, Thomas D. (1915), Koster, William J. (1939), Krumholz, Louis A. (1943), Lindeborg, R. G. (1941), McCabe, Britton C. (1943), Pickens, A. L. (1928), Raney, Edward C. (1943), Raney, Edward C. (1952), Raney, Edward C., and Robert M. Roecker. (1947), Raney, Edward C., and D. A. Webster. (1942), Scott, W. B. (1954), Seaman, E. A. (1950), Shelford, Victor E. (1911a), Snyder, Richard C. (1949), Spoor, W. A. (1935), Spoor, W. A. (1938), Toner, G. C. (1933), Van Duzen, Evelyn M. (1939), Vladykov, Vadim D. (1942), Webster, Dwight A. (1944), Weed, Alfred Cleveland. (1921), Welsh, W. W. (1916), Welter, Wilfred A. (1938),

Catostomus commersonnii commersonnii.
Krumholz, Louis A. (1943), Nelson, Edward M. (1948), Raney, Edward C., and Ernest A. Lachner. (1946a), Snyder, Richard C. (1949),

Catostomus commersonnii suckleyi (Girard, 1857).
Hendricks, Lawrence J. (1952),

Catostomus commersonnii sucklii (Girard, 1857).

Ellis, Max M., and B. B. Jaffa. (1918), Hubbs, Carl L., and Laura C. Hubbs. (1947),
Nelson, Edward M. (1948), Smith, Gerald R. (1966),

Catostomus commersonnii utawana Mather, 1890.
Dwarf white sucker.
Beamish, R. J., and E. J. Crossman. (1977), Dence, Wilford A. (1948), Hubbs, Carl L., and
Karl F. Lagler. (1941), Hubbs, Carl L., and Karl F. Lagler. (1947), Hubbs, Carl L., and
Karl F. Lagler. (1974), Lee, David S., and Carter R. Gilbert, Charles H. Hocutt, Robert E.
Jenkins, Don E. McAllister, Jay R. Stauffer, Jr. (1980), Raney, Edward C., and D. A.
Webster. (1942),

Catostomus communis.
Jordan, David Starr, and Barton Warren Evermann. (1896), Le Sueur, Charles Alexandre.
(1817), Rafinesque, Constantine Samuel. (1820b),

Catostomus conchos Meek, 1902.
Hubbs, Carl L., and Leonard P. Schultz. (1932), Lee, David S., and Carter R. Gilbert,
Charles H. Hocutt, Robert E. Jenkins, Don E. McAllister, Jay R. Stauffer, Jr. (1980), Meek,
Seth Eugene. (1902), Meek, Seth Eugene. (1904), Villar, José Alvarez del. (1970),

Catostomus congestus Baird and Girard, 1855.
Baird, Spencer Fullerton, and Charles Girard. (1855), Jordan, David Starr, and Barton
Warren Evermann. (1896),

Catotomus cristatus Cope, 1883.
Cope, Edward Drinker. (1883), Hay, Oliver Perry. (1902), Hay, Oliver Perry. (1927), Hay,
Oliver Perry. (1929), Hussakof, Louis. (1908), Minckley, W. L., and Dean A. Hendrickson,
Carl E. Bond. (1986), Smith, Gerald R. (1975), Uyeno, Teruya, and Robert Rush Miller.
(1963),

Catostomus cypho Lockington, 1881.
Kirsch, Philip Henry. (1889), Lockington, William Neale. (1881),

Catostomus cyprinus Le Sueur, 1817.
Günther, Albert C. (1868), Jordan, David Starr, and Barton Warren Evermann. (1896), Le
Sueur, Charles Alexandre. (1817), Rafinesque, Constantine Samuel. (1820b), Smith, Philip
W. (1979),

Catostomus discobolus Cope, 1872.
Bluehead Sucker.
Andreasen, J. K., and J. R. Barnes. (1975), Bailey, Reeve M., and John E. Fitch, Earl S.
Herald, Ernest A. Lachner, C. C. Lindsey, C. Richard Robins, W. B. Scott. (1970), Baxter,
George T., and James R. Simon. (1970), Bosley, C. E. (1960), Brienholt, J. C., and R. A.
Heckmann. (1980), Buth, Donald G. (1983), Carlander, Kenneth D. (1969), Carter, John G.,
and Vincent A. Lamarra, Ronald J. Ryel. (1986), Cope, Edward Drinker. (1871), Crabtree,
C. B., and Donald G. Buth. (1987), Dunham, A. E., and Gerald R. Smith, J. N. Taylor.
(1979), Eddy, Samuel. (1957), Eddy, Samuel. (1969), Evans, R. S., and R. A. Heckmann, J.
Palmieri. (1976), Ferris, Stephen D., and Gregory S. Whitt. (1978), Gilbert, Charles Henry,
and N. B. Scofield. (1898), Hubbs, Carl L., and Leonard P. Schultz. (1932), Jordan, David
Starr, and Barton Warren Evermann. (1896), Jordan, David Starr, and Charles Henry
Gilbert. (1883), Lee, David S., and Carter R. Gilbert, Charles H. Hocutt, Robert E. Jenkins,
Don E. McAllister, Jay R. Stauffer, Jr. (1980), Maddux, H. R., and W. G. Kepner. (1988),
McAda, Charles W., and Richard S. Wydoski. (1983), McAda, Charles W., and Richard S.
Wydoski. (1985), McDonald, D. B., and P. A. Dotson. (1960), Nelson, Edward M. (1948),
Palmieri, J., and R. Heckmann. (1976), Robins, C. Richard, and Reeve M. Bailey, Carl E.

Bond, James R. Brooker, Ernest A. Lachner, Robert N. Lea, W. B. Scott. (1980), Simpson, James C., and Richard L. Wallace. (1982), Smith, Gerald R. (1965), Smith, Gerald R. (1966), Smith, Gerald R. (1981a), Snyder, Darrel E., and Robert T. Muth. (1990),

Catostomus discobolus yarrowi (Jordan and Copeland, 1876).
  Zuni Mountain sucker.
  Crabtree, C. B., and Donald G. Buth. (1987), Smith, Gerald R., and J. G. Hall, R. K. Koehn, D. J. Innes. (1983),

Catostomus discobolus **X** *Catostomus platyrhynchus.*
  Smith, Gerald R. (1966),

Catostomus duquesnei Le Sueur, 1817.
  Forbes, Stephen Alfred., and Robert Earl Richardson. (1920), Le Sueur, Charles Alexandre. (1817),

Catostomus duquesni Le Sueur, 1817.
  Pittsburgh Sucker, White Sucker.
  Günther, Albert C. (1868), Jordan, David Starr, and Barton Warren Evermann. (1896), Rafinesque, Constantine Samuel. (1820b),

Catostomus duquesnii Le Sueur, 1817.
  Günther, Albert C. (1868), Jordan, David Starr, and Barton Warren Evermann. (1896), Le Sueur, Charles Alexandre. (1817), Smith, Philip W. (1979),

Catostomus ellipticus Miller and Smith, 1967.
  Smith, Gerald R. (1975),

Catostomus elongatus Le Sueur, 1817.
  Long sucker, Brown sucker.
  Forbes, Stephen Alfred., and Robert Earl Richardson. (1920), Günther, Albert C. (1868), Jordan, David Starr, and Barton Warren Evermann. (1896), Rafinesque, Constantine Samuel. (1820b), Smith, Philip W. (1979),

Catostomus erythrurus Rafinesque, 1818.
  Red-tail sucker, Red-horse, Horse-fish, Horse-sucker.
  Jordan, David Starr, and Barton Warren Evermann. (1896), Rafinesque, Constantine Samuel. (1818b), Rafinesque, Constantine Samuel. (1820b), Smith, Philip W. (1979),

Catostomus fasciatus Le Sueur.
  Forbes, Stephen Alfred., and Robert Earl Richardson. (1920), Günther, Albert C. (1868), Jordan, David Starr, and Barton Warren Evermann. (1896),

Catostomus fasciolaris Rafinesque, 1820.
  Rough-head Sucker, Pike sucker, Striped sucker.
  Günther, Albert C. (1868), Jordan, David Starr, and Barton Warren Evermann. (1896), Rafinesque, Constantine Samuel. (1820b),

Catostomus fecundus Cope and Yarrow, 1875.
  Webug Sucker.
  Bailey, Reeve M., and John E. Fitch, Earl S. Herald, Ernest A. Lachner, C. C. Lindsey, C. Richard Robins, W. B. Scott. (1970), Bailey, Reeve M., and Ernest A. Lachner, C. C. Lindsey, C. Richard Robins, Phil M. Roedel, W. B. Scott, Loren P. Woods. (1966), Cope, Edward Drinker, and H. C. Yarrow. (1875), Eddy, Samuel. (1969), Goode, C. Brown, and Theodore Nicholas Gill. (1903),.Hoffman, Glenn L. (1967), Jordan, David Starr. (1878c),

Jordan, David Starr. (1878d), Jordan, David Starr, and Barton Warren Evermann. (1896), Jordan, David Starr, and Charles Henry Gilbert. (1880), Jordan, David Starr, and Charles Henry Gilbert. (1883), Lee, David S., and Carter R. Gilbert, Charles H. Hocutt, Robert E. Jenkins, Don E. McAllister, Jay R. Stauffer, Jr. (1980), Minckley, W. L., and Dean A. Hendrickson, Carl E. Bond. (1986), Nelson, Edward M. (1948), Robins, C. Richard, and Reeve M. Bailey, Carl E. Bond, James R. Brooker, Ernest A. Lachner, Robert N. Lea, W. B. Scott. (1980), Simon, James R. (1946),

Catostomus flexuosus Rafinesque, 1820.
Kentucky Sucker.
Clay, W. M. (1975), Günther, Albert C. (1868), Jordan, David Starr, and Barton Warren Evermann. (1896), Rafinesque, Constantine Samuel. (1820b),

Catostomus forsterianus Richardson, 1823.
Jordan, David Starr, and Barton Warren Evermann. (1896), Low, A. P. (1896), Richardson, John R. (1823), Richardson, John R. (1836),

Catostomus fumeiventris Miller, 1973.
Owens Sucker.
Crabtree, C. B., and D. G. Buth. (1981), Hubbs, Carl L., and W. I. Follett, Lillian J. Dempster. (1979), Lee, David S., and Carter R. Gilbert, Charles H. Hocutt, Robert E. Jenkins, Don E. McAllister, Jay R. Stauffer, Jr. (1980), Miller, Robert Rush. (1973), Minckley, W. L., and Dean A. Hendrickson, Carl E. Bond. (1986), Moyle, Peter B. (1976), Pister, Edwin P. (1981), Robins, C. Richard, and Reeve M. Bailey, Carl E. Bond, James R. Brooker, Ernest A. Lachner, Robert N. Lea, W. B. Scott. (1980), Soltz, David L., and Robert J. Naiman. (1978),

Catostomus generosus Girard, 1856.
Girard, C. F. (1857), Jordan, David Starr, and Barton Warren Evermann. (1896), Smith, Gerald R. (1966),

Catostomus gibbosus Le Sueur, 1817.
Günther, Albert C. (1868), Le Sueur, Charles Alexandre. (1817), Rafinesque, Constantine Samuel. (1820b),

Catostomus gila Kirsch, 1889.
Gilbert, Charles Henry, and N. B. Scofield. (1898), Goode, C. Brown, and Theodore Nicholas Gill. (1903), Jordan, David Starr, and Barton Warren Evermann. (1896), Kirsch, Philip Henry. (1889),

Catostomus gracilis Kirtland, 1838.
Jordan, David Starr, and Barton Warren Evermann. (1896), Kirtland, Jared Potter. (1838),

Catostomus griseus (Girard, 1856).
Ellis, Max M. (1934), Goode, C. Brown, and Theodore Nicholas Gill. (1903), Günther, Albert C. (1868), Hubbs, Carl L., and Leonard P. Schultz. (1932), Jordan, David Starr, and Barton Warren Evermann. (1896), Jordan, David Starr, and Barton Warren Evermann. (1905), Nelson, Edward M. (1948), Schultz, Leonard P. (1947), Smith, Gerald R. (1966),

Catostomus guzmaniensis Girard, 1856.
Girard, C. F. (1857), Jordan, David Starr, and Barton Warren Evermann. (1896), Smith, Gerald R. (1966),

Catostomus heckelii de Fil.
Cagnolaro, L., and C. Violani. (1988),

Catostomus hudsonius Le Sueur, 1817.
> Günther, Albert C. (1868), Jordan, David Starr. (1878d), Jordan, David Starr, and Barton Warren Evermann. (1896), Le Sueur, Charles Alexandre. (1817), Rafinesque, Constantine Samuel. (1820b), Smith, Philip W. (1979),

Catostomus humboldtianus Snyder, 1908.
> Hoffman, Glenn L. (1967), Snyder, John Otterbein. (1908c),

Catostomus insignis Baird and Girard, 1855.
> **Sonora sucker.**
> Amin, Omar M. (1968), Bailey, Reeve M., and John E. Fitch, Earl S. Herald, Ernest A. Lachner, C. C. Lindsey, C. Richard Robins, W. B. Scott. (1970), Bailey, Reeve M., and Ernest A. Lachner, C. C. Lindsey, C. Richard Robins, Phil M. Roedel, W. B. Scott, Loren P. Woods. (1966), Baird, Spencer Fullerton, and Charles Girard. (1855), Branson, Branley A., and Clarence J. McCoy, Jr., Morgan E. Sisk. (1960), Clarkson, R. W., and W. L. Minckley. (1988), Cope, Edward Drinker, and H. C. Yarrow. (1875), Eddy, Samuel. (1969), Hubbs, Carl L., and Robert Rush Miller. (1951), Hubbs, Carl L., and Robert Rush Miller. (1953), Jakle, M. D., and T. A. Gatz. (1984), Jordan, David Starr. (1878d), Jordan, David Starr, and Barton Warren Evermann. (1896), Jordan, David Starr, and Charles Henry Gilbert. (1883), Koehn, Richard K. (1966), Koster, William J. (1957), Lee, David S., and Carter R. Gilbert, Charles H. Hocutt, Robert E. Jenkins, Don E. McAllister, Jay R. Stauffer, Jr. (1980), Miller, Robert Rush, and H. E. Winn. (1951), Miller, Rudolph J., and H. E. Evans. (1965), Minckley, W. L., and Dean A. Hendrickson, Carl E. Bond. (1986), Mpoame, M., and J. N. Rinne. (1983), Nelson, Edward M. (1948), Nelson, Edward M. (1955), Powers, D. A. (1972), Robins, C. Richard, and Reeve M. Bailey, Carl E. Bond, James R. Brooker, Ernest A. Lachner, Robert N. Lea, W. B. Scott. (1980), Smith, Gerald R. (1966), Villar, José Alvarez del. (1970), Wier, W., and L. F. Mayberry, H. G. Kinzer, P. R. Turner. (1983),

Catostomus insignis **X** *Catostomus clarki*
> Clarkson, R. W., and W. L. Minckley. (1988),

Catostomus labiatus Ayres, 1855.
> Ayres, William O. (1855), Cope, Edward Drinker. (1883), Cope, Edward Drinker. (1889a), Cope, Edward Drinker. (1889b), Günther, Albert C. (1868), Hay, Oliver Perry. (1902), Jordan, David Starr. (1878d), Jordan, David Starr, and Barton Warren Evermann. (1896), Jordan, David Starr, and Charles Henry Gilbert. (1883),

Catostomus lactarius Girard, 1857.
> Girard, C. F. (1857), Hubbs, Carl L., and Leonard P. Schultz. (1932), Jordan, David Starr, and Barton Warren Evermann. (1896),

Catostomus latipinnis Baird and Girard, 1854.
> **Flannelmouth Sucker, Flannel-Mouthed Sucker.**
> Bailey, Reeve M., and John E. Fitch, Earl S. Herald, Ernest A. Lachner, C. C. Lindsey, C. Richard Robins, W. B. Scott. (1970), Bailey, Reeve M., and Ernest A. Lachner, C. C. Lindsey, C. Richard Robins, Phil M. Roedel, W. B. Scott, Loren P. Woods. (1966), Baird, Spencer Fullerton, and Charles Girard. (1854), Baxter, George T., and James R. Simon. (1970), Brienholt, J. C., and R. A. Heckmann. (1980), Buth, Donald G., and R. W. Murphy, L. Ulmer. (1987), Carlander, Kenneth D. (1969), Carter, John G., and Vincent A. Lamarra, Ronald J. Ryel. (1986), Cross, Jeffrey N. (1985), Deacon, J. E., and P. B. Schumann, E. L. Stuenkel. (1987), Dunham, A. E., and Gerald R. Smith, J. N. Taylor. (1979), Eddy, Samuel. (1969), Fuiman, Lee A. (1983), Gilbert, Charles Henry, and N. B. Scofield. (1898), Goode, C. Brown, and Theodore Nicholas Gill. (1903), Greger, P. D., and

J. E. Deacon. (1988), Günther, Albert C. (1868), Herald, Earl S. (1967), Hubbs, Carl L., and W. I. Follett, Lillian J. Dempster. (1979), Hubbs, Carl L., and Robert Rush Miller. (1951), Hubbs, Carl L., and Robert Rush Miller. (1953), Hubbs, Carl L., and Leonard P. Schultz. (1932), Jordan, David Starr, and Barton Warren Evermann. (1896), Jordan, David Starr, and Barton Warren Evermann. (1905), Jordan, David Starr, and Charles Henry Gilbert. (1883), Karp, C. A., and H. M. Tyus. (1990), Koehn, Richard K. (1966), Koster, William J. (1957), Lee, David S., and Carter R. Gilbert, Charles H. Hocutt, Robert E. Jenkins, Don E. McAllister, Jay R. Stauffer, Jr. (1980), Malek, M., and G. McCallister. (1984), Miller, Robert Rush. (1963), Minckley, W. L., and Dean A. Hendrickson, Carl E. Bond. (1986), Robins, C. Richard, and Reeve M. Bailey, Carl E. Bond, James R. Brooker, Ernest A. Lachner, Robert N. Lea, W. B. Scott. (1980), Smith, Gerald R. (1966), Snyder, Darrel E., and Robert T. Muth. (1990), Uyeno, Teruya, and Robert Rush Miller. (1963), Walden, Howard T., 2d. (1964),

Catostomus latipinnis discobulus.
Hubbs, Carl L., and Laura C. Hubbs. (1947), Simon, James R. (1946), Smith, Gerald R. (1966),

Catostomus latipinnis X Xyrauchen texanus
Buth, Donald G., and R. W. Murphy, L. Ulmer. (1987),

Catostomus leopoldi Siebert and Minckley, 1986.
Siebert, Darrell J., and W. L. Minckley. (1986),

Catostomus lesueurii Richardson, 1823.
Jordan, David Starr, and Barton Warren Evermann. (1896), Richardson, John R. (1823),

Catostomus longirostris Le Sueur, 1817.
Jordan, David Starr, and Barton Warren Evermann. (1896), Jordan, David Starr, and Charles Henry Gilbert. (1883), Low, A. P. (1896), Smith, Philip W. (1979),

Catostomus longirostrum Le Sueur, 1817.
Jordan, David Starr, and Barton Warren Evermann. (1896), Le Sueur, Charles Alexandre. (1817), Obruchev, D. V. (ed.) (1967), Rafinesque, Constantine Samuel. (1820b),

Catostomus luxatus (Cope, 1879).
Lost River Sucker.
Andreasen, J. K. (1976), Bailey, Reeve M., and John E. Fitch, Earl S. Herald, Ernest A. Lachner, C. C. Lindsey, C. Richard Robins, W. B. Scott. (1970), Bailey, Reeve M., and Ernest A. Lachner, C. C. Lindsey, C. Richard Robins, Phil M. Roedel, W. B. Scott, Loren P. Woods. (1966), Eddy, Samuel. (1969), Ferris, Stephen D., and Gregory S. Whitt. (1978), Grinham, T., and D. K. Cone. (1990), Hubbs, Carl L., and W. I. Follett, Lillian J. Dempster. (1979), Lee, David S., and Carter R. Gilbert, Charles H. Hocutt, Robert E. Jenkins, Don E. McAllister, Jay R. Stauffer, Jr. (1980), Minckley, W. L., and Dean A. Hendrickson, Carl E. Bond. (1986), Moyle, Peter B. (1976), Robins, C. Richard, and Reeve M. Bailey, Carl E. Bond, James R. Brooker, Ernest A. Lachner, Robert N. Lea, W. B. Scott. (1980), Wyatt, E. J. (1979),

Catostomus macrocheilus Girard, 1857.
Largescale sucker, Columbia River Sucker.
Arai, Hisao P., and Dwight R. Mudry. (1983), Bailey, Reeve M., and John E. Fitch, Earl S. Herald, Ernest A. Lachner, C. C. Lindsey, C. Richard Robins, W. B. Scott. (1970), Bailey, Reeve M., and Ernest A. Lachner, C. C. Lindsey, C. Richard Robins, Phil M. Roedel, W. B. Scott, Loren P. Woods. (1966), Bangham, Ralph V., and James R. Adams. (1954), Beverly-Burton, Mary. (1984), Black, Edgar C. (1955), Brett, J. R., and A. L. Pritchard.

(1946a), Brett, J. R., and A. L. Pritchard. (1946b), Brown, C. J. D. (1971), Carl, G. Clifford. (1936), Carl, G. Clifford, and Wilbert Amie Clemens, Casimir Charles Lindsey. (1977), Carlander, Kenneth D. (1969), Clemens, W. A. (1939), Clemens, W. A., and D. S. Rawson, J. L. McHugh. (1939), Dauble, Dennis D. (1986), Dauble, Dennis D., and R. L. Buschbom. (1981), DeKay, James Ellsworth. (1842), Dunham, A. E., and Gerald R. Smith, J. N. Taylor. (1979), Dymond, J. R. (1936), Eddy, Samuel. (1957), Eddy, Samuel. (1969), Evermann, Barton Warren. (1893a), Ferris, Stephen D., and Gregory S. Whitt. (1978), Fickeisen, D. H., and J. C. Montgomery. (1978), Fujihara, M. P. and F. P. Hungate. (1971), Fujihara, M. P. and F. P. Hungate. (1972), Gadd, Ben. (1986), Girard, C. F. (1857), Godfrey, H. (1955), Goode, C. Brown, and Theodore Nicholas Gill. (1903), Günther, Albert C. (1868),.Hoffman, Glenn L. (1967), Johnson, A., and D. Norton, B. Yake. (1988), Jordan, David Starr. (1878d), Jordan, David Starr, and Barton Warren Evermann. (1896), Jordan, David Starr, and Barton Warren Evermann. (1905), Jordan, David Starr, and Charles Henry Gilbert. (1883), Krygier, B. B., and R. W. Macy. (1969), La Bolle, L. D., Jr., and H. W. Li, and B. C. Mundy. (1985), La Rivers, Ira. (1962), Lee, David S., and Carter R. Gilbert, Charles H. Hocutt, Robert E. Jenkins, Don E. McAllister, Jay R. Stauffer, Jr. (1980), Lindsey, Casimir Charles. (1956), Lindsey, Casimir Charles. (1957), Macphee, Craig. (1960), Mayr, Ernst. (1966), Mayr, Ernst. (1971), McCart, P., and N. Aspinwall. (1970), McKeown, B. A., and G. H. Geen, T. A. Watson, J. F. Powell, D. B. Parker. (1985), McPhail, J. D., and C. C. Lindsey. (1970), Miller, R. G. (1951), Miller, Robert Rush, and Ralph G. Miller. (1948), Miller, Rudolph J., and H. E. Evans. (1965), Minckley, W. L., and Dean A. Hendrickson, Carl E. Bond. (1986), Munro, J. A., and W. A. Clemens. (1937), Nelson, Edward M. (1948), Nelson, Edward M. (1955), Nelson, Joseph S. (1966), Nelson, Joseph S. (1968), Nelson, Joseph S. (1974), Nelson, Joseph S. (1977), Northcote, T. G., and G. F. Hartman. (1959), Nursall, J. R. (1963), Paetz, Martin J., and Joseph S. Nelson. (1970), Patten, Benjamin G. (1960), Peters, J. C. (ed.) (1964), Rehnberg, B. G., and C. B. Schreck. (1987), Reinking, L. N. (1983), Robins, C. Richard, and Reeve M. Bailey, Carl E. Bond, James R. Brooker, Ernest A. Lachner, Robert N. Lea, W. B. Scott. (1980), Rogers, I. H., and H. W. Mahood. (1982), Schell, S. C. (1973), Schoenthal, N. D. (1964), Schoffman, R. J. (1943), Schultz, Leonard P. (1936), Scott, W. B. (1958), Scott, W. B., and E. J. Crossman. (1969), Scott, W. B., and E. J. Crossman. (1973), Simpson, James C., and Richard L. Wallace. (1982), Smith, Gerald R. (1966), Smith, Gerald R. (1981a), Uglem, G. L. (1972), Uglem, G. L., and S. M. Beck. (1972), Walden, Howard T., 2d. (1964), Weisel, George F. (1960), Weisel, George F. (1967a), Weisel, George F. (1967b), Whitehouse, Francis C. (1946), Williams, D. D. (1978a), Wooding, Frederick H. (1959), Wydoski, Richard S., and Richard R. Whitney. (1979),

Catostomus macrolepidotus Le Sueur, 1817.
Jordan, David Starr, and Barton Warren Evermann. (1896), Le Sueur, Charles Alexandre. (1817), Rafinesque, Constantine Samuel. (1820b), Smith, Philip W. (1979),

Catostomus maculosus Le Sueur, 1817.
Günther, Albert C. (1868), Jordan, David Starr, and Barton Warren Evermann. (1896), Le Sueur, Charles Alexandre. (1817), Rafinesque, Constantine Samuel. (1820b),

Catostomus megastomus Rafinesque, 1820.
Big-mouth sucker.
Günther, Albert C. (1868), Jordan, David Starr, and Barton Warren Evermann. (1896), Rafinesque, Constantine Samuel. (1820b),

Catostomus melanops Rafinesque, 1820.
Forbes, Stephen Alfred., and Robert Earl Richardson. (1920), Jordan, David Starr. (1878b), Jordan, David Starr, and Barton Warren Evermann. (1896), Rafinesque, Constantine Samuel. (1820b), Smith, Philip W. (1979),

Catostomus melanotus.
> **Black-back Sucker, Black Sucker, Blue Sucker.**
> Rafinesque, Constantine Samuel. (1820b),

Catostomus microps Rutter, 1908.
> **Modoc Sucker.**
> Bailey, Reeve M., and John E. Fitch, Earl S. Herald, Ernest A. Lachner, C. C. Lindsey, C. Richard Robins, W. B. Scott. (1970), Bailey, Reeve M., and Ernest A. Lachner, C. C. Lindsey, C. Richard Robins, Phil M. Roedel, W. B. Scott, Loren P. Woods. (1966), Cooper, J. J. (1983), Eddy, Samuel. (1969), Hubbs, Carl L., and W. I. Follett, Lillian J. Dempster. (1979), Hubbs, Carl L., and Robert Rush Miller. (1951), Lee, David S., and Carter R. Gilbert, Charles H. Hocutt, Robert E. Jenkins, Don E. McAllister, Jay R. Stauffer, Jr. (1980), Martin, M. (1972), Minckley, W. L., and Dean A. Hendrickson, Carl E. Bond. (1986), Moyle, Peter B. (1976), Moyle, Peter B., and A. Marciochi. (1975), Nelson, Edward M. (1948), Nelson, Edward M. (1955), Ono, R. Dana, and James D. Williams, Anne Wagner. (1983), Robins, C. Richard, and Reeve M. Bailey, Carl E. Bond, James R. Brooker, Ernest A. Lachner, Robert N. Lea, W. B. Scott. (1980), Rutter, Cloudsley M. (1908), Schultz, Leonard P. (1936), Smith, Gerald R. (1966),

Catostomus mniotiltus Snyder.
> Hubbs, Clark. (1947), Nelson, Edward M. (1948), Snyder, John Otterbein. (1913),

Catostomus nanomyzon Mather, 1886.
> Jordan, David Starr, and Barton Warren Evermann. (1896), Mather, Frederic. (1886),

Catostomus nebulifer Garman, 1881.
> Jordan, David Starr, and Barton Warren Evermann. (1896), Jordan, David Starr, and Charles Henry Gilbert. (1883),

Catostomus nebuliferus Garman, 1881.
> Garman, Samuel. (1881), Jordan, David Starr. (1923), Smith, Gerald R. (1966),

Catostomus niger Rafinesque, 1820.
> **Black Buffalo-fish.**
> Rafinesque, Constantine Samuel. (1820b),

Catostomus nigricans Le Sueur, 1817.
> **Hogsucker, Hogmolly, Stone-Roller, Stone toter, hog molly, mullet, Stone Lugger, Hammer Head, Crawl-a-Bottom, Toter.**
> Breder, C. M., Jr. (1920), Forbes, Stephen Alfred., and Robert Earl Richardson. (1920), Fowler, Henry Weed. (1918), Goode, C. Brown, and Theodore Nicholas Gill. (1903), Günther, Albert C. (1868), Hubbs, Carl L. (1945), Jordan, David Starr. (1878d), Jordan, David Starr, and Barton Warren Evermann. (1896), Jordan, David Starr, and Charles Henry Gilbert. (1883), Larimore, R. W., and P. W. Smith. (1963), Meek, Seth Eugene. (1894), Meek, Seth Eugene, and S. F. Hildebrand. (1910), Pickens, A. L. (1928), Rafinesque, Constantine Samuel. (1820b), Shelford, Victor E. (1911a), Shelford, Victor E. (1937), Smith, Philip W. (1979),

Catostomus nigricans etowanus Jordan, 1877.
> Jordan, David Starr. (1877c), Jordan, David Starr, and Barton Warren Evermann. (1896),

Catostomus oblongus Mitchill.
> Rafinesque, Constantine Samuel. (1820b),

Catostomus occidentalis Ayres, 1854.
   Sacramento Sucker.
   Agassiz, John Louis Rodolphe. (1855), Anonymous. (1965a), Bailey, Reeve M., and John
   E. Fitch, Earl S. Herald, Ernest A. Lachner, C. C. Lindsey, C. Richard Robins, W. B.
   Scott. (1970), Bailey, Reeve M., and Ernest A. Lachner, C. C. Lindsey, C. Richard Robins,
   Phil M. Roedel, W. B. Scott, Loren P. Woods. (1966), Baltz, Donald M., and Peter B.
   Moyle. (1984), Baltz, D. M., and B. Vondracek, L. R. Brown, P. B. Moyle. (1987), Brittan,
   Martin R., and John D. Hopkirk, Jerrold D. Conners, Michael Martin. (1970), Burns, J. W.
   (1966), Carlander, Kenneth D. (1969), Casteel, Richard W., and Michael J. Rymer. (1981),
   Casteel, Richard W., and J. H. Williams, C. K. Throckmorton, et al. (1979), Cooper, J. J.
   (1983), Dempster, R. P., and P. Morales, F. X. Glennon. (1988), Eastman, Joseph T.
   (1980), Eddy, Samuel. (1957), Eddy, Samuel. (1969), Ferris, Stephen D., and Gregory S.
   Whitt. (1978), Goode, C. Brown, and Theodore Nicholas Gill. (1903), Günther, Albert C.
   (1868), Hoffman, Glenn L. (1967), Hopkirk, J. D. (1973), Hubbs, Carl L., and W. I. Follett,
   Lillian J. Dempster. (1979), Hubbs, Carl L., and Robert Rush Miller. (1951), Jordan, David
   Starr. (1878d), Jordan, David Starr, and Barton Warren Evermann. (1896), Jordan, David
   Starr, and Barton Warren Evermann. (1905), Jordan, David Starr, and Charles Henry
   Gilbert. (1883), Lee, David S., and Carter R. Gilbert, Charles H. Hocutt, Robert E. Jenkins,
   Don E. McAllister, Jay R. Stauffer, Jr. (1980), Li, H. W. (1973), Miller, Rudolph J., and H.
   E. Evans. (1965), Minckley, W. L., and Dean A. Hendrickson, Carl E. Bond. (1986),
   Moyle, Peter B. (1976), Moyle, Peter B., and Donald M. Baltz. (1985), Moyle, Peter B.,
   and Robert A. Daniels, Bruce Herbold, Donald M. Baltz. (1986), Moyle, Peter B., and
   Bruce Vondracek. (1983), Nelson, Edward M. (1948), Nelson, Edward M. (1955), Robins,
   C. Richard, and Reeve M. Bailey, Carl E. Bond, James R. Brooker, Ernest A. Lachner,
   Robert N. Lea, W. B. Scott. (1980), Schultz, Leonard P. (1952), Smith, Gerald R. (1966),
   Villa, Nick A. (1985), Walden, Howard T., 2d. (1964), Weisel, George F., and Eldon L.
   McLaury. (1964),

Catostomus occidentalis humboldtianum Snyder, 1908.
   Minckley, W. L., and Dean A. Hendrickson, Carl E. Bond. (1986),

Catostomus occidentalis humboldtianus Snyder, 1908.
   Hubbs, Carl L., and W. I. Follett, Lillian J. Dempster. (1979), Lee, David S., and Carter R.
   Gilbert, Charles H. Hocutt, Robert E. Jenkins, Don E. McAllister, Jay R. Stauffer, Jr.
   (1980), Minckley, W. L., and Dean A. Hendrickson, Carl E. Bond. (1986),

Catostomus occidentalis lacus-anserinus Fowler.
   Fowler, Henry Weed. (1914a), Schultz, Leonard P. (1936),

Catostomus occidentalis lacusanserinus Fowler.
   Lee, David S., and Carter R. Gilbert, Charles H. Hocutt, Robert E. Jenkins, Don E.
   McAllister, Jay R. Stauffer, Jr. (1980), Minckley, W. L., and Dean A. Hendrickson, Carl E.
   Bond. (1986),

Catostomus occidentalis mniotiltus Snyder, 1913.
   Lee, David S., and Carter R. Gilbert, Charles H. Hocutt, Robert E. Jenkins, Don E.
   McAllister, Jay R. Stauffer, Jr. (1980), Minckley, W. L., and Dean A. Hendrickson, Carl E.
   Bond. (1986),

Catostomus occidentalis occidentalis Ayres, 1854.
   Hubbs, Carl L., and W. I. Follett, Lillian J. Dempster. (1979), Lee, David S., and Carter R.
   Gilbert, Charles H. Hocutt, Robert E. Jenkins, Don E. McAllister, Jay R. Stauffer, Jr.
   (1980), Minckley, W. L., and Dean A. Hendrickson, Carl E. Bond. (1986),

Catostomus oneida De Kay, 1842.
   DeKay, James Ellsworth. (1842), Jordan, David Starr, and Barton Warren Evermann. (1896),

Catostomus oreganus Gilbert.
   Hubbs, Carl L., and Robert Rush Miller. (1951),

Catostomus owyhee.
   Minckley, W. L., and Dean A. Hendrickson, Carl E. Bond. (1986), Smith, Gerald R. (1975),

Catostomus pallidus De Kay, 1842.
   DeKay, James Ellsworth. (1842), Jordan, David Starr, and Barton Warren Evermann. (1896),

Catostomus planiceps Cuvier and Valenciennes, 1844.
   Cuvier, Georges, and Achille Valenciennes. (1844), Günther, Albert C. (1868), Jordan, David Starr, and Barton Warren Evermann. (1896),

Catostomus platyrhynchus (Cope, 1874).
   Mountain sucker, Northern Mountain sucker.
   Bailey, Reeve M., and John E. Fitch, Earl S. Herald, Ernest A. Lachner, C. C. Lindsey, C. Richard Robins, W. B. Scott. (1970), Baugh, T. (1979), Baxter, George T., and James R. Simon. (1970), Brown, C. J. D. (1971), Carl, G. Clifford, and Wilbert Amie Clemens, Casimir Charles Lindsey. (1977), Carlander, Kenneth D. (1969), Decker, L. M. (1989), Dunham, A. E., and Gerald R. Smith, J. N. Taylor. (1979), Eddy, Samuel. (1957), Eddy, Samuel. (1969), Erman, D. C. (1972), Evans, R. S., and R. A. Heckmann, J. Palmieri. (1976), Ferris, Stephen D., and Gregory S. Whitt. (1978), Gadd, Ben. (1986), Hauser, W. J. (1969), Henderson, N. E., and R. E. Peter. (1969), Heuser, W. J. (1975), Hubbs, Carl L., and W. I. Follett, Lillian J. Dempster. (1979), La Rivers, Ira. (1962), Lee, David S., and Carter R. Gilbert, Charles H. Hocutt, Robert E. Jenkins, Don E. McAllister, Jay R. Stauffer, Jr. (1980), McClane, Albert Jules. (1974), McPhail, J. D., and C. C. Lindsey. (1970), Moyle, Peter B. (1976), Paetz, Martin J., and Joseph S. Nelson. (1970), Palmieri, J., and R. Heckmann. (1976), Robins, C. Richard, and Reeve M. Bailey, Carl E. Bond, James R. Brooker, Ernest A. Lachner, Robert N. Lea, W. B. Scott. (1980), Scoppettone, G. Gary, and Mark Coleman, Gary A. Wedemeyer. (1986), Scott, W. B., and E. J. Crossman. (1969), Scott, W. B., and E. J. Crossman. (1973), Simpson, James C., and Richard L. Wallace. (1982), Smith, Gerald R. (1965), Smith, Gerald R. (1966), Snyder, Darrel E. (1983), Snyder, Darrel E., and Robert T. Muth. (1990), Willock, T. A. (1969), Wydoski, Richard S., and Richard R. Whitney. (1979),

Catostomus platyrhynchus X *Catostomus tahoensis.*
   Smith, Gerald R. (1966),

Catostomus plebeius Baird and Girard, 1855.
   Rio Grande Sucker.
   Crabtree, C. B., and Donald G. Buth. (1987), Günther, Albert C. (1868), Jordan, David Starr, and Barton Warren Evermann. (1896), Lee, David S., and Carter R. Gilbert, Charles H. Hocutt, Robert E. Jenkins, Don E. McAllister, Jay R. Stauffer, Jr. (1980), Robins, C. Richard, and Reeve M. Bailey, Carl E. Bond, James R. Brooker, Ernest A. Lachner, Robert N. Lea, W. B. Scott. (1980), Rinne, J. N. (1988), Smith, Gerald R. (1965), Smith, Gerald R. (1966), Smith, Gerald R. (1981a), Villar, José Alvarez del. (1970),

Catostomus plebejus Baird and Girard, 1855.
   Rio Grande Sucker.

164

Günther, Albert C. (1868), Jordan, David Starr, and H. E. Copeland. (1876), Smith, Gerald R. (1966), 1740,

Catostomus plebius Baird and Girard, 1855.
   Rio Grande Sucker.
   Bailey, Reeve M., and John E. Fitch, Earl S. Herald, Ernest A. Lachner, C. C. Lindsey, C. Richard Robins, W. B. Scott. (1970), Butler, J. L. (1960), Eddy, Samuel. (1969), Ferris, Stephen D., and Donald G. Buth, Gregory S. Whitt. (1982), Ferris, Stephen D., and Gregory S. Whitt. (1978), Rinne, J. N. (1985a), Zuckerman, L. D., and E. P. Bergersen. (1986),

Catostomus pocatello Gilbert and Evermann, 1894.
   Gilbert, Charles Henry, and Barton Evermann. (1894), Hubbs, Carl L., and Leonard P. Schultz. (1932), Jordan, David Starr, and Barton Warren Evermann. (1896), Jordan, David Starr, and Barton Warren Evermann. (1905),

Catostomus reddingi Cope.
   Cope, Edward Drinker. (1883), Hay, Oliver Perry. (1929), Hussakof, Louis. (1908), Uyeno, Teruya, and Robert Rush Miller. (1963),

Catostomus reticulatus Richardson, 1836.
   Jordan, David Starr, and Barton Warren Evermann. (1896), Richardson, John R. (1836),

Catostomus retropinnis Jordan, 1878.
   Hubbs, Carl L., and Leonard P. Schultz. (1932), Jordan, David Starr. (1878d), Jordan, David Starr, and Barton Warren Evermann. (1896),

Catostomus rex Rosa Smith Eigenmann, 1891.
   Eigenmann, Rosa Smith. (1891), Goode, C. Brown, and Theodore Nicholas Gill. (1903), Hubbs, Carl L., and Leonard P. Schultz. (1932), Jordan, David Starr, and Barton Warren Evermann. (1896),

Catostomus rhothœcus ThoburnIN: Jordan and Evermann, 1896. Fowler, Henry Weed. (1922), Jordan, David Starr. (1917), Jordan, David Starr, and Barton Warren Evermann. (1896),

Catostomus richardsonius Harper and Nichols, 1919.
   Harper, F., and J. T. Nichols. (1919),

Catostomus rimiculus Gilbert and Snyder **IN:** Gilbert, 1898.
   Klamath Smallscale sucker.
   Bailey, Reeve M., and John E. Fitch, Earl S. Herald, Ernest A. Lachner, C. C. Lindsey, C. Richard Robins, W. B. Scott. (1970), Bailey, Reeve M., and Ernest A. Lachner, C. C. Lindsey, C. Richard Robins, Phil M. Roedel, W. B. Scott, Loren P. Woods. (1966), Eddy, Samuel. (1969), Gilbert, Charles Henry (1898),.Hoffman, Glenn L. (1967), Hubbs, Carl L., and W. I. Follett, Lillian J. Dempster. (1979), Hubbs, Carl L., and Robert Rush Miller. (1951), Hubbs, Carl L., and Leonard P. Schultz. (1932), Lee, David S., and Carter R. Gilbert, Charles H. Hocutt, Robert E. Jenkins, Don E. McAllister, Jay R. Stauffer, Jr. (1980), Minckley, W. L., and Dean A. Hendrickson, Carl E. Bond. (1986), Moyle, Peter B. (1976), Nelson, Edward M. (1955), Robins, C. Richard, and Reeve M. Bailey, Carl E. Bond, James R. Brooker, Ernest A. Lachner, Robert N. Lea, W. B. Scott. (1980), Schultz, Leonard P. (1936), Smith, Gerald R. (1966),

Catostomus rostratus (Tilesius, 1813).
   Jordan, David Starr, and Barton Warren Evermann. (1905), Schultz, Leonard P. (1947),

Catostomus santaanae (Snyder, 1908).
   Santa Ana Sucker.
   Bailey, Reeve M., and John E. Fitch, Earl S. Herald, Ernest A. Lachner, C. C. Lindsey, C. Richard Robins, W. B. Scott. (1970), Buth, Donald G. (1983), Buth, Donald G., and C. B. Crabtree. (1982), Crabtree, C. B., and D. G. Buth. (1981), Eddy, Samuel. (1969), Greenfield, David Wayne, and Stephen T. Ross, Gary D. Deckert. (1970), Hubbs, Carl L., and W. I. Follett, Lillian J. Dempster. (1979), Lee, David S., and Carter R. Gilbert, Charles H. Hocutt, Robert E. Jenkins, Don E. McAllister, Jay R. Stauffer, Jr. (1980), Miller, Robert Rush. (1968), Moyle, Peter B. (1976), Robins, C. Richard, and Reeve M. Bailey, Carl E. Bond, James R. Brooker, Ernest A. Lachner, Robert N. Lea, W. B. Scott. (1980), Smith, Gerald R. (1965), Smith, Gerald R. (1966),

Catostomus setosns Le Sueur.
   Rafinesque, Constantine Samuel. (1820b),

Catostomus setosus Le Sueur.
   Rafinesque, Constantine Samuel. (1820b),

Catostomus shoshonensis Cope, 1883.
   Cope, Edward Drinker. (1883), Hay, Oliver Perry. (1902), Hay, Oliver Perry. (1927), Hay, Oliver Perry. (1929), Minckley, W. L., and Dean A. Hendrickson, Carl E. Bond. (1986), Smith, Gerald R. (1975), Uyeno, Teruya, and Robert Rush Miller. (1963),

Catostomus snyderi Gilbert, 1898.
   Klamath Largescale sucker.
   Andreasen, J. K. (1976), Bailey, Reeve M., and Ernest A. Lachner, C. C. Lindsey, C. Richard Robins, Phil M. Roedel, W. B. Scott, Loren P. Woods. (1966), Eddy, Samuel. (1969), Evermann, Barton Warren, and Seth Eugene Meek. (1898), Hoffman, Glenn L. (1967), Hubbs, Carl L., and W. I. Follett, Lillian J. Dempster. (1979), Hubbs, Carl L., and Robert Rush Miller. (1951), Hubbs, Carl L., and Leonard P. Schultz. (1932), Lee, David S., and Carter R. Gilbert, Charles H. Hocutt, Robert E. Jenkins, Don E. McAllister, Jay R. Stauffer, Jr. (1980), Minckley, W. L., and Dean A. Hendrickson, Carl E. Bond. (1986), Moyle, Peter B. (1976), Robins, C. Richard, and Reeve M. Bailey, Carl E. Bond, James R. Brooker, Ernest A. Lachner, Robert N. Lea, W. B. Scott. (1980), Schultz, Leonard P. (1936),

Catostomus sonorensis Meek, 1902.
   Hubbs, Carl L., and Robert Rush Miller. (1951), Meek, Seth Eugene. (1902), Meek, Seth Eugene. (1904),

Catostomus sucetta Le Sueur.
   Rafinesque, Constantine Samuel. (1820b),

Catostomus sucklii Girard, 1857.
   Girard, C. F. (1857), Jordan, David Starr, and Barton Warren Evermann. (1896),

Catostomus syncheilus Hubbs and Schultz, 1932.
   Hubbs, Carl L., and Robert Rush Miller. (1951), Hubbs, Carl L., and Leonard P. Schultz. (1932), Mayr, Ernst. (1966), Mayr, Ernst. (1971), Miller, Robert Rush, and Ralph G. Miller. (1948), Nelson, Edward M. (1948), Nelson, Edward M. (1955), Schultz, Leonard P. (1936), Smith, Gerald R. (1966),

Catostomus syncheilus palouseanus Schultz and Thompson, 1936.
   Schultz, Leonard P., and R. J. Thompson. (1936), Smith, Gerald R. (1966),

166

Catostomus syncheilus syncheilus Hubbs and Schultz, 1932. Schultz, Leonard P., and R. J. Thompson. (1936), Smith, Gerald R. (1966),

Catostomus tahoensis Gill and Jordan **IN:** Jordan, 1878.
Tahoe Sucker.
Bailey, Reeve M., and John E. Fitch, Earl S. Herald, Ernest A. Lachner, C. C. Lindsey, C. Richard Robins, W. B. Scott. (1970), Bailey, Reeve M., and Ernest A. Lachner, C. C. Lindsey, C. Richard Robins, Phil M. Roedel, W. B. Scott, Loren P. Woods. (1966), Carlander, Kenneth D. (1969), Cope, Edward Drinker. (1883), Decker, L. M. (1989), Dunham, A. E., and Gerald R. Smith, J. N. Taylor. (1979), Eddy, Samuel. (1957), Eddy, Samuel. (1969), Erman, D. C. (1972), Estep, Marilyn L. F., and Steven Vigg. (1985), Follett, W. I. (1967), Goode, C. Brown, and Theodore Nicholas Gill. (1903),.Hoffman, Glenn L. (1967), Hubbs, Carl L., and W. I. Follett, Lillian J. Dempster. (1979), Hubbs, Carl L., and Robert Rush Miller. (1951), Hubbs, Carl L., and Leonard P. Schultz. (1932), Jordan, David Starr. (1878c), Jordan, David Starr, and Barton Warren Evermann. (1896), Jordan, David Starr, and Charles Henry Gilbert. (1883), Jordan, David Starr, and Henry W. Henshaw. (1878), Kennedy, J. L., and P. A. Kucera. (1978), Kucera, P. A., and J. L. Kennedy. (1977), La Rivers, Ira. (1962), Lee, David S., and Carter R. Gilbert, Charles H. Hocutt, Robert E. Jenkins, Don E. McAllister, Jay R. Stauffer, Jr. (1980), Marrin, Donn L. (1983), Marrin, Donn L., and Don C. Erman, Bruce Von Dracek. (1984),Minckley, W. L., and Dean A. Hendrickson, Carl E. Bond. (1986), Moyle, Peter B. (1976), Nelson, Edward M. (1948), Robins, C. Richard, and Reeve M. Bailey, Carl E. Bond, James R. Brooker, Ernest A. Lachner, Robert N. Lea, W. B. Scott. (1980), Rutter, Cloudsley M. (1904), Scoppettone, G. Gary, and Mark Coleman, Gary A. Wedemeyer. (1986), Smith, Gerald R. (1966), Smith, Gerald R. (1981a), Smith, Gerald R. (1985), Snyder, D. E. (1983), Snyder, John Otterbein. (1917), Taylor, Dwight W., and Gerald R. Smith. (1981), Vigg, S. (1978), Vigg, S. (1980), Vondracek, B. C. (1982), Vondracek, B. C., and L. R. Brown, J. J. Cech, Jr. (1982), Vondracek, B. C., and J. J. Cech, Jr. (1980), Vondracek, B. C., and J. J. Cech, Jr., R. K. Buddington. (1989), Vondracek, B. C., and J. J. Cech, Jr., D. Longanecker. (1982),

Catostomus teres (Mitchill, 1815).
Common sucker, White sucker.
Clay, W. M. (1975), Forbes, Stephen Alfred., and Robert Earl Richardson. (1920), Gilbert, Charles Henry. (1885), Goode, G. Brown, and Tarleton H. Bean. (1879), Günther, Albert C. (1868),.Hoffman, Glenn L. (1967), Jordan, David Starr. (1878d), Jordan, David Starr, and Barton Warren Evermann. (1896), Meek, Seth Eugene. (1894), Mitchill, Samuel Latham. (1815), Rafinesque, Constantine Samuel. (1820b), Smith, Philip W. (1979), Storer, David Humphreys. (1867),

Catostomus texanus Abbott, 1861.
Abbott, Charles Conrad. (1861), Günther, Albert C. (1868), Jordan, David Starr, and Barton Warren Evermann. (1896), Minckley, W. L., and Dean A. Hendrickson, Carl E. Bond. (1986),

Catostomus tsiltcoosensis Evermann and Meek, 1898.
Evermann, Barton Warren, and Seth Eugene Meek. (1898), Minckley, W. L., and Dean A. Hendrickson, Carl E. Bond. (1986),

Catostomus tuberculatus Le Sueur, 1817.
Günther, Albert C. (1868), Le Sueur, Charles Alexandre. (1817), Nelson, E. W. (1878), Smith, Philip W. (1979),

Catostomus tuberculesus Le Sueur.
Rafinesque, Constantine Samuel. (1820b),

167

Catostomus utawana Mather, 1884.
>Jordan, David Starr, and Barton Warren Evermann. (1896),

Catostomus velifer Rafinesque, 1820.
>**Sailing Sucker.**
>Forbes, Stephen Alfred., and Robert Earl Richardson. (1920), Jordan, David Starr, and Barton Warren Evermann. (1896), Rafinesque, Constantine Samuel. (1820b), Smith, Philip W. (1979),

Catostomus vittatus Le Sueur, 1817.
>Günther, Albert C. (1868), Le Sueur, Charles Alexandre. (1817), Rafinesque, Constantine Samuel. (1820b),

Catostomus warnerensis Snyder, 1908.
>**Warner Sucker.**
>Bailey, Reeve M., and John E. Fitch, Earl S. Herald, Ernest A. Lachner, C. C. Lindsey, C. Richard Robins, W. B. Scott. (1970), Bailey, Reeve M., and Ernest A. Lachner, C. C. Lindsey, C. Richard Robins, Phil M. Roedel, W. B. Scott, Loren P. Woods. (1966), Eddy, Samuel. (1969), Hubbs, Carl L., and Leonard P. Schultz. (1932), Lee, David S., and Carter R. Gilbert, Charles H. Hocutt, Robert E. Jenkins, Don E. McAllister, Jay R. Stauffer, Jr. (1980), Minckley, W. L., and Dean A. Hendrickson, Carl E. Bond. (1986), Nelson, Edward M. (1948), Ono, R. Dana, and James D. Williams, Anne Wagner. (1983), Robins, C. Richard, and Reeve M. Bailey, Carl E. Bond, James R. Brooker, Ernest A. Lachner, Robert N. Lea, W. B. Scott. (1980), Schultz, Leonard P. (1936), Smith, Gerald R. (1966), Snyder, John Otterbein. (1908b), Snyder, John Otterbein. (1917),

Catostomus wigginsi Herre and Brock, 1936.
>Branson, Branley A., and Clarence J. McCoy, Jr., Morgan E. Sisk. (1960), Herre, A. W. C. T. (1936), Hubbs, Carl L., and Robert Rush Miller. (1951), Minckley, W. L., and Dean A. Hendrickson, Carl E. Bond. (1986), Villar, José Alvarez del. (1970),

Catostomus xanthopus Rafinesque, 1820.
>**Mud Sucker.**
>Günther, Albert C. (1868), Jordan, David Starr, and Barton Warren Evermann. (1896), Rafinesque, Constantine Samuel. (1820b),

Chasmistes Jordan, 1878.
>Arldt, Th. (1923), Behnke, Robert J. (1981), Cavender, Ted M. (1986), Cope, Edward Drinker. (1883), Eschmeyer, William N. (1990), Hay, Oliver Perry. (1927), Hay, Oliver Perry. (1929), Jordan, David Starr. (1878c), Jordan, David Starr. (1878d), Jordan, David Starr. (1907b), Jordan, David Starr. (1919), Jordan, David Starr. (1923), Jordan, David Starr, and Barton Warren Evermann. (1896), Jordan, David Starr, and Charles Henry Gilbert. (1883), Koehn, Richard K. (1969), Madsen, James H., Jr., and W. E. Miller. (1979), McClellan, P. H. (1977), Miller, Robert Rush. (1958), Miller, Robert Rush. (1965), Miller, Robert Rush, and Gerald R. Smith. (1981), Minckley, W. L., and Dean A. Hendrickson, Carl E. Bond. (1986), Moyle, Peter B., and Joseph J. Cech, Jr. (1982), Nelson, Edward M. (1949), Nelson, Joseph S. (1976), Nelson, Joseph S. (1984), Obruchev, D. V. (ed.) (1967), Orr, William N., and Elizabeth L. Orr. (1981), Romer, Alfred Sherwood. (1966), Smith, Gerald R. (1966), Smith, Gerald R. (1981a), Uyeno, Teruya, and Robert Rush Miller. (1962),

Chasmistes batrachops (Cope).

Hay, Oliver Perry. (1902), Hay, Oliver Perry. (1927), Hay, Oliver Perry. (1929), Hussakof, Louis. (1908), Minckley, W. L., and Dean A. Hendrickson, Carl E. Bond. (1986), Starks, Edwin C. (1907), Uyeno, Teruya, and Robert Rush Miller. (1963),

Chasmistes brevirostris Cope, 1879.

Shortnose Sucker.

Bailey, Reeve M., and John E. Fitch, Earl S. Herald, Ernest A. Lachner, C. C. Lindsey, C. Richard Robins, W. B. Scott. (1970), Bailey, Reeve M., and Ernest A. Lachner, C. C. Lindsey, C. Richard Robins, Phil M. Roedel, W. B. Scott, Loren P. Woods. (1966), Coots, M. (1965), Cope, Edward Drinker. (1879), Cope, Edward Drinker. (1883), Eastman, Joseph T. (1977), Eastman, Joseph T. (1980), Eddy, Samuel. (1969), Ferris, Stephen D., and Gregory S. Whitt. (1978), Gilbert, Charles Henry (1898), Goode, C. Brown, and Theodore Nicholas Gill. (1903), Hubbs, Carl L., and W. I. Follett, Lillian J. Dempster. (1979), Hubbs, Carl L., and Leonard P. Schultz. (1932), Jordan, David Starr, and Barton Warren Evermann. (1896), Jordan, David Starr, and Barton Warren Evermann. (1905), Jordan, David Starr, and Charles Henry Gilbert. (1883), Lee, David S., and Carter R. Gilbert, Charles H. Hocutt, Robert E. Jenkins, Don E. McAllister, Jay R. Stauffer, Jr. (1980), Minckley, W. L., and Dean A. Hendrickson, Carl E. Bond. (1986), Moyle, Peter B. (1976), Robins, C. Richard, and Reeve M. Bailey, Carl E. Bond, James R. Brooker, Ernest A. Lachner, Robert N. Lea, W. B. Scott. (1980), Schultz, Leonard P. (1936),

Chasmistes chamberlaini Rutter, 1904.

Hubbs, Carl L., and Leonard P. Schultz. (1932), Rutter, Cloudsley M. (1904), Snyder, John Otterbein. (1917),

Chasmistes copei Evermann and Meek, 1898.

Evermann, Barton Warren, and Seth Eugene Meek. (1898), Goode, C. Brown, and Theodore Nicholas Gill. (1903), Hubbs, Carl L., and Leonard P. Schultz. (1932), Jordan, David Starr, and Barton Warren Evermann. (1905), Schultz, Leonard P. (1936),

Chasmistes cujus Cope, 1883.

Cui-ui, Couia.

Bachanan, C. C., and M. W. Coleman. (1987), Bailey, Reeve M., and John E. Fitch, Earl S. Herald, Ernest A. Lachner, C. C. Lindsey, C. Richard Robins, W. B. Scott. (1970), Bailey, Reeve M., and Ernest A. Lachner, C. C. Lindsey, C. Richard Robins, Phil M. Roedel, W. B. Scott, Loren P. Woods. (1966), Carlander, Kenneth D. (1969), Chatto, D. A. (1979), Cope, Edward Drinker. (1883), Eddy, Samuel. (1957), Eddy, Samuel. (1969), Engel, J. M. (1978), Finnley, D. [Editor]. (1978a), Follett, W. I. (1967), Fowler, Henry Weed. (1914a), Jordan, David Starr, and Barton Warren Evermann. (1896), Jordan, David Starr, and Charles Henry Gilbert. (1883), Koch, D. L. (1973a), Koch, D. L. (1973b), Koch, D. L. (1976), Koch, D. L., and G. P. Contreras. (1972), Koch, D. L., and G. P. Contreras. (1973), La Rivers, Ira. (1962), Lee, David S., and Carter R. Gilbert, Charles H. Hocutt, Robert E. Jenkins, Don E. McAllister, Jay R. Stauffer, Jr. (1980), Miller, Rudolph J., and H. E. Evans. (1965), Minckley, W. L., and Dean A. Hendrickson, Carl E. Bond. (1986), Nelson, Edward M. (1948), Ono, R. Dana, and James D. Williams, Anne Wagner. (1983), Pister, Edwin P. (1981), Robins, C. Richard, and Reeve M. Bailey, Carl E. Bond, James R. Brooker, Ernest A. Lachner, Robert N. Lea, W. B. Scott. (1980), Scoppettone, G. G. (1988), Scoppettone, G. Gary, and Mark Coleman, Gary A. Wedemeyer. (1986), Scoppettone, G. Gary, and Gary A. Wedemeyer, Mark Coleman, Howard Burge. (1983), Sigler, W. F., and S. Vigg, M. Bres. (1985), Smith, Gerald R. (1985), Snyder, D. E. (1983), Sonnevil, G. M. (1978), Vigg, S. (1978), Vigg, S. (1980),

Chasmistes liorus Jordan, 1878.

June Sucker, June Sucker of Utah Lake.

Bailey, Reeve M., and John E. Fitch, Earl S. Herald, Ernest A. Lachner, C. C. Lindsey, C. Richard Robins, W. B. Scott. (1970), Bailey, Reeve M., and Ernest A. Lachner, C. C. Lindsey, C. Richard Robins, Phil M. Roedel, W. B. Scott, Loren P. Woods. (1966), Baxter, George T., and James R. Simon. (1970), Eddy, Samuel. (1969), Goode, C. Brown, and Theodore Nicholas Gill. (1903), Jordan, David Starr. (1878c), Jordan, David Starr. (1878d), Jordan, David Starr, and Barton Warren Evermann. (1896), Jordan, David Starr, and Barton Warren Evermann. (1905), Jordan, David Starr, and Charles Henry Gilbert. (1880), Jordan, David Starr, and Charles Henry Gilbert. (1883), Lee, David S., and Carter R. Gilbert, Charles H. Hocutt, Robert E. Jenkins, Don E. McAllister, Jay R. Stauffer, Jr. (1980), Minckley, W. L., and Dean A. Hendrickson, Carl E. Bond. (1986), Robins, C. Richard, and Reeve M. Bailey, Carl E. Bond, James R. Brooker, Ernest A. Lachner, Robert N. Lea, W. B. Scott. (1980), Scoppettone, G. Gary, and Mark Coleman, Gary A. Wedemeyer. (1986),

Chasmistes liorus mictus Miller and Smith, 1981.
June Sucker.
Miller, Robert Rush, and Gerald R. Smith. (1981),

Chasmistes luxatus Cope, 1879.
Cope, Edward Drinker. (1879), Cope, Edward Drinker. (1883), Goode, C. Brown, and Theodore Nicholas Gill. (1903), Jordan, David Starr, and Barton Warren Evermann. (1896), Jordan, David Starr, and Charles Henry Gilbert. (1883),

Chasmistes muriei Miller and Smith, 1981.
Snake River Sucker.
Miller, Robert Rush, and Gerald R. Smith. (1981), Minckley, W. L., and Dean A. Hendrickson, Carl E. Bond. (1986),

Chasmistes oregonus Starks, 1907.
Arldt, Th. (1907), Cope, Edward Drinker. (1883), Hay, Oliver Perry. (1902), Hay, Oliver Perry. (1927), Hay, Oliver Perry. (1929), Jordan, David Starr. (1907b), Starks, Edwin C. (1907),

Chasmistes spatulifer Miller and Smith, 1967.
Kimmel, Peter G. (1975), Linder, Allan D., and Dale G. Kosluchar. (1976), Miller, Robert Rush, and Gerald R. Smith. (1967), Minckley, W. L., and Dean A. Hendrickson, Carl E. Bond. (1986), Smith, Gerald R. (1975),

Chasmistes stomias Evermann and Meek, 1898.
Evermann, Barton Warren, and Seth Eugene Meek. (1898), Gilbert, Charles Henry (1898), Goode, C. Brown, and Theodore Nicholas Gill. (1903), Hubbs, Carl L., and Leonard P. Schultz. (1932), Jordan, David Starr, and Barton Warren Evermann. (1905), Schultz, Leonard P. (1936),

Chasmites.
Orr, William N., and Elizabeth L. Orr. (1981),

Chasmites cujus.
Estep, Marilyn L. F., and Steven Vigg. (1985),

Cotostomus anisopterus.
Buffalo Carp Sucker, Buffalo Carp, Buffalo perch, Buffalo Sucker, White Buffalo-Fish.
Rafinesque, Constantine Samuel. (1820b),

Cotostomus melanops.
Black-face Sucker.
Rafinesque, Constantine Samuel. (1820b),

Cotostomus rhothœcus Thoburn **IN:** Jordan and Evermann, 1896. Jordan, David Starr, and Barton Warren Evermann. (1896),

Cycelptus.
Miller, Robert Rush. (1958),

Cycleptus Rafinesque, 1819.
Black Horse.
Eschmeyer, William N. (1990), Jordan, David Starr. (1923), Jordan, David Starr, and Barton Warren Evermann. (1896), Meek, Seth Eugene. (1894), Miller, Robert Rush. (1958), Miller, Rudolph J., and H. E. Evans. (1965), Nelson, Edward M. (1948), Nelson, Edward M. (1949), Rafinesque, Constantine Samuel. (1820b),

Cycleptus elongatus (Le Sueur, 1817).
Blue sucker, Gourd-Seed Sucker, Suckerel, Missouri Sucker, Black-Horse.
Bailey, Reeve M., and Marvin O. Allum. (1962), Bailey, Reeve M., and John E. Fitch, Earl S. Herald, Ernest A. Lachner, C. C. Lindsey, C. Richard Robins, W. B. Scott. (1970), Bailey, Reeve M., and Ernest A. Lachner, C. C. Lindsey, C. Richard Robins, Phil M. Roedel, W. B. Scott, Loren P. Woods. (1966), Barnickol, P. G., and W. C. Starrett. (1951), Becker, George C. (1983), Blatchley, W. S. (1938), Boschung, Herbert T., Jr., and James D. Williams, Daniel W. Gotshall, David K. Caldwell, Melba C. Caldwell, Carol Nehring, Jordan Verner. (1983), Branson, Branley A. (1962), Breder, C. M., Jr., and D. E. Rosen. (1966), Brown, C. J. D. (1971), Buth, Donald G. (1983), Carlander, Kenneth D. (1969), Christenson, L. M. (1974), Cincotta, Dan A., and Robert L. Miles, Michael E. Hoeft, Gerald E. Lewis. (1986), Clay, W. M. (1975), Clemens, Howard P., and W. Waynon Johnson. (1964), Coker, R. E. (1930), Contreras-Balderas, S., and R. Rivera-T. (1972), Cooper, Edwin Lavern. (1983), Cowley, D. E., and J. E. Sublette. (1989), Cross, Frank B. (1967), Cross, Frank B., and Joseph T. Collins. (1975), Curry, Kevin D., and Anne Spacie. (1979), Deacon, James Everett. (1960), Douglas, Neil H. (1974), Eastman, Joseph T. (1977), Eddy, Samuel. (1957), Eddy, Samuel. (1969), Eddy, Samuel, and James C. Underhill. (1974), Elrod, J. H., and T. J. Hassler. (1971), Fago, Don. (1984a), Ferris, Stephen D., and Gregory S. Whitt. (1978), Fisher, H. J. (1962), Fogle, N. E. (1961a), Fogle, N. E. (1961b), Fogle, N. E. (1963a), Fogle, N. E. (1963b), Forbes, Stephen Alfred. (1884), Forbes, Stephen Alfred., and Robert Earl Richardson. (1908), Forbes, Stephen Alfred., and Robert Earl Richardson. (1920), Fowler, Henry Weed. (1945), Fowler, Henry Weed. (1948b), Gehlbach, F. R., and R. R. Miller. (1961), Goode, C. Brown, and Theodore Nicholas Gill. (1903), Hogue, J. J., Jr., and J. V. Conner, V. R. Kranz. (1981), Hubbs, Carl L., and Clark Hubbs. (1958), Jenkins, Robert M. (1953a), Jordan, David Starr. (1878a), Jordan, David Starr. (1929), Jordan, David Starr, and Barton Warren Evermann. (1896), Jordan, David Starr, and Barton Warren Evermann. (1905), Jordan, David Starr, and Charles Henry Gilbert. (1883), Koster, William J. (1957), Kuehn, J. H., and W. Niemuth, A. R. Peterson. (1961), Large, T. (1903), Lee, David S., and Carter R. Gilbert, Charles H. Hocutt, Robert E. Jenkins, Don E. McAllister, Jay R. Stauffer, Jr. (1980), Leiby, P. D., and D. C. Kritsky, D. D. Bauman. (1973), Les, B. L. (1979), Le Sueur, Charles Alexandre. (1817), Lindsey, Hague L., and James C. Randolph, John Carroll. (1983), Mcinerny, M. C. and J. Witteld. (1988), Meek, Seth Eugene. (1894), Miller, Rudolph J., and Henry W. Robinson. (1973), Moore, G. A., and Frank B. Cross. (1950), Moss, R. E., and J. W. Scanlan, C. S. Anderson. (1983), Moyle, J. B. (1975), Nelson, Edward M. (1948), Nelson, E. W. (1876), Nelson, Joseph S. (1976), Nelson, Joseph S. (1984), Nelson, W. R. (1962), O'Donnell, D. J. (1935), Pearson, William D., and Louis A. Krumholz (1984), Pflieger, William L. (1971), Pflieger, William L. (1975), Phillips, Gary L., and William D. Schmid,

James C. Underhill. (1982), Phillips, Gary L., and James C. Underhill. (1971), Pigg, J. (1982), Platt, D. R., and Frank B. Cross, D. Distler, O. S. Fent, E. R. Hall, M. Terman, J. Zimmerman, J. Walstrom. (1973), Rasmussen, J. L., editor. (1979), Robins, C. Richard, and Reeve M. Bailey, Carl E. Bond, James R. Brooker, Ernest A. Lachner, Robert N. Lea, W. B. Scott. (1980), Rupprecht, R. J., and L. A. Jahn. (1980), Scott, Donald C. (1951), Semmens,.K. J. (1985), Shields, J. T. (1955b), Shields, J. T. (1956), Shields, J. T. (1957b), Shields, J. T. (1958a), Smith, Gerald R. (1966), Smith, Gerald R. (1981b), Smith, Philip W. (1965), Smith, Philip W. (1973), Smith, Philip W. (1979), Smith, Philip W., and A. C. Lopinot, W. L. Pflieger. (1971), Sprague, J. W. (1959a), Swingle, W. E. (1965), Trautman, Milton B. (1957), Trautman, Milton B. (1981), Villar, José Alvarez del. (1970), Walden, Howard T., 2d. (1964), Yeager, Bruce L., and Kenneth J. Semmens. (1987),

Cycleptus nigrescens Rafinesque, 1819.
   Black Suckerel.
   Jordan, David Starr, and Barton Warren Evermann. (1896), Rafinesque, Constantine Samuel. (1819), Rafinesque, Constantine Samuel. (1820b),

Cycleptus robustus Sytchevskaya, 1986.
   Sytchevskaya, E. K. (1986),

Cyprinus catostomus Forster, 1773.
   Forster, J. R. (1773), Jordan, David Starr, and Barton Warren Evermann. (1896), Smith, Philip W. (1979),

Cyprinus commersonii La Cepède, 1803.
   Forbes, Stephen Alfred., and Robert Earl Richardson. (1920), Jordan, David Starr, and Barton Warren Evermann. (1896), La Cepède, Bernard Germain Étienne. (1803), Smith, Philip W. (1979),

Cyprinus oblongus Mitchill, 1815.
   Forbes, Stephen Alfred., and Robert Earl Richardson. (1920), Mitchill, Samuel Latham. (1815), Smith, Philip W. (1979),

Cyprinus rostratus Tilesius, 1813.
   Günther, Albert C. (1868), Tilesius von Tilenau, Wilhelm Gottlieb. (1813),

Cyprinus sucetta La Cepède, 1803.
   Smith, Philip W. (1979),

Cyprinus suerii Richardson, 1836.
   Günther, Albert C. (1868), Richardson, John R. (1836),

Cyprinus teres Mitchill, 1815.
   Jordan, David Starr, and Barton Warren Evermann. (1896), Mitchill, Samuel Latham. (1815),

Decactylus Rafinesque, 1820.
   Eschmeyer, William N. (1990), Jordan, David Starr. (1923), Rafinesque, Constantine Samuel. (1820b),

Decactylus bostoniensis (Le Sueur, 1817).
   Jordan, David Starr, and Barton Warren Evermann. (1896),

Deltistes Seale, 1896.
   Eschmeyer, William N. (1990), Jordan, David Starr. (1923), Nelson, Joseph S. (1984), Romer, Alfred Sherwood. (1966), Smith, Gerald R. (1966),

Deltistes ellipticus Miller and Smith, 1967.
   Miller, Robert Rush, and Gerald R. Smith. (1967), Minckley, W. L., and Dean A. Hendrickson, Carl E. Bond. (1986),

Deltistes luxatus
   Coots, M. (1965), Gilbert, Charles Henry (1898), Goode, C. Brown, and Theodore Nicholas Gill. (1903), Hubbs, Carl L., and Leonard P. Schultz. (1932), Jordan, David Starr, and Barton Warren Evermann. (1905), Minckley, W. L., and Dean A. Hendrickson, Carl E. Bond. (1986), Schultz, Leonard P. (1936),

Deltistes owyhee Miller and Smith, 1967.
   Miller, Robert Rush, and Gerald R. Smith. (1967),

Erimyzon Jordan, 1876.
   Chub Suckers.
   Eschmeyer, William N. (1990), Fuiman, Lee A. (1985), Jordan, David Starr. (1923), Jordan, David Starr, and Barton Warren Evermann. (1896), Meek, Seth Eugene. (1894), Miller, Robert Rush. (1958), Nelson, Edward M. (1948), Nelson, Edward M. (1949), Nelson, Joseph S. (1976), Nelson, Joseph S. (1984), Ribble, D. O., and M. H. Smith. (1983), Yeager, Bruce L., and Kenneth J. Semmens. (1987),

Erimyzon goodei Jordan, 1878.
   Goode, C. Brown, and Theodore Nicholas Gill. (1903), Jordan, David Starr. (1878d), Jordan, David Starr, and Barton Warren Evermann. (1896), Jordan, David Starr, and Charles Henry Gilbert. (1883),

Erimyzon luxus Sytchevskaya, 1986.
   Sytchevskaya, E. K. (1986),

Erimyzon melanops
   Smith, Philip W. (1979),

Erimyzon oblongus (Mitchill, 1815).
   Creek chubsucker.
   Anderson, W. D. (1964), Bagenal, T. B. (1978), Bailey, Reeve M., and John E. Fitch, Earl S. Herald, Ernest A. Lachner, C. C. Lindsey, C. Richard Robins, W. B. Scott. (1970), Bailey, Reeve M., and Ernest A. Lachner, C. C. Lindsey, C. Richard Robins, Phil M. Roedel, W. B. Scott, Loren P. Woods. (1966), Becker, George C. (1983), Behnke, Robert J., and Ralph M. Wetzel. (1960), Blatchley, W. S. (1938), Boschung, Herbert T., Jr., and James D. Williams, Daniel W. Gotshall, David K. Caldwell, Melba C. Caldwell, Carol Nehring, Jordan Verner. (1983), Breder, C. M., Jr., and D. E. Rosen. (1966), Carlander, Kenneth D. (1969), Carnes, W. C., Jr. (1958), Chaicharn, A., and W. L. Bullock. (1967), Clay, W. M. (1975), Cook, F. A. (1959), Cooper, Edwin Lavern. (1983), Curry, Kevin D., and Anne Spacie. (1984), Dorkin, John L., Jr. (1980), Douglas, Neil H. (1974), Eastman, Joseph T. (1977), Eddy, Samuel. (1969), Elser, H. J. (1961), Evans, James W., and Richard L. Noble. (1979), Everhart, W. H. (1958), Fago, Don. (1984b), Ferris, Stephen D., and Gregory S. Whitt. (1978), Flemer, D. A., and W. S. Woolcott. (1966), Forbes, Stephen Alfred. (1884), Forbes, Stephen Alfred., and Robert Earl Richardson. (1908), Forbes, Stephen Alfred., and Robert Earl Richardson. (1920), Forney, J. L. (1957a), Fuiman, Lee A. (1979), Funk, J. L., and R. S. Campbell. (1953), Gilbert, Carter R., and Benjamin R. Wall, Jr. (1985), Gilbert, Charles Henry. (1891), Greeley, J. R. (1936), Greene, C. W. (1935),

Grimes, L. R., and G. C. Miller. (1975), Grimes, L. R., and G. C. Miller. (1976), Hankinson, T. L. (1920),.Hoffman, Glenn L. (1967), Hubbs, Carl L., and Karl F. Lagler. (1974), Jordan, David Starr. (1876), Jordan, David Starr. (1878a), Jordan, David Starr, and Barton Warren Evermann. (1896), Kendall, William Converse. (1914), Kennicott, Robert. (1855), Large, T. (1903), Lee, David S., and Carter R. Gilbert, Charles H. Hocutt, Robert E. Jenkins, Don E. McAllister, Jay R. Stauffer, Jr. (1980), Lewis, W. M., and D. Elder. (1953), Lippson, Alice J., and R. L. Moran. (1974), Luce, W. (1933), Mackiewicz, J. S. (1974), Mansueti, A. J., and J. D. Hardy. (1967), Martin, R. G., and R. S. Campbell. (1953), McCollum, J. L., and C. J. Quertermus. (1980), Meek, Seth Eugene. (1891), Miller, Rudolph J., and Henry W. Robinson. (1973), Mitchill, Samuel Latham. (1815), Nelson, E. W. (1876), O'Donnell, D. J. (1935), Page, Lawrence M. (1982), Page, L. M., and C. E. Johnston. (1990), Pearson, William D., and Louis A. Krumholz (1984), Pflieger, William L. (1971), Pflieger, William L. (1975), Ritson, Philip C., and Janet L. Polk, Robert W. Malick, Jr. (1977), Robins, C. Richard, and Reeve M. Bailey, Carl E. Bond, James R. Brooker, Ernest A. Lachner, Robert N. Lea, W. B. Scott. (1980), Scarola, J. F. (1973), Scott, W. B. (1954), Scott, W. B. (1967), Skea, J. C., and H. A. Simonin, H. J. Dean, J. R. Colquhoun, J. J. Spagnoli, G. D. Veith. (1979), Smith, C. Lavett. (1986), Smith, Philip W. (1963), Smith, Philip W. (1965), Smith, Philip W. (1968), Smith, Philip W. (1971), Smith, Philip W. (1973), Smith, Philip W. (1979), Trautman, Milton B. (1957), Underhill, A. H. (1941), Wagner, Charles C., and Edwin L. Cooper. (1963), Walden, Howard T., 2d. (1964), Wang, Johnson C. S., and Ronnie J. Kernehan. (1979), Werner, Robert G. (1976a), Werner, Robert G. (1976b), Werner, Robert G. (1980), Whitworth, W. R., and P. L. Berrien, W. T. Keller. (1968),

Erimyzon oblongus claviformis (Girard).
Western Creek Chubsucker.
Bailey, Reeve M., and Gerald R. Smith. (1981), (1954), Clay, W. M. (1975), Hubbs, Carl L., and Karl F. Lagler. (1941), Hubbs, Carl L., and Karl F. Lagler. (1947), Hubbs, Carl L., and Karl F. Lagler. (1974), Larimore, R. W., and P. W. Smith. (1963), Lee, David S., and Carter R. Gilbert, Charles H. Hocutt, Robert E. Jenkins, Don E. McAllister, Jay R. Stauffer, Jr. (1980), Miller, Rudolph J., and H. E. Evans. (1965), Nelson, Edward M. (1948), Smith, Philip W. (1979), Trautman, Milton B. (1957), Trautman, Milton B. (1981), Welter, Wilfred A. (1938),

Erimyzon oblongus connectens Hubbs, 1930.
Hubbs, Carl L. (1930), Hubbs, Carl L., and Karl F. Lagler. (1974), Lee, David S., and Carter R. Gilbert, Charles H. Hocutt, Robert E. Jenkins, Don E. McAllister, Jay R. Stauffer, Jr. (1980),

Erimyzon oblongus oblongus (Mitchill, 1815).
Bailey, Reeve M., and Gerald R. Smith. (1981), (1954), Eastman, Joseph T. (1980), Harrington, Robert W., Jr. (1947), Hubbs, Carl L., and Karl F. Lagler. (1941), Hubbs, Carl L., and Karl F. Lagler. (1947), Hubbs, Carl L., and Karl F. Lagler. (1974), Lee, David S., and Carter R. Gilbert, Charles H. Hocutt, Robert E. Jenkins, Don E. McAllister, Jay R. Stauffer, Jr. (1980), Mansueti, Romeo. (1951), Mansueti, Romeo, and Harold J. Elser. (1953), McCabe, Britton C. (1943), Smith, Philip W. (1979),

Erimyzon sucetta (La Cepède, 1803).
Lake Chubsucker, Sweet sucker, Creek Fish, Chub Sucker.
Allen, E. R. (1946), Amin, Omar A. (1985), Amin, Omar M. (1982), Amin, O. M. (1985), Amin, Omar M. (1986a), Amin, Omar M. (1986b), Amin, O. M., and J. C. Vignieri. (1986), Anderson, W. D. (1964), Anonymous. (1965a), Bailey, Reeve M., and John E. Fitch, Earl S. Herald, Ernest A. Lachner, C. C. Lindsey, C. Richard Robins, W. B. Scott. (1970), Bailey, Reeve M., and Ernest A. Lachner, C. C. Lindsey, C. Richard Robins, Phil M. Roedel, W. B. Scott, Loren P. Woods. (1966), Bailey, Reeve M., and Gerald R. Smith.

174

(1981), (1954), Bajkov, A. (1928), Baker, M. R. (1986), Becker, George C. (1964b), Becker, George C. (1983), Bennett, G. W., and W. F. Childers. (1957), Bennett, G. W., and W. F. Childers. (1966), Bissett, E. D. R. (1927), Boschung, Herbert T., Jr., and James D. Williams, Daniel W. Gotshall, David K. Caldwell, Melba C. Caldwell, Carol Nehring, Jordan Verner. (1983), Brown, C. J. D., and R. C. Ball. (1943), Buth, Donald G. (1983), Cahn, A. R. (1927), Carlander, Kenneth D. (1955), Carlander, Kenneth D. (1969), Christensen, B. M., and R. L. Calentine. (1983), Clay, W. M. (1975), Cooper, Edwin Lavern. (1983), Cooper, Edwin Lavern, and C. C. Wagner, G. E. Krantz. (1971), Cooper, G. P. (1936a), Cooper, G. P. (1936b), Cooper, G. P., and R. N. Schafer. (1954), Cooper, G. P., and G. N. Washburn. (1949), Crossman, E. J. (1962), Crossman, E. J., and R. G. Ferguson. (1963), Dorkin, John L., Jr. (1980), Douglas, Neil H. (1974), Eddy, Samuel. (1957), Eddy, Samuel. (1969), Emery, Lee. (1976), Ewers, L. A., and M. W. Boesel. (1935), Fago, Don. (1984b), Ferris, Stephen D., and Gregory S. Whitt. (1978), Forbes, Stephen Alfred. (1884), Forbes, Stephen Alfred. (1890), Forbes, Stephen Alfred., and Robert Earl Richardson. (1908), Fowler, Henry Weed. (1919), Gerking, Shelby D. (1945), Goode, C. Brown, and Theodore Nicholas Gill. (1903), Goode, G. Brown, and Tarleton H. Bean. (1879), Greene, C. W. (1935), Grinham, T., and D. K. Cone. (1990), Hankinson, T. L. (1920), Harlan, J. R., and E. B. Speaker. (1956), Hildebrand, Samuel F., and William C. Schroeder. (1923), Hinks, David. (1943),.Hoffman, Glenn L. (1967), Hubbs, Carl L. (1921), Jordan, David Starr. (1878a), Jordan, David Starr, and Barton Warren Evermann. (1896), Jordan, David Starr, and Barton Warren Evermann. (1905), Jordan, David Starr, and Charles Henry Gilbert. (1883), Keleher, J. J., and B. Kooyman. (1957), Lambou, V. W. (1961), Large, T. (1903), Lee, David S., and Carter R. Gilbert, Charles H. Hocutt, Robert E. Jenkins, Don E. McAllister, Jay R. Stauffer, Jr. (1980), Leed, J. A., and T. V. Belanger. (1981), Louder, D. E. (1961), Louder, D. E. (1962), Martin, R. G., and R. S. Campbell. (1953), McClane, Albert Jules. (1974), Meek, Seth Eugene. (1894), Meek, Seth Eugene, and S. F. Hildebrand. (1910), Miller, Rudolph J., and H. E. Evans. (1965), Moody, H. L. (1957), Negus, M. T., and J. M. Aho, C. S. Anderson. (1987), Nelson, E. W. (1876), O'Donnell, D. J. (1935), Odum, Howard T., and David K. Caldwell. (1955), Pearson, William D., and Louis A. Krumholz (1984), Pflieger, William L. (1971), Pflieger, William L. (1975), Priegel, G. R. (1967), Richardson, R. E. (1913), Ricker, W. E. (1945), Riley, D. M. (1978), Robins, C. Richard, and Reeve M. Bailey, Carl E. Bond, James R. Brooker, Ernest A. Lachner, Robert N. Lea, W. B. Scott. (1980), Roosa, D. M. (1977), Rutherford, D. A., and A. A. Echelle, O. E. Maughan. (1985), Scott, W. B. (1954), Scott, W. B. (1967), Scott, W. B., and E. J. Crossman. (1969), Scott, W. B., and E. J. Crossman. (1973), Shaklee, J. B., and M. J. Champion, Gregory S. Whitt. (1974), Shelford, Victor E. (1911a), Shelford, Victor E. (1911b), Shelford, Victor E. (1937), Shireman, J. V., and R. L. Stetler, D. E. Colle. (1978), Smith, C. Lavett. (1986), Smith, Hugh M. (1893), Smith, Philip W. (1965), Smith, Philip W. (1973), Smith, Philip W. (1979), Storer, David Humphreys. (1867), Swift, Camm, and Ralph W. Yerger, Patrick R. Parrish. (1977), Trautman, Milton B. (1957), Underhill, A. H. (1941), Walden, Howard T., 2d. (1964), Webster, Dwight A. (1942), Werner, Robert G. (1976a), Werner, Robert G. (1976b), Werner, Robert G. (1980), Wiener, J. G., and J. P. Giesy, Jr. (1979), Williams, E. H., Jr. (1979), Williams, E. H., Jr., and W. A. Rogers. (1972), Williams, E. H., Jr., and W. A. Rogers. (1984),

Erimyzon sucetta kennerleyi.
Scott, W. B. (1952), Trautman, Milton B. (1957),

Erimyzon sucetta kennerlii (Girard).
Gerking, Shelby D. (1947), Hubbs, Carl L., and Karl F. Lagler. (1941), Hubbs, Carl L., and Karl F. Lagler. (1947), Hubbs, Carl L., and Karl F. Lagler. (1974), Lee, David S., and Carter R. Gilbert, Charles H. Hocutt, Robert E. Jenkins, Don E. McAllister, Jay R. Stauffer, Jr. (1980), Nelson, Edward M. (1948),

Erimyzon sucetta kennerlyi (Girard).
Western Lake Chubsucker.
Clay, W. M. (1975), Eastman, Joseph T. (1980), Scott, D. M. (1955), Trautman, Milton B. (1981),

Erimyzon sucetta oblongus (Mitchill, 1815).
Chub-sucker, Sweet Sucker, Creek-Fish.
Forbes, Stephen Alfred., and Robert Earl Richardson. (1920), Fowler, Henry Weed. (1914c), Fowler, Henry Weed. (1916a), Fowler, Henry Weed. (1916b), Fowler, Henry Weed. (1918), Fowler, Henry Weed. (1921), Jordan, David Starr. (1929), Jordan, David Starr, and Barton Warren Evermann. (1896), Jordan, David Starr, and Barton Warren Evermann. (1905), Jordan, David Starr, and Charles Henry Gilbert. (1883), Keim, Thomas D. (1915), Larimore, R. W., and P. W. Smith. (1963), Nichols, John Treadwell, and William K. Gregory. (1918), Smith, Philip W. (1979),

Erimyzon sucetta sucetta (La Cepède).
Breder, C. M., Jr. (1920), Brimley, C. S., and W. B. Mabee. (1925), Eastman, Joseph T. (1980), Fowler, Henry Weed. (1945), Jordan, David Starr. (1929), Lee, David S., and Carter R. Gilbert, Charles H. Hocutt, Robert E. Jenkins, Don E. McAllister, Jay R. Stauffer, Jr. (1980), Nelson, Edward M. (1948), Pickens, A. L. (1928), Reid, George K., Jr. (1950), Weed, Alfred Cleveland. (1921), Welsh, W. W. (1916),

Erimyzon tenuis (Agassiz, 1855).
Sharpfin chubsucker.
Agassiz, John Louis Rodolphe. (1855), Bailey, Reeve M., and John E. Fitch, Earl S. Herald, Ernest A. Lachner, C. C. Lindsey, C. Richard Robins, W. B. Scott. (1970), Bailey, Reeve M., and Ernest A. Lachner, C. C. Lindsey, C. Richard Robins, Phil M. Roedel, W. B. Scott, Loren P. Woods. (1966), Douglas, Neil H. (1974), Eddy, Samuel. (1969), Ferris, Stephen D., and Gregory S. Whitt. (1978), Gilbert, Carter R., and Benjamin R. Wall, Jr. (1985), Gunning, G. E., and T. M. Berra. (1969), Lee, David S., and Carter R. Gilbert, Charles H. Hocutt, Robert E. Jenkins, Don E. McAllister, Jay R. Stauffer, Jr. (1980), Miller, Rudolph J., and H. E. Evans. (1965), Robins, C. Richard, and Reeve M. Bailey, Carl E. Bond, James R. Brooker, Ernest A. Lachner, Robert N. Lea, W. B. Scott. (1980),

Eurystomus Rafinesque, 1820.
Eschmeyer, William N. (1990), Jordan, David Starr. (1923), Jordan, David Starr, and Barton Warren Evermann. (1896), Rafinesque, Constantine Samuel. (1820b),

Eurystomus megastomus Rafinesque, 1820.
Jordan, David Starr, and Barton Warren Evermann. (1896),

Exoglossum macropterum Rafinesque, 1820.
Günther, Albert C. (1868), Rafinesque, Constantine Samuel. (1820b),

Hylomyzon Agassiz, 1855.
Agassiz, John Louis Rodolphe. (1855), Eschmeyer, William N. (1990), Jordan, David Starr. (1923), Jordan, David Starr, and Barton Warren Evermann. (1896),

Hylomyzon nigricans (Le Sueur, 1817).
Agassiz, John Louis Rodolphe. (1855), Günther, Albert C. (1868), Jordan, David Starr, and Barton Warren Evermann. (1896),

Hypentelium Rafinesque, 1818.
Eschmeyer, William N. (1990), Jaffe, R., and E. A. Stemmler, B. D. Eitzer, R. A. Hites. (1985), Jordan, David Starr. (1923), Jordan, David Starr, and Barton Warren Evermann.

(1896), Nelson, Edward M. (1948), Nelson, Edward M. (1949), Nelson, Joseph S. (1976), Raney, Edward C., and Ernest A. Lachner. (1947), Smith, Gerald R. (1966), Swofford, D. L., and S. H. Berlocher. (1987), Trautman, Milton B. (1957), Woods, A. E., and R. F. Carlton, M. E. Casto, G. I. Gleason. (1979), Yeager, Bruce L., and Kenneth J. Semmens. (1987),

Hypentelium etowanum (Jordan, 1877).
Alabama hog sucker.
Amin, Omar M., and Ernest H. Williams, Jr. (1983), Bailey, Reeve M., and John E. Fitch, Earl S. Herald, Ernest A. Lachner, C. C. Lindsey, C. Richard Robins, W. B. Scott. (1970), Bailey, Reeve M., and Ernest A. Lachner, C. C. Lindsey, C. Richard Robins, Phil M. Roedel, W. B. Scott, Loren P. Woods. (1966), Boschung, Herbert T., Jr., and James D. Williams, Daniel W. Gotshall, David K. Caldwell, Melba C. Caldwell, Carol Nehring, Jordan Verner. (1983), Buth, Donald G. (1978), Buth, Donald G. (1980), Buth, Donald G. (1983), Carlander, Kenneth D. (1969), Chien, Shin Ming, and Wilmer A. Rogers. (1970), Cone, D. K., and A. O. Dechtiar. (1984), Eddy, Samuel. (1957), Eddy, Samuel. (1969), Ferris, Stephen D., and Gregory S. Whitt. (1978), Fuiman, Lee A. (1984), Gilbert, Charles Henry. (1891), Hubbs, Carl L., and Karl F. Lagler. (1974), Jenkins, Robert E. (1970), Johnson, Sterling K. (1971), Jordan, David Starr. (1877c), Mackiewicz, J. S. (1972), Miller, Rudolph J., and H. E. Evans. (1965), Robins, C. Richard, and Reeve M. Bailey, Carl E. Bond, James R. Brooker, Ernest A. Lachner, Robert N. Lea, W. B. Scott. (1980), Rogers, Wilmer A. (1967), Rogers, Wilmer A. (1968), Rogers, Wilmer A., and J. D. Mizelle. (1966), Shih, M. C., and W. A. Rogers. (1970), Stiles, R. A., and D. A. Etnier. (1971), Swingle, W. E. (1965), Walden, Howard T., 2d. (1964), Williams, E. H., Jr. (1974), Wiltz, J. W. (1986),

Hypentelium macropterum Rafinesque, 1818.
Jordan, David Starr, and Barton Warren Evermann. (1896), Rafinesque, Constantine Samuel. (1818a),

Hypentelium nigricans (Le Sueur, 1817).
Northern hog sucker, Hog Sucker, Stone Lugger, Stone Toter, Hammerhead, Crawl-a-bottom, Hog Mullet.
Anonymous. (1965a), Anonymous. (1978), Anonymous. (1981), Bailey, Reeve M., and Marvin O. Allum. (1962), Bailey, Reeve M., and John E. Fitch, Earl S. Herald, Ernest A. Lachner, C. C. Lindsey, C. Richard Robins, W. B. Scott. (1970), Bailey, Reeve M., and Ernest A. Lachner, C. C. Lindsey, C. Richard Robins, Phil M. Roedel, W. B. Scott, Loren P. Woods. (1966), Bailey, Reeve M., and Gerald R. Smith. (1981), (1954), Bauer, Bruce H., and Branley A. Branson, Strant T. Colwell. (1978), Becker, George C. (1966), Becker, George C. (1983), Bennett, D. H., and O. E. Maughan, D. B. Jester, Jr. (1985), Beverly-Burton, Mary. (1984), Blatchley, W. S. (1938), Boschung, Herbert T., Jr., and James D. Williams, Daniel W. Gotshall, David K. Caldwell, Melba C. Caldwell, Carol Nehring, Jordan Verner. (1983), Bouck, G. R., and R. C. Ball. (1967), Branson, Branley A., and Donald L. Batch. (1974), Breder, C. M., Jr., and D. E. Rosen. (1966), Brown, E. H., Jr. (1960), Buth, Donald G. (1977b), Buth, Donald G. (1978), Buth, Donald G. (1980), Buth, Donald G. (1983), Buynak, G. L., and H. W. Mohr, Jr. (1978b), Cahn, A. R. (1927), Call, R. E. (1887), Carlander, Kenneth D. (1948), Carlander, Kenneth D. (1969), Chapman, D. W. (1978), Cherry, D. S., and K. L. Dickson, J. Cairns, Jr., J. R. Stauffer. (1977), Chien, Shin Ming. (1969), Chung, Y.-T. (1980), Chung, Y.-T. (1981), Clay, W. M. (1975), Cochran, P. A. (1985), Cooper, Edwin Lavern. (1983), Cross, Frank B. (1967), Cross, Frank B., and Joseph T. Collins. (1975), Curry, Kevin D., and Anne Spacie. (1979), Curry, Kevin D., and Anne Spacie. (1984), Dorkin, John L., Jr. (1980), Douglas, Neil H. (1974), Eastman, Joseph T. (1977), Eastman, Joseph T. (1980), Eddy, Samuel. (1957), Eddy, Samuel. (1969), Eddy, Samuel, and T. Surber. (1947), Eddy, Samuel, and James C. Underhill. (1974), Elser, H. J. (1961), Emery, Lee. (1976), Evermann, Barton Warren, and

W. C. Kendall. (1895), Fago, Don. (1984b), Ferris, Stephen D., and Gregory S. Whitt. (1978), Fish, M. P. (1932), Forbes, Stephen Alfred. (1884), Forbes, Stephen Alfred., and Robert Earl Richardson. (1908), Freeman, H. W. (1952), Friedrich, George W. (1933), Fuiman, Lee A. (1979), Funk, J. L., and R. S. Campbell. (1953), Gale, N. L. and B. G. Wixson. (1986), Gerking, Shelby D. (1953), Gleason, Larry N. (1984), Gleason, Larry N., and B. M. Christensen, Yui Tan Chung. (1983), Greeley, J. R. (1927), Guilday, J. E., and H. W. Hamilton, E. Anderson, et al. (1978), Haas, Robert L. (1943), Hall, Gordon E., and R. M. Jenkins. (1953), Hallam, J. C. (1959), Hankinson, T. L. (1920), Hankinson, T. L. (1923), Harlan, J. R., and E. B. Speaker. (1956), Hendrix, S. S. (1973), Hendrix, S. S. (1978), Hinks, David. (1943),.Hoffman, Glenn L. (1967), Holey, M., and B. Hollender, M. Imhof, R. Jesien, R. Konopacky, M. Toneys, D. Coble. (1980), Hubbs, Carl L. (1945), Hubbs, Carl L., and Karl F. Lagler. (1941), Hubbs, Carl L., and Karl F. Lagler. (1947), Hubbs, Carl L., and Karl F. Lagler. (1974), Jackson, S. W., Jr. (1966), Jacobs, K. E., and W. D. Swink. (1983), Jenkins, Robert E. (1970), Jenkins, Robert M. (1953b), Jenkins, Robert M., and E. M. Leonard, G. E. Hall. (1952), Johnson, Sterling K. (1971), Jordan, David Starr. (1878a), Jordan, David Starr. (1929), Jordan, David Starr, and Barton Warren Evermann. (1896), Keleher, J. J., and B. Kooyman. (1957), Kennicott, Robert. (1855), Kreuzer, R. O., and J. G. Sivak. (1984), Large, T. (1903), Larimore, R. W., and P. W. Smith. (1963), Lee, David S., and Carter R. Gilbert, Charles H. Hocutt, Robert E. Jenkins, Don E. McAllister, Jay R. Stauffer, Jr. (1980), Le Sueur, Charles Alexandre. (1817), Lopinot, Alvin C. (1966a), Lopinot, Alvin C. (ed.). (1968), Malick, Robert W., Jr., and Wayne A. Potter. (1976), Marenchin, Ginger Lee, and David M. Sever. (1981), Martin, R. G., and R. S. Campbell. (1953), Maurakis, Eugene G., and William S. Woolcott. (1984), McClane, Albert Jules. (1974), McCleave, James David. (1964), Meek, Seth Eugene. (1891), Mergo, John C., Jr., and Andrew M. White. (1984), Metcalf, A. L. (1966), Miller, Rudolph J., and H. E. Evans. (1965), Miller, Rudolph J., and Henry W. Robinson. (1973), Mills, Paul A., Jr., and Charles H. Hocutt, Jay R. Stauffer, Jr. (1978), Minckley, W. L. (1963), Minckley, W. L., and R. H. Goodyear, J. E. Craddock. (1964), Muzzall, P. M. (1982a), Muzzall, P. M., and F. C. Rabalais. (1975), Nash, R. D. M., and Y. Sun, C. S. Clay. (1987), Nelson, Edward M. (1948), Nelson, E. W. (1876), Ney, J. J., and J. H. van Hassel. (1983), O'Donnell, D. J. (1935), Otnes, M. A. (1973), Page, Lawrence M. (1982), Pearson, William D., and Louis A. Krumholz (1984), Pflieger, William L. (1971), Pflieger, William L. (1975), Phillips, Gary L., and William D. Schmid, James C. Underhill. (1982), Potter, Wayne A., and Robert W. Malick, Jr., Janet L. Polk. (1976), Purkett, C. A., Jr. (1958b), Raney, Edward C. (1940), Raney, Edward C. (1952), Raney, Edward C., and Ernest A. Lachner. (1939), Raney, Edward C., and Ernest A. Lachner. (1946a), Raney, Edward C., and Ernest A. Lachner. (1946b), Raney, Edward C., and Ernest A. Lachner. (1947), Raney, Edward C., and Robert M. Roecker. (1947), Rankin, Edward T. (1986), Reed, Roger J. (1957), Reed, Roger J. (1959), Reighard, Jacob E. (1920), Ribble, D. O., and M. H. Smith. (1983), Ritson, Philip C., and Janet L. Polk, Robert W. Malick, Jr. (1977), Robins, C. Richard, and Reeve M. Bailey, Carl E. Bond, James R. Brooker, Ernest A. Lachner, Robert N. Lea, W. B. Scott. (1980), Sather, L. M., and C. W. Threinen. (1968), Schlosser, Isaac J. (1985), Schmidt, P. J. (1950), Scott, W. B. (1954), Scott, W. B. (1958), Scott, W. B. (1967), Scott, W. B., and E. J. Crossman. (1969), Scott, W. B., and E. J. Crossman. (1973), Sheldon, Andrew L. (1968), Smith, C. Lavett. (1986), Smith, Philip W. (1963), Smith, Philip W. (1965), Smith, Philip W. (1968), Smith, Philip W. (1973), Smith, Philip W. (1979), Snyder, Richard C. (1949), Stanley, D. R. (1988), Sun, Ying, and Richard Nash, C. S. Clay. (1985), Swingle, W. E. (1965), Trautman, Milton B. (1981), Walden, Howard T., 2d. (1964), Ward, C. M. (1960), Welter, Wilfred A. (1938), Werner, Robert G. (1980), Williams, D. D. (1977b), Williams, D. D. (1979), Williams, D. D. (1980a), Williams, D. D. (1980d), Williams, D. D. (1980e), Williams, D. D., and M. J. Ulmer. (1980), Wiltz, J. W. (1986), Ying Sun, and, R. Nash, C. S. Clay. (1985),

Hypentelium nigricans etowanum.
Fowler, Henry Weed. (1945),

Hypentelium nigricans nigricans.
Fowler, Henry Weed. (1945),

Hypentelium roanokense Raney and Lachner, 1947.
Roanoke hog sucker.
Bailey, Reeve M., and John E. Fitch, Earl S. Herald, Ernest A. Lachner, C. C. Lindsey, C. Richard Robins, W. B. Scott. (1970), Bailey, Reeve M., and Ernest A. Lachner, C. C. Lindsey, C. Richard Robins, Phil M. Roedel, W. B. Scott, Loren P. Woods. (1966), Boschung, Herbert T., Jr., and James D. Williams, Daniel W. Gotshall, David K. Caldwell, Melba C. Caldwell, Carol Nehring, Jordan Verner. (1983), Buth, Donald G. (1978), Buth, Donald G. (1980), Buth, Donald G. (1983), Carlander, Kenneth D. (1969), Eddy, Samuel. (1957), Eddy, Samuel. (1969), Jenkins, Robert E. (1970), Lee, David S., and Carter R. Gilbert, Charles H. Hocutt, Robert E. Jenkins, Don E. McAllister, Jay R. Stauffer, Jr. (1980), Miller, Rudolph J., and H. E. Evans. (1965), Raney, Edward C., and Ernest A. Lachner. (1947), Robins, C. Richard, and Reeve M. Bailey, Carl E. Bond, James R. Brooker, Ernest A. Lachner, Robert N. Lea, W. B. Scott. (1980), Snyder, Richard C. (1949), Walden, Howard T., 2d. (1964),

Ichthyobus bison.
Smith, Philip W. (1979),

Ichthyobus bubalus Rafinesque.
Goode, C. Brown, and Theodore Nicholas Gill. (1903), Günther, Albert C. (1868), Jordan, David Starr. (1878b), Jordan, David Starr, and Barton Warren Evermann. (1896), Smith, Philip W. (1979),

Ichthyobus carpio.
Forbes, Stephen Alfred., and Robert Earl Richardson. (1920), Smith, Philip W. (1979),

Ichthyobus cyanellus Nelson, 1876.
Jordan, David Starr. (1878b), Jordan, David Starr, and Barton Warren Evermann. (1896), Smith, Philip W. (1979),

Ichthyobus difformis.
Smith, Philip W. (1979),

Ichthyobus ischyrus Jordan, 1877.
Jordan, David Starr. (1877b), Jordan, David Starr. (1878b),

Ichthyobus ranchii Agassiz, 1855.
Agassiz, John Louis Rodolphe. (1855), Günther, Albert C. (1868),

Ichthyobus rauchi Agassiz, 1855.
Jordan, David Starr. (1878b),

Ichthyobus stolleyi Agassiz, 1855.
Agassiz, John Louis Rodolphe. (1855), Günther, Albert C. (1868),

Ichthyobus thompsoni.
Smith, Philip W. (1979),

Ichthyobus velifer.
Smith, Philip W. (1979),

Ictiobus Rafinesque, 1820.
Buffalo Fishes.
Afanasiev, V. I. (1985), Amin, Omar M. (1969), Andryushchenko, A. I., and V. I. Glebova. (1979), Angelescu, N. (1982), Angelescu, N., and G. Cazacu, C. Cazacu. (1980), Bailey, R. M., and W. N. Eschmeyer. (1988), Berner, Lester M. (1948), Borgstrom, Georg. (1978), Carlander, Kenneth D. (1978), Dorosev, S. I., and V. K. Vinogradov. (1976), Dyakonov, Yu. N. (1980), Erokhina, L. V., and N. V. Voropaev, A. K. Bogeruk, V. F. Krivtsov. (1976), Eschmeyer, William N. (1990), Gabel, J. A. (1974),.Hoffman, Glenn L. (1967), Hoffman, Glenn L., and Fred P. Meyer. (1974), Hollander, E. E., and J. W. Avault, Jr. (1975), Holloway, H. L., Jr. (1978), Johnson, D. W., and W. L. Minckley. (1972), Jordan, David Starr. (1923), Jordan, David Starr, and Barton Warren Evermann. (1896), Jordan, David Starr, and Charles Henry Gilbert. (1884), Lee, Lana, and David C. Corson, Brian D. Sykes. (1985), Lobchenko, V. V. (1981), McGeachin, R. B. (1986), Meek, Seth Eugene. (1894), Meyer, Fred P. (1967), Meyers, George Sprague. (1966), Miller, Robert Rush. (1958), Mills, Harlow B., and William C. Starrett, Frank C. Belrose. (1966), Minckley, W. L., and J. E. Johnson, J. N. Rinne, S. E. Willoughby. (1970), Moyle, Peter B., and Joseph J. Cech, Jr. (1982), Nelson, Edward M. (1948), Nelson, Edward M. (1949), Nelson, Joseph S. (1976), Nelson, Joseph S. (1984), Opinion 1582. (1990),.Perry, W. G., Jr., and J. W. Avault, Jr. (1976), Peterson, E. J., and E. W. Steucke, Jr., W. H. Lynch. (1966), Rafinesque, Constantine Samuel. (1820b), Rostlund, Erhard. (1951), Shilenko, Yu. V. and V. G. Krasnikov, N. V. Shilenko. (1986), Shumkov, M. A. (1985), Smith, Gerald R. (1963), Smith, Gerald R. (1966), Smith, Gerald R. (1981b), Starrett, William C., and William J. Harth, Philip W. Smith. (1960), Trautman, Milton B. (1957), Uyeno, Teruya, and Robert Rush Miller. (1962), Weigel, R. D., and J. A. Holman, A. A. Paloumpis. (1974), Willis, David W., and Lanny D. Jones. (1986), Wilson, R. L. (1968), Yeager, Bruce L., and Kenneth J. Semmens. (1987), Yurawecz, M. P., and J.-Y. Chen, B. J. Puma. (1986),

Ictiobus bison.
Jordan, David Starr, and Seth Eugene Meek. (1885),

Ictiobus bubalus (Rafinesque, 1818).
Smallmouth Buffalo, Small-Mouthed Buffalo, Sucker-Mouthed Buffalo, Small-Mouth Buffalo, Razor-Backed Buffalo, Quillback Buffalo.
Agassiz, John Louis Rodolphe. (1854), Angelescu, N., and G. Cazacu, C. Cazacu. (1980), Anonymous. (1961), Anonymous. (1965a), Anonymous. (1965b), Bailey, Reeve M., and Marvin O. Allum. (1962), Bailey, Reeve M., and John E. Fitch, Earl S. Herald, Ernest A. Lachner, C. C. Lindsey, C. Richard Robins, W. B. Scott. (1970), Bailey, Reeve M., and Ernest A. Lachner, C. C. Lindsey, C. Richard Robins, Phil M. Roedel, W. B. Scott, Loren P. Woods. (1966), Barnickol, P. G., and W. C. Starrett. (1951), Baughman, J. L. (1946), Becker, George C. (1983), Berigina, I. A. (1976), Berner, Lester M. (1948), Blatchley, W. S. (1938), Borges, M. H. (1950), Boschung, Herbert T., Jr., and James D. Williams, Daniel W. Gotshall, David K. Caldwell, Melba C. Caldwell, Carol Nehring, Jordan Verner. (1983), Branson, Branley A., and Donald L. Batch. (1974), Breder, C. M., Jr., and D. E. Rosen. (1966), Brown, C. J. D. (1971), Cahn, A. R. (1927), Caraiman, G., and Z. Pogan. (1981), Carlander, Kenneth D. (1949), Carlander, Kenneth D. (1969), Chien, Shin Ming, and Wilmer A. Rogers. (1970), Chlebeck, A., and G. L. Phillips. (1969), Christenson, L. M. (1957), Christenson, L. M., and L. L. Smith. (1965), Cicerello, Ronald R., and Robert S. Butler. (1985), Clay, W. M. (1975), Coker, R. E. (1930), Cooper, Edwin Lavern. (1983), Cross, Frank B. (1967), Cross, Frank B., and Joseph T. Collins. (1975), Curry, Kevin D., and Anne Spacie. (1979), Deacon, James Everett. (1960), Deacon, James Everett. (1961), Diercks, K. J., and T. G. Goldsberry. (1970), Dorkin, John L., Jr. (1980), Douglas, Neil H. (1974), Eastman, Joseph T. (1977), Eastman, Joseph T. (1980), Eddy, Samuel. (1957), Eddy, Samuel. (1969), Eddy, Samuel, and James C. Underhill. (1974), Elrod, J. H., and T. J. Hassler. (1971), Erokhina, L. V., and V. K. Vinogradov, V. V. Vychegzhanina. (1976),

Eschmeyer, R. W., and R. H. Stroud, A. M. Jones. (1944), Evermann, Barton Warren. (1899), Ferris, Stephen D., and Gregory S. Whitt. (1978), Finnell, Joe C. (1955), Fisher, H. J. (1962), Fogle, N. E. (1961a), Fogle, N. E. (1961b), Fogle, N. E. (1963a), Fogle, N. E. (1963b), Forbes, Stephen Alfred. (1884), Forbes, Stephen Alfred. (1890), Forbes, Stephen Alfred., and Robert Earl Richardson. (1908), Forbes, Stephen Alfred., and Robert Earl Richardson. (1920), Fowler, Henry Weed. (1945), Funk, J. L., and R. S. Campbell. (1953), Gammon, J. R. (1977), Gasaway, C. R. (1970), Georgescu, R., and P. Dascalescu, G. Caraiman. (1984), Giurca, R., and N. Angelescu. (1978), Gowanloch, J. N., and C. Gresham. (1965), Grinham, T., and D. K. Cone. (1990), Hall, Gordon E. (1951), Hall, Gordon E., and R. M. Jenkins. (1953), Hall, Gordon E., and George A. Moore. (1954), Hambrick, P. S., and R. E. Spieler. (1977), Hanson, W. D., and R. S. Campbell. (1963), Hargis, H. L. (1966), Hendricks, Lawrence J. (1956), Hinks, David. (1943), Hoese, H. Dickson, and Richard H. Moore. (1977), Houser, A. (1960), Hubbs, Carl L., and J. D. Black. (1940), Hubbs, Carl L., and Karl F. Lagler. (1941), Hubbs, Carl L., and Karl F. Lagler. (1947), Hubbs, Carl L., and Karl F. Lagler. (1974), Hubert, Wayne A., and Dennis N. Schmitt. (1985), Isom, B. G., and R. G. Hudson. (1984), Jenkins, Robert M. (1953a), Jenkins, Robert M. (1953b), Jenkins, Robert M., and J. C. Finnell. (1957), Jester, D. B. (1973), Jordan, David Starr. (1878a), Jordan, David Starr. (1929), Jordan, David Starr, and Alembert Winthrop Brayton. (1878), Jordan, David Starr, and Barton Warren Evermann. (1896), Jordan, David Starr, and Barton Warren Evermann. (1905), Jordan, David Starr, and Charles Henry Gilbert. (1884), Jordan, David Starr, and Seth Eugene Meek. (1885), Katz, M. (1954), Koster, William J. (1957), Krumholz, Louis A. (1943), Kurinnyi, S. A. (1984), Lambou, V. W. (1961), Large, T. (1903), Larimore, R. W., and P. W. Smith. (1963), Lee, David S., and Carter R. Gilbert, Charles H. Hocutt, Robert E. Jenkins, Don E. McAllister, Jay R. Stauffer, Jr. (1980), Linton, T. L. (1961), Lopinot, Alvin C. (1966a), Lopinot, Alvin C. (1967), Lopinot, Alvin C. (ed.). (1968), Martin, R. E. (1964a), Martin, R. E. (1964b), Martin, R. E., and S. I. Auerbach, D. J. Nelson. (1964), Martin, R. G., and R. S. Campbell. (1953), Matthews, W. J., and L. G. Hill, S. M. Schellhaass. (1985), Mauney, Morris, Jr. (1979), Maruney, Morris, Jr., and George L. Harp. (1979), McClane, Albert Jules. (1974), McComish, T. S. (1967), McNally, Tom. (1970), McPhail, J. D., and C. C. Lindsey. (1970), Meek, Seth Eugene. (1894), Meek, Seth Eugene, and S. F. Hildebrand. (1910), Mergo, John C., Jr., and Andrew M. White. (1984), Miller, Robert Rush. (1966), Miller, Rudolph J., and H. E. Evans. (1965), Miller, Rudolph J., and Henry W. Robinson. (1973), Mills, Paul A., Jr., and Charles H. Hocutt, Jay R. Stauffer, Jr. (1978), Minckley, W. L. (1959), Minckley, W. L. (1969), Minckley, W. L., and R. H. Goodyear, J. E. Craddock. (1964), Moen, T. E. (1960), Molya, S. P., and P. D. Arikov. (1988), Nelson, Edward M. (1948), Nelson, E. W. (1876), Nelson, W. R. (1961a), Nelson, W. R. (1962), Nelson, W. R. (1980), Niculescu-Duvaz, M., and R. Giurca, V. Popovici. (1979), Nord, R. C. (1967), O'Donnell, D. J. (1935), Patriarche, M. H. (1953), Pearson, William D., and Louis A. Krumholz (1984), Pflieger, William L. (1971), Pflieger, William L. (1975), Phillips, Gary L., and William D. Schmid, James C. Underhill. (1982), Pigg, J. (1987), Proffitt, M. A., and R. S. Benda. (1971), Purkett, C. A., Jr. (1958a), Purkett, C. A., Jr. (1958b), Pyefinch, K. A. (1964), Rafinesque, Constantine Samuel. (1818a), Robins, C. Richard, and Reeve M. Bailey, Carl E. Bond, James R. Brooker, Ernest A. Lachner, Robert N. Lea, W. B. Scott. (1980), Robinson, G. L., and L. A. Jahn. (1980), Savitz, J. (1987), Sandoz, O. (1960), Schoffman, R. J. (1944), Schoonover, R., and W. H. Thompson. (1954), Scott, W. B. (1958), Scott Cone, R., and K. Barbour, M. Russell, S. K. Simonet. (1986), Shields, J. T. (1955a), Shields, J. T. (1956), Shields, J. T. (1957a), Shields, J. T. (1957b), Shields, J. T. (1958a), Shields, J. T. (1958b), Shih, M. C., and W. A. Rogers. (1970), Smith, C. G., and W. M. Lewis, H. M. Kaplan. (1952), Smith, C. Lavett. (1962), Smith, Gerald R. (1981b), Smith, Philip W. (1973), Smith, Philip W. (1979), Sparks, Richard E., and William C. Starrett. (1975), Sprague, J. W. (1959a), Sprague, J. W. (1959b), Sprague, J. W. (1961), Swingle, W. E. (1965), Thompson, W. H. (1950), Trautman, Milton B. (1957), Trautman, Milton B. (1981), Uyeno, Teruya, and Robert Rush Miller. (1963), Villar, José Alvarez del. (1970), Walburg, C. H. (1964), Walburg, C. H. (1976), Walburg, C. H., and W. R. Nelson.

(1966), Walden, Howard T., 2d. (1964), Walker, M. C., and P. T. Frank. (1952), Ward, C. M. (1960), Werner, Robert G. (1976a), Werner, Robert G. (1976b), Whitaker, J. O., Jr., and R. A. Schlueter. (1975), Willis, David W. (1979), Willis, David W., and J. B. Owen. (1978), Winger, P. V., and J. K. Andreasen. (1985), Wisdom, J. L. A. (1972), Witt, Arthur, Jr. and Richard C. Marzolf. (1954), Wrenn, W. B., and B. G. Grinstead. (1968),

Ictiobus bulbalus (Rafinesque, 1818).
Amin, Omar M., and Ernest H. Williams, Jr. (1983), Anonymous. (1957), Berner, Lester M. (1951), Lowe, T. P., and T. W. May, W. G. Brumbaugh, D. A. Kane. (1985),

Ictiobus bubalus **X** *Ictiobus niger.*
Kurinnyi, S. A. (1984),

Ictiobus carpio Rafinesque.
Hubbs, Carl L., and J. D. Black. (1940), Jordan, David Starr, and Charles Henry Gilbert. (1884), Jordan, David Starr, and Seth Eugene Meek. (1885), Meek, Seth Eugene. (1894),

Ictiobus cutisanserinus.
Jordan, David Starr, and Seth Eugene Meek. (1885),

Ictiobus cyprinella (Valenciennes, 1844, **IN:** Cuvier and Valenciennes, 1844).
Red-Mouth Buffalo, Big-Mouth Buffalo.
Batraeva, M. N. and E. K. Saurskaya. (1982), Borgstrom, Georg. (1978), Deacon, James Everett. (1960), Emel'Yanova, N. G., and A. P. Makeeva. (1983), Forbes, Stephen Alfred., and Robert Earl Richardson. (1920), Hubbs, Carl L., and W. I. Follett, Lillian J. Dempster. (1979), Jordan, David Starr, and Barton Warren Evermann. (1896), Jordan, David Starr, and Barton Warren Evermann. (1905), Jordan, David Starr, and Charles Henry Gilbert. (1884), Meek, Seth Eugene. (1894), Miller, Rudolph J., and H. E. Evans. (1965), Smith, Philip W. (1979), Sterba, Günther. (1983),

Ictiobus cyprinellus (Valenciennes, 1844, **IN:** Cuvier and Valenciennes, 1844).
bigmouth buffalo, red-mouthed buffalo, red mouth buffalo fish, common buffalo fish.
Aadland, L. P., and J.J. Peterka. (1981), Andrews, L. M., and C. W. Threinen. (1968), Andryushchenko, A. I., and N. F. Grishchenko. (1985), Andryushchenko, A. I., and T. G. Litvinova, N. F. Grishchenko, E. P. Garbareva. (1986), Andryushchenko, A. I., and A. M. Tretyak. (1989), Andryushchenko, A. I., and N. V. Yurkevich. (1983), Angelescu, N., and G. Cazacu, C. Cazacu. (1980), Anonymous. (1915), Anonymous. (1921), Anonymous. (1961), Anonymous. (1965b), Averyanov, O. V., and V. N. Dubrovin, R. A. Aslanova. (1980), Badenko, L. V., and T. F. Shuvatova, V. I. Zhivonkina. (1983), Bailey, Reeve M. (1943a), Bailey, Reeve M. (1943b), Bailey, Reeve M., and Marvin O. Allum. (1962), Bailey, Reeve M., and John E. Fitch, Earl S. Herald, Ernest A. Lachner, C. C. Lindsey, C. Richard Robins, W. B. Scott. (1970), Bailey, Reeve M., and Ernest A. Lachner, C. C. Lindsey, C. Richard Robins, Phil M. Roedel, W. B. Scott, Loren P. Woods. (1966), Bailey, Reeve M., and Gerald R. Smith. (1981), (1954), Balan, A. I., and V. A. Prikhod'ko, I. M. Sherman, O. M. Tarasova, V. V. Isaevich, O. E. Semenyuk. (1977), Barnickol, P. G., and W. C. Starrett. (1951), Becker, George C. (1964a), Becker, George C. (1983), Beers, G. D. (1955), Berner, Lester M. (1951), Boschung, Herbert T., Jr., and James D. Williams, Daniel W. Gotshall, David K. Caldwell, Melba C. Caldwell, Carol Nehring, Jordan Verner. (1983), Brady, L., and A. Hulsey. (1959), Branson, Branley A. (1961), Branson, Branley A., and Donald L. Batch. (1974), Breder, C. M., Jr., and D. E. Rosen. (1966), Bronte, C. R., and D. W. Johnson. (1984), Brown, C. J. D. (1971), Burr, Brooks M., and R. C. Heidinger. (1983), Canfield, H. L. (1922), Caraiman, G., and Z. Pogan. (1981), Carlander, Kenneth D. (1949), Carlander, Kenneth D. (1952), Carlander, Kenneth D. (1955), Carlander, Kenneth D. (1969), Carlander, Kenneth D., and R. B. Moorman. (1949), Carlander, Kenneth D., and J. W. Parsons. (1949), Carson, R. (1943), Chlebeck, A., and G. L. Phillips. (1969),

Christenson, L. M. (1957), Clay, W. M. (1975), Cleary, R. E. (1956), Clemens, Howard P., and W. Waynon Johnson. (1964), Coble, Daniel W., and Gordon B. Farabee, Richard O. Anderson. (1985), Coker, R. E. (1930), Cooper, Edwin Lavern. (1983), Cross, Frank B. (1967), Cross, Frank B., and Joseph T. Collins. (1975), Cross, Frank B., and Artie L. Metcalf. (1963), Crossman, E. J., and R. G. Ferguson. (1963), Curry, Kevin D., and Anne Spacie. (1979), Davis, J. T. (1960), Douglas, Neil H. (1974), Eastman, Joseph T. (1977), Eastman, Joseph T. (1980), Eddy, Samuel. (1957), Eddy, Samuel. (1969), Eddy, Samuel, and Kenneth D. Carlander. (1939), Eddy, Samuel, and Kenneth D. Carlander. (1942), Eddy, Samuel, and T. Surber. (1947), Eddy, Samuel, and Roy C. Tasker, James C. Underhill. (1972), Eddy, Samuel, and James C. Underhill. (1974), Edwards, Elizabeth A. (1983), Elrod, J. H., and T. J. Hassler. (1971), Emery, Lee. (1976), Erokhina, L. V., and V. K. Vinogradov, V. V. Vychegzhanina. (1976), Fernholz, W. B., and V. E. Crawley. (1977), Ferris, Stephen D., and Gregory S. Whitt. (1978), Finke, A. H. (1967), Finnell, Joe C. (1955), Fogle, N. E. (1961a), Fogle, N. E. (1961b), Fogle, N. E. (1963a), Fogle, N. E. (1963b), Forbes, Stephen Alfred. (1884), Forbes, Stephen Alfred., and Robert Earl Richardson. (1908), Frey, D. G., and H. Pedracine. (1938), Frych, I. V., and A. M. Tretyak, V. V. Romanyuk. (1989), Funk, J. L., and R. S. Campbell. (1953), Galasun, P. T., and A. I. Andryushchenko, V. V. Grusevich. (1984), Garman, H., (1890), Georgescu, R., and P. Dascalescu, G. Caraiman. (1984), Giurca, R., and N. Angelescu. (1978), Gould, W. R. III, and W. H. Irwin. (1962), Gowanloch, J. N. (1951), Greer, J. K., and Frank B. Cross. (1956), Grinham, T., and D. K. Cone. (1990), Hall, Gordon E., and R. M. Jenkins. (1953), Hanson, W. D., and R. S. Campbell. (1963), Harlan, J. R., and E. B. Speaker. (1956), Helms, D. R. (1966), Herald, Earl S. (1967),.Hoffman, Glenn L. (1967), Hubbs, Carl L., and Karl F. Lagler. (1974), Jackson, S. W., Jr. (1966), Jenkins, Robert M. (1953a), Jenkins, Robert M. (1953b), Jenkins, Robert M., and J. C. Finnell. (1957), Jenkins, Robert M., and E. M. Leonard, G. E. Hall. (1952), Johnson, D. W., and W. L. Minckley. (1969), Johnson, M. C. (1959), Johnson, R. P. (1963), Jordan, David Starr. (1878a), Jordan, David Starr, and Barton Warren Evermann. (1923), Katz, M. (1954), Kernen, L. T. (1974), Koehn, Richard K., and D. W. Johnson. (1967), Lambou, V. W. (1961), Lantz, A. W. (1948b), Large, T. (1903), Larimore, R. W., and P. W. Smith. (1963), Lee, David S., and Carter R. Gilbert, Charles H. Hocutt, Robert E. Jenkins, Don E. McAllister, Jay R. Stauffer, Jr. (1980), Leiby, P. D., and D. C. Kritsky, C. A. Peterson. (1972), Lopinot, Alvin C. (1966a), Lopinot, Alvin C. (ed.). (1968), Lynch, T. M., and P. A. Buscemi, D. G. Lemons. (1953), Makeeva, A. P. (1980), Margaritov, N. (1988), Mayhew, J. (1964), McClane, Albert Jules. (1974), McComish, T. S. (1967), McNally, Tom. (1970), McPhail, J. D., and C. C. Lindsey. (1970), Mergo, John C., Jr., and Andrew M. White. (1984), Migdalski, E. C. (1955), Miller, N. J. (1971), Miller, Rudolph J., and Henry W. Robinson. (1973), Mitzner, L. (1966), Mitzner, L. (1971), Moen, T. E. (1954), 1125, Moen, T. E. (1960), Moen, T. E. (1974), Morris, M. A., and Brooks M. Burr. (1982), Moyle, Peter B. (1976), Nelson, E. W. (1876), Nelson, W. R. (1961a), Nelson, W. R. (1962), Newton, S. H., and C. J. Haskins, J. M. Martin. (1981), Niculescu-Duvaz, M., and R. Giurca, V. Popovici. (1979), Nikonova, R. S., and T. V. Solomatina. (1981), Novokshonov, Yu. D. (1981), O'Donnell, D. J. (1935), Osburn, Raymond Carroll. (1901), Patriarche, M. H. (1953), Pearson, William D., and Louis A. Krumholz (1984), Perry, W. G. (1976), Pflieger, William L. (1971), Pflieger, William L. (1975), Phillips, Gary L., and William D. Schmid, James C. Underhill. (1982), Priegel, G. R. (1967), Prieto, A., and M. Vinjoy, E. Fajer. (1988), Proffitt, M. A., and R. S. Benda. (1971), Raciunas, L. (1985a), Raciunas, L. (1985b), Ricker, W. E. (1962), Robins, C. Richard, and Reeve M. Bailey, Carl E. Bond, James R. Brooker, Ernest A. Lachner, Robert N. Lea, W. B. Scott. (1980), Rosenthal, H. L., and M. M. Eves, O. A. Cochran. (1970), Rostlund, Erhard. (1951), Scidmore, W. J., and D. E. Woods. (1960), Scott, W. B. (1967), Scott, W. B., and E. J. Crossman. (1969), Scott, W. B., and E. J. Crossman. (1973), Shields, J. T. (1955a), Shields, J. T. (1956), Shields, J. T. (1957a), Shields, J. T. (1957b), Shields, J. T. (1958a), Shields, J. T. (1958b), Smith, C. Lavett. (1962), Smith, C. Lavett. (1986), Smith, Gerald R. (1963), Smith, Gerald R. (1966), Smith, Gerald R. (1981b), Smith, Gerald R., and J. G. Lundberg. (1972), Smith, Philip W. (1973), Smith, Philip W.

(1979), Sparks, Richard E., and William C. Starrett. (1975), Sprague, J. W. (1959a), Sprague, J. W. (1959b), Sprague, J. W. (1961), Stanley, J. G., and J. B. Jones. (1976), Starostka, V. J., and R. L. Applegate. (1970), Stevenson, J. H. (1964), Stewart, Kenneth W., and Iain M. Suthers, Kelly Leavesley. (1985), Swingle, H. S. (1956), Swingle, H. S. (1957), Swingle, W. E. (1965), Torrans, E. L., and H. P. Clemens. (1981), Torrans, L., and F. Lowell, H. Clemens. (1986), Trautman, Milton B. (1957), Trautman, Milton B. (1981), Trombitskii, I. D. (1984), Trombitsky, I. D. (1987), Tuten, J. S., and J. W. Avault, Jr. (1981), Valenciennes, Achille. (1844), Verigina, I. A. (1976), Wagner, G. (1908), Walburg, C. H. (1964), Walburg, C. H. (1976), Walburg, C. H., and W. R. Nelson. (1966), Walden, Howard T., 2d. (1964), Werner, Robert G. (1976a), Werner, Robert G. (1976b), Werner, Robert G. (1980), Willis, David W. (1979), Willis, David W., and J. B. Owen. (1978), Yashouv, A. (1958), Yurkevich, N. V. (1978),

Ictiobus cyprinellus **X** *Ictiobus niger.*
Margaritov, N. (1988), Williamson, J., and R. O. Smitherman. (1976),

Ictiobus cyprinus Le Sueur.
Forbes, Stephen Alfred., and Robert Earl Richardson. (1920), Jordan, David Starr, and Charles Henry Gilbert. (1884), Jordan, David Starr, and Seth Eugene Meek. (1885), Smith, Philip W. (1979),

Ictiobus damalis.
Jordan, David Starr, and Seth Eugene Meek. (1885),

Ictiobus difformis (Cope).
Jordan, David Starr, and Seth Eugene Meek. (1885), Meek, Seth Eugene. (1894),

Ictiobus elongatus (Meek).
Hubbs, Carl L., and J. D. Black. (1940),

Ictiobus grayi.
Jordan, David Starr, and Seth Eugene Meek. (1885),

Ictiobus labiosus (Meek, 1904).
Villar, José Alvarez del. (1970),

Ictiobus meridionalis (Günther, 1868).
Jordan, David Starr, and Barton Warren Evermann. (1896), Miller, Robert Rush. (1966), Nelson, Joseph S. (1976), Nelson, Joseph S. (1984), Villar, José Alvarez del. (1970),

Ictiobus microstomus (Meek).
Hubbs, Carl L., and J. D. Black. (1940),

Ictiobus niger (Rafinesque, 1820).
Black buffalo.
Adams, L. A. (1931), Andryushchenko, A. I., and T. G. Litvinova. (1978), Bailey, Reeve M., and John E. Fitch, Earl S. Herald, Ernest A. Lachner, C. C. Lindsey, C. Richard Robins, W. B. Scott. (1970), Bailey, Reeve M., and Ernest A. Lachner, C. C. Lindsey, C. Richard Robins, Phil M. Roedel, W. B. Scott, Loren P. Woods. (1966), Bailey, Reeve M., and Gerald R. Smith. (1981), (1954), Barnickol, P. G., and W. C. Starrett. (1951), Becker, George C. (1983), Berner, Lester M. (1948), Blinova, R. D., and A. N. Burlakova, E. M. Zaitseva. (1980), Borges, M. H. (1950), Boschung, Herbert T., Jr., and James D. Williams, Daniel W. Gotshall, David K. Caldwell, Melba C. Caldwell, Carol Nehring, Jordan Verner. (1983), Boyadjiev, A. (1983), Breder, C. M., Jr., and D. E. Rosen. (1966), Buck, D. H., and Frank B. Cross. (1952), Cahn, A. R. (1927), Caraiman, G., and Z. Pogan. (1981),

Carlander, Kenneth D. (1969), Carlander, Kenneth D., and J. W. Parsons. (1949), Carson, R. (1943), Clay, W. M. (1975), Cross, Frank B. (1967), Cross, Frank B., and Joseph T. Collins. (1975), Crossman, E. J., and S. J. Nepszy. (1979), Curry, Kevin D., and Anne Spacie. (1979), Deacon, James Everett. (1960), Douglas, Neil H. (1974), Eastman, Joseph T. (1977), Eastman, Joseph T. (1980), Eddy, Samuel. (1957), Eddy, Samuel. (1969), Elkin, R. E., Jr. (1954), Emery, Lee. (1976), Erokhina, L. V., and V. K. Vinogradov, V. V. Vychegzhanina. (1976), Eschmeyer, R. W., and R. H. Stroud, A. M. Jones. (1944), Fago, Don. (1982), Ferris, Stephen D., and Gregory S. Whitt. (1978), Finnell, Joe C. (1955), Fisher, H. J. (1962), Forbes, Stephen Alfred. (1884), Forbes, Stephen Alfred., and Robert Earl Richardson. (1908), Gammon, J. R. (1973), Georgescu, R., and P. Dascalescu, G. Caraiman. (1984), Giurca, R., and N. Angelescu. (1978), Greer, J. K., and Frank B. Cross. (1956), Hall, Gordon E. (1951), Hall, Gordon E., and R. M. Jenkins. (1953), Hancock, H. M. (1955), Hanson, W. D., and R. S. Campbell. (1963),.Hoffman, Glenn L. (1967), Hubbs, Carl L. (1945), Hubbs, Carl L., and Karl F. Lagler. (1941), Hubbs, Carl L., and Karl F. Lagler. (1947), Hubbs, Carl L., and Karl F. Lagler. (1974), Jenkins, J. T., and H. A. Semken. (1972), Jenkins, Robert M. (1953a), Jenkins, Robert M., and J. C. Finnell. (1957), Jenkins, Robert M., and E. M. Leonard, G. E. Hall. (1952), Jordan, David Starr. (1878a), Koster, William J. (1957), Krumholz, Louis A. (1943), Kurinnyi, S. A. (1984), Lambou, V. W. (1961), Large, T. (1903), Larimore, R. W., and P. W. Smith. (1963), Lee, David S., and Carter R. Gilbert, Charles H. Hocutt, Robert E. Jenkins, Don E. McAllister, Jay R. Stauffer, Jr. (1980), Les, B. L. (1979), Lopinot, Alvin C. (ed.). (1968), Margaritov, N. (1988), McNally, Tom. (1970), Mergo, John C., Jr., and Andrew M. White. (1984), Miller, Rudolph J., and Henry W. Robinson. (1973), Moen, T. E. (1960), Moen, T. E. (1970), Molya, S. P., and P. D. Arikov. (1988), Neff, Nancy A. (1975), Nelson, Edward M. (1948), Nelson, E. W. (1876), Newton, S. H., and C. J. Haskins, J. M. Martin. (1981), Niculescu-Duvaz, M., and R. Giurca, V. Popovici. (1979), O'Donnell, D. J. (1935), Patriarche, M. H. (1953), Pearson, William D., and Louis A. Krumholz (1984), Perry, W. G. (1976), Pflieger, William L. (1971), Pflieger, William L. (1975), Prieto, A., and M. Vinjoy, E. Fajer. (1988), Robins, C. Richard, and Reeve M. Bailey, Carl E. Bond, James R. Brooker, Ernest A. Lachner, Robert N. Lea, W. B. Scott. (1980), Smith, C. Lavett. (1962), Smith, Gerald R. (1981b), Smith, Philip W. (1965), Smith, Philip W. (1979), Sparks, Richard E., and William C. Starrett. (1975), Stevenson, J. H. (1964), Trautman, Milton B. (1957), Trautman, Milton B. (1981), Villar, José Alvarez del. (1970), Walden, Howard T., 2d. (1964), Werner, Robert G. (1976a), Werner, Robert G. (1976b), Yeager, Lee E. (1936),

Ictiobus niger **X** *Ictiobus cyprinellus*
Margaritov, N. (1988),

Ictiobus selene
Jordan, David Starr, and Seth Eugene Meek. (1885),

Ictiobus thomsoni.
Jordan, David Starr, and Seth Eugene Meek. (1885),

Ictiobus timidus.
Jordan, David Starr, and Seth Eugene Meek. (1885),

Ictiobus tumidus.
Jordan, David Starr, and Barton Warren Evermann. (1896), Jordan, David Starr, and Charles Henry Gilbert. (1886),

Ictiobus urus (Agassiz, 1854).
Razor-backed buffalo, Mongrel Buffalo, Round Buffalo.

Adams, L. A. (1928), Blatchley, W. S. (1938), Breder, C. M., Jr., and D. E. Rosen. (1966), Forbes, Stephen Alfred., and Robert Earl Richardson. (1920), Gunter, Gordon. (1938), Jordan, David Starr. (1929), Jordan, David Starr, and Barton Warren Evermann. (1896), Jordan, David Starr, and Barton Warren Evermann. (1905), Jordan, David Starr, and Charles Henry Gilbert. (1884), Meek, Seth Eugene. (1894), Meek, Seth Eugene, and S. F. Hildebrand. (1910), Nelson, Edward M. (1948), Smith, Philip W. (1979),

Ictiobus velifer (Rafinesque, 1820).
Quill-back, skim-back, carp sucker.
Hubbs, Carl L., and J. D. Black. (1940), Jones, David T. (1929), Jordan, David Starr, and Barton Warren Evermann. (1896), Jordan, David Starr, and Charles Henry Gilbert. (1886), Jordan, David Starr, and Seth Eugene Meek. (1885), Meek, Seth Eugene. (1894),

Ictiorus
Eschmeyer, William N. (1990), Opinion 1582. (1990),.

Labeo cyprinus De Kay. 1842.
DeKay, James Ellsworth. (1842), Günther, Albert C. (1868),

Labeo elegans De Kay, 1842.
DeKay, James Ellsworth. (1842), Günther, Albert C. (1868), Jordan, David Starr, and Barton Warren Evermann. (1896),

Labeo elongatus De Kay, 1842.
DeKay, James Ellsworth. (1842), Girard, C. F. (1857), Jordan, David Starr, and Barton Warren Evermann. (1896),

Labeo esopus De Kay, 1842.
DeKay, James Ellsworth. (1842), Günther, Albert C. (1868),

Labeo gibbosus De Kay, 1842.
DeKay, James Ellsworth. (1842), Günther, Albert C. (1868),

Labeo oblongus De Kay, 1842.
DeKay, James Ellsworth. (1842), Günther, Albert C. (1868),

Lagochila Jordan and Brayton, 1877.
Eschmeyer, William N. (1990), Jordan, David Starr. (1923), Jordan, David Starr, and Alembert Winthrop Brayton. (1877), Meek, Seth Eugene. (1894), Miller, Robert Rush. (1958), Nelson, Edward M. (1948), Nelson, Edward M. (1949), Nelson, Joseph S. (1976), Nelson, Joseph S. (1984), Smith, Gerald R. (1966),

Lagochila lacera Jordan and Brayton, 1877.
Harelip Sucker, Hare-Lip Sucker, Split-Mouth Sucker, May Sucker, Pea-Lip Sucker, Rabbit-Mouth sucker, Cutlips.
Bailey, Reeve M., and John E. Fitch, Earl S. Herald, Ernest A. Lachner, C. C. Lindsey, C. Richard Robins, W. B. Scott. (1970), Bailey, Reeve M., and Ernest A. Lachner, C. C. Lindsey, C. Richard Robins, Phil M. Roedel, W. B. Scott, Loren P. Woods. (1966), Bailey, Reeve M., and Gerald R. Smith. (1981), (1954), Blatchley, W. S. (1938), Clay, W. M. (1975), Curry, Kevin D., and Anne Spacie. (1979), Eastman, Joseph T. (1977), Eastman, Joseph T. (1980), Eddy, Samuel. (1969), Forbes, Stephen Alfred., and Robert Earl Richardson. (1920), Hubbs, Carl L., and Karl F. Lagler. (1941), Hubbs, Carl L., and Karl F. Lagler. (1947), Hubbs, Carl L., and Karl F. Lagler. (1974), Jordan, David Starr. (1878b), Jordan, David Starr. (1878d), Jordan, David Starr. (1929), Jordan, David Starr, and Alembert Winthrop Brayton. (1877), Jordan, David Starr, and Barton Warren Evermann.

186

(1896), Jordan, David Starr, and Barton Warren Evermann. (1905), Lee, David S., and Carter R. Gilbert, Charles H. Hocutt, Robert E. Jenkins, Don E. McAllister, Jay R. Stauffer, Jr. (1980), Meek, Seth Eugene. (1894), Miller, Rudolph J., and H. E. Evans. (1965), Nelson, Edward M. (1948), Ono, R. Dana, and James D. Williams, Anne Wagner. (1983), Robins, C. Richard, and Reeve M. Bailey, Carl E. Bond, James R. Brooker, Ernest A. Lachner, Robert N. Lea, W. B. Scott. (1980), Trautman, Milton B. (1957), Trautman, Milton B. (1981), Werner, Robert G. (1976a), Werner, Robert G. (1976b),

Lipomyzon Cope, 1881.
Eschmeyer, William N. (1990), Fowler, Henry Weed. (1914a), Jordan, David Starr. (1923),

Lipomyzon brevirostris Cope, 1881.
Cope, Edward Drinker. (1881), Jordan, David Starr, and Barton Warren Evermann. (1896),

Maxostoma macrolepidotum.
Thompson, Peter. (1980),

Megapharynx Legendre, 1942.
Lee, David S., and Carter R. Gilbert, Charles H. Hocutt, Robert E. Jenkins, Don E. McAllister, Jay R. Stauffer, Jr. (1980), Legendre, Vianney. (1942), Legendre, Vianney. (1943a), Legendre, Vianney. (1943b), Nelson, Edward M. (1948), Nelson, Edward M. (1949),

Megapharynx valenciennesi (Jordan, 1885).
Hubbs, Carl L., and Karl F. Lagler. (1947), Hubbs, Carl L., and Karl F. Lagler. (1974), Legendre, Vianney. (1942),

Megastomatobus Fowler, 1913.
Eschmeyer, William N. (1990), Fowler, Henry Weed. (1914a), Jordan, David Starr. (1923), Nelson, Edward M. (1948), Nelson, Edward M. (1949),

Megastomatobus cyprinella (Valenciennes, 1844).
Gourdhead buffalo, Red-mouth Buffalo, Bigmouth Buffalo. Blatchley, W. S. (1938), Hinks, David. (1943), Hubbs, Carl L., and Karl F. Lagler. (1941), Hubbs, Carl L., and Karl F. Lagler. (1947), Jordan, David Starr. (1929), Krumholz, Louis A. (1943), Nelson, Edward M. (1948), Schoffman, R. J. (1943), Scott, W. B. (1958), Smith, Philip W. (1979), Yashouv, A. (1958),

Megastomatolus cyprinella (Valenciennes, 1844).
Evans, W. A. (1950),

Minomus Girard, 1856.
Eschmeyer, William N. (1990), Girard, C. F. (1857), Jordan, David Starr. (1923), Jordan, David Starr, and Barton Warren Evermann. (1896),

Minomus bairdus Cope, 1872.
Jordan, David Starr, and Barton Warren Evermann. (1896),

Minomus bardus Cope, 1872.
Jordan, David Starr, and Barton Warren Evermann. (1896),

Minomus clarki.
Smith, Gerald R. (1966),

Minomus clarkii.
   Smith, Gerald R. (1966),

Minomus delphinus Cope, 1872.
   Jordan, David Starr, and Barton Warren Evermann. (1896), Smith, Gerald R. (1966),

Minomus insignis Girard, 1857.
   Girard, C. F. (1857), Günther, Albert C. (1868), Jordan, David Starr, and Barton Warren Evermann. (1896),

Minomus jarrovii Cope, 1874.
   Cope, Edward Drinker. (1874c), Cope, Edward Drinker, and H. C. Yarrow. (1875), Jordan, David Starr. (1923), Smith, Gerald R. (1966),

Minomus platyrhynchus Cope, 1874.
   Cope, Edward Drinker. (1874c), Cope, Edward Drinker, and H. C. Yarrow. (1875), Jordan, David Starr, and Barton Warren Evermann. (1896),

Minomus plebius (Baird and Girard, 1855).
   Günther, Albert C. (1868), Smith, Gerald R. (1966),

Minomus plebejus (Baird and Girard, 1855).
   Günther, Albert C. (1868),

Minytrema Jordan, 1878.
   Spotted Suckers.
   Eschmeyer, William N. (1990), Fuiman, Lee A. (1985), Jordan, David Starr. (1878b), Jordan, David Starr. (1878d), Jordan, David Starr. (1923), Meek, Seth Eugene. (1894), Miller, Robert Rush. (1958), Nelson, Edward M. (1948), Nelson, Edward M. (1949), Nelson, Joseph S. (1976), Nelson, Joseph S. (1984), Yeager, Bruce L., and Kenneth J. Semmens. (1987),

Minytrema austrinum (Bean, 1879).
   Jordan, David Starr, and Barton Warren Evermann. (1896), Jordan, David Starr, and Charles Henry Gilbert. (1883),

Minytrema melanops (Rafinesque, 1820).
   Spotted Sucker, Winter Sucker, Striped Sucker.
   Agassiz, John Louis Rodolphe. (1854), Anderson, W. D. (1964), Bailey, Reeve M., and John E. Fitch, Earl S. Herald, Ernest A. Lachner, C. C. Lindsey, C. Richard Robins, W. B. Scott. (1970), Bailey, Reeve M., and Ernest A. Lachner, C. C. Lindsey, C. Richard Robins, Phil M. Roedel, W. B. Scott, Loren P. Woods. (1966), Bailey, Reeve M., and Gerald R. Smith. (1981), (1954), Becker, George C. (1983), Blatchley, W. S. (1938), Boschung, Herbert T., Jr., and James D. Williams, Daniel W. Gotshall, David K. Caldwell, Melba C. Caldwell, Carol Nehring, Jordan Verner. (1983), Branson, Branley A., and Donald L. Batch. (1974), Britton, J. C., and C. E. Murphy. (1977), Bur, M. T. (1976), Buth, Donald G. (1983), Carlander, Kenneth D. (1955), Carlander, Kenneth D. (1969), Chien, Shin Ming, and Wilmer A. Rogers. (1970), Christensen, B. M., and P. K. Wellner, L. N. Gleason. (1982), Christenson, L. M. (1957), Cincotta, Dan A., and Robert L. Miles, Michael E. Hoeft, Gerald E. Lewis. (1986), Clay, W. M. (1975), Combs, D. L., and J. P. Harley, J. C. Williams. (1977), Combs, D. L., and J. C. Williams, J. P. Harley. (1976), Coomer, C. E., Jr., and D. R. Holder, C. D. Swanson. (1977), Cooper, Edwin Lavern. (1983), Cross, Frank B. (1967), Cross, Frank B., and Joseph T. Collins. (1975), Crossman, E. J., and R. G. Ferguson. (1963), Curry, Kevin D., and Anne Spacie. (1979), Douglas, Neil H. (1974), Eastman, Joseph T. (1977), Eastman, Joseph T. (1980), Eddy, Samuel. (1957), Eddy,

Samuel. (1969), Eddy, Samuel, and Kenneth D. Carlander. (1942), Eddy, Samuel, and James C. Underhill. (1974), Elkin, R. E., Jr. (1954), Emery, Lee. (1976), Eshelman, Ralph E. (1975), Evans, James W., and Richard L. Noble. (1979), Fago, Don. (1984b), Fassbender, R. L., and J. J. Weber, L. M. Nelson. (1970), Ferris, Stephen D., and Gregory S. Whitt. (1978), Finnell, Joe C. (1955), Forbes, Stephen Alfred. (1884), Forbes, Stephen Alfred., and Robert Earl Richardson. (1908), Forbes, Stephen Alfred., and Robert Earl Richardson. (1920), Funk, J. L., and R. S. Campbell. (1953), Gleason, Larry N., and B. M. Christensen, Yui Tan Chung. (1983), Greene, C. W. (1935), Hall, Gordon E., and R. M. Jenkins. (1953), Grinham, T., and D. K. Cone. (1990), Harlan, J. R., and E. B. Speaker. (1956), Herald, Earl S. (1967), Herald, Earl S. (1979), Hildebrand, Samuel F., and William C. Schroeder. (1923),.Hoffman, Glenn L. (1967), Hoffman, C. H., and E. W. Surber. (1948), Hogue, J. J., Jr., and J. P. Buchanan. (1977), Hubbs, Carl L., and Karl F. Lagler. (1941), Hubbs, Carl L., and Karl F. Lagler. (1947), Hubbs, Carl L., and Karl F. Lagler. (1974), Hunn, J. B. (1972), Jackson, S. W., Jr. (1954), Jackson, S. W., Jr. (1957), Jackson, S. W., Jr. (1966), Jenkins, Robert M. (1953b), Jenkins, Robert M., and J. C. Finnell. (1957), Jordan, David Starr. (1878a), Jordan, David Starr. (1878b), Jordan, David Starr. (1929), Jordan, David Starr, and Barton Warren Evermann. (1896), Jordan, David Starr, and Barton Warren Evermann. (1905), Jordan, David Starr, and Charles Henry Gilbert. (1883), Krumholz, Louis A. (1943), Lambou, V. W. (1961), Large, T. (1903), Larimore, R. W., and P. W. Smith. (1963), Lee, David S., and Carter R. Gilbert, Charles H. Hocutt, Robert E. Jenkins, Don E. McAllister, Jay R. Stauffer, Jr. (1980), Lopinot, Alvin C. (ed.). (1968), Martin, R. G., and R. S. Campbell. (1953), Maruney, Morris, Jr., and George L. Harp. (1979), McClane, Albert Jules. (1974), McSwain, L. E., and R. M. Gennings. (1972), Meek, Seth Eugene. (1891), Meek, Seth Eugene. (1894), Meek, Seth Eugene, and S. F. Hildebrand. (1910), Miller, Rudolph J., and H. E. Evans. (1965), Miller, Rudolph J., and Henry W. Robinson. (1973), Minckley, W. L. (1963), Minckley, W. L., and R. H. Goodyear, J. E. Craddock. (1964), Nelson, Edward M. (1948), Nelson, E. W. (1876), Noland, W. E. (1951), O'Donnell, D. J. (1935), Parker, B., and P. McKee. (1984a), Pearson, William D., and Louis A. Krumholz (1984), Pflieger, William L. (1971), Pflieger, William L. (1975), Phillips, Gary L., and William D. Schmid, James C. Underhill. (1982), Phillips, Gary L., and James C. Underhill. (1971), Pickens, A. L. (1928), Priegel, G. R. (1967), Rafinesque, Constantine Samuel. (1820a), Roberts, J. R. (1967), Robins, C. Richard, and Reeve M. Bailey, Carl E. Bond, James R. Brooker, Ernest A. Lachner, Robert N. Lea, W. B. Scott. (1980), Rogers, Wilmer A. (1967), Scott, W. B. (1967), Scott, W. B., and E. J. Crossman. (1969), Scott, W. B., and E. J. Crossman. (1973), Shih, M. C., and W. A. Rogers. (1970), Smith, C. G., and W. M. Lewis, H. M. Kaplan. (1952), Smith, C. Lavett. (1986), Smith, Gerald R. (1981b), Smith, Philip W. (1963), Smith, Philip W. (1965), Smith, Philip W. (1968), Smith, Philip W. (1973), Smith, Philip W. (1979), Sterba, Günther. (1983), Swift, Camm, and Ralph W. Yerger, Patrick R. Parrish. (1977), Swingle, W. E. (1965), Trautman, Milton B. (1957), Trautman, Milton B. (1981), Tsuyuki, H., and E. Roberts, R. H. Kerr, J. F. Uthe, L. W. Clarke. (1967), Viosca, Percy, Jr. (1952), 1622, Welter, Wilfred A. (1938), Werner, Robert G. (1976a), Werner, Robert G. (1976b), Werner, Robert G. (1980), White, D. S. (1975), White, D. S. (1977), White, D. S., and K. H. Haag. (1977), Williams, E. H., Jr., and W. A. Rogers. (1982), Williams, E. H., Jr., and W. A. Rogers. (1984), Winger, P. V., and D. P. Schultz, W. W. Johnson. (Undated),

Minytrema shevyrevi.
Sytchevskaya, 1986 Sytchevskaya, E. K. (1986),

Mofoxostoma congestum (Baird and Girard).
Villar, José Alvarez del. (1970),

Moxostoma Rafinesque, 1820.
Red Horse.

Agassiz, John Louis Rodolphe. (1855), Black, J. J. (1984), Branson, Branley A., and George A. Moore. (1962), Buth, Donald G. (1978), Buth, Donald G. (1979a), Buth, Donald G. (1982), Curry, Kevin D., and Anne Spacie. (1984), Donahue, J., and R. Stuckenrath, J. M. Adovasio, et al. (1978), Eschmeyer, William N. (1990), Fowler, Henry Weed. (1914a), Fuiman, Lee A. (1985), Günther, Albert C. (1868), Hocutt, C. H. (1979), Jacobs, K. E., and W. D. Swink. (1983), Jordan, David Starr. (1923), Lagler, Karl F., and John E. Bardach, Robert Rush Miller. (1962), Lowe, T. P., and T. W. May, W. G. Brumbaugh, D. A. Kane. (1985), Massé, G. (1977), Meek, Seth Eugene. (1894), Mergo, John C., Jr., and Andrew M. White. (1984), Miller, Robert Rush. (1958), Moyle, Peter B., and Joseph J. Cech, Jr. (1982), Myers, George Sprague. (1949), Nelson, Edward M. (1948), Nelson, Edward M. (1949), Nelson, Joseph S. (1976), Nelson, Joseph S. (1984), Rafinesque, Constantine Samuel. (1820b), Ramamoorthy, S., and J. W. Moore, L. George. (1985), Raney, Edward C., and Robert M. Roecker. (1947), Richardson, Laurence R. (1942), Roberts, Tyson R. (1973), Robins, C. Richards, and Edward C. Raney. (1956), Robins, C. Richards, and Edward C. Raney. (1957a), Robins, C. Richards, and Edward C. Raney. (1957b), Romer, Alfred Sherwood. (1966), Scott, W. B. (1954), Scott, W. B. (1967), Smith, Gerald R. (1981b), Smith, Michael L., and Ted M. Cavender, Robert R. Miller. (1975), Smith, S. H. (1968), Sterba, Günther. (1983), Swink, W. D., and K. E. Jacobs. (1983), Williams, E. H., Jr., and W. A. Rogers. (1982),

Moxostoma albidum (Girard, 1857).
Jordan, David Starr, and Barton Warren Evermann. (1896), Jordan, David Starr, and Charles Henry Gilbert. (1883),

Moxostoma album Cope, 1870.
Jordan, David Starr. (1878d), Jordan, David Starr, and Barton Warren Evermann. (1896), Jordan, David Starr, and Charles Henry Gilbert. (1883),

Moxostoma alleghaniensis Nichols, 1911.
Nichols, John Treadwell. (1911),

Moxostoma anisurum (Rafinesque, 1820).
Silver redhorse, White-Nosed Sucker.
Atton, F. M., and R. P. Johnson. (1955), Bailey, Reeve M., and John E. Fitch, Earl S. Herald, Ernest A. Lachner, C. C. Lindsey, C. Richard Robins, W. B. Scott. (1970), Bailey, Reeve M., and Ernest A. Lachner, C. C. Lindsey, C. Richard Robins, Phil M. Roedel, W. B. Scott, Loren P. Woods. (1966), Bailey, Reeve M., and Gerald R. Smith. (1981), (1954), Barwick, D. H., and P. L. Hudson. (undated), Becker, George C. (1983), Bensley, B. A. (1915), Beverly-Burton, Mary. (1984), Blatchley, W. S. (1938), Breder, C. M., Jr., and D. E. Rosen. (1966), Bur, M. T. (1976), Buth, Donald G. (1978), Carlander, Kenneth D. (1944b), Carlander, Kenneth D. (1948), Carlander, Kenneth D. (1969), Clay, W. M. (1975), Cooper, Edwin Lavern. (1983), Crossman, E. J. (1976), Curry, Kevin D., and Anne Spacie. (1979), Dechtiar, A. O. (1972a), Dechtiar, A. O. (1972b), Eastman, Joseph T. (1977), Eastman, Joseph T. (1980), Eddy, Samuel. (1957), Eddy, Samuel. (1969), Eddy, Samuel, and Roy C. Tasker, James C. Underhill. (1972), Eddy, Samuel, and James C. Underhill. (1974), Emery, Lee. (1976), Fago, Don. (1984b), Fish, M. P. (1932), Forbes, Stephen Alfred. (1884), Forbes, Stephen Alfred., and Robert Earl Richardson. (1908), Forbes, Stephen Alfred., and Robert Earl Richardson. (1920), Fowler, Henry Weed. (1945), Grinham, T., and D. K. Cone. (1990), Haas, Robert L. (1943), Harlan, J. R., and E. B. Speaker. (1956), Harrison, H. M. (1950), Henderson, N. E., and R. E. Peter. (1969),.Hoffman, Glenn L. (1967), Hinks, David. (1943), Hubbs, Carl L., and Karl F. Lagler. (1941), Hubbs, Carl L., and Karl F. Lagler. (1947), Hubbs, Carl L., and Karl F. Lagler. (1974), Hubert, Wayne A., and Dennis N. Schmitt. (1985), Jenkins, Robert E. (1970), Jordan, David Starr. (1878a), Jordan, David Starr. (1929), Jordan, David Starr, and Barton Warren Evermann. (1896), Jordan, David Starr, and Barton Warren Evermann.

(1905), Jordan, David Starr, and Charles Henry Gilbert. (1883), Keleher, J. J., and B. Kooyman. (1957), Kennicott, Robert. (1855), Krumholz, Louis A. (1943), Lagler, Karl F., and John E. Bardach, Robert Rush Miller. (1962), Large, T. (1903), Larimore, R. W., and P. W. Smith. (1963), Lee, David S., and Carter R. Gilbert, Charles H. Hocutt, Robert E. Jenkins, Don E. McAllister, Jay R. Stauffer, Jr. (1980), McAllister, Don E., and Brian W. Coad. (1974), McClane, Albert Jules. (1974), McLain, A. L., and B. R. Smith, H. H. Moore. (1965), Meek, Seth Eugene, and S. F. Hildebrand. (1910), Mergo, John C., Jr., and Andrew M. White. (1982), Meyer, W. H. (1961), Meyer, W. H. (1962), Miller, Rudolph J., and H. E. Evans. (1965), Minckley, W. L., and R. H. Goodyear, J. E. Craddock. (1964), Morgan, R. P., II, and R. E. Smith, Jr., J. R. Stauffer, Jr. (1983), Nelson, Edward M. (1948), Nelson, E. W. (1876), Paetz, Martin J., and Joseph S. Nelson. (1970), Pearson, William D., and Louis A. Krumholz (1984), Pflieger, William L. (1971), Pflieger, William L. (1975), Phillips, Gary L., and William D. Schmid, James C. Underhill. (1982), Purkett, C. A., Jr. (1958b), Rafinesque, Constantine Samuel. (1820a), Richardson, Laurence R. (1938), Robins, C. Richard, and Reeve M. Bailey, Carl E. Bond, James R. Brooker, Ernest A. Lachner, Robert N. Lea, W. B. Scott. (1980), Scott, W. B. (1954), Scott, W. B. (1958), Scott, W. B. (1967), Scott, W. B., and E. J. Crossman. (1969), Scott, W. B., and E. J. Crossman. (1973), Seegert, Greg. (1986), Sibley, C. K. (1929), Smith, C. G. (1977), Smith, C. Lavett. (1986), Smith, Gerald R. (1966), Smith, Gerald R. (1981b), Smith, Hugh M. (1893), Smith, Philip W. (1965), Smith, Philip W. (1973), Smith, Philip W. (1979), Toner, G. C. (1933), Trautman, Milton B. (1957), Trautman, Milton B. (1981), Vladykov, Vadim D. (1942), Welter, Wilfred A. (1938), Werner, Robert G. (1976a), Werner, Robert G. (1976b), Werner, Robert G. (1980), Whitaker, J. O., and D. C. Wallace. (1966), Wooding, Frederick H. (1959),

Moxostoma anisurus (Rafinesque, 1820).
Jordan, David Starr, and Barton Warren Evermann. (1896),

Moxostoma ariommum Robins and Raney, 1956.
Bigeye jumprock.
Bailey, Reeve M., and John E. Fitch, Earl S. Herald, Ernest A. Lachner, C. C. Lindsey, C. Richard Robins, W. B. Scott. (1970), Bailey, Reeve M., and Ernest A. Lachner, C. C. Lindsey, C. Richard Robins, Phil M. Roedel, W. B. Scott, Loren P. Woods. (1966), Buth, Donald G. (1978), Eddy, Samuel. (1969), Jenkins, Robert E. (1970), Lee, David S., and Carter R. Gilbert, Charles H. Hocutt, Robert E. Jenkins, Don E. McAllister, Jay R. Stauffer, Jr. (1980), Robins, C. Richard. (1961), Robins, C. Richard, and Reeve M. Bailey, Carl E. Bond, James R. Brooker, Ernest A. Lachner, Robert N. Lea, W. B. Scott. (1980), Robins, C. Richards, and Edward C. Raney. (1956),

Moxostoma (Thoburnia) atripinne Bailey, 1959.
Blackfin sucker.
Bailey, Reeve M. (1959), Bailey, Reeve M., and John E. Fitch, Earl S. Herald, Ernest A. Lachner, C. C. Lindsey, C. Richard Robins, W. B. Scott. (1970), Bailey, Reeve M., and Ernest A. Lachner, C. C. Lindsey, C. Richard Robins, Phil M. Roedel, W. B. Scott, Loren P. Woods. (1966), Carlander, Kenneth D. (1969), Clay, W. M. (1975), Eddy, Samuel. (1969), Jenkins, Robert E. (1970), Lee, David S., and Carter R. Gilbert, Charles H. Hocutt, Robert E. Jenkins, Don E. McAllister, Jay R. Stauffer, Jr. (1980), Robins, C. Richard, and Reeve M. Bailey, Carl E. Bond, James R. Brooker, Ernest A. Lachner, Robert N. Lea, W. B. Scott. (1980), Timmons, T. J., and J. S. Ramsey. (1983), Timmons, T. J., and W. A. Rogers. (1977),

Moxostoma aureolum (Le Sueur, 1817).
Common Red-Horse, Mullet, White Sucker, Large-Scaled Sucker.
Blatchley, W. S. (1938), Carlander, Kenneth D. (1948), Carlander, Kenneth D., and Lloyd L. Smith, Jr. (1945), Comeau, Napoléon A. (1915), Cross, Frank B., and Artie L. Metcalf.

(1963), Dugal, L. C. (1962), Dymond, J. R., and W. B. Scott. (1941), Forbes, Stephen Alfred., and Robert Earl Richardson. (1920), Friedrich, George W. (1933), Greenbank, J. (1957), Grinham, T., and D. K. Cone. (1990), Haas, Robert L. (1943), Hall, Gordon E., and George A. Moore. (1954), Hankinson, T. L. (1923), Hinks, David. (1943), Hubbs, Carl L., and Karl F. Lagler. (1941), Hubbs, Carl L., and Karl F. Lagler. (1947), Jordan, David Starr. (1929), Jordan, David Starr, and Barton Warren Evermann. (1896), Jordan, David Starr, and Barton Warren Evermann. (1905), Keleher, J. J., and B. Kooyman. (1957), Krumholz, Louis A. (1943), La Monte, Francesca. (1958), Lantz, A. W. (1948b), Larimore, R. W., and P. W. Smith. (1963), Lindeborg, R. G. (1941), Lower, A. R. M. (1915), Meek, Seth Eugene, and S. F. Hildebrand. (1910), Minckley, W. L., and Frank B. Cross. (1960), Moore, G. A., and Frank B. Cross. (1950), Nelson, Edward M. (1948), Nigrelli, R. F. (1948), Reighard, Jacob E. (1920), Riggs, C. D., and G. A. Moore. (1963), Robins, C. Richards, and Edward C. Raney. (1957a), Scott, W. B. (1954), Scott, W. B. (1958), Shelford, Victor E. (1911a), Shelford, Victor E. (1937), Simon, James R. (1946), Smith, Philip W. (1979), Trautman, Milton B. (1981), Vladykov, Vadim D. (1933), Vladykov, Vadim D. (1942), Walters, Vladimir. (1953), Walters, V. (1955), Weed, Alfred Cleveland. (1921), Wooding, Frederick H. (1959),

Moxostoma aureolum pisolabrum Trautman and Martin, 1951. Deacon, James Everett. (1960), Riggs, C. D., and G. A. Moore. (1963), Trautman, Milton B., and R. G. Martin. (1951),

Moxostoma aureolus (Le Sueur, 1817).
   Goode, C. Brown, and Theodore Nicholas Gill. (1903),

Moxostoma austrinum (Bean, 1879).
West Mexican redhorse.
   Buth, Donald G. (1978), Jenkins, Robert E. (1970), Jordan, David Starr, and Barton Warren Evermann. (1896), Lee, David S., and Carter R. Gilbert, Charles H. Hocutt, Robert E. Jenkins, Don E. McAllister, Jay R. Stauffer, Jr. (1980), Minckley, W. L., and Dean A. Hendrickson, Carl E. Bond. (1986),

Moxostoma austrinum austrinum (Bean, 1879).
   Villar, José Alvarez del. (1970),

Moxostoma austrinum milleri Robins and Raney, 1957.
   Buth, Donald G. (1978), Lee, David S., and Carter R. Gilbert, Charles H. Hocutt, Robert E. Jenkins, Don E. McAllister, Jay R. Stauffer, Jr. (1980), Robins, C. Richards, and Edward C. Raney. (1957b), Villar, José Alvarez del. (1970),

Moxostoma breviceps (Cope, 1870).
Short-headed Red-Horse.
   Bailey, Reeve M., and Ernest A. Lachner, C. C. Lindsey, C. Richard Robins, Phil M. Roedel, W. B. Scott, Loren P. Woods. (1966), Blatchley, W. S. (1938), Breder, C. M., Jr., and D. E. Rosen. (1966), Carlander, Kenneth D. (1969), Cope, Edward Drinker. (1870), Eddy, Samuel. (1957), Eddy, Samuel. (1969), Forbes, Stephen Alfred., and Robert Earl Richardson. (1920), Grinham, T., and D. K. Cone. (1990),.Hoffman, Glenn L. (1967), Jordan, David Starr, and Barton Warren Evermann. (1896), Jordan, David Starr, and Barton Warren Evermann. (1905), Larimore, R. W., and P. W. Smith. (1963), Meek, Seth Eugene, and S. F. Hildebrand. (1910), Miller, Rudolph J., and H. E. Evans. (1965), Minckley, W. L. (1963), Minckley, W. L., and R. H. Goodyear, J. E. Craddock. (1964), Riggs, C. D., and G. A. Moore. (1963), Robins, C. Richards, and Edward C. Raney. (1957a), Shelford, Victor E. (1911a), Shelford, Victor E. (1937), Smith, Philip W. (1979), Trautman, Milton B. (1957), Ward, C. M. (1960), Whitaker, J. O., and D. C. Wallace. (1966),

Moxostoma bucco (Cope, 1872).
>Jordan, David Starr, and Barton Warren Evermann. (1896), Jordan, David Starr, and Charles Henry Gilbert. (1883),

Moxostoma campbelli Girard, 1857.
>Girard, C. F. (1857), Günther, Albert C. (1868), Jordan, David Starr, and Barton Warren Evermann. (1896),

Moxostoma carinatum (Cope, 1870).
>**River redhorse.**
>Anonymous. (1965a), Bailey, Reeve M., and John E. Fitch, Earl S. Herald, Ernest A. Lachner, C. C. Lindsey, C. Richard Robins, W. B. Scott. (1970), Bailey, Reeve M., and Ernest A. Lachner, C. C. Lindsey, C. Richard Robins, Phil M. Roedel, W. B. Scott, Loren P. Woods. (1966), Bailey, Reeve M., and Gerald R. Smith. (1981), (1954), Becker, George C. (1976), Becker, George C. (1983), Boschung, Herbert T., Jr., and James D. Williams, Daniel W. Gotshall, David K. Caldwell, Melba C. Caldwell, Carol Nehring, Jordan Verner. (1983), Buth, Donald G. (1978), Clay, W. M. (1975), Cooper, Edwin Lavern. (1983), Cope, Edward Drinker. (1870), Cross, Frank B. (1967), Cross, Frank B., and Joseph T. Collins. (1975), Curry, Kevin D., and Anne Spacie. (1979), Douglas, Neil H. (1974), Eastman, Joseph T. (1977), Eddy, Samuel. (1957), Eddy, Samuel. (1969), Eddy, Samuel, and James C. Underhill. (1974), Elkin, R. E., Jr. (1954), Fago, Don. (1982), Fago, Don. (1984b), Finnell, Joe C. (1955), Forbes, Stephen Alfred. (1884), Forbes, Stephen Alfred. (1890), Forbes, Stephen Alfred., and Robert Earl Richardson. (1908), Gerking, Shelby D. (1945), Guilday, J. E., and H. W. Hamilton, E. Anderson, et al. (1978), Hackney, P. A., and W. M. Tatum, S. L. Spencer. (1968), Hall, Gordon E., and R. M. Jenkins. (1953), Hall, Gordon E., and George A. Moore. (1954), Howell, W. Mike, and David E. Butts. (1983), Hubbs, Carl L., and Karl F. Lagler. (1974), Jackson, S. W., Jr. (1954), Jacobs, K. E., and W. D. Swink. (1983), Jenkins, Robert E. (1970), Jenkins, Robert M. (1953b), Jordan, David Starr. (1878a), Large, T. (1903), Lee, David S., and Carter R. Gilbert, Charles H. Hocutt, Robert E. Jenkins, Don E. McAllister, Jay R. Stauffer, Jr. (1980), Lopinot, Alvin C., and Philip W. Smith. (1973), Martin, R. G., and R. S. Campbell. (1953), McAllister, Don E., and Brian W. Coad. (1974), Miller, Rudolph J., and Henry W. Robinson. (1973), Mills, Paul A., Jr., and Charles H. Hocutt, Jay R. Stauffer, Jr. (1978), Nelson, E. W. (1876), O'Donnell, D. J. (1935), Parker, B. J. (1988), Parker, B., and P. McKee. (1984b), Patriarche, M. H. (1953), Pearson, William D., and Louis A. Krumholz (1984), Pflieger, William L. (1971), Pflieger, William L. (1975), Phillips, Gary L., and William D. Schmid, James C. Underhill. (1982), Phillips, Gary L., and James C. Underhill. (1971), Platt, D. R., and Frank B. Cross, D. Distler, O. S. Fent, E. R. Hall, M. Terman, J. Zimmerman, J. Walstrom. (1973), Purkett, C. A., Jr. (1958b), Robins, C. Richard, and Reeve M. Bailey, Carl E. Bond, James R. Brooker, Ernest A. Lachner, Robert N. Lea, W. B. Scott. (1980), Robins, C. Richards, and Edward C. Raney. (1957a), Rogers, Wilmer A. (1969), Roosa, D. M. (1977), Scott, W. B. (1958), Scott, W. B. (1967), Scott, W. B., and E. J. Crossman. (1969), Scott, W. B., and E. J. Crossman. (1973), Seegert, Greg. (1986), Smith, C. Lavett. (1986), Smith, Philip W. (1965), Smith, Philip W. (1973), Smith, Philip W. (1979), Swingle, W. E. (1965), Tatum, W. M., and P. A. Hackney. (1973), Trautman, Milton B. (1957), Trautman, Milton B. (1981), Ward, C. M. (1960), Werner, Robert G. (1976a), Werner, Robert G. (1976b), Werner, Robert G. (1980), White, A. M., and Milton B. Trautman. (1981), Williams, E. H., Jr. (1978), Yerger, R. W., and R. D. Suttkus. (1962), Yoder, Chris O., and Raymond A. Beaumier. (1986),

Moxostoma carinatus.
>Scott, W. B. (1954),

Moxostoma carpio (Rafinesque, 1820).
> Jordan, David Starr, and Barton Warren Evermann. (1896), Jordan, David Starr, and Charles Henry Gilbert. (1883), Smith, Philip W. (1979),

Moxostoma cervinum (Cope, 1868).
> **Black jumprock.**
> Bailey, Reeve M., and John E. Fitch, Earl S. Herald, Ernest A. Lachner, C. C. Lindsey, C. Richard Robins, W. B. Scott. (1970), Bailey, Reeve M., and Ernest A. Lachner, C. C. Lindsey, C. Richard Robins, Phil M. Roedel, W. B. Scott, Loren P. Woods. (1966), Boschung, Herbert T., Jr., and James D. Williams, Daniel W. Gotshall, David K. Caldwell, Melba C. Caldwell, Carol Nehring, Jordan Verner. (1983), Buth, Donald G. (1978), Eddy, Samuel. (1969), Ferris, Stephen D., and Gregory S. Whitt. (1978), Jenkins, Robert E. (1970), Jordan, David Starr. (1878d), Jordan, David Starr, and Barton Warren Evermann. (1896), Jordan, David Starr, and Charles Henry Gilbert. (1883), Lee, David S., and Carter R. Gilbert, Charles H. Hocutt, Robert E. Jenkins, Don E. McAllister, Jay R. Stauffer, Jr. (1980), Pickens, A. L. (1928), Raney, Edward C., and Ernest A. Lachner. (1946a), Robins, C. Richard, and Reeve M. Bailey, Carl E. Bond, James R. Brooker, Ernest A. Lachner, Robert N. Lea, W. B. Scott. (1980),

Moxostoma claviformis Girard, 1857.
> Girard, C. F. (1857), Günther, Albert C. (1868),

Moxostoma collapsum (Cope, 1870).
> **Small-Mouthed Red Horse.**
> Bailey, Reeve M., and Ernest A. Lachner, C. C. Lindsey, C. Richard Robins, Phil M. Roedel, W. B. Scott, Loren P. Woods. (1966), Eddy, Samuel. (1969), Fowler, Henry Weed. (1945), Jordan, David Starr. (1929), Jordan, David Starr, and Barton Warren Evermann. (1896), Miller, Rudolph J., and H. E. Evans. (1965), Smith, Gerald R. (1966), Smith, Hugh M. (1893),

Moxostoma congestum (Baird and Girard, 1855).
> **Gray redhorse, Texas Red Horse.**
> Bailey, Reeve M., and John E. Fitch, Earl S. Herald, Ernest A. Lachner, C. C. Lindsey, C. Richard Robins, W. B. Scott. (1970), Bailey, Reeve M., and Ernest A. Lachner, C. C. Lindsey, C. Richard Robins, Phil M. Roedel, W. B. Scott, Loren P. Woods. (1966), Buth, Donald G. (1978), Carlander, Kenneth D. (1969), Cowley, D. E., and J. E. Sublette. (1989), Dietz, E. M. C., and K. C. Jurgens. (1963), Eddy, Samuel. (1957), Eddy, Samuel. (1969), Ferris, Stephen D., and Gregory S. Whitt. (1978), Fowler, Henry Weed. (1904), Jenkins, Robert E. (1970), Jordan, David Starr, and Barton Warren Evermann. (1896), Koster, William J. (1957), Lee, David S., and Carter R. Gilbert, Charles H. Hocutt, Robert E. Jenkins, Don E. McAllister, Jay R. Stauffer, Jr. (1980), Martin, R. F. (1986), Nelson, Joseph S. (1976), Nelson, Joseph S. (1984), Robins, C. Richard, and Reeve M. Bailey, Carl E. Bond, James R. Brooker, Ernest A. Lachner, Robert N. Lea, W. B. Scott. (1980), Robins, C. Richards, and Edward C. Raney. (1957a), Robinson, Dorthea Trevino. (1959), Xiong Quanimo. (1988),

Moxostoma congestum albidum Robins and Raney, 1975.
> Lee, David S., and Carter R. Gilbert, Charles H. Hocutt, Robert E. Jenkins, Don E. McAllister, Jay R. Stauffer, Jr. (1980), Villar, José Alvarez del. (1970),

Moxostoma congestum congestum (Baird and Girard, 1854).
> Lee, David S., and Carter R. Gilbert, Charles H. Hocutt, Robert E. Jenkins, Don E. McAllister, Jay R. Stauffer, Jr. (1980), Villar, José Alvarez del. (1970),

Moxostoma conus (Cope, 1870).

Jordan, David Starr. (1878d), Jordan, David Starr, and Barton Warren Evermann. (1896), Jordan, David Starr, and Charles Henry Gilbert. (1883),

Moxostoma coregonus (Cope).
Blue Mullet.
Bailey, Reeve M., and Ernest A. Lachner, C. C. Lindsey, C. Richard Robins, Phil M. Roedel, W. B. Scott, Loren P. Woods. (1966), Eddy, Samuel. (1969), Jordan, David Starr. (1878d), Jordan, David Starr, and Barton Warren Evermann. (1896), Jordan, David Starr, and Charles Henry Gilbert. (1883), Miller, Rudolph J., and H. E. Evans. (1965), Robins, C. Richards, and Edward C. Raney. (1957a),

Moxostoma crassilabre (Cope, 1870).
Golden Mullet.
Fowler, Henry Weed. (1945), Jordan, David Starr. (1890), Jordan, David Starr. (1929), Jordan, David Starr, and Barton Warren Evermann. (1896), Jordan, David Starr, and Barton Warren Evermann. (1905), Jordan, David Starr, and Charles Henry Gilbert. (1883), Smith, Hugh M. (1893),

Moxostoma duquesnei (Le Sueur, 1817).
Black redhorse, Common red horse, mullet, Allegheny Red Horse.
Bailey, Reeve M., and John E. Fitch, Earl S. Herald, Ernest A. Lachner, C. C. Lindsey, C. Richard Robins, W. B. Scott. (1970), Bailey, Reeve M., and Ernest A. Lachner, C. C. Lindsey, C. Richard Robins, Phil M. Roedel, W. B. Scott, Loren P. Woods. (1966), Bailey, Reeve M., and Gerald R. Smith. (1981), (1954), Bauer, Bruce H., and Branley A. Branson, Strant T. Colwell. (1978), Becker, George C. (1983), Boschung, Herbert T., Jr., and James D. Williams, Daniel W. Gotshall, David K. Caldwell, Melba C. Caldwell, Carol Nehring, Jordan Verner. (1983), Bowman, M. L. (1954), Bowman, M. L. (1959), Bowman, M. L. (1970), Branson, Branley A., and Donald L. Batch. (1974), Buth, Donald G. (1978), Buth, Donald G. (1983), Carlander, Kenneth D. (1969), Clay, W. M. (1975), Cooper, Edwin Lavern. (1983), Cross, Frank B. (1967), Cross, Frank B., and Joseph T. Collins. (1975), Curry, Kevin D., and Anne Spacie. (1979), Curry, Kevin D., and Anne Spacie. (1984), Eastman, Joseph T. (1977), Eddy, Samuel. (1957), Eddy, Samuel. (1969), Eddy, Samuel, and James C. Underhill. (1974), Emery, Lee. (1976), Evermann, Barton Warren, and W. C. Kendall. (1895), Ferris, Stephen D., and Gregory S. Whitt. (1978), Forbes, Stephen Alfred., and Robert Earl Richardson. (1908), Fowler, Henry Weed. (1945), Funk, J. L. (1957), Gale, N. L. and B. G. Wixson. (1986), Gilbert, Charles Henry. (1891), Greene, C. W. (1935), Guilday, J. E., and H. W. Hamilton, E. Anderson, et al. (1978), Hall, Gordon E., and R. M. Jenkins. (1953),.Hoffman, Glenn L. (1967), Jackson, S. W., Jr. (1966), Jenkins, Robert E. (1970), Kennicott, Robert. (1855), Kott, E., and R. E. Jenkins, G. Humphreys. (1979), Larimore, R. W., and P. W. Smith. (1963), Lee, David S., and Carter R. Gilbert, Charles H. Hocutt, Robert E. Jenkins, Don E. McAllister, Jay R. Stauffer, Jr. (1980), Mackiewicz, J. S. (1972), Marin, R. G., and R. S. Campbell. (1953), Martin, R. G., and R. S. Campbell. (1953), Meek, Seth Eugene. (1894), Miller, Rudolph J., and Henry W. Robinson. (1973), Mills, Paul A., Jr., and Charles H. Hocutt, Jay R. Stauffer, Jr. (1978), Minckley, W. L., and R. H. Goodyear, J. E. Craddock. (1964), Moyle, J. B. (1975), Patriarche, M. H. (1953), Patriarche, M. H., and R. S. Campbell. (1958), Pearson, William D., and Louis A. Krumholz (1984), Pflieger, William L. (1971), Pflieger, William L. (1975), Phillips, Gary L., and William D. Schmid, James C. Underhill. (1982), Phillips, Gary L., and James C. Underhill. (1971), Purkett, C. A., Jr. (1958b), Robins, C. Richard, and Reeve M. Bailey, Carl E. Bond, James R. Brooker, Ernest A. Lachner, Robert N. Lea, W. B. Scott. (1980), Roosa, D. M. (1977), Schmitt, Christopher J., and F. James Dwyer, Susan E. Finger. (1984), Schmitt, Christopher J., and S. E. Finger. (1987), Scott, W. B. (1958), Scott, W. B. (1967), Scott, W. B., and E. J. Crossman. (1969), Scott, W. B., and E. J. Crossman. (1973), Seegert, Greg. (1986), Sibley, C. K. (1929), Smith, C. G. (1977), Smith, C. Lavett. (1986), Smith, Gerald R. (1963), Smith, Philip W. (1965), Smith, Philip W. (1973), Smith, Philip

195

W. (1979), Trautman, Milton B. (1957), Trautman, Milton B. (1981), Uyeno, Teruya, and Robert Rush Miller. (1963), Ward, C. M. (1960), Werner, Robert G. (1976a), Werner, Robert G. (1976b), Werner, Robert G. (1980), Yerger, R. W., and R. D. Suttkus. (1962),

Moxostoma duquesni (Le Sueur, 1817).
Black redhorse.
Holey, M., and B. Hollender, M. Imhof, R. Jesien, R. Konopacky, M. Toneys, D. Coble. (1980),

Moxostoma duquesnii (Le Sueur, 1817).
Allegheny Red Horse.
Hubbs, Carl L., and Karl F. Lagler. (1947), Hubbs, Carl L., and Karl F. Lagler. (1974), Jordan, David Starr. (1929), Miller, Rudolph J., and H. E. Evans. (1965), Nelson, Edward M. (1948), Scott, W. B. (1954),

Moxostoma duquesnii duquesnii (Le Sueur, 1817).
Black redhorse.
Haas, Robert L. (1943), Hubbs, Carl L., and Karl F. Lagler. (1941), Raney, Edward C. (1939),

Moxostoma erythrurum (Rafinesque, 1818).
Golden redhorse.
Aliff, J.U., and D. Smith, H. Lucas. (1977), Amin, O. M. (1981), Amin, Omar M. (1986b), Anonymous. (1978), Anonymous. (1981), Bailey, Reeve M., and Marvin O. Allum. (1962), Bailey, Reeve M., and John E. Fitch, Earl S. Herald, Ernest A. Lachner, C. C. Lindsey, C. Richard Robins, W. B. Scott. (1970), Bailey, Reeve M., and Ernest A. Lachner, C. C. Lindsey, C. Richard Robins, Phil M. Roedel, W. B. Scott, Loren P. Woods. (1966), Bailey, Reeve M., and Gerald R. Smith. (1981), (1954), Bauer, Bruce H., and Branley A. Branson, Strant T. Colwell. (1978), Becker, George C. (1983), Beverly-Burton, Mary. (1984), Boschung, Herbert T., Jr., and James D. Williams, Daniel W. Gotshall, David K. Caldwell, Melba C. Caldwell, Carol Nehring, Jordan Verner. (1983), Branson, Branley A., and Donald L. Batch. (1974), Breder, C. M., Jr., and D. E. Rosen. (1966), Brown, E. H., Jr. (1960), Bur, M. T. (1976), Buth, Donald G. (1978), Buth, Donald G. (1983), Call, R. E. (1887), Carlander, Kenneth D. (1969), Clarke, R. F., and J. W. Clarke. (1984), Clay, W. M. (1975), Combs, D. L., and J. P. Harley, J. C. Williams. (1977), Combs, D. L., and J. C. Williams, J. P. Harley. (1976), Cooper, Edwin Lavern. (1983), Cross, Frank B. (1967), Cross, Frank B., and Joseph T. Collins. (1975), Curry, Kevin D., and Anne Spacie. (1979), Curry, Kevin D., and Anne Spacie. (1984), Deacon, James Everett. (1960), Deacon, James Everett. (1961), Dechtiar, A. O. (1972a), Dechtiar, A. O. (1972b), Dorkin, John L., Jr. (1980), Eastman, Joseph T. (1977), Eastman, Joseph T. (1980), Eddy, Samuel. (1957), Eddy, Samuel. (1969), Eddy, Samuel, and Roy C. Tasker, James C. Underhill. (1972), Eddy, Samuel, and James C. Underhill. (1974), Elkin, R. E., Jr. (1954), Emery, Lee. (1976), Eschmeyer, R. W. (1942), Eschmeyer, R. W., and R. H. Stroud, A. M. Jones. (1944), Fago, Don. (1984b), Fernholz, W. B., and V. E. Crawley. (1977), Ferris, Stephen D., and Gregory S. Whitt. (1978), Finnell, Joe C. (1955), Forbes, Stephen Alfred. (1884), Forbes, Stephen Alfred., and Robert Earl Richardson. (1908), Fowler, Henry Weed. (1945), Franzin, W. G., and B. R. Parker, S. M. Harbicht. (1986), Fredrickson, L. H., and M. J. Ulmer. (1965), Fuiman, Lee A., and D. C. Witman. (1979), Funk, J. L. (1957), Gammon, J. R. (1973), Gammon, J. R. (1977), Gerking, Shelby D. (1953), Greene, C. W. (1935), Greer, J. K., and Frank B. Cross. (1956), Guilday, J. E., and H. W. Hamilton, E. Anderson, et al. (1978), Hall, Gordon E., and George A. Moore. (1954), Hankinson, T. L. (1932), Hanson, W. D., and R. S. Campbell. (1963), Hargis, H. L. (1966), Harrison, H. M. (1950),.Hoffman, Glenn L. (1967), Houser, A. (1960), Hubbs, Carl L., and Karl F. Lagler. (1941), Hubbs, Carl L., and Karl F. Lagler. (1947), Hubbs, Carl L., and Karl F. Lagler. (1974), Jackson, S. W., Jr. (1954), Jackson, S. W., Jr. (1966), Jenkins, Robert E. (1970), Jenkins, Robert M.,

and J. C. Finnell. (1957), Jenkins, Robert M., and E. M. Leonard, G. E. Hall. (1952), Jordan, David Starr. (1878a), Krumholz, Louis A. (1943), Krumholz, Louis A. (1956), Lagler, Karl F., and John E. Bardach, Robert Rush Miller. (1962), Large, T. (1903), Larimore, R. W., and P. W. Smith. (1963), Layher, W. G., and K. L. Brunson. (1986), Lee, David S., and Carter R. Gilbert, Charles H. Hocutt, Robert E. Jenkins, Don E. McAllister, Jay R. Stauffer, Jr. (1980), Lewis, W. M. (1957), Lewis, W. M., and D. Elder. (1953), Lopinot, Alvin C. (1966a), Mackiewicz, J. S. (1972), Marenchin, Ginger Lee, and David M. Sever. (1981), Marin, R. G., and R. S. Campbell. (1953), Martin, R. E., and S. I. Auerbach, D. J. Nelson. (1964), Maruney, Morris, Jr., and George L. Harp. (1979), Maurakis, Eugene G., and William S. Woolcott. (1984), Meek, Seth Eugene. (1891), Meyer, W. H. (1962), Miller, Rudolph J., and H. E. Evans. (1965), Miller, Rudolph J., and Henry W. Robinson. (1973), Mills, Paul A., Jr., and Charles H. Hocutt, Jay R. Stauffer, Jr. (1978), Minckley, W. L. (1963), Minckley, W. L., and R. H. Goodyear, J. E. Craddock. (1964), Morgan, R. P., II, and R. E. Smith, Jr., J. R. Stauffer, Jr. (1983), Nelson, Edward M. (1948), Nelson, E. W. (1876), O'Donnell, D. J. (1935), Page, Lawrence M. (1982), Patriarche, M. H., and R. S. Campbell. (1958), Pearson, William D., and Louis A. Krumholz (1984), Pflieger, William L. (1971), Pflieger, William L. (1975), Phillips, Gary L., and William D. Schmid, James C. Underhill. (1982), Purkett, C. A., Jr. (1958b), Rafinesque, Constantine Samuel. (1818b), Raney, Edward C. (1952), Reighard, Jacob E. (1920), Roach, L. S. (1948b), Robins, C. Richard, and Reeve M. Bailey, Carl E. Bond, James R. Brooker, Ernest A. Lachner, Robert N. Lea, W. B. Scott. (1980), Schmitt, Christopher J., and F. James Dwyer, Susan E. Finger. (1984), Scott, W. B. (1954), Scott, W. B. (1958), Scott, W. B. (1967), Scott, W. B., and E. J. Crossman. (1969), Scott, W. B., and E. J. Crossman. (1973), Seegert, Greg. (1986), Smith, C. G. (1977), Smith, C. Lavett. (1986), Smith, Gerald R. (1963), Smith, Gerald R. (1981b), Smith, Philip W. (1965), Smith, Philip W. (1973), Smith, Philip W. (1979), Swingle, W. E. (1965), Trautman, Milton B. (1957), Trautman, Milton B. (1981), Uthe, J. F. (1965), Ward, C. M. (1960), Werner, Robert G. (1976a), Werner, Robert G. (1976b), Werner, Robert G. (1980), Xiong Quanimo. (1988), Zabik, M. E., and B. Olson, T. M. Johnson. (1978),

Moxostoma fungidens Sytchevskaya, 1986.
Sytchevskaya, E. K. (1986),

Moxostoma hamiltoni (Raney and Lachner, 1946).
   Rustyside sucker.
   Bailey, Reeve M., and John E. Fitch, Earl S. Herald, Ernest A. Lachner, C. C. Lindsey, C. Richard Robins, W. B. Scott. (1970), Bailey, Reeve M., and Ernest A. Lachner, C. C. Lindsey, C. Richard Robins, Phil M. Roedel, W. B. Scott, Loren P. Woods. (1966), Buth, Donald G. (1977a), Buth, Donald G. (1978), Eddy, Samuel. (1969), Jenkins, Robert E. (1970), Lee, David S., and Carter R. Gilbert, Charles H. Hocutt, Robert E. Jenkins, Don E. McAllister, Jay R. Stauffer, Jr. (1980), Robins, C. Richard. (1961), Robins, C. Richard, and Reeve M. Bailey, Carl E. Bond, James R. Brooker, Ernest A. Lachner, Robert N. Lea, W. B. Scott. (1980),

Moxostoma hubbsi Legendre, 1952.
   Copper redhorse.
   Bailey, Reeve M., and John E. Fitch, Earl S. Herald, Ernest A. Lachner, C. C. Lindsey, C. Richard Robins, W. B. Scott. (1970), Bailey, Reeve M., and Ernest A. Lachner, C. C. Lindsey, C. Richard Robins, Phil M. Roedel, W. B. Scott, Loren P. Woods. (1966), Buth, Donald G. (1978), Buth, Donald G. (1982), Eastman, Joseph T. (1977), Eddy, Samuel. (1969), Hubbs, Carl L., and Karl F. Lagler. (1974), Jenkins, Robert E. (1970), Lee, David S., and Carter R. Gilbert, Charles H. Hocutt, Robert E. Jenkins, Don E. McAllister, Jay R. Stauffer, Jr. (1980), Legendre, Vianney. (1942), Massé, G. (1977), Mongeau, J. -R., and P. Dumont, L. Cloutier. (1986), Mongeau, J. -R., and P. Dumont, L. Cloutier, A.-M. Clement. (1988), Ono, R. Dana, and James D. Williams, Anne Wagner. (1983), Robins, C. Richard,

and Reeve M. Bailey, Carl E. Bond, James R. Brooker, Ernest A. Lachner, Robert N. Lea, W. B. Scott. (1980), Scott, W. B. (1954), Scott, W. B. (1958), Scott, W. B. (1967), Scott, W. B., and E. J. Crossman. (1969), Scott, W. B., and E. J. Crossman. (1973), Trautman, Milton B. (1981), Werner, Robert G. (1976a), Werner, Robert G. (1976b),

Moxostoma kennerlii Girard, 1857.
Girard, C. F. (1857), Günther, Albert C. (1868),

Moxostoma kennerlyi Girard, 1857.
Girard, C. F. (1857), Jordan, David Starr, and Barton Warren Evermann. (1896),

Moxostoma lachneri Robins and Raney, 1956.
Greater jumprock.
Bailey, Reeve M., and John E. Fitch, Earl S. Herald, Ernest A. Lachner, C. C. Lindsey, C. Richard Robins, W. B. Scott. (1970), Bailey, Reeve M., and Ernest A. Lachner, C. C. Lindsey, C. Richard Robins, Phil M. Roedel, W. B. Scott, Loren P. Woods. (1966), Boschung, Herbert T., Jr., and James D. Williams, Daniel W. Gotshall, David K. Caldwell, Melba C. Caldwell, Carol Nehring, Jordan Verner. (1983), Burr, Brooks M. (1979), Buth, Donald G. (1978), Buth, Donald G. (1982), Eddy, Samuel. (1969), Jenkins, Robert E. (1970), Lee, David S., and Carter R. Gilbert, Charles H. Hocutt, Robert E. Jenkins, Don E. McAllister, Jay R. Stauffer, Jr. (1980), Robins, C. Richard, and Reeve M. Bailey, Carl E. Bond, James R. Brooker, Ernest A. Lachner, Robert N. Lea, W. B. Scott. (1980), Robins, C. Richards, and Edward C. Raney. (1956),

Moxostoma lachrymale (Cope).
Bailey, Reeve M., and Ernest A. Lachner, C. C. Lindsey, C. Richard Robins, Phil M. Roedel, W. B. Scott, Loren P. Woods. (1966), Eddy, Samuel. (1969),

Moxostoma lesueuri (Richardson, 1823).
Jordan, David Starr, and Barton Warren Evermann. (1896), Walters, Vladimir. (1955),

Moxostoma lesueurii (Richardson).
Dymond, J. R., and J. L. Hart. (1927), Jordan, David Starr. (1929), Smith, Philip W. (1979),

Moxostoma macrolepidotum (Le Sueur, 1817).
Shorthead redhorse, Eastern Red Horse, White Sucker.
Bailey, Reeve M., and John E. Fitch, Earl S. Herald, Ernest A. Lachner, C. C. Lindsey, C. Richard Robins, W. B. Scott. (1970), Bailey, Reeve M., and Ernest A. Lachner, C. C. Lindsey, C. Richard Robins, Phil M. Roedel, W. B. Scott, Loren P. Woods. (1966), Bailey, Reeve M., and Gerald R. Smith. (1981), (1954), Baker, S. C., and M. L. Armstrong. (1987), Barnickol, P. G., and W. C. Starrett. (1951), Baxter, George T., and James R. Simon. (1970), Becker, George C. (1983), Beverly-Burton, Mary. (1984), Branson, Branley A., and Donald L. Batch. (1974), Branson, Branley A., and Donald L. Batch, S. Rice. (1981), Breder, C. M., Jr., and D. E. Rosen. (1966), Brown, C. J. D. (1971), Bur, M. T. (1976), Buth, Donald G. (1978), Buth, Donald G. (1979c), Buth, Donald G. (1983), Buynak, G. L., and H. W. Mohr, Jr. (1979), Carlander, Kenneth D. (1943), Carlander, Kenneth D. (1944a), Carlander, Kenneth D. (1944b), Carlander, Kenneth D. (1949), Carlander, Kenneth D. (1969), Carlander, Kenneth D., and J. W. Parsons. (1949), Christenson, L. M. (1957), Coker, R. E. (1930), Comeau, Napoléon A. (1915), Cooper, Edwin Lavern. (1983), Cross, Frank B. (1967), Cross, Frank B., and Joseph T. Collins. (1975), Crossman, E. J. (1976), Curry, Kevin D., and Anne Spacie. (1979), Curry, Kevin D., and Anne Spacie. (1984), Dechtiar, A. O. (1972b), Dorkin, John L., Jr. (1980), Dugal, L. C. (1962), Dymond, J. R. (1964), Eastman, Joseph T. (1977), Eastman, Joseph T. (1980), Eddy, Samuel. (1969), Eddy, Samuel, and Kenneth D. Carlander. (1942), Eddy,

Samuel, and Roy C. Tasker, James C. Underhill. (1972), Eddy, Samuel, and James C. Underhill. (1974), Elrod, J. H., and T. J. Hassler. (1971), Elser, H. J. (1961), Emery, Lee. (1976), Fago, Don. (1984b), Fernholz, W. B., and V. E. Crawley. (1977), Ferris, Stephen D., and Gregory S. Whitt. (1978), Fish, M. P. (1932), Fogle, N. E. (1961a), Fogle, N. E. (1961b), Fogle, N. E. (1963a), Fogle, N. E. (1963b), Forbes, Stephen Alfred. (1884), Forbes, Stephen Alfred., and Robert Earl Richardson. (1908), Fowler, Henry Weed. (1945), Fredrickson, L. H., and M. J. Ulmer. (1965), Fuiman, Lee A. (1979), Gasaway, C. R. (1970), Gobas, F. A. P. C., and D. C. G. Muir, D. Mackay. (1989), Goode, C. Brown, and Theodore Nicholas Gill. (1903), Greeley, J. R. (1936), Greenbank, J. (1950), Greenbank, J. (1957), Hall, Gordon E., and R. M. Jenkins. (1953), Hanson, W. D., and R. S. Campbell. (1963), Harrison, H. M. (1950), Henderson, N. E., and R. E. Peter. (1969),.Hoffman, Glenn L. (1967), Hubert, Wayne A., and Dennis N. Schmitt. (1985), Huggins, Donald G., and Randall E. Moss. (1975), Jenkins, Robert E. (1970), Jenkins, Robert M. (1953b), Jordan, David Starr. (1878a), Jordan, David Starr. (1929), Jordan, David Starr, and Barton Warren Evermann. (1896), Jordan, David Starr, and Barton Warren Evermann. (1923), Keleher, J. J., and B. Kooyman. (1957), Kennicott, Robert. (1855), Kuehn, J. H. (1949), Lachner, E. A. (1967), Lagler, Karl F., and John E. Bardach, Robert Rush Miller. (1962), Lantz, A. W. (1948b), Large, T. (1903), Lee, David S., and Carter R. Gilbert, Charles H. Hocutt, Robert E. Jenkins, Don E. McAllister, Jay R. Stauffer, Jr. (1980), Le Sueur, Charles Alexandre. (1817), Lindsey, Hague L., and James C. Randolph, John Carroll. (1983), Lower, A. R. M. (1915), Luce, W. (1933), Malick, Robert W., Jr., and Wayne A. Potter. (1976), Mansueti, A. J., and J. D. Hardy. (1967), Martin, R. G., and R. S. Campbell. (1953), Maurakis, Eugene G., and William S. Woolcott. (1984), McAllister, Don E., and Brian W. Coad. (1974), McClane, Albert Jules. (1974), McPhail, J. D., and C. C. Lindsey. (1970), Meek, Seth Eugene. (1894), Meyer, W. H. (1962), Miller, Rudolph J., and H. E. Evans. (1965), Miller, Rudolph J., and Henry W. Robinson. (1973), Minckley, W. L. (1963), Moore, G. A., and Frank B. Cross. (1950), Nelson, E. W. (1876), Nelson, Joseph S. (1976), Nelson, Joseph S. (1984), Nelson, W. R. (1961a), Nelson, W. R. (1962), Nichols, John Treadwell, and William K. Gregory. (1918), O'Donnell, D. J. (1935), Paetz, Martin J., and Joseph S. Nelson. (1970), Page, Lawrence M. (1982), Pearson, William D., and Louis A. Krumholz (1984), Peters, J. C. (ed.) (1964), Pflieger, William L. (1971), Pflieger, William L. (1975), Phillips, Gary L., and William D. Schmid, James C. Underhill. (1982), Potter, Wayne A., and Robert W. Malick, Jr., Janet L. Polk. (1976), Purkett, C. A., Jr. (1958a), Purkett, C. A., Jr. (1958b), Reed, E. B. (1962), Reighard, Jacob E. (1920), Ritson, Philip C., and Janet L. Polk, Robert W. Malick, Jr. (1977), Roberts, J. R., and A. S. W. De Frietas, M. A. J. Gidney. (1977), Robins, C. Richard, and Reeve M. Bailey, Carl E. Bond, James R. Brooker, Ernest A. Lachner, Robert N. Lea, W. B. Scott. (1980), Robins, C. Richards, and Edward C. Raney. (1957a), Robinson, G. L., and L. A. Jahn. (1980), Sanderson, A. E., Jr. (1958), Scott, W. B. (1967), Scott, W. B., and E. J. Crossman. (1969), Scott, W. B., and E. J. Crossman. (1973), Seegert, Greg. (1986), Shields, J. T. (1957a), Shields, J. T. (1957b), Shields, J. T. (1958a), Sibley, C. K. (1929), Smith, C. Lavett. (1986), Smith, Gerald R. (1963), Smith, Gerald R. (1981b), Smith, Philip W. (1965), Smith, Philip W. (1973), Smith, Philip W. (1979), Sprague, J. W. (1959a), Stanley, D. R. (1988), Stevens, E. D., and F. E. J. Fry. (1974), Stewart, Kenneth W., and Iain M. Suthers, Kelly Leavesley. (1985), Sule, Michael J., and Thomas M. Skelly. (1985), Thompson, W. H. (1950), Threinen, C. W., and W. T. Helm. (1952), Trautman, Milton B. (1957), Uthe, J. F. (1965), Vladykov, Vadim D. (1933), Walburg, C. H. (1964), Walden, Howard T., 2d. (1964), Werner, Robert G. (1976a), Werner, Robert G. (1976b), Werner, Robert G. (1980), Williams, D. D. (1977b), Williams, D. D. (1979), Williams, D. D. (1980c), Williams, D. D. (1980d), Williams, D. D., and M. J. Ulmer. (1980), Willock, T. A. (1969), Wobeser, G., and N. O. Nielsen, R. H. Dunlop, F. M. Atton. (1970),

Moxostoma macrolepidotum breviceps (Cope, 1870).
Ohio Shorthead Redhorse.

Bauer, Bruce H., and Branley A. Branson, Strant T. Colwell. (1978), Clay, W. M. (1975), Comiskey, C. E., and D. A. Etnier. (1972), Jenkins, Robert E. (1970), Lee, David S., and Carter R. Gilbert, Charles H. Hocutt, Robert E. Jenkins, Don E. McAllister, Jay R. Stauffer, Jr. (1980), Smith, C. Lavett. (1986), Trautman, Milton B. (1981),

Moxostoma macrolepidotum macrolepidotum (Le Sueur, 1817).
Northern Shorthead Redhorse.
Bailey, Reeve M., and Marvin O. Allum. (1962), Clay, W. M. (1975), Hubbs, Carl L., and Karl F. Lagler. (1974), Jenkins, Robert E. (1970), Larimore, R. W., and P. W. Smith. (1963), Lee, David S., and Carter R. Gilbert, Charles H. Hocutt, Robert E. Jenkins, Don E. McAllister, Jay R. Stauffer, Jr. (1980), Smith, C. Lavett. (1986), Trautman, Milton B. (1981),

Moxostoma macrolepidotum pisolabrum Trautman and Martin, 1951.
Carlander, Kenneth D. (1944b), Fogle, N. E. (1961b), Fry, F. E. J. (1960), Hall, Gordon E., and R. M. Jenkins. (1953), Hankinson, T. L. (1920), Jenkins, Robert E. (1970), Lee, David S., and Carter R. Gilbert, Charles H. Hocutt, Robert E. Jenkins, Don E. McAllister, Jay R. Stauffer, Jr. (1980), Meyer, W. H. (1962), Moore, G. A., and Frank B. Cross. (1950), Nelson, W. R. (1961a), Nelson, W. R. (1962), Nurnberger, P. K. (1930), Peters, J. C. (ed.) (1964), Purkett, C. A., Jr. (1958a), Reed, E. B. (1962), Reighard, Jacob E. (1920), Riggs, C. D., and G. A. Moore. (1963), Shields, J. T. (1955a), Shields, J. T. (1956), Shields, J. T. (1957a), Shields, J. T. (1957b), Shields, J. T. (1958a), Sprague, J. W. (1959a), Starrett, William C. (1958),

Moxostoma mascotae Regan, 1907.
Regan, Charles Tate. (1907), Villar, José Alvarez del. (1970),

Moxostoma melanops (Rafinesque, 1820).
Spotted Sucker, Winter Sucker, Striped Sucker.
Tsuyuki, H., and E. Roberts, R. H. Kerr, J. F. Uthe, L. W. Clarke. (1967),

Moxostoma oblongum (Mitchill, 1815).
Forbes, Stephen Alfred., and Robert Earl Richardson. (1920), Günther, Albert C. (1868), Jordan, David Starr, and Barton Warren Evermann. (1896),

Moxostoma oblongus (Mitchill, 1815).
Agassiz, John Louis Rodolphe. (1855), Günther, Albert C. (1868), Jordan, David Starr, and Barton Warren Evermann. (1896),

Moxostoma pappillosum (Cope, 1870).
Suckermouth redhorse, V-lip redhorse, White Mullet.
Buth, Donald G. (1978), Fowler, Henry Weed. (1945), Jenkins, Robert E. (1970), Jordan, David Starr. (1878d), Jordan, David Starr. (1929), Jordan, David Starr, and Barton Warren Evermann. (1896), Jordan, David Starr, and Barton Warren Evermann. (1905), Jordan, David Starr, and Charles Henry Gilbert. (1883), Lee, David S., and Carter R. Gilbert, Charles H. Hocutt, Robert E. Jenkins, Don E. McAllister, Jay R. Stauffer, Jr. (1980), Miller, Rudolph J., and H. E. Evans. (1965), Pickens, A. L. (1928), Robins, C. Richard, and Reeve M. Bailey, Carl E. Bond, James R. Brooker, Ernest A. Lachner, Robert N. Lea, W. B. Scott. (1980),

Moxostoma parvidens Regan, 1907.
Regan, Charles Tate. (1907),

Moxostoma pidiense (Cope, 1870).
Evermann, Barton Warren. (1916), Jordan, David Starr. (1878d), Jordan, David Starr, and Barton Warren Evermann. (1896), Jordan, David Starr, and Charles Henry Gilbert. (1883),

Moxostoma poecilura.
Fowler, Henry Weed. (1945),

Moxostoma pœcilurum (Jordan, 1877).
Blacktail redhorse.
Amin, Omar M., and Ernest H. Williams, Jr. (1983), Anonymous. (1958a), Bailey, Reeve M., and John E. Fitch, Earl S. Herald, Ernest A. Lachner, C. C. Lindsey, C. Richard Robins, W. B. Scott. (1970), Bailey, Reeve M., and Ernest A. Lachner, C. C. Lindsey, C. Richard Robins, Phil M. Roedel, W. B. Scott, Loren P. Woods. (1966), Boschung, Herbert T., Jr., and James D. Williams, Daniel W. Gotshall, David K. Caldwell, Melba C. Caldwell, Carol Nehring, Jordan Verner. (1983), Burr, Brooks M., and D. A. Carney. (1984), Buth, Donald G. (1978), Carlander, Kenneth D. (1969), Chien, Shin Ming, and Wilmer A. Rogers. (1970), Douglas, Neil H. (1974), Eddy, Samuel. (1957), Eddy, Samuel. (1969), Evans, James W., and Richard L. Noble. (1979), Fingerman, Sue Whitsell, and Royal D. Suttkus. (1961), Garth, W. A., and J. S. Dendy. (1952), Herald, Earl S. (1967), Herald, Earl S. (1979), Jenkins, Robert E. (1970), Jordan, David Starr. (1878d), Jordan, David Starr, and Barton Warren Evermann. (1896), Jordan, David Starr, and Charles Henry Gilbert. (1883), Kilgen, R. H. (1974a), Kilgen, R. H. (1974b), Kilken, R. H. (1972), Lee, David S., and Carter R. Gilbert, Charles H. Hocutt, Robert E. Jenkins, Don E. McAllister, Jay R. Stauffer, Jr. (1980), Miller, Rudolph J., and H. E. Evans. (1965), Nelson, Edward M. (1948), Robins, C. Richard, and Reeve M. Bailey, Carl E. Bond, James R. Brooker, Ernest A. Lachner, Robert N. Lea, W. B. Scott. (1980), Rogers, Wilmer A. (1967), Swingle, W. E. (1965), Viosca, Percy, Jr. (1936), Viosca, Percy, Jr. (1937), Williams, E. H., Jr. (1974), Williams, E. H., Jr. (1980), Xiong Quanimo. (1988),

Moxostoma rhotheca.
Eddy, Samuel. (1969), Flemer, D. A., and W. S. Woolcott. (1966),

Moxostoma rhothoecum (Thoburn **IN:** Jordan and Evermann, 1896).
Torrent sucker.
Bailey, Reeve M., and John E. Fitch, Earl S. Herald, Ernest A. Lachner, C. C. Lindsey, C. Richard Robins, W. B. Scott. (1970), Bailey, Reeve M., and Ernest A. Lachner, C. C. Lindsey, C. Richard Robins, Phil M. Roedel, W. B. Scott, Loren P. Woods. (1966), Buth, Donald G. (1977a), Carlander, Kenneth D. (1969), Eddy, Samuel. (1957), Ferris, Stephen D., and Gregory S. Whitt. (1978), Flemer, D. A., and W. S. Woolcott. (1966), Gilbert, Carter R. (1961), Jenkins, Robert E. (1970), Jordan, David Starr, and Barton Warren Evermann. (1896), Lee, David S., and Carter R. Gilbert, Charles H. Hocutt, Robert E. Jenkins, Don E. McAllister, Jay R. Stauffer, Jr. (1980), Raney, Edward C., and Ernest A. Lachner. (1946c), Robins, C. Richard. (1961), Robins, C. Richard, and Reeve M. Bailey, Carl E. Bond, James R. Brooker, Ernest A. Lachner, Robert N. Lea, W. B. Scott. (1980),

Moxostoma robustrum (Cope, 1870).
Smith, Michael L. (1981),

Moxostoma robustum (Cope, 1870).
Smallfin redhorse.
Bailey, Reeve M., and John E. Fitch, Earl S. Herald, Ernest A. Lachner, C. C. Lindsey, C. Richard Robins, W. B. Scott. (1970), Bailey, Reeve M., and Ernest A. Lachner, C. C. Lindsey, C. Richard Robins, Phil M. Roedel, W. B. Scott, Loren P. Woods. (1966), Buth, Donald G. (1978), Eddy, Samuel. (1969), Fowler, Henry Weed. (1945), Jenkins, Robert E. (1970), Jordan, David Starr, and Barton Warren Evermann. (1896), Lee, David S., and

201

Carter R. Gilbert, Charles H. Hocutt, Robert E. Jenkins, Don E. McAllister, Jay R. Stauffer, Jr. (1980), Robins, C. Richard, and Reeve M. Bailey, Carl E. Bond, James R. Brooker, Ernest A. Lachner, Robert N. Lea, W. B. Scott. (1980),

Moxostoma rubresque Hubbs, 1930.
Keleher, J. J., and B. Kooyman. (1957), Lantz, A. W. (1948a), Lantz, A. W. (1966), Lantz, A. W. (1969), Ricker, W. E. (1962), Schmidt, P. J. (1949), Schmidt, P. J. (1950), Tarr, H. L. A. (1952),

Moxostoma rubreques Hubbs, 1930.
Hinks, David. (1943),.Hoffman, Glenn L. (1967), Hubbs, Carl L. (1930), Hubbs, Carl L., and Karl F. Lagler. (1941), Hubbs, Carl L., and Karl F. Lagler. (1947), Nelson, Edward M. (1948), Robins, C. Richards, and Edward C. Raney. (1957a), Smith, Philip W. (1979), Trautman, Milton B. (1981), Vladykov, Vadim D. (1942),

Moxostoma rupiscartes Jordan and Jenkins **IN:** Jordan, 1889.
Striped jumprock, Jump-rocks.
Bailey, Reeve M., and John E. Fitch, Earl S. Herald, Ernest A. Lachner, C. C. Lindsey, C. Richard Robins, W. B. Scott. (1970), Bailey, Reeve M., and Ernest A. Lachner, C. C. Lindsey, C. Richard Robins, Phil M. Roedel, W. B. Scott, Loren P. Woods. (1966), Boschung, Herbert T., Jr., and James D. Williams, Daniel W. Gotshall, David K. Caldwell, Melba C. Caldwell, Carol Nehring, Jordan Verner. (1983), Buth, Donald G. (1978), Eddy, Samuel. (1969), Jenkins, Robert E. (1970), Jordan, David Starr. (1889), Jordan, David Starr, and Barton Warren Evermann. (1896), Lee, David S., and Carter R. Gilbert, Charles H. Hocutt, Robert E. Jenkins, Don E. McAllister, Jay R. Stauffer, Jr. (1980), McClane, Albert Jules. (1974), Pickens, A. L. (1928), Raney, Edward C., and Ernest A. Lachner. (1946a), Robins, C. Richard, and Reeve M. Bailey, Carl E. Bond, James R. Brooker, Ernest A. Lachner, Robert N. Lea, W. B. Scott. (1980),

Moxostoma tenue Agassiz, 1855.
Agassiz, John Louis Rodolphe. (1855), Günther, Albert C. (1868), Jordan, David Starr, and Barton Warren Evermann. (1896),

Moxostoma thalassinum (Cope, 1870).
Jordan, David Starr, and Barton Warren Evermann. (1896),

Moxostoma thalassinus Cope, 1870.
Jordan, David Starr. (1878d), Jordan, David Starr, and Barton Warren Evermann. (1896), Jordan, David Starr, and Charles Henry Gilbert. (1883),

Moxostoma trisignatum Cope and Yarrow, 1876.
Cope, Edward Drinker, and H. C. Yarrow. (1875), Jordan, David Starr, and Barton Warren Evermann. (1896),

Moxostoma valenciennesi Jordan, 1885.
Greater redhorse.
Bailey, Reeve M., and John E. Fitch, Earl S. Herald, Ernest A. Lachner, C. C. Lindsey, C. Richard Robins, W. B. Scott. (1970), Bailey, Reeve M., and Ernest A. Lachner, C. C. Lindsey, C. Richard Robins, Phil M. Roedel, W. B. Scott, Loren P. Woods. (1966), Bailey, Reeve M., and Gerald R. Smith. (1981), (1954), Becker, George C. (1966), Becker, George C. (1983), Burr, Brooks M., and D. A. Carney. (1984), Burr, Brooks M., and M. A. Morris. (1977), Buth, Donald G. (1978), Buth, Donald G. (1979a), Cooper, Edwin Lavern. (1983), Dunst, R. C., and T. Wirth. (1972), Dymond, J. R., and J. L. Hart, A. L. Pritchard. (1929), Eastman, Joseph T. (1977), Eddy, Samuel. (1969), Eddy, Samuel, and Roy C. Tasker, James C. Underhill. (1972), Eddy, Samuel, and James C. Underhill. (1974), Fago,

Don. (1982), Fago, Don. (1984b), Forbes, Stephen Alfred., and Robert Earl Richardson. (1908), Fourine, J. W., and J. J. Black, A. D. Vethaak. (1988), Greene, C. W. (1935), Hubbs, Carl L. (1930), Hubbs, Carl L., and Karl F. Lagler. (1974), Jenkins, Robert E. (1970), Jenkins, Robert E., and D. J. Jenkins. (1980), Jordan, David Starr. (1885a), Jordan, David Starr, and Barton Warren Evermann. (1896), Keleher, J. J., and B. Kooyman. (1957), Lantz, A. W. (1948a), Lantz, A. W. (1966), Lantz, A. W. (1969), Lee, David S., and Carter R. Gilbert, Charles H. Hocutt, Robert E. Jenkins, Don E. McAllister, Jay R. Stauffer, Jr. (1980), Legendre, Vianney. (1942), Les, B. L. (1979), McAllister, Don E., and Brian W. Coad. (1974), Pearson, William D., and Louis A. Krumholz (1984), Phillips, Gary L., and William D. Schmid, James C. Underhill. (1982), Ricker, W. E. (1962), Rimsky-Korsakoff, V. N. (1930), Robins, C. Richard, and Reeve M. Bailey, Carl E. Bond, James R. Brooker, Ernest A. Lachner, Robert N. Lea, W. B. Scott. (1980), Robins, C. Richards, and Edward C. Raney. (1957a), Schmidt, P. J. (1949), Schmidt, P. J. (1950), Scott, W. B. (1954), Scott, W. B. (1958), Scott, W. B. (1967), Scott, W. B., and E. J. Crossman. (1969), Scott, W. B., and E. J. Crossman. (1973), Seegert, Greg. (1986), Smith, C. Lavett. (1986), Smith, Philip W. (1973), Smith, Philip W. (1979), Smith, Philip W., and A. C. Lopinot, W. L. Pflieger. (1971), Tarr, H. L. A. (1952), Taylor, W. R. (1954), Trautman, Milton B. (1957), Trautman, Milton B. (1981), Werner, Robert G. (1976a), Werner, Robert G. (1976b), Werner, Robert G. (1980), Whitaker, J. O., and D. C. Wallace. (1966), Yoder, Chris O., and Raymond A. Beaumier. (1986),

Moxostoma velatum (Cope, 1870).
Jordan, David Starr, and Barton Warren Evermann. (1896), Jordan, David Starr, and Charles Henry Gilbert. (1883), Smith, Hugh M. (1893),

Moxostoma victoriæ Girard, 1857.
Girard, C. F. (1857), Günther, Albert C. (1868), Jordan, David Starr, and Barton Warren Evermann. (1896), Robins, C. Richards, and Edward C. Raney. (1957a),

Myxocyprinus Gill, 1878.
Eschmeyer, William N. (1990), Ferris, Stephen D., and Gregory S. Whitt. (1978), Fowler, Henry Weed. (1958), Jordan, David Starr. (1923), Lagler, Karl F., and John E. Bardach, Robert Rush Miller. (1962), Lee, David S., and Carter R. Gilbert, Charles H. Hocutt, Robert E. Jenkins, Don E. McAllister, Jay R. Stauffer, Jr. (1980), Miller, Robert Rush. (1958), Moyle, Peter B., and Joseph J. Cech, Jr. (1982), Nelson, Edward M. (1948), Nelson, Edward M. (1949), Nelson, Edward M. (1976), Smith, Gerald R. (1966), Ueno, K., and A. Nagase, J.-J. Ye. (1988),

Myxocyprinus asiaticus (Bleeker, 1864).
Chang, C.-Y., and G. I. Ji. (1978), Eastman, Joseph T. (1980), Fang, P. W. (1934), Herald, Earl S. (1967), Lagler, Karl F., and John E. Bardach, Robert Rush Miller. (1962), Lo, Y.-I., and H.-W. Wu. (1979), Moyle, Peter B., and Joseph J. Cech, Jr. (1982), Nelson, Edward M. (1948), Nelson, Joseph S. (1976), Nelson, Joseph S. (1984), Quanwei, Xiong, and Xia Shenglin. (1985), Ramaswami, L. S. (1957), Rendahl, H. (1932), Tsoi, S. C. M., and S.-C. Lee, W.-C. Chao. (1989), Ueno, K., and A. Nagase, J.-J. Ye. (1988), Yu, Z., and Z. Deng, M. Cai, X. Deng, H. Jiang, J. Yi, J. Tian. (1988),

Myxocyprinus asiaticus asiaticus (Bleeker, 1864).
Bleeker, P. (1864), Nichols, John Treadwell. (1943),

Myxocyprinus asiaticus chinensis (Dabry de Thiersant, 1872).
Huo-shao-pien.
Nichols, John Treadwell. (1943),

Myxocyprinus asiaticus fukiensis Nichols, 1925.
    Nichols, John Treadwell. (1925), Nichols, John Treadwell. (1928), Nichols, John Treadwell. (1943),

Myxocyprinus asiaticus nankinensis Tchang, 1929.
    Nichols, John Treadwell. (1943), Tchang, T.-L. (1929),

Myxostoma
    Jordan. Jordan, David Starr. (1923), Jordan, David Starr, and Alembert Winthrop Brayton. (1877),

Myxostoma aureola.
    Nelson, E. W. (1878),

Myxostoma aureolum.
    Forbes, Stephen Alfred., and Robert Earl Richardson. (1920), Smith, Philip W. (1979),

Myxostoma austrina Bean, 1879.
    Bean, Tarleton Hoffman. (1879), Jordan, David Starr, and Barton Warren Evermann. (1896),

Myxostoma carpio.
    Forbes, Stephen Alfred., and Robert Earl Richardson. (1920), Smith, Philip W. (1979),

Myxostoma euryops Jordan, 1877.
    Jordan, David Starr. (1877c), Jordan, David Starr, and Barton Warren Evermann. (1896),

Myxostoma macrolepidota (Le Sueur, 1817).
    Nelson, E. W. (1878),

Myxostoma macrolepidotum (Le Sueur, 1817).
    Smith, Philip W. (1979),

Myxostoma macrolepidotum duquesnii.
    Forbes, Stephen Alfred., and Robert Earl Richardson. (1920), Smith, Philip W. (1979),

Myxostoma pœcilura Jordan, 1877.
    Jordan, David Starr. (1877a), Jordan, David Starr, and Barton Warren Evermann. (1896),

Myxostoma velatum.
    Smith, Philip W. (1979),

Notolepidomyzon Fowler, 1913.
    Eschmeyer, William N. (1990), Fowler, Henry Weed. (1914a), Jordan, David Starr. (1923), Smith, Gerald R. (1966), Tanner, V. M. (1942),

Notolepidomyzon clarki.
    Smith, Gerald R. (1966),

Notolepidomyzon generosus (Girard, 1856).
    Smith, Gerald R. (1966),

Notolepidomyzon intermedius Tanner, 1942.
    Smith, Gerald R. (1966), Tanner, V. M. (1942),

Notolepidomyzon plebeius.
    Smith, Gerald R. (1966),

Notolepidomyzon santa-anae (Snyder, 1908).
    Smith, Gerald R. (1966),

Notolepidomyzon santae-anae (Snyder, 1908).
    Smith, Gerald R. (1966),

Notolepidomyzon utahensis Tanner, 1932.
    Minckley, W. L., and Dean A. Hendrickson, Carl E. Bond. (1986), Smith, Gerald R.
    (1966), Tanner, V. M. (1942),

Pantosteus Cope, 1875.
    Mountain suckers.
    Cope, Edward Drinker, and H. C. Yarrow. (1875), Dunham, A. E., and Gerald R. Smith, J.
    N. Taylor. (1979), Eschmeyer, William N. (1990), Evermann, Barton Warren. (1893b),
    Ferris, Stephen D., and Gregory S. Whitt. (1978), Fowler, Henry Weed. (1914a), Hubbs,
    Carl L., and Laura C. Hubbs, R. E. Johnson. (1943), Jordan, David Starr. (1923), Jordan,
    David Starr, and Barton Warren Evermann. (1896), Koehn, Richard K. (1969), Miller,
    Robert Rush. (1958), Minckley, W. L., and Dean A. Hendrickson, Carl E. Bond. (1986),
    Moyle, Peter B., and Joseph J. Cech, Jr. (1982), Nelson, Edward M. (1948), Nelson,
    Edward M. (1949), Nelson, Joseph S. (1976), Romer, Alfred Sherwood. (1966), Smith,
    Gerald R. (1965), Smith, Gerald R. (1966),

Pantosteus arœopus (Jordan, 1878).
    Jordan, David Starr, and Barton Warren Evermann. (1896), Smith, Gerald R. (1966),

Pantosteus arizonœ Gilbert, 1896 **IN:** Jordan and Evermann, 1896.
    Fowler, Henry Weed. (1914a), Gilbert, Charles Henry, and N. B. Scofield. (1898), Jordan,
    David Starr, and Barton Warren Evermann. (1896), Smith, Gerald R. (1966),

Pantosteus bardus Cope.
    Cope, Edward Drinker, and H. C. Yarrow. (1875),

Pantosteus clarki (Baird and Girard, 1854).
    Bailey, Reeve M., and Ernest A. Lachner, C. C. Lindsey, C. Richard Robins, Phil M.
    Roedel, W. B. Scott, Loren P. Woods. (1966), Jordan, David Starr, and Barton Warren
    Evermann. (1896), Jordan, David Starr, and Charles Henry Gilbert. (1883), Koehn, Richard
    K. (1966), Koster, William J. (1957), Lee, David S., and Carter R. Gilbert, Charles H.
    Hocutt, Robert E. Jenkins, Don E. McAllister, Jay R. Stauffer, Jr. (1980), Minckley, W. L.,
    and Dean A. Hendrickson, Carl E. Bond. (1986), Smith, Gerald R. (1966),

Pantosteus clarkii.
    Nelson, Edward M. (1948),

Pantosteus columbianus Eigenmann and Smith, 1893.
    Bridgelip Sucker.
    Eigenmann, Carl H., and Rosa Smith. (1893), Lee, David S., and Carter R. Gilbert, Charles
    H. Hocutt, Robert E. Jenkins, Don E. McAllister, Jay R. Stauffer, Jr. (1980), Smith, Gerald
    R. (1966),

Pantosteus delphinus (Cope, 1872).
    Blueheaded Sucker.

Bailey, Reeve M., and Ernest A. Lachner, C. C. Lindsey, C. Richard Robins, Phil M. Roedel, W. B. Scott, Loren P. Woods. (1966), Carlander, Kenneth D. (1969), Cope, Edward Drinker, and H. C. Yarrow. (1875), Goode, C. Brown, and Theodore Nicholas Gill. (1903), Hubbs, Carl L., and Laura C. Hubbs. (1947), Jordan, David Starr, and Barton Warren Evermann. (1896), Koster, William J. (1957), Lee, David S., and Carter R. Gilbert, Charles H. Hocutt, Robert E. Jenkins, Don E. McAllister, Jay R. Stauffer, Jr. (1980), Miller, Rudolph J., and H. E. Evans. (1965), Nelson, Edward M. (1948), Simon, James R. (1946), Smith, Gerald R. (1966),

Pantosteus delphinus delphinus (Cope, 1872).
Hubbs, Carl L., and Laura C. Hubbs. (1947), Smith, Gerald R. (1966),

Pantosteus delphinus jordani.
Smith, Gerald R. (1966),

Pantosteus delphinus utahensis (Tanner).
Smith, Gerald R. (1966),

Pantosteus discobulus.
Minckley, W. L., and Dean A. Hendrickson, Carl E. Bond. (1986), Smith, Gerald R. (1966),

Pantosteus discobulus yarrowi.
Minckley, W. L., and Dean A. Hendrickson, Carl E. Bond. (1986),

Pantosteus discobulus jarrowi.
Minckley, W. L., and Dean A. Hendrickson, Carl E. Bond. (1986),

Pantosteus generosus (Girard, 1856).
Mountain sucker.
Goode, C. Brown, and Theodore Nicholas Gill. (1903), Jordan, David Starr, and Barton Warren Evermann. (1896), Jordan, David Starr, and Charles Henry Gilbert. (1883), Smith, Gerald R. (1966),

Pantosteus guzmaniensis (Girard, 1856).
Jordan, David Starr, and Barton Warren Evermann. (1896), Smith, Gerald R. (1966),

Pantosteus intermedius Tanner, 1942.
Bailey, Reeve M., and Ernest A. Lachner, C. C. Lindsey, C. Richard Robins, Phil M. Roedel, W. B. Scott, Loren P. Woods. (1966), Smith, Gerald R. (1966),

Pantosteus jarrovii Cope and Yarrow, 1875.
Cope, Edward Drinker, and H. C. Yarrow. (1875), Jordan, David Starr, and Barton Warren Evermann. (1896), Smith, Gerald R. (1966),

Pantosteus jordani Evermann, 1893.
Bond, Carl E. (1953), Eigenmann, Carl H. (1895), Eigenmann, Carl H., and Rosa Smith. (1893), Evermann, Barton Warren. (1893b), Evermann, Barton Warren. (1896), Goode, C. Brown, and Theodore Nicholas Gill. (1903),.Hoffman, Glenn L. (1967), Jordan, David Starr. (1929), Jordan, David Starr, and Barton Warren Evermann. (1896), Jordan, David Starr, and Barton Warren Evermann. (1905), Miller, Rudolph J., and H. E. Evans. (1965), Schultz, Leonard P. (1936), Scott, W. B. (1957), Scott, W. B. (1958), Scott, W. B., and E. J. Crossman. (1969), Simon, James R. (1946), Smith, Gerald R. (1966),

Pantosteus lahontan Rutter, 1904.
> Bailey, Reeve M., and Ernest A. Lachner, C. C. Lindsey, C. Richard Robins, Phil M. Roedel, W. B. Scott, Loren P. Woods. (1966), Minckley, W. L., and Dean A. Hendrickson, Carl E. Bond. (1986), Nelson, Edward M. (1948), Rutter, Cloudsley M. (1904), Smith, Gerald R. (1966),

Pantosteus macrocheilus Girard.
> Evermann, Barton Warren. (1896),

Pantosteus platyrhynchus (Cope, 1874).
> **Northern Mountain Sucker.**
> Bailey, Reeve M., and Marvin O. Allum. (1962), Bailey, Reeve M., and Ernest A. Lachner, C. C. Lindsey, C. Richard Robins, Phil M. Roedel, W. B. Scott, Loren P. Woods. (1966), Goode, C. Brown, and Theodore Nicholas Gill. (1903),.Hoffman, Glenn L. (1967), Jordan, David Starr, and Barton Warren Evermann. (1896), Jordan, David Starr, and Charles Henry Gilbert. (1883), McPhail, J. D., and C. C. Lindsey. (1970), Minckley, W. L., and Dean A. Hendrickson, Carl E. Bond. (1986), Nelson, Edward M. (1948), Simon, James R. (1946), Smith, Gerald R. (1966), Snyder, John Otterbein. (1924), Willock, T. A. (1969),

Pantosteus plebeius (Baird and Girard, 1854).
> Bailey, Reeve M., and Ernest A. Lachner, C. C. Lindsey, C. Richard Robins, Phil M. Roedel, W. B. Scott, Loren P. Woods. (1966), Breder, C. M., Jr., and D. E. Rosen. (1966), Jordan, David Starr. (1878d), Jordan, David Starr, and Barton Warren Evermann. (1896), Jordan, David Starr, and Charles Henry Gilbert. (1883), Koehn, Richard K. (1966), Koster, William J. (1957), Minckley, W. L., and Dean A. Hendrickson, Carl E. Bond. (1986), Nelson, Edward M. (1948), Smith, Gerald R. (1966),

Pantosteus santaanae Snyder, 1908.
> Bailey, Reeve M., and Ernest A. Lachner, C. C. Lindsey, C. Richard Robins, Phil M. Roedel, W. B. Scott, Loren P. Woods. (1966), Lee, David S., and Carter R. Gilbert, Charles H. Hocutt, Robert E. Jenkins, Don E. McAllister, Jay R. Stauffer, Jr. (1980), Minckley, W. L., and Dean A. Hendrickson, Carl E. Bond. (1986), Smith, Gerald R. (1966),

Pantosteus santa-anae Snyder, 1908.
> Nelson, Edward M. (1948), Smith, Gerald R. (1966), Snyder, John Otterbein. (1908a),

Pantosteus santanae Snyder, 1908.
> Smith, Gerald R. (1966),

Pantosteus utahensis (Tanner, 1932).
> Lee, David S., and Carter R. Gilbert, Charles H. Hocutt, Robert E. Jenkins, Don E. McAllister, Jay R. Stauffer, Jr. (1980), Nelson, Edward M. (1948),

Pantosteus virescens Cope, 1875.
> Bailey, Reeve M., and Ernest A. Lachner, C. C. Lindsey, C. Richard Robins, Phil M. Roedel, W. B. Scott, Loren P. Woods. (1966), Cope, Edward Drinker, and H. C. Yarrow. (1875), Jordan, David Starr. (1878e), Jordan, David Starr, and Barton Warren Evermann. (1896), Jordan, David Starr, and Charles Henry Gilbert. (1883), Smith, Gerald R. (1966), Snyder, John Otterbein. (1924),

Pantosteus yarrowi.
> Smith, Gerald R. (1966),

Pithecomyzon Fowler, 1913.
> Eschmeyer, William N. (1990), Fowler, Henry Weed. (1914a), Jordan, David Starr. (1923),

Placopharynx Cope, 1870.
> Cope, Edward Drinker. (1870), Eschmeyer, William N. (1990), Jordan, David Starr. (1923), Jordan, David Starr, and Barton Warren Evermann. (1896), Meek, Seth Eugene. (1894), Nelson, Edward M. (1948), Nelson, Edward M. (1949),

Placopharynx carinatns.
> Smith, Philip W. (1979),

Placopharynx carinatus Cope, 1870.
> Blatchley, W. S. (1938), Cope, Edward Drinker. (1870), Cross, Frank B., and G. A. Moore. (1952), Forbes, Stephen Alfred., and Robert Earl Richardson. (1920), Fowler, Henry Weed. (1945), Hubbs, Carl L., and Karl F. Lagler. (1941), Hubbs, Carl L., and Karl F. Lagler. (1947), Jordan, David Starr. (1878d), Jordan, David Starr. (1929), Jordan, David Starr, and Barton Warren Evermann. (1896), Jordan, David Starr, and Charles Henry Gilbert. (1883), Meek, Seth Eugene. (1894), Nelson, Edward M. (1948), Smith, Philip W. (1979), Trautman, Milton B. (1981), Vladykov, Vadim D. (1942),

Placopharynx duquesnei (Le Sueur, 1817).
> **Pavement-Toothed Red-Horse.**
> Forbes, Stephen Alfred., and Robert Earl Richardson. (1920), Smith, Philip W. (1979),

Placopharynx duquesnii (Le Sueur, 1817).
> Jordan, David Starr, and Barton Warren Evermann. (1896), Jordan, David Starr, and Barton Warren Evermann. (1905),

Procatostomus constablei Whitfield, 1890.
> Whitfield, Robert Parr. (1890), Not a member of the Catostomidae, but rather the Family Gonorynchidae, = Notogoneus osculus Cope, 1885.

Proictiobus zaissanicus Sychevskaya, 1984.
> Sychevskaya, E. K. (1984),

Ptychostomus Agassiz, 1855.
> Eschmeyer, William N. (1990), Jordan, David Starr. (1923), Jordan, David Starr, and Alembert Winthrop Brayton. (1877),

Ptychostomus albidus Girard, 1857.
> Girard, C. F. (1857), Jordan, David Starr, and Barton Warren Evermann. (1896),

Ptychostomus albus Cope, 1870.
> Cope, Edward Drinker. (1870), Jordan, David Starr, and Barton Warren Evermann. (1896),

Ptychostomus aureolus (Le Sueur, 1817).
> Agassiz, John Louis Rodolphe. (1855), Jordan, David Starr, and Barton Warren Evermann. (1896),

Ptychostomus breviceps Cope, 1870.
> Cope, Edward Drinker. (1870), Forbes, Stephen Alfred., and Robert Earl Richardson. (1920), Jordan, David Starr, and Barton Warren Evermann. (1896),

Ptychostomus bucco Cope, 1872.
> Cope, Edward Drinker. (1871), Jordan, David Starr, and Barton Warren Evermann. (1896),

Ptychostomus cervinus (Cope, 1868).
Cope, Edward Drinker. (1870), Fowler, Henry Weed. (1914a), Jordan, David Starr, and Barton Warren Evermann. (1896),

Ptychostomus collapsus Cope, 1870.
Cope, Edward Drinker. (1870), Jordan, David Starr, and Barton Warren Evermann. (1896),

Ptychostomus congestus (Baird and Girard, 1855).
Günther, Albert C. (1868),

Ptychostomus conus Cope, 1870.
Cope, Edward Drinker. (1870), Jordan, David Starr, and Barton Warren Evermann. (1896),

Ptychostomus coregonus Cope, 1870.
Cope, Edward Drinker. (1870), Jordan, David Starr, and Barton Warren Evermann. (1896),

Ptychostomus crassilabris Cope, 1870.
Cope, Edward Drinker. (1870), Jordan, David Starr, and Barton Warren Evermann. (1896),

Ptychostomus duquesnei (Le Sueur, 1817).
Cope, Edward Drinker. (1870), Jordan, David Starr, and Barton Warren Evermann. (1896),

Ptychostomus duquesnii (Le Sueur, 1817).
Günther, Albert C. (1868),

Ptychostomus erythrurus.
Cope, Edward Drinker. (1870), Jordan, David Starr, and Barton Warren Evermann. (1896),

Ptychostomus haydeni Girard, 1857.
Girard, C. F. (1857), Günther, Albert C. (1868), Jordan, David Starr, and Barton Warren Evermann. (1896), Robins, C. Richards, and Edward C. Raney. (1957a),

Ptychostomus lachrymalis Cope, 1870.
Cope, Edward Drinker. (1870), Jordan, David Starr, and Barton Warren Evermann. (1896),

Ptychostomus melanops (Rafinesque, 1820).
Agassiz, John Louis Rodolphe. (1855), Günther, Albert C. (1868),

Ptychostomus oneida.
Cope, Edward Drinker. (1870), Jordan, David Starr, and Barton Warren Evermann. (1896),

Ptychostomus papillosus Cope, 1870.
Cope, Edward Drinker. (1870), Jordan, David Starr, and Barton Warren Evermann. (1896),

Ptychostomus pidiensis.
Cope, Edward Drinker. (1870), Jordan, David Starr, and Barton Warren Evermann. (1896),

Ptychostomus robustus Cope, 1870.
Cope, Edward Drinker. (1870), Jordan, David Starr, and Barton Warren Evermann. (1896),

Ptychostomus thalassinus Cope, 1870.
Cope, Edward Drinker. (1870),

Ptychostomus velatus Cope, 1870.
Cope, Edward Drinker. (1870), Jordan, David Starr, and Barton Warren Evermann. (1896),

Quassilabia Jordan and Brayton, 1878.
> Eschmeyer, William N. (1990), Jordan, David Starr. (1878b), Jordan, David Starr. (1878c), Jordan, David Starr. (1878d), Jordan, David Starr. (1923), Jordan, David Starr, and Barton Warren Evermann. (1896),

Quassilabia lacera (Jordan and Brayton, 1877).
> **Harelip Sucker.**
> Goode, C. Brown, and Theodore Nicholas Gill. (1903), Jordan, David Starr. (1878b), Jordan, David Starr, and Barton Warren Evermann. (1896), Jordan, David Starr, and Charles Henry Gilbert. (1883), Meek, Seth Eugene. (1894),

Rhytidostomus
> Eschmeyer, William N. (1990),

Rhytidostomus elongatus (Le Sueur, 1817).
> Jordan, David Starr, and Barton Warren Evermann. (1896),

Rutilus melanurus Rafinesque, 1820.
> Jordan, David Starr, and Barton Warren Evermann. (1896), Rafinesque, Constantine Samuel. (1820b),

Scartomyzon Fowler, 1913.
> Eschmeyer, William N. (1990), Fowler, Henry Weed. (1914a), Lee, David S., and Carter R. Gilbert, Charles H. Hocutt, Robert E. Jenkins, Don E. McAllister, Jay R. Stauffer, Jr. (1980), Nelson, Joseph S. (1976), Nelson, Joseph S. (1984), Robins, C. Richards, and Edward C. Raney. (1957a), Robins, C. Richards, and Edward C. Raney. (1957b), Smith, Gerald R. (1966), Smith, Michael L., and Ted M. Cavender, Robert R. Miller. (1975),

Scartomyzon cervinus (Cope).
> **Jumprocks, Jumping Mullet.**
> Jordan, David Starr. (1929),

Scartomyzon rupiscartes (Jordan and Jenkins).
> Jordan, David Starr. (1929),

Sclerognathus Cuvier and Valenciennes, 1844.
> Eschmeyer, William N. (1990), Günther, Albert C. (1868),

Sclerognathus asiaticus (Bleeker, 1864).
> Günther, Albert C. (1868),

Sclerognathus chinensis Günther, 1889.
> Günther, Albert C. (1889),

Sclerognathus cyprinella Valenciennes **IN:** Cuvier and Valenciennes, 1844.
> Forbes, Stephen Alfred., and Robert Earl Richardson. (1920), Fowler, Henry Weed. (1914a), Günther, Albert C. (1868), Jordan, David Starr, and Barton Warren Evermann. (1896), Smith, Philip W. (1979), Valenciennes, Achille. (1844),

Sclerognathus cyprinus.
> Günther, Albert C. (1868), Trautman, Milton B. (1981),

Sclerognathus elongatus (Le Sueur, 1817).
> Günther, Albert C. (1868), Jordan, David Starr, and Barton Warren Evermann. (1896),

Sclerognathus meridionalis Günther, 1868.
   Günther, Albert C. (1868), Jordan, David Starr, and Barton Warren Evermann. (1896),

Sclerognathus urus (Agassiz, 1855).
   Forbes, Stephen Alfred., and Robert Earl Richardson. (1920), Günther, Albert C. (1868), Jordan, David Starr, and Barton Warren Evermann. (1896), Leidy, Joseph. (1875),

Stomocatus Bonaparte, 1840.
   Eschmeyer, William N. (1990), Jordan, David Starr. (1923),

Stomocatus catostomus (Forster, 1773).
   Jordan, David Starr. (1923),

Teretulus Rafinesque, 1820.
   Eschmeyer, William N. (1990), Jordan, David Starr. (1923), Rafinesque, Constantine Samuel. (1820b),

Teretulus anisurus.
   Smith, Philip W. (1979),

Teretulus aureolum.
   Forbes, Stephen Alfred., and Robert Earl Richardson. (1920), Smith, Philip W. (1979),

Teretulus aureolus Rafinesque, 1820.
   Jordan, David Starr, and Barton Warren Evermann. (1896),

Teretulus carpio.
   Forbes, Stephen Alfred., and Robert Earl Richardson. (1920), Smith, Philip W. (1979),

Teretulus cervinus Cope, 1868.
   Cope, Edward Drinker. (1868), Jordan, David Starr, and Barton Warren Evermann. (1896),

Teretulus duquesnii.
   Forbes, Stephen Alfred., and Robert Earl Richardson. (1920), Smith, Philip W. (1979),

Teretulus macrolepidotum.
   Smith, Philip W. (1979),

Teretulus velatus.
   Smith, Philip W. (1979),

Thoburnia Jordan and Snyder, 1917.
   Buth, Donald G. (1979b), Eschmeyer, William N. (1990), Jordan, David Starr. (1923), Lee, David S., and Carter R. Gilbert, Charles H. Hocutt, Robert E. Jenkins, Don E. McAllister, Jay R. Stauffer, Jr. (1980), Miller, Robert Rush. (1958), Nelson, Edward M. (1948), Nelson, Edward M. (1949), Nelson, Joseph S. (1984), Raney, Edward C., and Ernest A. Lachner. (1946a),

Thoburnia atripinnis.
   Miller, Rudolph J., and H. E. Evans. (1965),

Thoburnia hamiltoni Raney and Lachner, 1946.
   Miller, Rudolph J., and H. E. Evans. (1965), Raney, Edward C., and Ernest A. Lachner. (1946a),

Thoburnia rhothoeca.
>Jordan, David Starr. (1929), Miller, Robert Rush. (1946), Miller, Rudolph J., and H. E. Evans. (1965), Nelson, Edward M. (1948), Raney, Edward C., and Ernest A. Lachner. (1946c),

Vasnetzovia Sytchevskaya, 1986.
>Sytchevskaya, E. K. (1986),

Vasnetzovia artemica Sytchevskaya, 1986.
>Sytchevskaya, E. K. (1986),

Xyrauchen Kirsch, 1889.
>Eschmeyer, William N. (1990), Jordan, David Starr, and Barton Warren Evermann. (1896), Koehn, Richard K. (1969), Miller, Robert Rush. (1958), Nelson, Edward M. (1948), Nelson, Edward M. (1949), Nelson, Edward M. (1955), Nelson, Joseph S. (1976), Nelson, Joseph S. (1984), Smith, Gerald R. (1966), Snyder, John Otterbein. (1916),

Xyrauchen cypho (Lockington, 1881).
>**Razor-Back Sucker, Hump-Backed Sucker.**
>Gilbert, Charles Henry, and N. B. Scofield. (1898), Goode, C. Brown, and Theodore Nicholas Gill. (1903), Jordan, David Starr. (1891), Jordan, David Starr, and Barton Warren Evermann. (1896), Jordan, David Starr, and Barton Warren Evermann. (1905), Jordan, David Starr, and Charles Henry Gilbert. (1883), Kirsch, Philip Henry. (1889),

Xyrauchen rotundus Sytchevskaya, 1986.
>Sytchevskaya, E. K. (1986),

Xyrauchen texanus (Abbott, 1861).
>**Razorback sucker, Humpback sucker.**
>Bailey, Reeve M., and John E. Fitch, Earl S. Herald, Ernest A. Lachner, C. C. Lindsey, C. Richard Robins, W. B. Scott. (1970), Bailey, Reeve M., and Ernest A. Lachner, C. C. Lindsey, C. Richard Robins, Phil M. Roedel, W. B. Scott, Loren P. Woods. (1966), Baxter, George T., and James R. Simon. (1970), Berry, C. R., Jr. (1984), Boschung, Herbert T., Jr., and James D. Williams, Daniel W. Gotshall, David K. Caldwell, Melba C. Caldwell, Carol Nehring, Jordan Verner. (1983), Bozek, M. A., and L. J. Paulson, G. R. Wilde. (1990), Bulkley, R. V., and R. Pimental. (1983), Buth, Donald G., and R. W. Murphy, L. Ulmer. (1987), Carlander, Kenneth D. (1969), Carter, John G., and R. A. Valdez, Ronald J. Ryel, Vincent A. Lamarra. (1985), Casteel, Richard W. (1976), Day, D. (1979), Dill, W. A. (1944), Douglas, P. A. (1952), Douglas, P. A. (1957), Eastman, Joseph T. (1977), Eastman, Joseph T. (1980), Eddy, Samuel. (1957), Eddy, Samuel. (1969), Ferris, Stephen D., and Gregory S. Whitt. (1978), Finnley, D. [Editor]. (1978b), Hamman, R. L. (1985), Hamman, R. L. (1987), Herald, Earl S. (1967), Herald, Earl S. (1979), Holden, P. B., and C. B. Stalnaker. (1975a), Holden, P. B., and C. B. Stalnaker. (1975b), Hubbs, Carl L., and W. I. Follett, Lillian J. Dempster. (1979), Hubbs, Carl L., and Robert Rush Miller. (1953), La Rivers, Ira. (1962), Lanigan, S. H., and H. M. Tyus. (1989), Lee, David S., and Carter R. Gilbert, Charles H. Hocutt, Robert E. Jenkins, Don E. McAllister, Jay R. Stauffer, Jr. (1980), Marsh, Paul C. (1985), Marsh, Paul C., and J. E. Brooks. (1989), Marsh, P. C., and W. L. Minckley. (1989), McAda, Charles W., and Richard S. Wydoski. (1980), McClane, Albert Jules. (1974), McDonald, D. B., and P. A. Dotson. (1960), Minckley, C. O., and S. W. Carothers. (1979), Minckley, W. L. (1983), Minckley, W. L., and E. S. Gustafson. (1982), Minckley, W. L., and Dean A. Hendrickson, Carl E. Bond. (1986), Moyle, Peter B. (1976), Moyle, Peter B., and Joseph J. Cech, Jr. (1982), Mpoame, M., and J. N. Rinne. (1983), Mueller, G. (1989), Naiman, Robert J. (1981), Nelson, Edward M. (1948), Ono, R. Dana, and James D. Williams, Anne Wagner. (1983), Robins, C. Richard, and Reeve M.

Bailey, Carl E. Bond, James R. Brooker, Ernest A. Lachner, Robert N. Lea, W. B. Scott. (1980), Scoppettone, G. Gary, and Mark Coleman, Gary A. Wedemeyer. (1986), Simon, James R. (1946), Snyder, Darrel E., and Robert T. Muth. (1990), Tyus, H. M. (1987), Tyus, H. M. (1988), Tyus, H. M., and C. A. Karp. (1989), Tyus, H. M., and W. L. Minckley. (1989), Villar, José Alvarez del. (1970), Walden, Howard T., 2d. (1964),

Xyrauchen texanus X *Catostomus latipinnis*
Buth, Donald G., and R. W. Murphy, L. Ulmer. (1987),

Xyrauchen uncompahgre Jordan and Evermann, **IN:** Jordan, 1891.
Jordan, David Starr. (1891), Jordan, David Starr, and Barton Warren Evermann. (1896), Jordan, David Starr, and Barton Warren Evermann. (1905),

Thompson: Illinois is 'Sucker State'

By United Press International

SPRINGFIELD, Ill. — Gov. James R. Thompson said Monday there's something fishy going on in the Legislature, but lawmakers and other officials said the state's chief executive is all wet.

Although the Legislature has sent him a bill (H2725) calling on the state's school children to pick a state fish, Thompson said he believes Illinois already has a gilled representative. He said he thinks the state fish is the sucker, a bottom-feeding species that is fairly common in most of the state's waterways.

Thompson said Illinois carries the unofficial title of the sucker state because of the fish.

"When I was at the Shedd Aquarium the other day, I was told by the director that we already have a state fish and it's the sucker. Now if we already have a state fish, it doesn't surprise me it's the sucker, but if we already have one, I've got to find out what this bill means," said Thompson when asked if he will sign the fish bill into law.

"Does this bill mean the Legislature is dissatisfied with having the sucker as the state fish of Illinois or does this bill mean the Legislature is ignorant of the fact that the sucker is the state fish of Illinois? And if so, maybe we've been passing a bill for state fish when we should have been concentrating on things like the budget and education and economic development."

William Braker, director of the Shedd Aquarium in Chicago confirmed he told Thompson he believes the sucker already is the state fish, although it might never have been put into law.

"The sucker's about as close to the state fish as you can get. That's why people in Illinois are called suckers" Braker said.

"Many years ago there was such a large number of suckers that went up the rivers particularly in the northwest part of Illinois, that we became known as the sucker state. Apparently the sucker runs in the spring were so thick, people would say you could walk on them. That's an exaggeration, but I think their runs were like that of the salmon."

But Jim Graham, a spokesman for the secretary of state's office, said there is no reference in Illinois law to the sucker — or any other species — being the state fish.

"According to the state statutes, there is a state animal, a state mineral, a state bird and everything else, but there's no reference to a state fish," Graham said.

Rep. Richard Mautino, a Spring Valley Democrat who sponsored the fish bill, said he also believes Illinois does not have a state fish.

Bruner, John Clay. 1991. Bibliography of the Family Catostomidae (Cypriniformes). Provincial Museum of Alberta. Natural History Occasional Paper No. 14:1-213.

ERRATA:

Preface
p. v.   Col. 1,   line 1. change "2000 references" to "2004 references"
p. v.   Col. 1,   line 24. change "2000 papers" to "2004 papers"
p. v.   Col. 1,   line 31. change "thirty five" to "fifty four"
p. v.   Col. 1,   line 32. change "2000 references" to "2004 references"
p. v.   Col. 1,   line 47. change "Éienne La Cepéde's" to "Étienne La Cepède's"
p. v.   Col. 2,   line 33. change "Society of American" to "Society of America"
p. vi. Col. 2,   line 22. change "148 references" to "164 references"

ACKNOWLEDGEMENTS
p. vii. Col. 1,   line 6. change "Anaylst" to "Analyst"

AUTHOR INDEX
p. 1   line 29. change "1990" to "1990a"
p. 1   line 32. change "1990" to "1990b"
p. 2   line 6. change "1990" to "1989"
p. 2   line 6. move reference "Amin, O. M. 1981." after "Amin, Omar. M. 1977b."
p. 3   line 30. insert the following reference after Andryushchenko, A. I., and V. I., Glebova. 1979.

Andryushchenko, A. I., and N. F. Grishcenko. 1985. [in Russian] The upper temperature threshold for survival in the big mouth buffalo during early ontogenesis. Rybnoe Khoz., Kiev No. 39:28-31.
p. 3   line 36. change "HEP..Rybn." to "HEP. Rybn."
p. 5   line 21. change "conditions" to "condition"
p. 5   line 27. change "M. W. Coleman" to "M. E. Coleman"
p. 10   line 14. change "Behmer, D. J. 1969" to "Behmer, D. J. 1969b" and move to line 16 and change "fecunditiy" to "fecundity"
p. 10   line 16. change "Behmer, D. J. 1969" to "Behmer, D. J. 1969a" and move to line 14
p. 10   line 26. change "Harvey. 1986" to "Harvey. 1986a"
p. 10   line 29. change "Harvey. 1986" to "Harvey. 1986b"
p. 10   line 33. change "to levels" to "to elevated levels"
p. 11   line 4. change "Micropterus dolomieui" to "*Micropterus dolomieui*"
p. 14   line 10. change "Kh, M." to "Kh. and M."
p. 15   line 3. change "Pritchard. 1946" to "Pritchard. 1946a"
p. 15   line 4. change "Stations.Issue" to "Stations. Issue"
p. 15   line 5. change "Pritchard. 1946" to "Pritchard. 1946b"
p. 16   line 21. remove "Vol. . Sci."
p. 17   line 6. change "Syst.. Ecol." to "Syst. Ecol."
p. 18   line 35. change "Columbia.British" to "Columbia. British"
p. 21   line 27. change "in vitro" to "*in vitro*"
p. 23   line 36. change "Burleigh," to "*Burleigh,*"
p. 25   line 13. change "Colorado.Annual" to "Colorado. Annual"
p. 25   line 23. change "[Lipomyzon]" to "[*Lipomyzon*]"
p. 28   line 12. change "1895.Geological" to "1895. Geological"
p. 29   line 13. change "the108th" to "the 108th"
p. 31   line 35. change "Arthur, Hermanutz," to "Arthur, R. Hermanutz,"
p. 33   line 14. change "removed..Vopr" to "removed Vopr"
p. 34   line 22. change "494 Evermann" to "Evermann"
p. 34   line 35. change "1907.The" to "1907. The"
p. 35   line 21. change "horst" to "host"
p. 36   line 15. change "in their coding" to "in their protein coding"
p. 37   lines 30 and 32. change "Alfred.," to "Alfred,"
p. 37   line 12. change "1914.c" to "1914c."

Bruner, John Clay. 1991. Bibliography of the Family Catostomidae (Cypriniformes). Provincial Museum of Alberta. Natural History Occasional Paper No. 14:1-213.

p. 39   line 5. change "history.Advances" to "history. Advances"
p. 39   line 21. change "form" to "from"
p. 40   line 6. change "Triganodistomum" to "*Triganodistomum*"
p. 40   line 6. change "Fessisentis" to "*Fessisentis*"
p. 40   line 36. change "Chondrococcus columnaris" to "*Chondrococcus columnaris*"
p. 41   line 28. insert the following reference after Gasaway, C. R. 1970.
        Gee, R. J. 1989. A morphological study of the nervous system of the praesoma of *Octospinifer macilentus* (Acanthocephala: Noechinorhynchidae). J. Morphol. Vol. 196(1):23-31.
p. 42   line 3. change "Nova" to "Noua"
p. 42   line 6. change "1947 " to "1947. "
p. 42   lines 18 and 20. change "Henry " to "Henry. "
p. 43   line 14. change "refernce" to "reference"
p. 44   line 31. insert the following before "Fishes of El Dorado" Greer, J. K., and Frank B. Cross. 1956."
p. 45   line 14. change "Vol. 68:2290-2298." to "Vol. 68(11):2290-2298."
p. 47   line 33. change "Drabl s" to "Drabløs"
p. 47   line 34. change "As" to "Ås"
p. 48   line 1. change "sucker. *Catostomus*" to "sucker *Catostomus*"
p. 49   line 1. insert the following reference before Heinermann, P. H., and M. A. Ali. 1989.
        Heierhorst, J., and S. D. Morley, J. Figueroa, C. Krentler, K. Lederis, D. Richter. 1989. Vasotocin and isotocin precursors from the white sucker *Catostomus commersoni*.: cloning and sequence analysis of the cDNAs. Proc. Natl. Acad. Sci. USA Vol. 86(14):5242-5246.
p. 49   line 7. change "1989.Trace" to "1989. Trace"
p. 49   line 21. change "Hocutt, JrAprelininary" to "Hocutt, Jr., C. R. Gilbert. 1979. A prelininary"
p. 51   line 15. change "1977.Temperature" to "1977. Temperature"
p. 51   line 18. change "1975." to "1975a."
p. 51   line 21. change "1975." to "1975b."
p. 52   line 16. change "Materials for a revision" to "Hubbs, Carl L. 1930. Materials for a revision"
p. 53   line 23. change "AcademyVol" to "Academy of Science 1974 (1975). Vol"
p. 56   line 26. change "addenda.antedates" to "addenda, antedates"
p. 59   line 1. change "behavioral" to "behavioural"
p. 59   line 28. change "Hinks.Studies" to "Hinks. Studies"
p. 61   line 3. change "cadium binding" to "cadium toxicity by white suckers: cadium binding"
p. 61   line 20. change "1973." to "1973a."
p. 61   line 23. change "1973." to "1973b."
p. 65   line 22. change "*urophysis*" to "urophysis"
p. 66   line 1. change "esp_ce" to "espèce"
p. 68   line 2. change "Moldavia.Fishes" to "Moldavia. Fishes"
p. 68   line 27. change "Fisheries.Special" to "Fisheries. Special"
p. 69   line 5. change "Glutenmann" to "Gutenmann"
p. 69   line 16. change "edition.Blackwell" to "edition. Blackwell"
p. 69   line 37. change "MacKay, W. C." to "Mackay, W. C."
p. 69   line 37. change "*commersoni*" to "*commersonii*"
p. 70   line 1. change "MacKay, W. C.," to "Mackay, W. C.,"
p. 70   line 2. change "*commersoni*," to "*commersonii*,"
p. 71   line 12. change "phosporylase" to "phosphorylase"
p. 71   line 28. change "Vol. 18(1):95-102" to "Vol. 78(1):95-102"
p. 75   line 10. change "1980.Early" to "1980. Early"
p. 75   line 20. change "J. Witteld" to "J. W. Held"
p. 77   line 16. change "(B).Vol." to "(B). Vol."
p. 77   line 29. change "1955.Fish" to "1955. Fish"
p. 77   line 33. change "Science.Washington," to "Science. Washington,"

Bruner, John Clay. 1991. Bibliography of the Family Catostomidae (Cypriniformes). Provincial Museum of Alberta. Natural History Occasional Paper No. 14:1-213.

p. 78   line 12. change "Cyprinodon" to "*Cyprinodon*"
p. 80   lines 21 and 22. change "Quebec" to "Québec"
p. 81   line 9. change "Vol. 29(10):2505-2511." to "Vol. 29(10):2506-2511."
p. 83   line 22. change "3).Mus." to "3). Mus."
p. 85   line 20. change "Nickol, B. b.," to "Nickol, B. B.,"
p. 87   line 17. change "Ostland, v. E.," to "Ostland, V. E.," and "faitfish" to "baitfish"
p. 87   line 18. change "Org. (2):163-166" to "Org. 2(3):163-166"
p. 88   line 25. change "Ottawa.167pp." to "Ottawa. 167pp."
p. 88   line 29. change "buffalo.Proceedings" to "buffalo. Proceedings"
p. 88   line 18. change "Peterson, P. H., and d. J. " to "Peterson, P. H., and D. J. "
p. 89   line 3. change "Notropis rubellus." to "*Notropis rubellus*."
p. 90   line 39. change "Comm.,," to "Comm.,"
p. 91   line 29. change "l'inté_rieur" to "l'intérieur"
p. 93   line 27. change "Reickhow, K. H., and" to "Reckhow, K. H., and" and move entire reference to line 12
p. 95   line 18. change "Roberto, Julis, C." to "Roberto Julis, C."
p. 96   line 10. change "1967.Studies" to "1967. Studies"
p. 98   line 2. change "Quebec" to "Québec" and "Que." to "Qué."
p. 98   line 14. change "preation" to "predation"
p. 99   line 14. change "Service.Fish" to "Service. Fish"
p. 101   line 4. change "Semmens,,K. J." to "Semmens, K. J."
p. 101   line 5. change "Vol. 47(2);19-120." to "Vol. 47(2):19-120."
p. 104   line 15. change "Hayes,." to "Hayes."
p. 104   line 34. change "fiah" to "fish"
p. 104   line 35. change "<F 2>et al.<F>" to "*et al.*"
p. 108   line 3. change "Circ.178" to "Circ. 178"
p. 109   line 21. change "1987" to "1987a."
p. 109   line 22. change "Canada..J." to "Canada. J."
p. 109   line 23. change "1987" to "1987b."
p. 110   line 22. change "1813.Iconum" to "1813. Iconum"
p. 111   line 13. change "Harvey. 1987." to "Harvey. 1987a."
p. 111   line 16. change "Harvey. 1987." to "Harvey. 1987b."
p. 111   line 36. change "Biochem. Vol." to "Biochem. Physiol. B. Comp. Biochem. Vol."
p. 112   line 20. change "Manage.." to "Manage."
p. 112   line 25. change "Nagase, J.-J." to "Nagase, Y.-J."
p. 113   line 32. change "Van Coillle," to "Van Coille,"
p. 114   line 30. change "Rep.No." to "Rep. No."
p. 115   line 27. change "Vondracek, B.," to "Vondracek, B. C.,"
p. 120   line 19. change "Williams, D. D. 1980." to "Williams, D. D. 1980a."
p. 120   line 21. change "Williams, D. D. 1980." to "Williams, D. D. 1980b."
p. 120   line 23. change "Williams, D. D. 1980." to "Williams, D. D. 1980c."
p. 120   line 25. change "Williams, D. D. 1980." to "Williams, D. D. 1980d."
p. 120   line 28. change "Williams, D. D. 1980." to "Williams, D. D. 1980e."
p. 121   line 1. change "1979.," to "1979."
p. 122   line 17. change "battey" to "battery"
p. 123   line 22. change "Wu, H.-w.," to "Wu, H.-W.,"
p. 123   line 35. change "*elongatus*.." to "*elongatus*."
p. 124   line 9. change "1988.Preliminary" to "1988. Preliminary"
p. 124   line 13. change "1986." to "1986a."
p. 124   line 16. change "1986." to "1986b."
p. 124   line 19. change "of the" to "of and the"

Bruner, John Clay. 1991. Bibliography of the Family Catostomidae (Cypriniformes). Provincial Museum of Alberta. Natural History Occasional Paper No. 14:1-213.

<u>INDEX TO SCIENTIFIC NAMES</u>
CATOSTOMIDAE
p. 133 line 29. change "1190" to "Nelson, Joseph S. (1984), "

Catostomus commersoni
p. 149 line 15. change "Amedjo, S. D., and John C. Holmes. (1990)" to "Amedjo, S. D., and John C. Holmes. (1989)"
p. 150 line 36. change "Eaton, J., and J. Arthur, Hermanutz," to "Eaton, J., and J. Arthur, R. Hermanutz,"
p. 152 line 10. change "Glutenmann" to "Gutenmann"

Cycleptus elongatus
p. 171 line 46. change "and J. Witteld." to "J. W. Held."

Erimyzon sucetta
p. 175 line 19. change "(1943),.Hoffman, Glenn L. (1967)," to "(1943), Hoffman, Glenn L. (1967),"

Bruner, John Clay. 1991. Bibliography of the Family Catostomidae (Cypriniformes). Provincial Museum of Alberta. Natural History Occasional Paper No. 14:1-213.

ERRATA:

Preface

p. v.   Col. 1,   line 1.   change "2000 references" to "2004 references"
p. v.   Col. 1,   line 24.   change "2000 papers" to "2004 papers"
p. v.   Col. 1,   line 31.   change "thirty five" to "fifty four"
p. v.   Col. 1,   line 32.   change "2000 references" to "2004 references"
p. v.   Col. 1,   line 47.   change "Éienne La Cepéde's" to "Étienne La Cepède's"
p. v.   Col. 2,   line 33.   change "Society of American" to "Society of America"
p. vi. Col. 2,   line 22.   change "148 references" to "164 references"

ACKNOWLEDGEMENTS

p. vii. Col. 1,   line 6.   change "Anaylst" to "Analyst"

AUTHOR INDEX

p. 1   line 29.   change "1990" to "1990a"
p. 1   line 32.   change "1990" to "1990b"
p. 2   line 6.   change "1990" to "1989"
p. 2   line 6.   move reference "Amin, O. M.   1981." after "Amin, Omar. M.   1977b."
p. 3   line 30.   insert the following reference after Andryushchenko, A. I., and V. I., Glebova.   1979.

   Andryushchenko, A. I., and N. F. Grishcenko.   1985. [in Russian] The upper temperature threshold for survival in the big mouth buffalo during early ontogenesis. Rybnoe Khoz., Kiev No. 39:28-31.

p. 3   line 36. change "HEP..Rybn." to "HEP. Rybn."
p. 5   line 21. change "conditions" to "condition"
p. 5   line 27. change "M. W. Coleman" to "M. E. Coleman"
p. 10   line 14. change "Behmer, D. J.   1969" to "Behmer, D. J.   1969b" and move to line 16 and change "fecunditiy" to "fecundity"
p. 10   line 16. change "Behmer, D. J.   1969" to "Behmer, D. J.   1969a" and move to line 14
p. 10   line 26. change "Harvey.   1986" to "Harvey.   1986a"
p. 10   line 29. change "Harvey.   1986" to "Harvey.   1986b"
p. 10   line 33. change "to levels" to "to elevated levels"
p. 11   line 4. change "Micropterus dolomieui" to "*Micropterus dolomieui*"
p. 14   line 10. change "Kh, M." to "Kh. and M."
p. 15   line 3. change "Pritchard.   1946" to "Pritchard.   1946a"
p. 15   line 4. change "Stations.Issue" to "Stations.   Issue"
p. 15   line 5. change "Pritchard.   1946" to "Pritchard.   1946b"
p. 16   line 21. remove "Vol. . Sci."
p. 17   line 6. change "Syst.. Ecol." to "Syst. Ecol."
p. 18   line 35. change "Columbia.British" to "Columbia.   British"
p. 21   line 27. change "in vitro" to "*in vitro*"
p. 23   line 36. change "Burleigh," to "*Burleigh,*"
p. 25   line 13. change "Colorado.Annual" to "Colorado.   Annual"
p. 25   line 23. change "[Lipomyzon]" to "[*Lipomyzon*]"
p. 26   line 2.   change "639-700," to "635-703,"
p. 28   line 12. change "1895.Geological" to "1895.   Geological"
p. 29   line 13. change "the108th" to "the 108th"
p. 31   line 35. change "Arthur,   Hermanutz," to "Arthur, R.   Hermanutz,"
p. 33   line 14. change "removed..Vopr" to "removed Vopr"
p. 34   line 22.   change "494   Evermann" to "Evermann"
p. 34   line 35. change "1907.The" to "1907.   The"
p. 35   line 21.   change "horst" to "host"
p. 36   line 15.   change "in their coding" to "in their protein coding"

Bruner, John Clay. 1991. Bibliography of the Family Catostomidae (Cypriniformes). Provincial
Museum of Alberta. Natural History Occasional Paper No. 14:1-213.

p. 37   lines 30 and 32.   change "Alfred.," to "Alfred,"
p. 37   line 12.   change "1914.c" to "1914c."
p. 39   line 5.   change "history.Advances" to "history.   Advances"
p. 39   line 21.   change "form" to "from"
p. 40   line 6. change "Triganodistomum" to "*Triganodistomum*"
p. 40   line 6. change "Fessisentis" to "*Fessisentis*"
p. 40   line 36. change "Chondrococcus columnaris" to "*Chondrococcus   columnaris*"
p. 41   line 28.   insert the following reference after Gasaway, C. R.   1970.
        Gee, R. J.   1989.   A morphological study of the nervous system of the praesoma of
Octospinifer   macilentus   (Acanthocephala: Noechinorhynchidae).   J. Morphol.   Vol.
196(1):23-31.
p. 42   line 3. change "Nova" to "Noua"
p. 42   line 6. change "1947   " to "1947.   "
p. 42   lines 18 and 20. change "Henry   " to "Henry.   "
p. 43   line 14.   change "refernce" to "reference"
p. 44   line 31. insert the following before "Fishes of El Dorado"   Greer, J. K., and Frank B.
Cross.   1956."
p. 45   line 14. change "Vol. 68:2290-2298." to "Vol. 68(11):2290-2298."
p. 47   line 33. change "Drabl s" to "Drabløs"
p. 47   line 34. change "As" to "Ås"
p. 48   line 1. change "sucker.   *Catostomus*" to "sucker *Catostomus*"
p. 48   line 38.   insert the following reference before Heinermann, P. H., and M. A. Ali.   1989.
        Heierhorst, J., and S. D. Morley, J. Figueroa, C. Krentler, K. Lederis, D. Richter.   1989.
Vasotocin and isotocin precursors from the white sucker *Catostomus   commersoni*.: cloning
and sequence analysis of the cDNAs.   Proc. Natl. Acad. Sci. USA   Vol. 86(14):5242-5246.
p. 49   line 7. change "1989.Trace" to "1989.   Trace"
p. 49   line 21. change "Hocutt, JrAprelininary" to "Hocutt, Jr., C. R. Gilbert.   1979.   A
prelininary"
p. 51   line 15. change "1977.Temperature" to "1977.   Temperature"
p. 51   line 18. change "1975." to "1975a."
p. 51   line 21. change "1975." to "1975b."
p. 52   line 16. change "Materials for a revision"   to "Hubbs, Carl L.   1930.   Materials for a
revision"
p. 53   line 23. change "AcademyVol" to "Academy of Science 1974 (1975).   Vol"
p. 56   line 26. change "addenda.antedates" to "addenda, antedates"
p. 59   line 1.   change "behavioral" to "behavioural"
p. 59   line 28. change "Hinks.Studies" to "Hinks.   Studies"
p. 61   line 3. change "cadium binding" to "cadium toxicity by white suckers: cadium
binding"
p. 61   line 20. change "1973." to "1973a."
p. 61   line 23. change "1973." to "1973b."
p. 65   line 22. change "*urophysis*" to "urophysis"
p. 66   line 1. change "esp_ce" to "espèce"
p. 68   line 2. change "<u>Moldavia.Fishes</u>" to "<u>Moldavia.</u> <u>Fishes</u>"
p. 68   line 27. change "Fisheries.Special" to "Fisheries.   Special"
p. 69   line 5. change "Glutenmann" to "Gutenmann"
p. 69   line 16. change "edition.Blackwell" to "edition.   Blackwell"
p. 69   line 37. change "MacKay, W. C." to "Mackay, W. C."
p. 69   line 37. change "*commersoni*" to "*commersonii*"
p. 70   line 1. change "MacKay, W. C.," to "Mackay, W. C.,"
p. 70   line 2. change "*commersoni*," to "*commersonii*,"
p. 71   line 12.   change "phosporylase" to "phosphorylase"
p. 71   line 28. change "Vol. 18(1):95-102" to "Vol. 78(1):95-102"

page 2

Bruner, John Clay. 1991. Bibliography of the Family Catostomidae (Cypriniformes). Provincial Museum of Alberta. Natural History Occasional Paper No. 14:1-213.

p. 75   line 10. change "1980.Early" to "1980.   Early"
p. 75   line 20. change "J. Witteld" to "J. W. Held"
p. 77   line 16. change "(B).Vol." to "(B).   Vol."
p. 77   line 29. change "1955.Fish" to "1955.   Fish"
p. 77   line 33. change "Science.Washington," to "Science.   Washington,"
p. 78   line 12. change "Cyprinodon" to "*Cyprinodon*"
p. 80   lines 21 and 22. change "Quebec" to "Québec"
p. 81   line 9. change "Vol. 29(10):2505-2511." to "Vol. 29(10):2506-2511."
p. 83   line 22. change "3).Mus." to "3).   Mus."
p. 85   line 20. change "Nickol, B. b.," to "Nickol, B. B.,"
p. 87   line 17. change "Ostland, v. E.," to "Ostland, V. E.," and "faitfish" to "baitfish"
p. 87   line 18. change "Org. (2):163-166" to "Org. 2(3):163-166"
p. 88   line 25. change "Ottawa.167pp." to "Ottawa.   167pp."
p. 88   line 29. change "buffalo.Proceedings" to "buffalo.   Proceedings"
p. 88   line 18. change "Peterson, P. H., and d. J. " to "Peterson, P. H., and D. J. "
p. 89   line 3. change "Notropis rubellus." to "*Notropis rubellus.*"
p. 90   line 39. change "Comm.,," to "Comm.,"
p. 91   line 29. change "l'inté_rieur" to "l'intérieur"
p. 93   line 27. change "Reickhow, K. H., and" to "Reckhow, K. H., and" and move entire reference to line 12
p. 95   line 18. change "Roberto, Julis, C." to "Roberto Julis, C."
p. 96   line 10. change "1967.Studies" to "1967.   Studies"
p. 98   line 2. change "Quebec" to "Québec" and "Que." to "Qué."
p. 98   line 14. change "preation" to "predation"
p. 99   line 14. change "Service.Fish" to "Service.   Fish"
p. 101 line 4. change "Semmens,,K. J." to "Semmens, K. J."
p. 101 line 5. change "Vol. 47(2);19-120." to "Vol. 47(2):19-120."
p. 104 line 15. change "Hayes,." to "Hayes."
p. 104 line 34. change "fiah" to "fish"
p. 104 line 35. change "<F 2>et al.<F>" to "*et al.*"
p. 108 line 3. change "Circ.178" to "Circ.   178"
p. 109 line 21. change "1987" to "1987a."
p. 109 line 22. change "Canada..J." to "Canada.   J."
p. 109 line 23. change "1987" to "1987b."
p. 110 line 22. change "1813.Iconum" to "1813.   Iconum"
p. 111 line 13. change "Harvey. 1987." to "Harvey.   1987a."
p. 111 line 16. change "Harvey. 1987." to "Harvey.   1987b."
p. 111 line 36. change "Biochem.   Vol." to "Biochem. Physiol. B.   Comp. Biochem.   Vol."
p. 112 line 20. change "Manage.." to "Manage."
p. 112 line 25. change "Nagase, J.-J." to "Nagase, Y.-J."
p. 113 line 32. change "Van Coillle," to "Van Coille,"
p. 114 line 30. change "Rep.No." to "Rep.   No."
p. 115 lines 27. change "Vondracek, B.," to "Vondracek, B. C.,"
p. 120 line 19. change "Williams, D. D. 1980." to "Williams, D. D.   1980a."
p. 120 line 21. change "Williams, D. D.   1980." to "Williams, D. D.   1980b."
p. 120 line 23. change "Williams, D. D.   1980." to "Williams, D. D.   1980c."
p. 120 line 25. change "Williams, D. D.   1980." to "Williams, D. D.   1980d."
p. 120 line 28. change "Williams, D. D.   1980." to "Williams, D. D.   1980e."
p. 121 line 1. change "1979.," to "1979."
p. 122 line 17. change "battey" to "battery"
p. 123 line 22. change "Wu, H.-w.," to "Wu, H.-W.,"
p. 123 line 35. change "*elongatus..*" to "*elongatus.*"
p. 124 line 9. change "1988.Preliminary" to "1988.   Preliminary"
p. 124 line 13. change "1986." to "1986a."

Bruner, John Clay. 1991. Bibliography of the Family Catostomidae (Cypriniformes). Provincial Museum of Alberta. Natural History Occasional Paper No. 14:1-213.

p. 124 line 16. change "1986." to "1986b."
p. 124 line 19. change "of the" to "of and the"

INDEX TO SCIENTIFIC NAMES
CATOSTOMIDAE
p. 133 line 29. change "1190" to "Nelson, Joseph S. (1984), "

Amblodon Rafinesque, 1819.
p. 134 line 6. change "Rafinesque, 1818." to "Rafinesque, 1819. "

Catostomus commersoni
p. 149 line 15. change "Amedjo, S. D., and John C. Holmes. (1990)" to "Amedjo, S. D., and John C. Holmes. (1989)"
p. 150 line 36. change "Eaton, J., and J. Arthur, Hermanutz," to "Eaton, J., and J. Arthur, R. Hermanutz,"
p. 152 line 10. change "Glutenmann" to "Gutenmann"

Cycleptus elongatus
p. 171 line 46. change "and J. Witteld." to "J. W. Held."

Decadactylus
p. 172 line 42. add "*Decadactylus*, Eschmeyer and Bailey (1990)."

Deltistes luxatus
p. 173 line 9. add "Jordan, David Starr, and Barton Warren Evermann. (1898)."

Erimyzon sucetta
p. 175 line 19. change "(1943),.Hoffman, Glenn L. (1967)," to "(1943), Hoffman, Glenn L. (1967),"

Exoglossum lesurianum Rafinesque, 1818.
p. 176 line 36. add "*Exoglossum lesurianum* Rafinesque, 1818. Eschmeyer and Bailey (1990)"

Ictiorus
p. 186 line 12. change "*Ictiorus*" to "*Ictiorus* Rafinesque, 1820"

Maxillingua Rafinesque, 1818.
p. 187 line 12. add "*Maxillingua* Rafinesque, 1818. Eschmeyer and Bailey (1990)"

Myostoma Meek, 1904.
p. 203 line 27. add "*Myostoma* Meek, 1904. Meek, Seth Eugene. (1904)."

Pantosteus Cope, 1875.
p. 205 line 10. change "*Pantosteus* Cope, 1875." to "*Pantosteus* Cope, 1875 *IN:* Cope and Yarrow, 1875"

Quassilabia Jordan and Brayton, 1878.
p. 210 line 1. change "*Quassilabia* Jordan and Brayton, 1878." to "*Quassilabia* Jordan and Brayton, 1878. *IN:* Jordan, 1878."

Rhytidostomus Heckel, 1843.
p. 210 line 10. change "*Rhytidostomus* " to "*Rhytidostomus* Heckel, 1843."

Bruner, John Clay. 1991. Bibliography of the Family Catostomidae (Cypriniformes). Provincial Museum of Alberta. Natural History Occasional Paper No. 14:1-213.

Sclerognathus Cuvier and Valenciennes, 1844.
p. 210 line 28.   change "*Sclerognathus* Cuvier and Valenciennes, 1844." to "*Sclerognathus* Valenciennes, 1844 *IN:* Cuvier and Valenciennes, 1844."

Thoburnia Jordan and Snyder, 1917
p. 211 line 29.   change "*Thoburnia* Jordan and Snyder, 1917" to "*Thoburnia* Jordan and Snyder, 1917 *IN:* Jordan, 1917."

Xyrauchen Kirsch, 1889.
p. 212 line 9.   change "*Xyrauchen* Kirsch, 1889." to "*Xyrauchen* Eigenemann and Kirsch 1889 *IN:* Kirsch, 1889."